Social, Political, and Economic Contexts in Public Relations:
Theory and Cases

COMMUNICATION
TEXTBOOK SERIES
Jennings Bryant—Editor

Public Relations
James E. Grunig—Advisor

TOTH/HEATH • Rhetorical and Critical Approaches to Public Relations

GRUNIG • Excellence in Public Relations and Communication Management

CULBERTSON/JEFFERS/STONE/ TERRELL • Social, Political, and Economic Contexts in Public Relations: Theory and Cases

SOCIAL, POLITICAL, AND ECONOMIC CONTEXTS IN PUBLIC RELATIONS:

Theory and Cases

HUGH M. CULBERTSON
Ohio University
DENNIS W. JEFFERS
Central Michigan University
DONNA BESSER STONE
University of Tennessee, Chattanooga
MARTIN TERRELL
Ohio University

LEA

LAWRENCE ERLBAUM ASSOCIATES, PUBLISHERS
1993   Hillsdale, New Jersey   Hove and London

Lawrence Erlbaum Associates, Inc., Publishers
365 Broadway
Hillsdale, New Jersey 07642

Library of Congress Cataloging-in-Publication Data

Social, political, and economic contexts in public
   relations : theory and cases / Hugh M. Culbertson . . . [et al.].
      p. cm.
   Includes bibliographical references and index.
   ISBN 0-8058-1013-7 (cloth) ISBN 0-8058-1288-1 (paperback)
    1. Issues management.   2. Issues management—Case studies.
   3. Public relations.   4. Public relations—Case studies.
   I. Culbertson, Hugh M.
   HD59.5.S78   1992
   658.4'01—dc20   92-18398
                                                CIP

Printed in the United States of America
10 9 8 7 6 5 4 3 2 1

Contents

PART III: SIX VARIED CASES

PART IV: CONCLUSION

Foreword

In the 1920s, Edward L. Bernays wrote two books, *Crystallizing Public Opinion* and *Propaganda,* in which he described why and how the practice of public relations should be based on the theories and methods of the social and behavioral sciences. In 1966, Edward J. Robinson wrote *Communication and Public Relations,* in which he did the same but in much greater detail. Both Bernays and Robinson filled their books with the prominent theories and methods of their day. Because of that legacy, few educators and practitioners today dispute the idea—at least in public—that the profession should be based on the theories and methods of social and behavioral science. In actual practice, however—in 1922, in 1966, and in 1993—far more practitioners talk about theory and research than use it.

When asked why, most practitioners will say they have no time or resources to use theory or research. When I have researched the backgrounds of practitioners, I also have found that few have the education or knowledge to actually use theory or research. Practitioners will also point out that theory has to be made practical—that they must be given concrete examples of how theory has actually been put into practice. In books and classes on public relations, we often teach theory and practice separately: We expect readers and students to figure out how to integrate the two. Most case study books and courses are especially bad. They describe cases without a theoretical framework to understand and evaluate them.

In *Social, Political, and Economic Contexts in Public Relations,* Culbertson, Jeffers, Stone, and Terrell have changed the status quo of case studies in public relations. They have provided us a book of case studies that integrates the theoretical and the applied. In the first six chapters, they identify and explain concepts that practitioners can and have used to understand and research the context of a public relations problem. In their chapter on issues management, they show how this recent innovation in management can be integrated into the overall public relations function and how it can be made more symmetrical, in line with current scholarly theories of public relations. In the following chapter, they describe research methods that practitioners can use to study the environment of their organization—the context that produces the issues about which they must communicate. Then, in three successive chapters, they identify relevant social, economic, and political concepts that can be used to understand that context and how to communicate with publics that are strategic to the organization.

The authors then turn to their cases—of a police department, a livestock magazine, a motel franchise, a Black Studies program in a university, employees of a municipal government, and osteopathic medicine. They ground their description of each case study in the theories and methods of the theoretical chapters. Unlike case studies described in most public relations books and courses, these communication programs actually were based on the theories and methods described. They are not after-the-fact attempts to force-feed theory and research into a case that did not actually use them. The authors' descriptions of the cases are credible, too, because the authors actually worked on the material.

The cases drive home the point that every organization and every practitioner can use theory and research in their work if they know how to do so. These studies do not come from large organizations with unlimited resources. They come from small organizations, whose public relations people usually would say, "We don't have the time or money to do research or to stop and use theory in our planning."

Throughout the chapters on the case studies and especially in the last chapter, the authors also use the outcome of the cases to reflect on their theory. When he wrote *Communication and Public Relations* in 1966, Robinson wrote that public relations practitioners should be applied behavioral and social scientists. These cases document programs in which practitioners actually functioned in that way. Scientists use theories to plan research. Then they use the research to reconstruct and improve the theories. Public relations practitioners, if they actually functioned as applied scientists, would use theory to plan programs and then use the success or failure of the program to revise the theory.

The authors explain how that process unfolded in these cases. They describe the background of the case, the research that was conducted, and the communication strategies that they recommended after doing the research. Then they reflect on the social, political, and economic theories that were used. In the last chapter, like good scientists, they reviewed their theory in light of the cases—suggesting how and why the cases were successful and how the theories should be revised in light of the cases.

Case studies are important in the body of knowledge of nearly every profession. In the more advanced professions, those case studies are integrated by the theoretical concepts that hold the body of knowledge together. In this volume, the authors have taken a giant step toward making public relations an advanced profession. They have shown how Edward Bernays' idea in the 1920s and Edward J. Robinson's idea in the 1960s can be and actually has been practiced in public relations.

James E. Grunig
University of Maryland
Advisory Editor, Public Relations Subseries

Preface

Two commissions within the Public Relations Society of America have recently defined courses in case-study analysis, research methods, and behavioral-science theory as central to acceptable public-relations curricula.

To date, these three "streams" within the field have been quite independent of each other. However, that appears to be changing. In particular, the growing number of PhD's now teaching in the field surely see the need for an integrative, applied-theory approach to the study of public relations cases.

The need for practitioners to study the social, political, and economic contexts of clients has been apparent for some time as issues management and environmental scanning became common in modern public relations. However, scholars have offered few, if any, solid theoretical frameworks for such study. This volume uses 17 theoretical perspectives to build such a framework.

Studying the social, political, and economic contexts of a client's projects and programs also requires a wide variety of qualitative and quantitative research methods. *Qualitative* approaches include background reading; database searching; in-depth interviews of client leaders, consumers and competitors (often including foes!); and focus groups. *Quantitative* methods include formal content analyses of media coverage, annual reports, and other messages along with large-sample surveys and field experiments. Because of budget and time limitations as well as conceptual focus, some public-relations projects entail more—and more varied—research than do others.

This volume includes an overview chapter on how these methods build on each other. Also, the 6 cases presented in Part III vary greatly as to types, complexity, and variety of research involved.

All four coauthors participated in the writing and editing of each chapter. However, Culbertson was the primary author of chapters 1, 3, 4, 5, 7, 12, and 13; Jeffers of chapters 6, 8 and 11; Stone of chapters 2 and 9; and Terrell of chapter 10. Chapter 12, on osteopathic medicine, was coauthored by Culbertson, Carl J. Denbow, and Guido H. Stempel III.

Acknowledgments

In writing this book, we drew on a life-time of inspiration and insight from professors, colleagues, students, and clients too numerous to mention. In particular, clients with whom we worked in studying the six cases contributed a great deal. We thank them very sincerely.

Also, we appreciate greatly several important recommendations and insights provided in the early stages of writing by Dr. James E. Grunig, professor of Journalism, University of Maryland. And each of us thanks his or her coauthors for stimulation, suggestions, constructive criticism, and many acts of kindness.

Following are acknowledgments by individual coauthors:

Martin Terrell deeply appreciates the faith, patience and breadth of perspective provided by his wife, Stephanie, at each stage of the project. Her support provided the inspiration needed to take on and complete this effort while Terrell worked full-time as a fund raiser during his university's largest-ever capital campaign.

The primary coauthors, all former students of Dr. Hugh M. Culbertson, owe him a special debt of gratitude for his encouragement, research, and teaching. All of these activities have proven valuable in our development.

M. T.

With great pleasure, Donna Stone extends heartfelt thanks to friend and colleague Kini Kedig, corporate supervisor of franchise relations, who unlocked the doors of the motel chain in which she played a key role. Also, thanks go to David Jones, senior vice-president of the Hotel Services Division of that chain, for continuing his open-communication policy. Both represent true public relations excellence.

A special debt of gratitude goes to Dr. Hugh M. Culbertson, a gentle, discerning man who recognizes even a faint spark of potential.

In addition, heartfelt thanks are offered to Betsy Ann Plank for information about a case offered in this text, and for her unstinting support of public relations education.

Finally, and most importantly, Stone give thanks to Dr. Gerald Stone, her favorite professor, husband, and dearest friend.

D. B. S.

Dennis Jeffers acknowledges the contribution of the more than 25 years of teaching, counseling and friendship of Dr. Hugh Culbertson to Jeffers' personal and professional career.

Also, Jeffers acknowledges the support and patience of the three most important persons in his life: his wife, Sue, and his sons, Andrew and Benjamin. During this project, as with other major endeavors in his life, they served as a source of strength.

D. W. J.

Hugh Culbertson acknowledges the pivotal role in this project played by his coauthors, all bright, able, stimulating former students who have made him proud in countless ways.

Drs. Carl J. Denbow and Guido H. Stempel III have contributed a great deal to the research reported in chapter 12—and to the perspective reflected throughout this volume. In addition, seminal ideas came from Drs. David K. Berlo, Carl J. Couch, the late Verling C. Troldahl, and the late Milton Rokeach, all former professors at Michigan State University, and from Gerald R. Miller, still a professor there. Also, Culbertson greatly appreciates many insights and much encouragement over 35 years from his dear friend and colleague, Dr. Juan Jamias, professor-emeritus at the University of the Philippines-Los Banos.

Confidentiality precludes identifying the police chief and several osteopathic physicians and educators with whom we worked, but their contributions were enormous.

Culbertson also owes a great debt to his wife, Charlene, who has supported him throughout and endured much frustration, and to his son, Steve, and daughter, Karen.

Finally, Culbertson offers sincere thanks to his "Chinese son-in-laws," Tang Siwei and Shuguang Zhang, and his "Chinese daughters"—Chen Ni, Chen Jiang, Liu Li, Liu Xia, Xu Chun, Ren Haihua, Yu Xinlu, Song Manhong, Zhou Xin, Chen Guang, Chen Yu-Qin, Yang Bin, and Min He—for helping him understand something of what two-way symmetric public relations really means.

H. M. C.

BACKGROUND

1 Introduction: Where This Book Is Coming From

For at least 80 years, the public relations profession/vocation has struggled to define itself. One person often regarded as a co-founder of the field, Ivy Ledbetter Lee, based his practice largely on case-by-case application of certain basic principles such as the need for openness and for doing good works if one is to receive favorable publicity. By and large, these principles have to do with one-way communication from practitioner and client to key publics (Cutlip, Center, & Broom, 1985).

Another co-founder, Edward L. Bernays, argued that public relations could best develop as an applied social science. In his view, psychological and sociological insights aid in gathering and interpreting data about public relations, needs, and preferences. Such a process seemed essential if public relations was to become a two-way street that Bernays saw as essential in establishing a mutually supportive relationship between client and public (Grunig & Hunt, 1984, pp. 37–41).

EVOLUTION OF CASE-RELATED PUBLIC RELATIONS EDUCATION

As public relations education has evolved, professors and the case-related courses they teach have gravitated toward either of two clusters:

Some emphasize publicity writing and techniques as Lee urged. Such content sometimes gains coverage largely in practical public relations principles courses, creating a market for texts such as Seitel (1987) and Reilly (1981). In recent years, publicity writing and techniques course have multiplied as separate entities, often utilizing texts such as Newsom and Wollert (1988) and Bivins (1988), as well as worktexts like Simon (1983).

Others stress behavioral science theory as advocated by Bernays. Such a focus has been urged by two commissions of the Foundation for Public Research and Education (Commission on Public Relations Education, 1975; National Commission on Graduate Study in Public Relations, 1985, pp. 5–12). Also, in a recent survey of educators, Culbertson (1985) documented substantial and growing emphasis on communication theory among public relations educators, especially among the growing number with doctoral degrees. Further, such a trend is suggested by the apparent success of recent editions of principles texts (Cutlip, Center, & Broom, 1985; Grunig & Hunt, 1984) that focus heavily on social science theory and research.

Further, the previously noted commissions reported and endorsed a growth in courses on public relations problems and cases (Commission on Public Relations Education, 1975, p. 11) and management (National Commission on Graduate Study in Public Relations, 1985, p. 10). Such courses draw on the notion, derived in part from years of teaching and study at the Harvard Business School (Christiansen with Hansen, 1987), that one can best prepare for management and planning by looking holistically and in depth at particular problems studied within a broad context. Texts such as Canfield (1968) and Center and Jackson (1990) exemplify such an approach to public relations teaching.

As management-and-cases instruction has evolved, it has gravitated toward the Lee tradition (emphasizing publicity writing and application of widely accepted but intuitively based principles) rather than the social science focus of Bernays. Texts such as Canfield (1968) and Center and Jackson (1990) devote very little attention to social science concepts and research as applied to case analysis. Also, the previously noted principles texts and recent writings on public relations theory (Pavlik, 1987) seldom apply theory in depth to specific cases.

Why is there a lack of bridges between case analysis and theory in the field? Perhaps the relatively few scholars doing theory-building research feel compelled to build more and better theory before concentrating on ways to use it (Broom, Cox, Krueger, & Liebler, 1989). Certainly it seems reasonable to build a good mousetrap before one sells or tries to use it much! However, scholars have long argued that, in development of a body of knowledge, practice affects inquiry as much as inquiry affects practice (Conant, 1951, p. 39). Thus introduction of behavioral science theory into the analysis of specific cases seems apt to benefit both.

THE AUTHORS' PERSPECTIVE

Against such a backdrop, the senior author has taught public relations principles at a major university for 26 years. In an attempt to define the class, he talked with and observed many successful practitioners who came to speak. As he listened to and questioned these people, he noted that the successful practitioners—and those most excited about their work—seemed widely read and able to analyze client problems and challenges in light of factors external to the client organization per se. Such practitioners had intellectual curiosity. They were really excited about looking at their clients and employers in broad social, political, and economic contexts.

Early on, the senior author began defining sensitivity to such contexts as a major goal of the principles course. How can people develop such a skill? He could offer few concrete suggestions beyond reading a lot and widely; interviewing leaders of the client organization and selected others in a detached, probing way; and looking for both aids and barriers to meeting publics' needs and gaining their support. He offered examples. But mostly he sent students into uncharted waters as they wrote papers on client public relations postures and problems.

Things proceeded with little change until, in the mid-1980s, an especially bright, bold student challenged the author after class one day. "What is this SPE [social, political, and economic] context business?" the student asked. "Surely you can do better than give us a few examples, tell us to read a lot, and send us to the Reader's Guide for Periodical Literature."

That response set the author to thinking and chatting with the second and third authors, both former advisees. Fortunately, all of us had been or soon would be doing applied research both to build and test theory and to help clients in concrete ways. We began trying to set down on paper what social science concepts helped us—sometimes without our realizing it—to design our research and interpret our data.

In 1989, the two senior authors presented a paper to the public relations division of the Association for Education in Journalism spelling out their use of several concepts within their own work. Three such notions had to do with the social context, two each with the political and economic contexts (Culbertson & Jeffers, 1992). Response to the paper suggested we'd struck a note in tune with what others were thinking. That, in turn, led us to invite our two colleagues to join us in writing this volume. They helped us expand the number of relevant concepts into the dozens and then to prune it so this volume would be of workable length.

As we write this, our definition of elements in the SPE context is still evolving. The number of potentially useful concepts is almost endless. We proceeded largely by groping—focusing on ideas that seem most useful to us.

As we studied, the social context occupied us more than the political and economic ones. Perhaps this stemmed in part from the fact that, on the whole, we were trained in communication and social psychology, not in political science or economics.

However, as we proceeded, we decided there was a deeper reason. Consideration of the political context focuses on gaining support from officials—on power relationships having to do with clients and the public at large. And economic context has to do largely with the distribution of resources.

Against this background, we pondered the oft-noted suggestions by Grunig and Hunt (1984, pp. 42–43) and Cutlip, Center, and Broom (1985, pp. 17–19) that two-way symmetric public relations offers more complete and generally fruitful service to society in most (not all) settings than do other types. This model involves great emphasis on:

> Listening to clients, seriously and respectfully, with every bit as much effort as one exerts in speaking to them. One cannot simply read, chat with as many people as possible, and hope to understand fully how the client organization and its actual or potential programs are viewed from the public's perspective. This last phrase is crucial. The word *symmetry,* as used here, asserts that one must learn public viewpoints and needs and adjust client behavior and approaches to these. One cannot simply seek to bring the public around, through persuasion, to the client's own set of preferences, intentions, or points of view.
>
> Doing research designed to clarify the public's needs as it defines them, not as it should define them in order to best serve the client organization. Such research differs in focus from that done in *asymmetric* approaches. There the primary goal is to develop and test persuasive appeals that may later bring the public around to the client's definition of the world (Grunig & Hunt, 1984, pp. 37–41).

In trying to apply these notions to definition of the SPE context, we found the social context to be paramount in understanding socially based public needs and how these can best be met. This required facilitating certain kinds of interaction between client and public. Economics and politics are important come planning and budgeting time, to be sure. But we argue that they generally have less to do, day to day, than the social context with studying publics, their needs, and how to meet them in creative, fruitful ways.

It seems necessary now to further justify focusing on the social, political, and economic contexts rather than slicing up the world in other ways.

Why the SPE Contexts?

To begin, the second word in the phrase public relations centers on ways in which people share meaning, take each other into account, influence others, and gain understanding as well as support and participation. Such social relations are focal points of social psychology. However, applied scholars and practitioners can best deal with them by borrowing from psychology, communication, and public-opinion research. These areas figure prominently in our analysis.

Public relations efforts deal to some degree with gaining resources and assessing their value to people. These resources include person power (time, skill, and willingness to behave in a certain way), money, and material goods. Questions of resource value are a major concern of economics. Of particular interest are the basic economic concepts of demand elasticity and marginal utility. Both deal with the amount a person is willing to pay for something in money or in labor and other inputs often assigned dollar-and-cent values.

Also of interest to practitioners is the question of how and where one obtains resources. Should they come from broad or narrow publics, and which ones? Do these publics actually have the resources to give? Can the client organization provide something in return so publics are willing to pay in some form? Are resources that the client needs controlled by bureaucrats or elected officials—analyzed basically as technocrats and politicians, respectively, in Bower's book, *The Two Faces of Management* (1983)? And is it most feasible and appropriate to seek support from government, from the private sector, or from both? These are but a few questions that economists can help answer.

Of course, economic analysis borrows profitably from social psychology. Two schools of thought in the latter discipline are especially useful here.

First, *exchange theory* in social psychology builds on the basic economic proposition that people normally work or pay only when they receive something in return that they see as justifying their inputs. And second, *standard-of-comparison theory* in psychology relates closely to the economic notion of diminishing marginal utility. Using the amount that Joan Smith consumed recently as a standard of comparison, theory suggests her third or fifth hamburger consumed at lunch will have less value than her first!

It is often said that resources translate into power and vice versa. And understanding power within an institutional setting is a major task of political science. Central here are questions of who has power, whether that power is based on coercion, persuasion, or exchange of material resources, and what processes and strategies figure in the gaining and losing of power.

Obviously, many of these processes and strategies have been examined by social psychologists. This points up, once again, the need for interdisciplinary study of public relations contexts. And it strengthens our argument in favor of the social context's centrality.

Issues Management: A Related Focus

Early on, we realized that management scholars had attempted to plan—and do research designed to support that effort—in ways that take broad organizational contexts into account. Carried out under such headings as "issues management" and "environmental scanning," the work shows up in public relations (Chase, 1977; Cutlip, Center, & Broom, 1985, pp. 15–16). We review the literature in both public relations and management on these concepts in chapter 2.

This review supports two basic conclusions. First, issues managers and environmental scanners draw on social science concepts to evaluate client contexts in ways from which public relations people can profit. Second, however, writings on issues management such as Miles (1987) have an asymmetric ring not quite in tune with the symmetric approach advocated here for public relations. Issues managers consider audience needs, all right. But in many if not most cases, client needs seem in subtle ways to come first. Audience concerns and reactions tend to gain thorough airing only insofar as they seem consistent with and supportive of the client organization.

Multiple Methodologies Needed

As we looked at our own research, methodological issues intrigued us. Theory-building studies often use one or at most two methodologies. However, in serving the needs of our clients, we felt compelled to draw on several methodologies: a systematic review of social-science and other professional or trade literature, in-depth interviews of experts and others highly involved in some way with our clients, focus groups, structured surveys, and even participant observation.

Time and money constraints sometimes led us to include fewer research strategies than might seem ideal. But we found the various approaches building on each other in ways not fully captured by the many research-methods books and chapters that approach them separately. Chapter 3 considers related methodological issues, describing particular sequences of strategies that we pursued in the studies reported here.

In Part III we present six studies that we have done for diverse clients: a corporation, a cause-oriented university center, a professional society, a police department, a city government, and a trade association. Each chapter covers a separate research effort, focusing in turn on:

1. Review of literature that helps define context at a national or international level.

2. Review of the local SPE contexts, where pertinent, based on direct observation, in-depth interviews and attention to relevant mass media.

3. Brief description of research methodology for the sequence of steps that we followed, clarifying how Step 1 strengthens Step 2, etc.

4. Presentation of findings interpreted in light of the SPE elements.

5. Consideration of specific courses of action suggested by, supported by, and/or called into question by the reported research. In some instances, the actions or policies discussed stem directly from our research. In other cases, basic ideas originated elsewhere but are assessed more fully and rigorously as a result of the study or studies reported. Each course of action is followed by a rationale favoring and/or opposing it. In line with the case-study teaching method, instructors may call attention to the courses of action and ask students to develop their own rationales, based on the research provided and other material, before reading the rationales provided.

6. A brief review of research findings and concepts that ties them concretely to the 17 elements as developed in chapters 4–6. Such "tying back" for conceptual refinement constitutes a separate section in some chapters but is integrated within

sections 4 and 5 in the list described previously, in other cases. This material is of particular interest to instructors who focus on theoretical development. Others may skip over this portion rather lightly.

In some chapters, these six sections appear in sequence. With other cases, the listed subject matter is included but is organized in a somewhat different way. Differing approaches were called for by different problems, and it seemed unwise to organize all six cases in precisely the same way.

The structure used here is patterned after that advocated by Christiansen with Hansen (1987) at the Harvard Business School. At Harvard, students first receive a description of a client organization's situation as it appears to managers at a key decision point. Case write-ups then present background information and suggest possible options before leading students back to the decision point with an assignment to consider all relevant angles, come up with actions or policies, and defend these.

Harvard Case-Study Approach Serves as Model

At Harvard, free-wheeling, nondirective discussion is emphasized and appears to work well even with large, diverse classes (Christiansen with Hansen, 1987, pp. 17–49). Public relations professors and students probably are receptive to such an approach because they have already used and studied similar methods such as the nominal group technique (McElreath, 1984) and game playing (Masel-Waters, 1984).

In line with the Harvard approach, good students will surely propose policies and actions that we have not thought of. Our list of possible steps is not presented as exhaustive.

In Part IV, chapter 13 provides an overview of the SPE contexts in light of the research and analysis given earlier. Illustrative conclusions based on each contextual element are discussed so as to sharpen understanding of that element.

It seems appropriate to conclude this chapter by commenting on the four authors and why they presume to develop such a volume.

ABOUT THE AUTHORS

In total, the four have amassed about 39 years of teaching experience and 23 years as public relations practitioners. Two, Culbertson and Jeffers, have spent most of their careers in teaching and research. The other two, Stone and Terrell, have had backgrounds primarily as practitioners. Among them, the four authors have had substantial involvement in all four often mentioned facets of public relations practice: corporate, agency, nonprofit, and professional/trade association.

The three most senior authors have all presented refereed papers on public relations theory and research at national-society meetings. In all, the authors have published about 70 books, book chapters, and refereed articles.

Culbertson was the second recipient of the annual Pathfinder Award given by the Foundation for Public Relations Research and Education to honor outstanding public relations scholarship. Also, the Public Relations Society of America chose him as its 1990 Educator of the Year. Jeffers and Stone have received top-paper awards from the Public Relations Division, Association for Education in Journalism and Mass Communication.

In concluding, we return to a theme raised earlier. Our definition of the SPE context is still evolving; in fact, we call it a crude attempt at this point. As theoretical tools and practical experience develop, we hope other scholars and practitioners will help build that better mousetrap.

One further point. Study of the SPE context requires considerable rigor and effort. We tried to make this volume as user friendly as possible. But understanding the concepts and relating them to each other takes time and effort. We caution readers not to assume they can master a case or theoretical chapter in 15 or 30 minutes. We hope the exercise proves stimulating and useful. However, good things seldom come easily.

REFERENCES

Bivins, T. (1988). *Handbook for public relations writing*. Lincolnwood, IL: National Textbook.

Bower, J. L. (1983). *The two faces of management*. New York: Mentor.

Broom, G. M., Cox, M. S., Krueger, E. A., & Liebler, C. M. (1989). The gap between professional and research agendas in public relations. In J. E. Grunig & L. A. Grunig (Eds.), *Public relations research annual* (Vol. 1, pp. 141–154). Hillsdale, NJ: Lawrence Erlbaum Associates.

Canfield, B. R. (1968). *Public relations: Principles, cases & problems*. Homewood, IL: Richard D. Irwin.

Center, A. H., & Jackson, P. (1990). *Public relations practices: Managerial case studies and problems*. Englewood Cliffs, NJ: Prentice-Hall.

Chase, W. H. (1977). Public issue management: The new science. *Public Relations Journal, 33*, 25–26.

Christiansen, C. R. with Hansen, A. J. (1987). *Teaching and the case method*. Boston: Harvard Business School Publishing Division.

Commission on Public Relations Education (1975). *A design for public relations education*. New York: Foundation for Public Relations Research and Education.

Conant, J. B. (1951). *Science and common sense*. New Haven, CT: Yale University Press.

Culbertson, H. M. (1985). Practitioner roles: Their meaning for educators. *Public Relations Review, 11*, 5–21.

Culbertson, H. M., & Jeffers, D. W. (1992). The social, political and economic contexts: Keys in educating true public relations professionals. *Public Relations Review, 18*, 53–65.

Cutlip, S. M., Center, A. H., & Broom, G. M. (1985). *Effective public relations*. Englewood Cliffs, NJ: Prentice-Hall.

Grunig, J. E., & Hunt, T. (1984). *Managing public relations*. New York: Holt, Rinehart & Winston.

Masel-Waters, L. (1984). Playing the game: Ethics situations for public relations courses. *Public Relations Research & Education, 1*, 46–54.

Mc Elreath, M. P. (1984). Playing the game: Ethics situations for public relations course. *Public Relations Research & Education, 1,* 55–60.

Miles, R. H. (1987). *Managing the corporate social environment: A grounded theory.* Englewood Cliffs, NJ: Prentice-Hall.

National Commission on Graduate Study in Public Relations (1985). *Advancing public relations education: Recommended curriculum for graduate public relations education.* New York: Foundation for Public Relations Research and Education.

Newsom, D., & Wollert, J. A. (1988). *Media writing: Preparing information for the mass media.* Belmont, CA: Wadsworth.

Pavlik, J. V. (1987). *Public relations: What research tells us.* Beverly Hills, CA: Sage.

Reilly, R. T. (1981). *Public relations in action.* Englewood Cliffs, NJ: Prentice-Hall.

Seitel, F. P. (1987). *The practice of public relations.* Columbus, OH: Charles Merrill.

Simon, R. (1983). *Publicity and public relations worktext.* Columbus, OH: Grid.

2 Issues Management: Decision Making in Action

DECISION MAKING IN ACTION

Public relations—management by communications—covers several conceptual and practical categories, including issues management (IM). As a systematic approach, IM recognizes, then selects, environmental issues that warrant planned organizational activity. Chiefly, IM is concerned with its own operations, and only with those external interactions that help meet internal needs.

In recent years, IM and the related concept of environmental scanning have gained much attention in the public relations literature. IM specialists pioneered the study of social, political, and economic contexts. However, IM differs from the approach offered here in at least two ways.

First, IM literature often has an asymmetric ring. That is, the client organization practicing IM focuses on context primarily in ways designed to insure its own survival and enhancement. Traditionally, the client organization comes first. On the other hand, we argue that study of the SPE context can and should give at least as much priority to the needs of external publics as to those of the clients. This equal attention more closely resembles the two-way symmetric model of public relations than does IM.

Second, context implies a focus on events, people, and problems external to an organization. Although IM scans the external environment, the focus is the process within the client organization that insures effective analysis of outside forces, then translation into strategy and tactics. Thus, IM serves as a link between the SPE context and organizational decision making and action.

Issue Defined

An issue is an ongoing public policy dispute affecting organizational performance, such as any continuing trend, event, or condition that affects an organization. For example, an issue might be diversity, or lack of it, in a plan, program, or organization. Indeed, there were unanticipated public outcries over the "Circa 1492" museum exhibit in Washington, DC, to the extent of down playing Columbus' discovery (or some say destruction) of America. The exhibit, perhaps the entire commemoration of the Columbus landing, evokes various responses depending on the individual or group perspectives.

Other issues are educational reform, changes in the tax structure, and health insurance. The slippery nature of these topics is but one element they all share. Each is an ongoing issue with multiple factors touching several areas in the social, political, and economic contexts. Further, they are especially relevant during an election year, an aspect adding to their slipperiness!

Although areas of business are slippery, or difficult to understand, some things are certain. One is the 5% rule of thumb. Any 5% increase or decrease in business performance is regarded as significant (Newman, 1989). This guideline accounts for IM flourishing in business circles. The focus is on internal procedures as a reaction to outside factors. In this way, IM differs from the social, political, and economic contexts perspectives that emphasize symmetrical communications.

Jones and Chase System

Shelby (1986) wrote, "Issues management aims for a positive, pro-active response to emerging issues that . . . impact on the organization" (pp. 4–5). The Jones and Chase (1979) Issues Management Process Model is "a resource for integrating diverse line and staff functions into a systems process for public policy management." The model consists of concentric circles illustrating steps to manage issues: (a) identification, (b) analysis, (c) developing strategy options for change, (d) action programming, and (e) evaluation.

Jones and Chase, contending public policy is at the heart of their model, created five classifications useful in defining issues.

Category	Definition
1. type	social, political, economic, technological
2. impact and response source	business system, industry, corporation, subsidiary, department
3. geography	international, national, regional, state, local
4. span of control	noncontrollable, semicontrollable, controllable
5. salience	immediacy, prominence

Those researchers, two of the first to offer cogent data on IM, also presented the issues identification guidelines of Robert Moore, coordinator of emerging issues for The Conference Board. These top-to-middle level activities are: recognition, discussion, formal research, selection for senior management consideration, strategic planning, and publication scanning.

Chase (1984) later offered "both the rationale and disciplines for effective issue/policy management" (p. 5). He gave brief background data and linked the interests among citizens, business, and government. However, Crable & Vibbert (1985) criticized Chase for not specifying the power, influence, and authority exerted in those relationships.

VARIETY OF INTERPRETATIONS

Despite the efforts of Chase, the literature reveals no clear consensus in defining IM. That helps explain the fog surrounding this misunderstood topic. Humans are rational animals, but at least one researcher contends they are rationalizing animals trying to appear reasonable (Aronson, 1980). Small wonder, then, that interpretations of concepts about human behavior, including IM, vary.

Credibility

Certainly a realm of growing concern to private, commercial, and governmental sectors, IM has endured the strife of any young specialty area. First, credibility is low. In an effort to raise it, practitioners make new claims. In an apparent attempt to establish final ownership of the concept, each claimant comes up with a different name denoting associated tasks, such as: advocacy advertising, boundary spanning, corporate planning, crisis management, forecasting, futurism, human resource management, intelligence activities, management styles, public affairs, public policy, and strategic IM (Grunig, 1988; Hainsworth & Meng, 1988; Heath, 1990).

Whatever the jargon, IM draws on social science concepts to evaluate client context for management planning. In short, IM enables an organization (or any assigned unit) to increase knowledge about itself and internal–external environments and publics for meaningful decision making. This process helps the organization cope with proliferating social, political, and economic changes. However, the asymmetric ring clearly resounds as business invokes IM to focus primarily on its own needs. Usually, external publics gain attention only when interaction or reaction fulfills organizational needs.

Public Relations Responsibility

However, in the last decade, responsibility for identifying issues has gravitated to public relations. With this seemingly minor change comes a broader management perspective. The organizational ability to adapt and influence the environment depends in part on the degree to which public relations is involved in the decision-making process (Dozier, 1986; Ehling & Hesse, 1983).

Unquestionably, IM is risky business (Heath & Nelson, 1986). Issues create phenomenal opportunities but also pose dangers for an organization. Related global and localized changes include:

1. shifts in wealth and power throughout the world;
2. a new type of worker: adventurous, artistic, seeking unlimited access to all information that increases knowledge;
3. information overload;
4. increased legal liabilities;
5. inability of business to hide anything from the public, government, or media;
6. a growing need for business to work with media in expeditious, fruitful ways;
7. ethics that seem to be achieving higher priority; and
8. problem solving that is both complex and public (Pinsdorf, 1987).

Consumerism, social reform, and political activism all affect business decision making. Groups that constantly monitor ethical and political decisions of business are especially pertinent. Today, almost all businesses face some issues—product safety, health care, sexual harassment, racism, right to know, privacy, air and water pollution, etc.

Pre-IM Considerations

Efficient planning and strategy become more important as organizational management grows in complexity. Before setting goals and identifying issues, organizations must spell out their purposes. Historically, many corporations tried to maintain a low profile so management could make decisions unilaterally. Still, IM evolved in business to improve effectiveness of anticipating, assessing, and responding to strategic topics (Callaghan, 1984).

Analysis of organizational behavior yields several frameworks applicable to top managers and stakeholders. One approach covers different levels of analysis, considering contextual variables and "ever-present constraints" (Janis, 1989). There are four key assumptions:

1. A strong, positive relationship exists between procedural quality that drives fundamental policy decisions and successful outcomes.

2. Most top-level managers are capable of following procedures to arrive at high-quality decisions.

3. Policy makers usually exert little effort to use quality procedures in a policy decision if they believe the issue is unimportant, especially in terms of what is at stake for the organization.

4. When dealing with an issue, even one with serious consequences, policymakers pay too much attention to constraints and excessively depend on simplistic, ineffective decision rules.

Generally, managers understand the cost of vigilant problem solving as described by Janis. There is obvious need for efficient use of time, effort, and money. Managers do not demand resources to deal with a given issue unless the stakes seem high. Even executives accustomed to viewing the larger picture tend to track only a few problems. Janis bemoaned the lack of research about problem recognition as a guide for impending or current conflict.

Particular beliefs about vital national interests are among factors that influence national policymakers' judgments on issue significance. Such judgments, in turn, guide choice of issues that merit information search and evaluation or other dedication of resources. Cultural beliefs are equally important.

People perceive a problem to be important when they detect a difference between the way things are (e.g., situations and actors) and the way they want things to be. Additionally, linkages of one problem to another are considered, along with the extent to which the newly perceived problem is interpreted as threatening.

If too many problems simultaneously confront the policymaker, something must be dropped from the agenda. Selecting which issues to drop may depend on the level of ambiguity underlying available information. Coping with vague data or highly variable circumstances can produce stress, frustration, or confusion. In chapter 4, this volume provides a thorough discussion of cultural beliefs that helps managers assess issue importance.

WINNERS AND LOSERS

Changing Times and Environmental Cues

People often do not change quite as rapidly as other elements in the environment, despite pressure to do so (Bridges, 1986). Ability and willingness to change is a prerequisite for realizing the American Dream. Today, managers of corporations, nonprofits and government agencies must be able to tolerate high and frequent ambiguity. Stages individuals go through to reduce uncertainty are unclear. According to Bridges, executives often have shallow understanding of the powerful consequences of change.

"Why do some leaders become losers?" executives ask. Foster (1986) aptly quoted Sir Leuan Maddock from the *New Scientist,* 1982:

To cherish traditions, old buildings, ancient cultures and graceful lifestyles is a worthy thing—but in the world of technology to cling to outmoded methods of manufacture, old product lines, old markets, or old attitudes among management and workers is a prescription for suicide. (p. 26)

Foster concluded that leaders and managers can not assume tomorrow will be just like today. Substantial change is likely. Firms such as IBM, Hewlett-Packard, Johnson & Johnson, Procter & Gamble, and Illinois Bell realize change occurs rapidly. However, those corporate innovators believe environments are predictable, analyzable, inevitable, and manageable. They see major advantages in sustaining innovative high performance. And they realize that nonassertive, unimaginative corporate behavior is often more risky than innovation and change.

Betsy A. Plank, Assistant Vice President, Corporate Communications, Illinois Bell, explained how Illinois Bell invoked IM and SPE context monitoring to abbreviate, if not preclude, impending danger of public telephone abuse by drug dealers. Plank (personal communications February 6, 12, and 18, 1992) noted that initially, it was alert Community Relations managers who recognized unusual activity. During evening hours in some disadvantaged Chicago neighborhoods, drug dealers usurped public telephones, using them as offices for illegal trading.

IM specialists at Illinois Bell identified numerous problems and the potential costly and hostile backlash. From an overall organizational perspective, reputation, integrity, and corporate responsibility were literally on the line. Illegal use of telephone services enabling drug traffic to thrive almost caused organizational short circuits!

Customer Service was concerned about citizens without residential telephone service being cut off, if not isolated, from the community—particularly in emergency situations. Marketing feared problems would compel city leaders to force the company to remove many public telephones, a bottom line loss estimated at $1.2 million.

With IM research and analysis that prompted top-management involvement, Plank said the entire organization pushed to find a solution. The collaboration of one of Bell's Quality of Work Life Committees, an employee group of community relations and operations and marketing employees, creatively came up with a solution to protect neighborhoods and telephones. The result, according to Plank, accounted for public and organizational concerns:

After many months of meeting with city officials, community and company people, the decision came down. In nighttime hours, those public phones are automatically converted to use only with operator assistance. Since this forces a "paper trail" of usage, drug dealers no longer risk using the phones, whose calls could then be traced by police. Citizens now have reclaimed those public phones for legitimate use, including toll-free emergency 911, information 411, and repair 611.

The announcement of the solution, unique in the U.S. at that time, was made by the city's mayor, applauded by the community, customers, and the police, and received national media attention.

The role of IM in researching and analyzing the situation and prompting priority action was essential to avoiding potential problems for community, company, and public. (February 12, 1992)

Prime examples of unimaginative behavior contributed to risks taken by Dow and Du Pont (Szwape & Seeger, 1989) provide different scenarios. Both corporations, fully aware of the destruction to the environment, continued to produce environmentally dangerous chemicals, despite public complaints and governmental warnings.

According to Habermas (1975), a legitimate organization and its actions are approved by society. Therefore, behavior counter to environmental safety called into question the legitimacy—their right to exist—of those two chemical giants. Yet, both responded through techniques common to a closed communication system. They tried to alter governmental reports, forestall negative legislation, actively conceal information from the media and public, and campaign to prolong research and truth-finding stages of investigations.

Innovation Recommended

In a similar vein, Fink (1986) advised a pre-emptive approach to issues, looking "for the opportunity that exists in every crisis: manage it, get control of it, benefit from it. Somebody will, why shouldn't it be you?" (p. 224).

Executives must be trained to examine every extraordinary occurrence, subtle or overt, managing fluid situations with scrupulous information processing. Before serious planning, the framework and parameters for plans need to be established. Hence, priorities and policies can not lead to violent conflict with government agencies or with any higher authority inside the client organization.

"Public relations organizes relations with publics to accomplish business strategy," according to Newman (1989). He counseled practitioners on the importance of concentrating on three to six issues at any one time. In selecting issues, managers should weigh organizational purposes. This process helps gauge the probability of a problem occurring, the significance of its impact on the organization, and the potential time frame for events.

Current events underscore the need for corporations to monitor internal and external environments. Examples are the decline of communism in Europe, the Middle East summit conference, and employee and customer class-action liability claims facing companies such as The Manville Corporation, A. H. Robins Co., and Continental Airlines. Also relevant are exposure of toxic waste disposal practices of supposedly "clean" companies, and indictment of top managers for criminal acts (even murder) arising from employee work conditions (Epstein, 1987).

Spirit of Cooperation and A Competitive Edge

Buller's research (1988a) indicated that firms gain competitive advantage partly by integrating strategic planning and human resource functions. The level of integration depends on external business environments. Many companies already associate human resources and strategic planning. Research indicates that companies integrating the two areas with other functions enjoy a competitive edge. Especially important are the quality and levels at which meshing strategic planning and human resources, taken together, fit with the external environment.

The competitive crisis in the United States underscores the imperative of cooperation. In fact, many organizations survive only by cooperating. American corporations gain a reality check with a glance at Japanese successes. Prosperity in the Far East is based on importance of interdependence there among social institutions that actively seek partners (Waddock, 1988).

The rapport between business and government, business and schools, and business and nonprofits is becoming more evident in the United States. Awareness of a decline in competition among sectors of society contributes to a national willingness to discuss issues. Partners establish issues such as community development, employment training for the disadvantaged, employee upgrading, and education.

Cooperating organizations also find ways to strengthen coalitions for dealing with the problems. These partnerships help society by cooperating as long as they do not engage in such practices as price fixing and bribe taking. Collusion destroys healthy competition. Also, resulting bigness hampers adaptiveness and responsiveness to public needs.

Asking a few questions tightens bonds between business and members of several environments:

1. Are all important stakeholders included?
2. Is there a civic entrepreneur or group available to champion the partnership?
3. Can partner representatives make decisions in partnership meetings?
4. Is top management committed?
5. Are stakeholders willing to cooperate?
6. Is power within partnership evenly balanced?
7. How much do the partners know about each other and the problems and issues?

IM resembles agenda setting, because both focus on the emergence and identification of new areas of interest. However, IM goes beyond agenda setting to solve salient problems and foster dialogue among diverse groups for advanced planning (Powers, 1987). Corporate planning must occur over time, encompassing strategic, project, and operational aspects (Meidan, 1986).

McGinnis (1985) pointed to the importance of business creatively and imaginatively living with environmental ambiguity. Any type of change generates conflict because of disruption in who holds resources and power (Greenhalgh, 1986).

MANAGING CONFLICT

Role Taking Useful

Presumably, conflict can be managed, assuming no substantial interference with ongoing relationships among those involved. Conflict is not a logical, material phenomenon, but an intangible in the minds of people. The phenomenon's symptoms include human brooding, arguing, fighting, or confusion—real elements that have to be dealt with. Empathy and understanding of the situation (viewed as role taking in symbolic interaction theory) are necessary for managing conflict.

Persuasion is basic to conflict management and provides a rationale to re-think views. Hence, people cultivate new perspectives that enhance reconciliation, rather than divisiveness. Often, third-party intervention helps.

A systematic approach to conflict management hinges in part on the context in which conflict occurs, the history of relationships, and the time available. During conflict, managers should emphasize agreement, not decision. If agreement can be reached, decision usually follows soon. The imperative is for all parties to accurately understand one another regardless of whether they achieve agreement.

Managers need to explore their individual standards of comparison and beliefs that shape interpretation and recognize differences among themselves. In this context, conflict management removes affective barriers to agreement. Even so, agreement does not mean the conflict has gone away, but ideally it does imply commitment to action that serves the interests of all contending parties.

Conflict-Theory Model

The Janis and Mann conflict-theory model (1977, p. 55) helps determine when communication variables readily precede the IM process. The model poses four simple, albeit important, questions:

1. Are the risks serious if I don't change?
2. Are the risks serious if I do change?
3. Is it realistic to hope to find a better solution?
4. Is there sufficient time to search and deliberate?

The two noted psychologists conceded the importance of other important variables that define antecedent conditions. These include a panic reaction to individual environmental cues, personalities, and predispositional characteristics that determine sensitivity to indications of change.

Good managers can manage context.   In fact, those who manage only content can do little more than improve organizational efficiency in a procedural sense. True effectiveness eludes such managers (Davis, 1982). Context encompasses the unquestioned assumptions through which all experience is filtered. Although context per se has no meaning, it provides the basis from which content is derived. Thus, context creates reality, which in turn creates the content.

The context emerges from drawing a boundary or frame around the issue, event, or people. Anything within the boundary is content. Asking a question determines the boundaries of the inquiry. A question centers attention, providing direction for answers. Participants look closely at that which they know they do not know. The wrong question yields the wrong data, and participants are side tracked. This problem, discussed later, is inherent in decision making.

Still, a key to a strategic-smart organization is leadership capable of transforming the context in which the task is held. Leadership defines a new role for itself. Symbolic interactionists refer to this ability as role making, as opposed to taking and defending an existing role. Davis pointed to a paradox here. Leaders often have a stake in perpetuating problems so as to keep their jobs.

Argyris (1974) explained the contribution of a win–win dynamic to higher levels of organizational performance. Individuals inside the organization have to realize they can't succeed unless the entire organization prospers. Any internal, counterproductive employee competition endangers organizational survival.

Davis (1982) substantiated the concept. Each job's importance stems from its implications for the organization and for all members. The most important task is the one not yet done. Doing the job is the reward, resulting in a stronger organization with fewer conflicts. This positive sentiment also serves as an umbrella concept governing IM.

The uniqueness of the Janis–Mann model is "the specification of conditions relating to conflict, hope, and time pressure" (pp. 172–178) that either foster diligent information searches and processing or precipitate defective decision patterns. These scholars define five coping patterns of decision makers:

1. Vigilance—thoroughly collects, then evaluates data for planned action (e.g., canvassing alternatives, weighing costs and consequences, detailing plans)
2. Unconflicted inertia—feels no danger or need to change; ignoring warnings
3. Unconflicted change—carries out new forms of action without resistance
4. Defensive avoidance—blocks any hint of ideas/actions that induce anxiety
5. Hyper-vigilance—shows hasty situational evaluation, then snap judgment; usually panic thinking from insufficient time and data

Deliberate interventions counteract the beliefs and perceptions responsible for poor coping patterns. All of the patterns listed, except vigilance, hamper important decision making. Studies indicate certain fundamental reactions to high stress.

However, behavior becomes quite subtle during decisional conflicts involving less stress. At such times, the more ambiguous the threat, the more the decision maker's perceptions determine actions.

During emergencies, regardless of the degree of threat, a person may use the cognitive approach that includes personal estimates of the: (a) probability danger will materialize, (b) severity of personal losses if danger materializes, and (c) probable advantages or disadvantages of alternatives available for averting or minimizing the danger.

Given needed preparation and calmness, people are capable of making the same kinds of decisions in emergency situations as for less consequential decisions. Methods are similar, with full use of cognitive judgments in collecting data and weighing criteria.

Decision Making as a Natural Aspect

The decision-making process is a natural aspect of business at every management level, whether or not it's carried out intentionally or consciously. The very act of not making a decision about monitoring the environment or publics is, in itself, a de facto decision.

Identification of issues is critical and usually is done through environmental or boundary scanning. This task often is quite informal. However, ideally IM is a linear process in which public opinion crystalizes, then public policy is made. Grievances often arise, and litigation may follow severe conflict. Modern IM-oriented companies do not wait for environmental changes. Rather they look for trends and detect patterns in the external environment.

Some companies such as Gannett have admitted that policy outcomes were not to their liking because of "relatively minimal external affairs operations." In that firm not too long ago, a legal department handled such affairs while public relations was composed of "one male practitioner and three ladies" and upper management was not involved (Miles, 1987, p. 183).

Organizational survival depends, in part, on the ability to deal with a variety of audiences (Gibson, 1980). Some organizations are structured in specific ways to handle those audiences. Grunig (1988) confirmed that environment affects organizational structure. She reported that some practitioners astutely recognize the need for segmenting audiences. Her work supports the idea that public opinion threatens organizational autonomy more than the direct influence of government.

Social science research indicates numerous circumstances that work against what Janis and Mann (1977) called optimal approaches to receiving and using information. Policymakers in large organizations often use less than ideal methods.

Any issue or crisis can harm an organization's reputation, the ability to make a profit, or even survivability. In fact, the implications of issues change the organization. Those policymakers who fail to recognize stages of issue evolution (signal detection, preparation prevention, containment or damage limitation, recovery, and learning) jeopardize their organizations, often beyond repair. Crisis and contingency plans point to better alternatives (Lerbinger, 1989).

Sociologists find that decision makers are influenced by their social institutions, habits, and traditions. Frequently, these factors converge so people act irrationally. Although not ideal, this approach can lead to action. That, in turn, may be better than no action at all.

Implications are great, because most important decisions are made in groups rather than by individuals (Walsh, Henderson, & Deighton, 1988). Group processing of information directly affects decisions. The Janis and Mann (1977) and Janis (1982) well-known term *groupthink* sounds a warning. Groups in which members look, act, and talk alike are big on agreement but small on perspective. Considerable research examines those processes (Culbertson, 1989).

Walsh and Fahey (1986) showed that group politics helped determine whose knowledge structures shaped a group's collective structure. Researchers found that negotiated belief structures establish cognitive orientations within a given group. This construct stems in part from psychological schema theory.

Schema theory, elaborated in chapter 4, holds that people build knowledge structures (schemata) to provide form and structure for information environments. Realized coverage and realized consensus are systematically related to the question at hand and to the big picture. A schema works somewhat like a template, affecting what information is attended to and how it is interpreted. In this way, people simplify reality, organizing information so it makes sense to them.

Do schemata lead to accurate, functional definitions of the environment? According to Hogarth (1988) desirable belief structures do. However, many scholars doubt that most managers can overcome selective perception to accurately read complex information.

Law of Requisite Variety: Diversity of Ideas = Diversity of Environment

The law of requisite variety holds that the diversity of ideas and viewpoints within a manager's self-regulating system should equal diversity of the environment. Complex information domains require complex belief structures. Awareness of many assumptions and beliefs of all group members during decision making contributes to effective decisions. Without such awareness, the wrong problem may be solved! This notion of breathing life into the wrong problem is referred to as the "error of the third kind," by Raiffa (1968).

In light of diversity implications, scholars and practitioners attend to ethics and social responsibility of business behavior. According to Naisbitt and Aburdene's *Re-Inventing the Corporation* (1985), being people oriented is not the same as being nice to people.

Listening carefully to internal audiences is every bit as important as scanning external environments. The two do not act independently of each other. Studies of osteopathic medicine, detailed in chapter 12, point to the equally important and frequently interdependent internal and external publics (Culbertson & Stempel, 1982).

Understanding all publics is vital to issues management. Having a finger on the pulse of the people guides business globally so even governments change (Moskowitz, 1987). Mobil Oil, a leader in corporate advocacy, exhibits concern with corporate image as well as social and political issues that help determine public policy. By evoking elaborate, transcendent frames of reference, Mobil scans and addresses a broad and varied environment (Williamson, 1982).

Bhambri (1984) looked at how different companies are organized to deal with public policies. He asked two questions: (a) What is the difference in the internal dynamics of the IM process in "responsive" and "unresponsive" companies? and (b) How and why do these differences develop with organizational experience over time?

He found two distinct patterns relative to public policy. First, adaptive organizations are receptive to change. Secondly, other groups are protective and eager to justify the status quo. The two types tend to differ as to values in place when an organization was established.

Researchers have featured such matters only within specific parts of society. For example, in medicine, work has centered on inpatient clinics and emergency units (EUs) as policymakers tried to resolve conflicts while protecting their bottom lines (Georgopoulous, 1988). Many nonemergency cases received treatment at inpatient clinics and emergency units, increasing power of these two entities within their overall hospitals and clinics.

Transformation Leadership and Ethics

Leadership and management studies neglect ethical values despite the surge of extensive corporate misdeeds made public. Corruption of business leaders, especially at high levels, is an ever-present media theme.

Flagrant breaches of public trust call attention to the need for leaders, not managers. Those who merely shuffle paper are not leaders and will not succeed. "In business organizations, as in the family, politics flourish in the absence of content and expression of talents" (Zaleznik, 1989, p. 21).

Obviously, managerial skills are necessary but not sufficient as most organizations need to transform themselves. Leaders must understand internal and external environments, involving a host of issues to project future organizational outcomes (Tichey & Devanna, 1986).

Transformation leadership inspires people rather than using them. The latter is manipulative, but the former excites people to follow capable leaders and perform beyond the call of duty. The moral aspects of leadership and social responsibility are crucial (Kalwies, 1988).

Such leadership, based on self-mastery, builds on consistent faith in human ingenuity and can favorably affect a work force. Self-actualizing leaders set people before profits, provide individual growth, and promote slow, incremental changes in employee behavior. People and organizations in this mode profit from and enjoy fundamental changes.

Forecasting

Studies in decision-maker forecasting deal with accuracy and uncertainty predictions. Forecasting assumes several forms along at least three continua (Turk, 1986):

conservative⟵——————————————————————⟶**radical**
future is like the past   utopian futures ignore
                                                           real world complexities

qualitative⟵——————————————————————⟶**quantitative**
perceived future with   facts, figures, and statistically
judgmental changes in life   measurable quality phenomena

subjective⟵——————————————————————⟶**objective**
forecaster as artist   empirical or quasi-empirical
                                                           scientific method

This type of research is interesting and has practical value. Still, not much is known about systematic forecasting or planning with high uncertainty about the future.

Forecasting techniques help apply strategic management to organizational development. Buller (1988b) suggested six activities needed in strategic management: (a) creating a state of readiness, (b) strategy formulation, (c) strategy implementation, (d) managing organizational decline, (e) mergers/acquisitions, and (f) developing leadership skills.

Specifically, organizational development concepts and practices that enhance strategic decision making are: diagnosis, team building, open system planning, survey feedback, intergroup activities, role analysis, coaching and counseling, education and training, structural activities, life and career-planning activities, action research, and process consultation.

Barriers to Action

Additionally, conditions are created to expedite implementing decisions. Fundamental barriers are differences in values, skills, knowledge, and actual outcomes of organizational operations. Strategic managers have to be sensitive to human elements of change. Pluralism, legitimacy of dissent, and a fluid power structure all enhance organizational development.

Indicators of sensitivity are accomplished through broader formal education and experience. Public relations practitioners must expand their knowledge to resolve conflicts among organization and development values of top management, particularly in profitability and uses of power and politics. Success demands that managers grasp broad perspectives and skill in integrative thinking such as that found by General Electric and Minnesota Mining and Manufacturing.

IM helps corporate social performance. Business literature is replete with management planning and strategy predicated on identifying issues. Amey (1986) discussed planning as "designing the desired future" and dealing with uncertainty and change. Business commonly makes performance the target of tactical plans. The rationale for planning is derived from, among others, Ackoff (1970, pp. 2–4), who described an organization as a complex structure requiring a systems approach.

Context Shapes Content

Levy (1986) drew from communication and psychology theories to discuss how context shapes content and to show that what people see is determined by what they believe. He argued that organizational members must plan change, drawing on internal and external experts as well as the managers themselves.

Planned changes often require: (a) purposeful, explicit decisions for a program of change, (b) a total program of change, (c) internal and external professional guidance, and (d) strategy of collaboration and power sharing between change agents and the client system. Planning helps the system change organizational environment to merge with organizational goals. Survival is achieved through adaptation. And some firms do more than survive (Limerick & Cunnington, 1989).

However, many CEOs in practice seem deliberately to avoid buying such assumptions as the need for teamwork and an open system. Nonetheless, especially in the last 10 years, corporate activity has expanded to identify, analyze, and respond to growing issues. Experience shows that strategic plans fail when leadership influence in the power structure and organizational dynamics is not recognized. Boundary scanning is best achieved by those who are well connected internally and externally (Tushman & Scanlan, 1981).

Resource Allocation

Researchers are quick to point out that all manner of decisions require allocation of resources (Ansoff, 1988). Newman (1989) discussed this concept as particularly relevant to competition or in usurping the competitive advantage.

He defined a competitor as any entity, human or organizational, that vies for the same resources. Often the strategy is depriving competitors of essential assets or basic resources. A more positive object here, of course, devises an allocation pattern to meet organizational needs. Reaching consensus is difficult, especially during times of diminishing resources, as individuals protect their areas of interest (Milter, 1986).

Actually, some situations only appear as no-win propositions able to do little more than deplete resources. The executive challenge is to create a different alternative, consonant with personal ethics and public responsibility. Environmental analysis may well lead to redefinition of elements to account for exceptional cases and stakeholder needs. A clear example was the Bush Administration's redefinition of *terrorists* and *assassination*—terms that had interfered with covert government attempts to disengage Noriega from power.

Building Consensus

Complexity of the modern business world demands innovative methods to meet society's needs. A holistic understanding of stakeholders and publics requires the anticipatory approach. Managers who are passionate diligently assemble relevant information for evaluation, integration, and action and move beyond linear thinking to complex strategy (Morris, 1987).

Just as corporate managers change, so do the social, political, and economic issues. The call to set priorities places a higher value on establishing issue impact. Corporations concentrate on shorter time-frame planning with a look inward at corporate objectives and competitive success. The result is "competitive co-opera- tion." As expected, consensus building emerges successfully (Littlejohn, 1986).

Actually, consensus building is good for business. Favorable public opinion of business is personally gratifying, and in most instances, it encourages economic stability. Further, it is a critical dimension of corporate legitimacy. Although there are cycles of more or less public faith in business, a society can not function without confidence in its leaders and institutions (Silk & Vogel, 1976).

Weakening of public trust today often stems from governmental actions. The consumer-confidence crisis is pervasive because of perceived manipulations such as managed news, credibility gap, or false advertising (Johannesen, 1981). Problems accompanying the dual role of advocate and information source compound ethical dilemmas (Sterba, 1990).

Simply by virtue of size, many corporations are positioned as consequential members of the national social order. They exert influence because in not deciding to act on an issue there is, in effect, a decision (Kuhn & Berg, 1969). Until a company decides what it is, it can not fully participate in the political process, as its own role is unarticulated. Hence, the organization can not identify, analyze, or properly evaluate issues (Sethi, 1982).

As underscored by Peters and Waterman (1982), excellent companies stay close to the consumer. The rationale for a positive public interest has to do with the entire public. IM is a viable tool to recognize, accept, and respond to social issues. A corporation positions itself by thinking and talking about ways to contribute to a better way of life and help people realize their personal objectives. Ferguson, Weigold, and Gibbs (1984) found a strong association between the ratio of public relations/public affairs officers to total officers and social responsibility activities.

Using simple logic and knowledge of human nature yields better questions and practical answers for issue-related actions. Although criteria may be subjective, a system that insures consistent decision making is objective in a scientific sense. IM invokes logical and ethical guidelines to preclude policy pitfalls as corporations behave in accord with social performance and profit objectives in a shifting, global environment.

SUMMARY AND CONCLUSIONS

Problem-solving practitioners assist in setting priorities. And IM looks to organizational processes for actions aimed at external audiences. Unquestionably, as the organization better understands itself, operational wheels roll smoothly.

Yet, practitioners concede their control resides solely within the organization, not in any outside environment. Hence, credence is given to social, political, and economic contexts that encompass IM. This expanded view well serves practitioners in most roles. IM helps an organization to know itself. Also, through the social, political, and economic contexts, an organization comprehends the needs of external publics. In tandem, this knowledge equips practitioners to facilitate behavior among publics, bringing people together, potentially to satisfy organizational and public interests.

IM, in sum, helps insure broad, effective collection and analysis of data about social, political, and economic contexts. Also, IM decision-making sophistication is needed if conclusions from such analysis contribute to strategy and tactics that serve society and client.

REFERENCES

Ackoff, R. (1970). *A concept of corporate planning.* New York: Wiley.

Amey, L. R. (1986). *Corporate planning: A systems view.* New York: Praeger.

Ansoff, I. H. (1988). *The new corporate strategy.* New York: Wiley.

Argyris, C. (1974). *Behind the front page.* San Francisco: Jossey-Bass.

Aronson, E. (1980). The rationalizing animal. In H. J. Leavitt, L. R. Pondy, & D. M. Boje (Eds.), *Readings in managerial psychology* (3rd ed., p. 173). Chicago: The University of Chicago Press.

Bhambri, A. (1984). The internal dynamics of corporate responsiveness to public policy issues: An exploratory study. *Dissertation Abstracts International, 45/04A,* AAC8416922.

Bridges, W. (1986). Managing organizational transitions. *Organizational Development, 15,* 24–33.

Buller, P. F. (1988a). For successful strategic change: Blend organizational practices with strategic management. *Organizational Dynamics, 16,* 42–55.

Buller, P. F. (1988b). Successful partnerships: Human resources and strategic planning at eight top firms. *Organizational Development, 17,* 27–43.

Callaghan, C. T. (1984). The management of strategic issues: An exploratory study of the concept and practice of issue management (intelligence, theory). *Dissertation Abstracts International, 45/09A,* AAC8426773.

Chase, W. H. (1984). *Issues management: Origins of the future.* Stamford, CT: Issues Action Publishing.

Crable, R. E., & Vibbert, S. L. (1985). Managing issues and influencing public policy. *Public Relations Review, 11*(2):3–15.

Culbertson, H. M. (1989). Breadth of perspective: An important concept for public relations. In J. E. Grunig & L. A. Grunig (Eds.), *Public relations research annual* (pp. 3–25). Hillsdale, NJ: Lawrence Erlbaum Associates.

Culbertson, H. M., & Stempel, G. H. III. (1982). *A study of the public relations posture of osteopathic medicine.* Columbus, OH: Ohio Osteopathic Association.

Davis, S. M. (1982). Transforming organizations: The key to strategy is context. *Organizational Development, 10,* 64–80.

Dozier, D. (1986, August). *The environmental scanning function of public relations practitioners and participants in management decision making.* Paper presented at the annual meeting of the Association For Education in Journalism and Mass Communication. Norman, OK.

Ehling, W. P., & Hesse, M. B. (1983). Use of "issue management" in public relations. *Public Relations Review, 9,* 18–26.

Epstein, E. M. (1987). The corporate social policy process: Beyond business ethics, corporate social responsibility, and corporate social responsiveness. *California Management Review, 29,* 99–114.

Ferguson, M. A., Weigold, M. F., & Gibbs, J. D. (1984, August). *The relationship of public relations and board-level boundary-spanning: Roles to corporate social responsibility.* Paper presented at the meeting of the Association of Journalism and Mass Communication.

Fink, S. (1986). *Crisis management: Planning for the inevitable.* New York: Amacom.

Foster, R. N. (1986). *Innovation: The attacker's advantage.* New York: Summit.

Georgopoulous, B. S. (1988). Organizational structure, problem-solving and effectiveness: A comparative study of hospital emergency services. *Organizational Studies, 9,* 273–275.

Gibson, D. C. (1980). Neither god nor devil: A rhetorical perspective on the political myths of J. Edgar Hoover. *Dissertation Abstracts International, 44/12A,* 3539.

Greenhalgh, L. (1986). SMR Forum: Managing conflict. *Sloan Management Review, 27,* 45–51.

Grunig, L. A. (1988). Variation in relations with environmental publics. *Public Relations Review, 14,* 46–58.

Habermas, J. (1975). *Legitimation crisis.* Boston: Beacon.

Hainsworth, B., & Meng, M. (1988). How corporations define issue management. *Public Relations Review, 14(4),* 18–28.

Heath, R. (1990). Corporate issues management: Theoretical underpinnings and research foundation. In J. Grunig & L. Grunig (Eds.), *Public relations research annual* (Vol. 2, pp. 29–65). Hillsdale, NJ: Lawrence Erlbaum Associates.

Heath, R. L., & Nelson, R. A. (1986). *Issues management: Corporate public policymaking in an information society.* Beverly Hills, CA: Sage.

Hogarth, R. M. (1988). *Judgement and choice: The psychology of decision* (2nd ed.). Chicester, England: Wiley.

Janis, I. L. (1982). *Groupthink: Psychological studies of policy decisions and fiascos.* Boston: Houghton Mifflin.

Janis, I. L. (1989). *Crucial decisions: Leadership in policymaking and crisis management.* New York: The Free Press.

Janis, I. L., & Mann, L. (1977). *Decision making: A psychological analysis of conflict, choice, and commitment.* New York: The Free Press.

Johannesen, R. L. (1981). *Ethics in human communication.* Prospect Heights, IL: Waveland.

Jones, B. L., & Chase, W. H. (1979). Managing public policy issues. *Public Relations Review, 5*, 3–23.

Kalwies, H. (1988). Ethical leadership: The foundation for organizational growth. *The Howard Journal of Communication, 1*(3), 113–130.

Kuhn, J. W., & Berg, I. (1969). *Values in a business society: Issues and analyses.* New York: Harcourt, Brace & World.

Lerbinger, O. (1989, October). *Managing corporate crises.* Paper presented at the meeting of the Public Relations Society of America, Dallas, TX.

Levy, A. (1986). Second-order planned change: Definition and conceptualization. *Organizational Dynamics, 15*, 5–20.

Littlejohn, S. E. (1986). Competition and cooperation: New trends in corporate public issue identification and resolution. *California Management Review, 29*, 109–123.

Limerick, D., & Cunnington, B. (1989). Management development: A look to the future. *Management Decision, 27*, 10–13.

McGinnis, M. A. (1985). The key to strategic planning: Integrating analysis and intuitions. *Sloan Management Review, 26*, 45–52.

Meidan, A. (1986). Chapter 4: Methods and approaches to corporate planning. *Management Decision, 24*, 44–54.

Miles, R. H. (1987). *Managing the corporate social environment: A grounded theory.* Englewood Cliffs, NJ: Prentice-Hall.

Milter, R. G. (1986). Resource allocation models and the budgeting process. In J. Rohrbaugh & A. T. McCartt (Eds.) *Applying decision support systems in higher education: New directions for institutional research* (No. 49, pp. 75–89). San Francisco: Jossey-Bass.

Morris, E. (1987). Vision and strategy: A focus for the future. *Journal of Business Strategy, 8*, 51–58.

Moskowitz, M. (1987). *The global marketplace: 102 of the most influential companies outside America.* New York: Macmillan.

Naisbitt, J., & Aburdene, P. (1985). *Re-inventing the corporation.* New York: Warner.

Newman, L. (1989, October). *Issues management.* Paper presented at the meeting of the Public Relations Society of America, Dallas, TX.

Peters, T. J., & Waterman, R. H., Jr. (1982). *In search of excellence.* New York: Harper & Row.

Pinsdorf, M. K. (1987). *Communicating when your company is under siege: Surviving public crisis.* Lexington, MA: Lexington Books.

Powers, P. E. (1987). Systemic issues management: An interactive approach. *Dissertation Abstracts International, 49/04B,* AAC8810405.

Raiffa, H. (1968). *Decision analysis: Introductory lectures on choices under uncertainty.* Reading, MA: Addison-Wesley.

Sethi, S. P. (1982). *Up against the corporate wall: Modern corporations and social issues of the eighties* (2nd ed.). Englewood Cliffs, NJ: Prentice-Hall.

Shelby, A. N. (1986). *Issues management: A new direction for public relations professionals.* Paper presented at the meeting of the International Communication Association (ICA), Chicago, IL.

Silk, L., & Vogel, D. (1976). *Ethics & profits: The crisis of confidence in American business.* New York: Simon & Schuster.

Sterba, J. P. (1990). *Morality in practice* (3rd ed.). Belmont, CA: Wadsworth.

Szwape, C., & Seeger, M. W. (1989). Legitimizing strategies in the chemical industries: A case study of DuPont de Nemoires and Dow Chemical Company. Paper presented at the International Communication Association Conference, San Francisco, CA.

Tichey, N. M., & Devanna, M. A. (1986). *The transformational leader.* New York: Wiley.

Turk, J. V. (1986). Forecasting tomorrow's public relations. *Public Relations Review, 12*, 12–21.

Tushman, M. L., & Scanlan, T. J. (1981). Boundary spanning individuals: Their role in information transfer and their antecedents. *Academy of Management Journal, 24*, 289–305.

Waddock, S. A. (1988). Building successful social partnerships. *Sloan Management Review, 29,* 17–23.

Walsh, J. P., & Fahey, L. (1986). The role of negotiated belief structures in strategy making. *Journal of Management, 12,* 325–338.

Walsh, J. P., Henderson, C. M., & Deighton, J. (1988). Negotiated belief structures and decision performance: An empirical investigation. *Organizational Behavior and Human Decision Processes, 42,* 194–216.

Williamson, L. A. (1982). Transcendence, ethics, and Mobil Oil: A rhetorical investigation. *Dissertation Abstracts International, 43/06A,* AAC8225786.

Zaleznik, A. (1989). *The managerial mystique: Restoring leadership in business* (p. 21). New York: Harper & Row.

3 Researching the SPE Context: A Montage of Methods

First, a disclaimer. This is not a research–methods chapter. It gives few specific nuts-and-bolts principles and tips. Instead, we focus on certain issues that come up in front-end public relations research and on ways in which various approaches fit in rather logical (though certainly not invariant) sequences, because one method supports and leads into another.

We agree wholeheartedly with two commissions on public relations education (Commission on Public Relations Education, 1975; National Commission on Graduate Study in Public Relations, 1985), as well as with leading practitioners (Lindenmann, 1990), that research methods are crucial in modern public relations. Practitioners must be involved in conducting research if they are to use it effectively. They cannot simply hand it over to professionals and then look at results when it's done.

Study of the SPE context should accompany (or ideally, follow) instruction on the basics of data analysis, collection, and interpretation. Thus, we assume our readers have (or soon will have) exposure to methods texts such as those written or edited by Brody and Stone (1989), Broom and Dozier (1990), and Stempel and Westley (1989).

Brody and Stone (1989, pp. 6–17) distinguished between *informal* and *formal research,* defining the latter as hinging on statistical methods. They described informal research basically as structured reading and talking to informed people, so as to monitor current and emerging trends and to gain background information. However, these authors noted that the formal vs. informal distinction is a misnomer (p. 6), partly because it's often equated with *quantitative* vs. *qualitative.* Such books as Richard A. Krueger's *Focus Groups: A Practical Guide for Research* (1988) make it clear that qualitative techniques involve much systematic, formal planning and implementation in data collection as well as analysis.

Broom and Dozier (1990, p. 27) located research methods along a continuum from very informal (casual media scanning, accidental interviews, and anecdotal reports) at one extreme to very formal (censuses and large-sample surveys of publics and media content) at the other. These authors suggested that, in general, practitioners, researchers, and clients begin by using informal techniques to detect emerging, changing, and previously undetected problems and issues. Formal approaches then follow to show whether and where a problem exists and to reveal at least some of the factors creating it so as to pave the way for solutions.

It is desirable, but not essential, that front-end researchers use most or all of the methods discussed below in a given project. Each approach sheds a unique kind of light on a client's SPE context. However, time and space constraints often rear their ugly heads. For example, in our studies of police (see chapter 7, this volume) and municipal-employee (chapter 11, this volume) relations, we did fairly simple studies with informal reading and interviewing of experts or participants followed by formal surveys. On the other hand, the analyses of livestock magazines (chapter 8) and osteopathic medicine (chapter 12, this volume) each involved at least four to six types of research carried out over about a decade.

We now discuss five specific research techniques that we found useful. In each case, we give some basics on how to carry out a certain type of study, what that study contributes to the entire research mosaic, and how it sets the stage for and builds on other types.

SOME SPECIFIC RESEARCH TECHNIQUES

Background Reading with Library and Computer

Almost any good practitioner reads as a first step in learning what a client has to offer and in what context. Such reading proceeds in at least two steps:

> Browsing to find out what topics show up often and rather suddenly in specialized magazines, overview books, and databases. For example, our study of osteopathic medicine involved a 1991 replication and extension of a survey done about 10 years earlier. Each project began with several days of rather unstructured browsing in the reading room at our osteopathic medical college. Several areas of concern and developments—wellness, health maintenance organizations, AIDS, hospital bankruptcies, and malpractice insurance, to name a few— showed up often in 1991, but not in the early 1980s. Such topics played a key role in the 1991 survey and are emphasized in chapter 12, this volume.

> Structured, issue-oriented searching to discern important issues, reasons for their emergence, proposals on how to approach them, and arguments for and against those proposals. Listing elements helps one identify key words and key names that are essential for a later database or literature search.

Details on carrying out an information search are beyond the scope of this volume. A useful resource is *Search Strategies in Mass Communication* by Jean Ward and Kathleen A. Hansen (1987). Here we simply list several types of sources and how they are useful.

Newsmagazines and publications of opinion and analysis are especially helpful in browsing. For example, *Time* and *Newsweek* provided colorful, timely articles on problems and innovative solutions in police public relations. Such items told what to look for as we sought depth in the academic literature of police science and social psychology. Also, newsmagazine and newspaper articles provided some quotes that livened up our own rather technical, sometimes dry reports. *Atlantic Monthly, Nation,* and other magazines of opinion and analysis gave rich background for our study of a Center for Afro-American Studies (see chapter 10, this volume).

Trade magazines serve specific industries, occupations, and professions. Some are sponsored by professional or trade associations, whereas others are independent. These publications explain how problems are defined by various interest groups and practitioners. In our research, *The Chronicle of Higher Education,* which reports on developments within and governance of colleges and universities, discussed the role, growth, and decline of Afro-American Studies Centers around the nation. Also, *Buckeye Osteopathic Physician,* monthly magazine of the Ohio Osteopathic Association, reported association views on issues ranging from malpractice insurance to doctor–patient relations.

Breadth of perspective is critical in choosing trade magazines. For instance, when we boned up on health insurance problems, we found quite different viewpoints in *HMO Magazine,* representing one segment of the insurance industry; *The New Physician,* which addresses primarily young medical doctors; and *Buckeye Osteopathic Physician.*

Academic journals report on original research and conceptual issues in detail. These publications are written largely by and for academicians. They tend to be tough sledding because of their technical language. However, not all journals are highly technical. Communication and social science publications such as *Journalism Quarterly, Administrative Science Quarterly,* and *Public Relations Review* discussed principles central to our research on police–community relations and the inner workings of municipal government. Also, in our police research, the *Journal of Police Science and Administration* provided important insights on the role of today's cop. And articles in *Mental Hygiene* clarified differences in viewpoint between mental health workers and police.

Recent books of readings in applied disciplines often discuss current issues and concepts with clarity, depth, and insight. Such books tend to have little jargon—and to define that which they do present—partly because they are designed for undergraduate or introductory graduate level classes.

In the police study, for example, a book edited by Snibbe and Snibbe (1973) discusses several topic areas central to our research. These include police occupational culture, changing police roles, police–community relations, and how cops do or do not get along with health care workers. Of course, additional sources were needed to update an 18-year-old book. However, this volume and others like it often contain classic, rather timeless, conceptual discussions. Three such chapters from Snibbe and Snibbe (1973) found their way into our list of references for chapter 7, this volume.

Periodicals that synthesize public opinion research also play a key role in SPE context research. After all, public opinion is a central focus of public relations. A bimonthly, *The American Enterprise* (formerly *Public Opinion*), reports and interprets trend data from reputable polls in a public opinion report and other features. Also, each issue of the academic journal, *Public Opinion Quarterly,* has long featured a somewhat similar analysis in each issue on a given topic. And *Gallup Reports* (formerly *The Gallup Poll Monthly*) regularly summarizes data collected by its parent polling organization.

Best selling books also merit attention, though they are sometimes superficial and one sided. Such volumes often provided needed "devil's advocate" arguments and material. In analyzing an Afro-American Studies Center, for example, we could scarcely avoid taking note of—and in some areas, arguing against—a book by Allan Bloom entitled *The Closing of the American Mind.* Bloom stirred up something of a hornet's nest by alleging that Women's Studies, Black Studies, and ethnically oriented programs at American universities have provided a haven for rhetoric about social justice but little first-rate intellectual inquiry (1987, pp. 313–335).

Also, publications of the United States Census Bureau are a gold mine of information—especially descriptive data about income, race, sex, education, etc., at the city, county, and state levels. In studying police public relations, we used census data on the number of people in town without high school diplomas and the percentage of families that fell below the poverty level as defined by the United States government. Such data became especially meaningful to our client when we compared the town under study with nearby municipalities of comparable size.

As noted earlier, browsing provides key authors' names and key words important in exploring issues. Key names and words are indispensable when using periodical indexes and computerized databases. And such tools move center stage as one begins a focused, issue-oriented literature search. We now consider these two index forms.

Periodical Indexes.   Publications of this type in hard-copy form fall into two categories. General-interest indexes provide citations (dates of publication and page numbers) in magazines and key newspapers read by the population as a whole. Examples include *The New York Times Index* and the *Washington Post Index,* each of which covers articles within its parent newspaper. Of these, *The New York Times Index* is especially useful. Published twice each month and cumulated into a single volume at the end of the year, it gives thorough coverage befitting the *Times* as a "newspaper of record." A single speech may appear in this index under six or eight different alphabetized subject headings such as "energy" and "crime."

Perhaps even more useful for the observer with little expertise in the area under study is the *Reader's Guide to Periodical Literature.* This biweekly paperback publication indexes articles in more than 100 familiar and oft-used magazines. Items are listed by subject and author.

A somewhat less detailed but very useful resource on current events is *Facts on File,* a weekly digest of world news. This publication, like the others discussed here, is found in most major city and university libraries. It is especially helpful in finding when a law was passed, a key speech was made, or some other event occurred that may have a bearing on an SPE context.

More specialized periodical indexes include *Communication Abstracts* (covering dozens of journals that deal with communication), *Sociological Abstracts,* the *Psychological Abstracts,* the *Education Index,* and many other services covering academic journals in various disciplines. Of course, these services prove useful only to those who have studied the disciplines involved in some depth. Without such background, searchers are apt to feel lost in a deluge of meaningless information.

Computerized Databases. In recent years, as books and periodicals have multiplied, communication professionals and educators might have drowned in information without computers. After all, data is useless unless one can find the right bit of it at the right time.

News media now subscribe to databases in large numbers (Izard, Culbertson, & Lambert, 1990, p. 361) and public relations agencies are beginning to do so. One such service, *Nexis,* provides full texts of articles from more than 160 newspapers, newsletters, wire services, and magazines. Costs seem high at first glance but not when one considers the tremendous expense of subscribing to and storing the array of publications covered.

Published organization directories sprung up in such large numbers that someone saw a need for a directory of directories! And, in like manner, vending services serve as middle persons, putting users in touch with relevant computerized databases. One such service, *Dialog,* taps into more than 250 databases covering specialized areas that range from packaging to dogs and the Philippines to child abuse.

Computerized databases provide output on at least three levels:

Full text from services such as *Nexis.* Here one may first get a count of the number of items available. In research for chapter 7, this volume, for example, *Dialog* informed us that it had 6,779 items dealing in some way with police. That figure was overwhelming, and we immediately asked our librarian to enter a much narrower term, "Police Neighborhood or Town Watch." This yielded a very workable 31 items, some of which we ordered in full-text form and received by mail in a few days.

Abstracts that summarize articles in roughly 100-250 words. Say a search turns up 100 abstracts. Chances are the user will discard several as irrelevant and glean all needed information from some other articles simply by reading their abstracts. This may leave only about one third or one half of all items for which one must look up full texts in a library or download (print out) those texts on a computer.

Citations that give only publication name, volume and issue numbers, page numbers, date, and sometimes length in words. Clearly the less detail one receives about an article, the lower the cost. And citations often fill the bill, because they tell one where to look. Further, the more one knows about a field, the better able one becomes to judge an item's potential importance from the author, the publication, the title, and/or the abstract.

Databases often identify articles by topic category. The user must then get acquainted with the service's directory of categories to figure out which ones meet a given need.

Other systems count and pinpoint all articles that include designated words anywhere within their text. The latter type of search sometimes yields many irrelevant citations, as articles often include only one or two mentions of the specified words and little content relating to them. However, such words and article counts may indicate how salient a topic is in the media. For example, in the early stages of our health care study, a search of national media revealed only a very few articles that contained the word *osteopathy* or *osteopathic* (Culbertson & Stempel, 1983). That confirmed our belief that this school of medicine was virtually invisible in the press. (Small wonder, then, that later audience research pinpointed a lack of awareness as osteopathy's main public relations problem.)

CompuServe, Inc., a leading firm in *videotex,* a facet of electronic publishing, now offers several services for public relations practitioners. Videotex permits subscribers to call up a directory of stored articles on their computers and download items of particular interest. One such service, the Public Relations and Marketing Forum (PRSIG), permits practitioners to ask and answer questions of each other and to exchange information. Brody and Stone (1989, pp. 101–118) illustrated and discussed how such services work.

Last, but not least, among the databases discussed here is the Public Relations Society of America (PRSA) *Body of Knowledge.* Developed since the mid-1980s by a team of professors and practitioners, this service provides about 1,000 carefully indexed 250-word abstracts on diverse social science topics related to public relations. The *Body of Knowledge* is updated periodically and can be obtained as hard copy, with inserts going into a loose-leaf binder or on a computer disk. PRSA offers this and other computer-related services through its office at 33 Irving Place in New York City.

In-Depth Interviews of Experts and Influential Participants

Reading normally helps the SPE-context researcher define, in broad outline, important issues and questions of concern to a client. However, published sources seldom provide all relevant arguments. In particular, they do not do justice to local, highly specialized, or emerging issues, proposals, and pros or cons. That's where unstructured interviews with well-informed and influential observers take over. For example:

> In the Afro-American Studies analysis, interviewees might include the university provost, engineering professors (who tend to be somewhat conservative on curricular matters), fine-arts professors (likely to be a bit avant garde and liberal), and student leaders. One or two women's studies professors at the same university might also play a part, as their nondegree program leading to a certificate upon graduation can be viewed as one of many possible frames of reference in looking at Afro-American Studies.

> In the osteopathic research, we focused on top administrators within a nearby College of Osteopathic Medicine and the state and national osteopathic associations. In particular, we singled out doctors of osteopathy who had championed the formation of that college a few years earlier. And we interviewed several medical doctors to get their devil's advocate view (which actually turned out to be quite favorable) on osteopathy as a competing school of health care.

As these examples make clear, diversity of viewpoints is important at this stage. We want to grasp all relevant perspectives. In particular, we need to avoid becoming wedded to our client's assumptions as to what issues are important and how they should be viewed. Such a "wedding" would make us "yes" people inclined to lead clients down blind alleys.

In collecting and analyzing data from such unstructured interviews, we generally proceeded in five steps. These were followed closely in our osteopathic research (see chapter 12, this volume). And they were approximated in other studies.

First, we prepared an interview guide with about 30 open-end questions. Each item sought reaction to or elaboration of an issue or argument that seemed salient in light of our reading. The guide left considerable space for taking notes after each question.

Second, we arranged appointments, usually in interviewee offices, for about 1 hour. These locations were chosen because they were convenient for respondents, and people usually feel at ease in familiar surroundings. Researchers, like all humans, should be as considerate as possible.

Third, we arrived for each interview with an audiotape recorder and a 90-minute cassette. At the outset, we explained that we wanted to insure accuracy by recording interviews. All respondents appreciated the need for such a precaution and felt comfortable with the recorder. (Of course, some people in a general-population sample might not.) We also took notes to capture key points as the interview progressed. After all, mechanical devices sometimes fail, and recorders are no exception! During the interview, we asked many probe questions, mostly ad libbed, to follow up on comments that we did not understand fully, that really failed to answer our initial questions, and that suggested intriguing and potentially important leads.

Fourth, we typed verbatim transcripts on our computers while questions and answers were still fresh in our minds, usually within a day or two after an interview. Where comments seemed hard to follow, we replayed them two or three times to get the wording correct. Sometimes, when a respondent said one thing but seemed in context to mean another, we called her or him for clarification. And we made parenthetical comments in transcripts to insure that, when we wrote later for client or public consumption, we would give the intended meaning rather than a string of words taken out of context.

Fifth, after all in-depth interviews were completed, we wrote an integrated, but partial and carefully paraphrased, transcript of all responses to aid synthesis. Here we looked at all questions, one at a time, commenting parenthetically on ways in which one answer clarified another. In writing this synthesis, a three-stage procedure seemed helpful:

> We read all answers to a given question, taking particular note of points that showed up two or more times. These comments apparently reflected some shared meaning among informed observers, so we saw them as especially salient.
>
> We included verbatim quotes in quotation marks where they might help us emphasize, clarify, and entertain a bit in writing a chapter for this volume or an article. Reports on a survey can be quite dry and boring. Quotes often liven things up when used in moderation. (Of course, these quotes must not misrepresent or emphasize a particular point more than seems justified in light of the data set viewed as a whole.)
>
> After summarizing responses to one or several related questions, we typed in clearly labeled notes or comments of our own discussing underlying meanings and possible implications of the comments made. We later included such comments—or reported on follow-up research to clarify them—when we wrote for public consumption.

In writing reports and articles (and chapters for this volume), we incorporated many quotes and paraphrases from the interview synthesis just described along with percentages, average or mean ratings, correlations coefficients, and other quantitative information based on the survey described in step four.

At this point, we came up with an elaborated set of questions, in a similar interviewer guide, for use in focus groups. It should be noted that focus groups were important in some of our studies, but not all. We used them in the 1981 research on osteopathic medicine but not in the 1991 follow-up where we had less time and a smaller budget. Also, chapter 8 (this volume) indicates that focus groups played a part in the livestock-magazine research.

Focus Groups

In the osteopathic study, we conducted two focus groups, each with about 12 osteopathic physicians attending a state convention. And, in the livestock-magazine research, focus groups of similar size were convened during workshops designed basically for training editors. Groups larger than this do not work well, as some members invariably say very little. (Time constraints intervene, and it takes nerve and assertiveness to address a large group.) In his book on focus-group methodology, Krueger (1988, p. 93) reported that 7–10 members are typical, but that minigroups of 4–6 are becoming increasingly popular.

Basically, we asked questions, tape-recorded answers, probed, and wrote follow-up transcripts very much as with the interviews of experts and participants. Of course, with 12 people speaking, we could not record who said what. And we could take notes only on a few highlights as they came up.

In general, we regarded focus groups as a source of insight in developing and interpreting structured questions used in later large-sample surveys. Our groups were not representative of clearly defined larger populations. Furthermore, while retaining all-important spontaneity, we could not control responses, so all members spoke clearly to each point raised. However, Krueger (1988, pp. 29–30), Larissa Grunig (1990) and others argued persuasively that, when properly constituted and conducted, focus-group sessions yield valid, reliable, and representative data that stands alone.

Focus groups fall on a continuum. At one extreme are *representative* groups chosen very carefully, sometimes with random or quota sampling, so they represent larger populations accurately. On the other hand, researchers often use *blue-ribbon* groups chosen because their expertise and experience enable then to articulate questions, issues, and arguments. Our osteopathic focus groups were clearly of the blue-ribbon variety, whereas the livestock magazine editors seemed quite representative of their occupational group. We believe that, in many settings, focus-group data of the representative variety can stand alone. However, results from blue-ribbon respondents do not indicate the thinking of larger populations.

Space limitations preclude a full discussion of focus groups here. However, we emphasize several points advanced by Krueger (1988):

1. Probe questions are often needed to help members clarify subtle meanings for products, people, and issues. In the absence of such probing, important ideas may "slip away into the mist" before they are clarified and placed in context.

2. In general, focus groups should be structured so people within a given group are quite similar as to level of knowledge and ability to articulate. Otherwise, the "lesser lights" may say very little. Also, members of a group should have fairly similar attitudes and opinions on the topics discussed. This helps insure focus and discourage heated arguments. *Variation in focus-group research is desirable, but it should reside primarily between, and not within, groups* [italics added].

3. Instructions, comments, and moderator gestures should encourage a *supportive* environment. Many focus groups engage in "brainstorming" wherein all participants say what comes to mind—even when it seems outlandish—before striving for synthesis and consensus.

4. Since focus groups involve several people, the number and variety of ideas expressed tends to be greater than with individual interviews. Thus the job of synthesis—identifying "big ideas" and themes—is especially challenging but very important. (pp. 106–121)

By the time focus-group data is analyzed, the SPE-context researcher should have a handle on the questions that need study. The next research phase seeks answers.

Structured, Large-Sample Surveys

In the osteopathic and livestock-magazine studies, we collected a great deal of data from both professionals (physicians in one case, editors in the other) and message receivers. The need to do this is indicated by the two-way symmetric model of Grunig and Hunt (1984, ch. 2), that suggests that practitioners must spend a great deal of time and effort listening, as well as speaking, to their audiences. It follows that the public relations posture of a professional or occupational group hinges at least as much on what the professionals and workers think and do as it does on what publics think and do.

Professionals often make comments that lead the researcher to ask questions that she or he hadn't thought of despite completion of the three phases described earlier in this chapter. Thus it makes sense to survey professionals first and then broader audiences. In general, this was our strategy.

Coorientation theory, discussed in chapter 4, suggests it's important to find out where client-organization members and their publics agree or disagree on certain points. However, that's only part of the story and not necessarily the most important part. People take each other into account on the basis of what each believes the other thinks or would do. Thus it's important to discern a given respondent's own views and actions while also inquiring as to what she or he ascribes to the other party (professionals or audience members).

Such relational analyses pose major methodological problems beyond the scope of this volume. Certainly our research did not do all it could in studying coorientational variables. Nonetheless, some important findings in this realm are apparent:

1. In the livestock-magazine research (reported in chapter 8, this volume), female journalists tend to feel they are discriminated against in hiring, promotions, and salary. However, men working in the magazine field believe they and women are both on the same level playing field. And, although the data aren't too clear on this, there is a suggestion that men do not realize that they and women editors differ in defining the role and plight of women.

2. In the same study (chapter 8, this volume), editors apparently feel presentation of diverse and conflicting views within their magazines would weaken lobbying by leading government officials to regard the parent livestock associations as lacking in unity. However, editors apparently have little hard evidence to test such hypotheses about possible reactions of government officials.

3. In the study of municipal officials (chapter 11, this volume), rules prevent city workers from taking a few minutes off while working to help a citizen cut down a tree, etc. However, citizens view the workers as people, not as rule-governed robots. Understanding of one party by the other is desperately needed in such cases.

4. In the police study (chapter 7, this volume), local police administrators apparently did not fully comprehend, prior to our study, the varying priorities of different audience segments. For example, retired folks and women strongly support street patrols partly because they often feel vulnerable.

5. In the health care study (chapter 12, this volume), citizens tend to regard osteopathic hospitals as *good* while D. O.s see them as *excellent*. Fortunately, perhaps, our data show that physicians correctly perceive the difference in viewpoint between themselves and the population as a whole. Demonstrating such differences proves useful in showing hospital administrators that, potentially, there is broad political support within the health-care field for education about hospitals.

Many other coorientation relationships showed up in our data. In studying them, one must collect reliable data from both groups about the same basic issues. And this, in turn, requires that a researcher remember two points:

Professionals tend to be highly motivated and very articulate in talking about their professions. Thus one can safely conduct longer interviews with them than with a lay or general-population sample. In the osteopathic research, for example, we attained a high 85% response rate despite administering a 40-minute questionnaire to physicians by telephone. However, in the follow-up general-population phone survey, we cut the interview to about 10–12 minutes but still achieved only about 60% response. Most people with low or moderate involvement in the topic studied are reluctant to take an hour—or even 30–40 minutes—out of their busy schedules. On the other hand, 5–10 minutes seem more like a coffee break, and a request for just this much time doesn't often lead to a refusal.

In general, professionals can answer questions about their own field with much precision and confidence. However, lay people usually think in more general terms, and questions asked of them must be worded accordingly. In the osteopathic survey, for example, each physician had little trouble estimating the percentage of patients who had received manipulative treatment in his or her office during the past year. However, when asked to guesstimate the frequency of manipulation by D. O.'s, lay people could not give percentages. They could deal with broader, less precise adjective phrases (all patients, most, some, a few, or none at all). Although general, such responses proved useful. About 40% of all Ohioans estimated that doctors of osteopathy manipulated all or most of their patients. But the mean estimate by physicians was 32%—clearly much less than all or most. Thus, the data clearly identify an area of misunderstanding about osteopathy.

Several books offer thorough discussions of questionnaire construction (see especially Izard et al., 1990, pp. 187–210) and data analysis (see other volumes mentioned in the second paragraph of this chapter). Here we simply mention a few tips and principles of questionnaire construction that we have found important.

First, inexperienced researchers facing that blank piece of paper or computer screen may suffer from a kind of writer's block unless and until they define clearly what variables or characteristics are to be measured. A good way to get started is to take a blank sheet of paper. Write "independent variables" at the top of the left side and "dependent variables" in the upper right. Then write the names of key variables in each category.

Remember that the dependent variables are the ones a person is really interested in measuring and understanding. They include such things as knowledge level, credibility, acceptance or rejection of an idea, and so on. Social science literature, knowledge of our topic area, definition of what audience behaviors your client needs to promote, and common sense all suggest what such variables may be.

Independent variables, on the other hand, are used to divide the sample into parts and then describe each part with respect to the dependent measures. One does this for two basic reasons:

To identify audience segments with varied views and intentions. Such segments may differ as to what interests them (e.g., only young mothers may be interested in pediatric information whereas elderly grandparents may not) and what affects them (e.g., a Protestant may find safe-sex ads persuasive whereas a Roman Catholic may not). Such differences, in turn, may play a key role in mapping out communication strategy and tactics.

To indicate, however tentatively, what may have contributed to acceptance or rejection of the client, the presence or absence of votes, lack or possession of knowledge, and other "payoff behavior." If conservatives oppose service activities by policy more than liberals do, political stance (liberal vs. conservative) may contribute to such opposition. Of course, other factors such as income level or education may really account for such a relationship. Language which even suggests the word cause drives many social scientists to the verge of heart attacks! However, in applied research, such thinking inevitably comes to the fore.

Second, once the variables are listed, draw lines between specific dependent variables and a few independent measures that seem, based on theory or common sense, apt to correlate with them. Such line drawing is often needed to keep the researcher from drowning in data. Say, for example, that you have 20 items in a questionnaire with each measuring one variable (unlikely, but conceivable). If you cross-tabulate each variable with each other variable, you would wind up with $20 \times 20 - 20 = 380$ possible cross-tabulations (the 20 being subtracted because a variable cannot be cross-tabulated against itself). No one could make sense out of that many analyses! But thoughtful line drawing cuts the number of cross-tabulations to about 5–20 that seem plausible and interesting. (Of course, one never exhausts a set of data. It's always wise to keep data so further analyses can be run in the future.)

Third, remember that certain types of questions are especially useful. Each serves a different general purpose. Four such types warrant mention here:

1. Semantic differential and other rating scales. These get at overall, global impressions that people have of clients and of objects in their SPE contexts. Such ratings are especially important where people know little about the client and have little to offer but global impressions. However, rating scales are almost impossible to handle in telephone interviews—now probably the most common strategy for data collection in the United States today.

2. Agree–disagree items. Here one writes a declarative sentence and asks respondents to indicate their levels of agreement or disagreement with it. Four choices—*agree strongly, agree somewhat, disagree somewhat,* and *disagree strongly*—are usually provided. Sometimes a *neither agree nor disagree* response is added to provide an out where the respondent simply has no opinion. Such Likert type items are easy to administer by phone. They encourage one to relate to item content at a personal level, enhancing validity in the view of some scholars. And items can be chosen carefully to reflect specific arguments and opinions that fairly knowledgeable, involved respondents may hold.

3. Knowledge-test items. In recent years, public relations people seemingly have moved toward defining themselves as educators rather than persuaders (Grunig & Hunt, 1984, chapter 2). Consequently, knowledge level has assumed added importance as a dependent (as well as an independent) variable in applied communication research. Thus many studies presumably need to include at least some fairly brief, 3–5 item indexes of knowledge level. Constructing a good knowledge test is difficult but worth the effort. Four basic points deserve mention here.

First, in general, use *open-ended questions* that ask respondents to provide their own answers rather than choose from among several in a list. True–false and multiple choice questions allow for some correct answers by guessing, and few if any testing experts have solved this problem adequately.

Second, be sure *items on a knowledge test vary as to difficulty level,* with some being easy, some hard, and others arrayed in between. Only then does the test discriminate well at all points from high to low knowledge levels.

Third, be sure that *respondents who do well or poorly on the entire test tend also to do well or poorly on each individual item.* Researchers call this criterion *internal consistency,* and its purpose is to insure that all items on the test measure, to some degree, the same underlying dimension or variable. Without such consistency, reporting a single test score based on all items is misleading or vague. It lumps apples and oranges together and calls them fruit, and that doesn't tell you very much. Internal consistency and difficulty level can both be measured in a pretest given to 30–50 respondents before one collects data in earnest. Then items that aren't needed or don't measure up can be eliminated.

Fourth, develop at least some items that require that people *use* knowledge rather than simply recall it from memory. Use usually entails *knowledge of concepts, trends, and relationships.* Also, it involves *demonstrating knowledge rather than testifying that one does or does not have it.* Self-testimonials often are inaccurate, as few of us like to admit—even to ourselves—that we are ignorant.

4. Rating or ranking items that indicate relative importance or prestige level. Only recently have researchers done justice to the concept of salience in public opinion research. People may feel the American Cancer Society is very commendable as gauged by rating scales or agree–disagree items. Yet they may consider it less important than supporting research on AIDS. Also, citizens may feel a given university is doing everything right but still argue that it lacks *prestige* when compared with Harvard, Stanford, Michigan, or Middle Tennessee State. Items that ask people to rank-order various programs, people, and organizations as to importance or prestige often yield useful information. And what's more, these items force people to view a client organization in light of other organizations within its context.

Finally, Izard et al. (1990, pp. 198–205) discussed many tips for wording items in a questionnaire. We pause to mention just a few tips here relating to oft-made errors in SPE-context research.

1. Avoid double-barreled questions that really combine two or more questions in one. For example: "Do you feel the United States should enhance world peace by pulling all troops out of the Middle East?" This item really includes three components: Should the United States enhance world peace? Should it pull all troops out of the Middle East? And would the second step probably contribute to the first? When a person says no to such a question, researchers never know which component he or she is saying no to.

2. Avoid vaguely worded questions. Where possible, ask if people read the local daily newspaper every day, 2–3 days per week, 4–6 days per week, each week, or less often than once per week. Don't ask if they read regularly, often, seldom, or never. Different people interpret these last options in different ways.

3. Avoid emotionally loaded words such as Communist or whore. Such terms tend to stir people's emotions so they give inaccurate or imprecise answers.

4. When asking a "yes or no" type question, be sure to include both options in the item. Ask: Do you favor or oppose a continuing United States role in the Middle East? Studies show that inertia influences people's behavior. Thus many may not choose a given answer because you don't provide it for them.

5. With multiple choice questions, be sure the options provided are exhaustive and mutually exclusive. In other words, see to it that all respondents find it appropriate to check one and only one of the responses listed.

We now look briefly at a final research approach found in our studies.

Content Analysis

The literature review in step one involves content analysis of a sort. However, researchers define quantitative content analysis as systematic study that entails some numbers and counting.

We made little use of such numbers in the studies reported here, so we discuss this approach only in passing. A more extended treatment is found in chapters 7 and 8, both by Guido H. Stempel III, in *Research Methods in Mass Communication* (1989), edited by Stempel and the late Bruce H. Westley.

Researchers use content analysis to gauge placement of news articles and features but not often in studies of the SPE context. In a project related to the health care research summarized in chapter 12, this volume, Stempel and Culbertson (1984) found that physicians were usually quoted two or more times per story in health care coverage by Ohio newspapers. Thus, physicians were defined as quite dominant— effective and assertive in making their points to the press, so reporters often viewed them as news sources. However, although hospital administrative personnel were often objects of coverage, they were seldom quoted. Thus, they were prominent in the media but not very active, as news sources, in communicating their definitions of issues and problems. Such analysis sheds light on media relations.

Chapter 8, this volume, reports an analysis of mastheads in livestock-association magazines. Here we counted the number of women, compared with men, who played different roles on these magazines. Such counts gave some clue to the status of women on livestock magazine staffs and to the number in management, editorial, and production roles.

Neither of these content studies stands alone. Both are interpreted in light of interpretations and responses by media personnel, news sources, and/or audience members. Studies of content seldom shed much light on its impact or on the processes that created it.

Nonetheless, content analysis has a place in SPE-context research. In particular, specialized and opinion magazines often merit attention, because they discuss emerging issues before these matters reach the attention of general-circulation media.

SUMMARY AND CONCLUSIONS

We summarize this chapter by noting briefly the role of each of the types of research discussed.

Background reading and research help one identify issues that people in various professional and journalistic groups regard as fairly salient. Also, such study reveals suggested approaches to resolving issues (which, by definition, entail some disagreement). Light is shed on pros and cons of proposed solutions.

Open-end interviews of experts and participants suggest questions that need to be asked to understand and predict reactions by clients and publics. Such interviews provide viewpoints that are apt to be more up-to-date and fully developed than those found in databases and periodicals. Production of the latter involves some time lag. And materials in any library tend to focus on the international, national, or state scene rather than on any specific locale. Furthermore, interviews provide elaboration because the interviewer can ask questions and get answers. (Admittedly, some computer services also are interactive. But even these provide only preplanned answers when the user types in a question!)

Focus groups give further elaboration with the benefit of creative thought promoted by interaction and mutual stimulation among respondents. Also, in some cases, focus-group data provide a representative picture of how clearly defined groups of people think and act.

Structured, large-sample surveys tell how large (and sometimes varied) populations of people do or might think and act vis-a-vis the client's programs. The three research strategies just listed help frame the questions. Surveys begin, at least, to suggest answers.

Finally, content analyses serve several purposes. They provide an early-warning system to identify issues that are just emerging or are gaining in salience. They help validate interview and focus-group data about the status of people within professional groups and publics. And they help answer two important questions about press relations of certain actors. First, how prominent are these actors as objects of coverage? And second, how dominant or assertive are they, as news sources, in presenting their views to the media.

We close by noting that the five research approaches discussed in this chapter do not exhaust the possibilities. Broom and Dozier (1990, pp. 1–88) showed many types of research to serve many purposes, as does our chapter 2, this volume (on issues management and environmental scanning). However, the five strategies covered here play a central role in studying SPE contexts.

REFERENCES

Bloom, A. (1987). *The closing of the American mind.* New York: Simon & Schuster.

Brody, E. W., & Stone, G. C. (1989). *Public relations research.* New York: Praeger.

Broom, G. M., & Dozier, D. M. (1990). *Using research in public relations: Applications to program management.* Englewood Cliffs, NJ: Prentice-Hall.

Commission on Public Relations Education (1975). *A design for public relations education.* New York: Foundation for Public Relations Research and Education.

Culbertson, H. M., & Stempel, G. H., III (1983, October). A study of medical coverage in eleven Ohio metropolitan newspapers. *Buckeye Osteopathic Physician,* pp. 4–11.

Grunig, J. E., & Hunt, T. (1984). *Managing public relations.* New York: Holt, Rinehart & Winston.

Grunig, L. A. (1990). Using focus group research in public relations. *Public Relations Review, 16,* 36–49.

Izard, R. S., Culbertson, H. M., & Lambert, D. A. (1990). *Fundamentals of news reporting.* Dubuque, IA: Kendall-Hunt.

Krueger, R. A. (1988). *Focus groups: A practical guide for applied research.* Newbury Park, CA: Sage.

Lindenmann, W. K. (1990). Research, evaluation and measurement: A national perspective. *Public Relations Review, 16,* 3–16.

National Commission on Graduate Study in Public Relations (1985). *Advancing public relations education: Recommended curriculum for graduate public relations education.* New York: Foundation for Public Relations Research and Education.

Snibbe, J. R., & Snibbe, H. M., (Eds.). (1973). *The urban policeman in transition: A psychological and sociological review.* Springfield, IL: Thomas.

Stempel, G. H., III, & Culbertson, H. M. (1984). The prominence and dominance of news sources in newspaper medical coverage. *Journalism Quarterly, 61,* 671–676.

Stempel, G. H., III, & Westley, B. H. (1989). *Research methods in mass communication.* Englewood Cliffs, NJ: Prentice-Hall.

Ward, J., & Hansen, K. A. (1987). *Search strategies in mass communication.* New York: Longman.

II A THEORETICAL BASE

4 The Social Context: No Human Is an Island

Sociologists such as Mead (1955) and Turner (1962) argued persuasively that humans are really human largely because they are social creatures. As infants, we observe how others react to our own behavior. We imitate their reactions to us. And thus we learn to view ourselves as objects—to plan our behavior so we can adapt in relating to others. All this is basic to human functioning.

Such a view implies that relating is, at base, a two-way process among humans. And Grunig and Hunt (1984), among others, suggested that the most fruitful and complete types of public relations are two way, hence interpersonal and social.

In light of this, the social context obviously plays an important part in understanding the public relations posture of any individual, program, or organization. For further development of this argument, see Culbertson (1991).

Countless theoretical perspectives and concepts play a part in defining the social context. Here we focus on five general areas of study that we found useful: cultural and subcultural beliefs, beliefs about one's own situation, frames of reference, the nature and number of personal contacts occurring, and coorientation processes.

TWO GUIDING DIMENSIONS

We focused on these concepts as we designed and interpreted research. Before choosing them, we scanned a wide range of theories and studies. The five perspectives chosen are not closely integrated. They did not jump out at us on the basis of an overriding framework or scheme.

However, we purposely included theories that vary along two dimensions often used to talk about social science. Viewpoints that vary on these two attributes

51

proved helpful in designing, interpreting, and using research. The characteristics are a focus on content vs. structure and on micro vs. macro levels (focusing on the individual, the small group of interacting persons, a large occupational or other subgroup, or society as a whole).

First, content refers to what people believe and how they behave. On the other hand, structure deals with relationships among one or many persons' beliefs and/or behaviors—on how these things are organized. For example, a politician on the far left (a Communist) and one on the far right (a member of the John Birch Society) differ dramatically as to belief content. To begin with, the Communist advocates state ownership of industries and businesses, whereas the John Bircher favors private ownership and free-market capitalism.

The two differ on many issues. However, when it comes to structure, extremists of the left and right tend to be quite similar as viewed by those who study the psychological and social dynamics of politics. As Lipset and Raab (1973, pp. 7–12) pointed out, zealots of many types often view the world in simple terms, tracing complex events and problems to a few clearly defined causes. Also, ardent Communists and John Birchers both tend to turn their backs on new ideas different from their own. And either type of citizen strongly resists changing personal opinions.

In a different realm, a great baseball player and a great ballet dancer differ greatly as to the content of their actions while performing. The ball player runs as hard as he can, mostly straight ahead, to catch up with a fly ball. The dancer stands on her toes as she glides around the stage in circles. Yet both performers show grace and continuity of movement—matters of structure. Neither the sports fan nor the dance lover can easily explain in words what the outfielder and dancer have in common. Yet the two would undoubtedly agree that the commonality is there, that it has to do with movement (hence relationships from one point to another) through time and space, and that it can be called grace.

Our second dimension centers on level of analysis—what economists call the distinction between macro and micro. Some theories focus on causal or influence factors, called independent variables that describe an individual human. Other scholars lean toward traits that define large groups of people or even society as a whole. In the middle, others operate at the social-interactional level, examining ways in which up to a few dozen or hundred people relate to and interact with each other at a one-on-one, personal level.

We explore these distinctions further at the end of this chapter, suggesting where the five perspectives that we chose stand on these two dimensions. Before that discussion can make sense, however, it is necessary to look in some detail at each theoretical perspective.

Two points deserve emphasis here. First, research and concepts in the five realms addressed in this chapter overlap; we separated them largely for ease and clarity of discussion. Second, although much of the research cited here has to do with beliefs held by and about Americans in the 1980s, it must be viewed as, at best, suggestive and illustrative. Beliefs and behavior change, and some of the findings noted surely will no longer hold by the time this volume comes off the press.

FIVE THEORETICAL PERSPECTIVES

Cultural and Subcultural Beliefs

Behavior and beliefs do not always seem consistent. People often assert that someone is terrible only to greet that individual with open arms at a party or in church. However, beliefs that are widely shared, are supported by social norms and customs, and are passed from generation to generation have great power. They can lead people to drink excessively, enter a convent, or risk their lives in battle.

Such beliefs constitute part of culture—the heritage shared by most or all members of a society or large subgroup thereof as a result of socialization. These beliefs include basic premises about what is, what's right, and what's important.

American communication research tends to ignore such beliefs—perhaps partly because they are shared by large groups of people. Thus they tend to contribute to uniformity, not variation, among individuals. And statistical methodology tends to focus on identifying sources of variation.

However, in the 1980s, several social critics and scientists attempted to measure people's basic beliefs: how they cluster together, how they conflict, and how they bear on patterns of behavior. Also, a body of research documents that linking one's organization, program, or personality to a positively valued belief can enhance acceptance and popularity. Linkage to a negative object, on the other hand, can contribute to rejection (Anderson, 1981; Culbertson & Stempel, 1985; Fishbein & Ajzen, 1981; Rosenberg, 1960; Woelfel, Cody, Gillham, & Holmes, 1980).

We categorize belief research in two ways: who holds the beliefs studied and which objects the beliefs help describe.

First, who holds them? Some beliefs are shared by most or all individuals within a society or a large subgroup thereof. We call these *cultural beliefs*. Other notions are important because, although they deal with broad societal issues and result from society-wide socialization, they impact behavior in ways unique to persons in a given subculture or vocation. We call these beliefs *subcultural*.

Second, what do the beliefs deal with? Some focus on institutions and how people relate to them and on related positions regarding broad moral and ethical issues. Other beliefs specify or relate to appropriate behavior, goals, and performance, often within a given vocational subgroup.

Combining these two factors yields four types of beliefs (see Tab. 4.1). We now review some illustrative studies on each of the four types.

1. Cultural Beliefs About Institutions and How People Relate to Them. In 1986, a research firm called Oxford Analytica concluded that a rural ethic remains

TABLE 4.1
Major Authors Cited in Dealing With Cultural and Subcultural Beliefs Defined as to
Topic and Group Holding Them

Group Holding Beliefs	Topic	
	Institutions and how people relate to them, with related positions on broad social-moral issues	Belief holder's proper standards of conduct and life goals
Most people within society as a whole or large subgroup (Cultural beliefs)	I. Hall; Ladd; Oxford Analytica	II. Yankelovich
Most people within a given vocational subgroup as result of overall societal or occupational experience, socialization (Subcultural beliefs)	III. Ganz, Lichter, Rothman and Lichter; Parenti; Efron	IV. Culbertson, Johnstone, Slawski & Bowman; Weaver & Wilhoit

Note. Roman numerals denote sections of text dealing with beliefs in the four cells.

alive and well in America. Stemming in part from the fact that America was a rural society until quite recently and in part from news emphasis on urban social blight, this ethic holds that rural life is wholesome, healthy, productive, and quite free of evil hedonistic impulses and behavior (Oxford Analytica, 1986, pp. 100–107).

Gans (1980, pp. 48–50) noted that many Americans apparently link other beliefs to this one so as to create public relations problems for some people. In particular:

Post-World War II developers of suburbia came under fire because idealizers of rural life portrayed the developers' construction efforts as despoiling the land in a relentless search for profits. Little note was taken of the fact that development provided needed housing.

Near worship of small towns, small firms, and family farms contributed to a fairly widespread view that conglomerates, federal bureaucracies, and other institutions are inefficient, inhuman, and not responsive to people's needs.

Idealization of individual humans exercising free choice, rooted in rural and small-town lifestyles contributed in some measure to a negative view of the computer as a robot that lacks free will and deprives people of control over their own lives.

A second cultural belief important in understanding American politics during the 1980s, according to Oxford Analytica (1986, pp. 180–181), holds that Americans, conquerors of a vast frontier and long-time admirers of cowboys who did much of the conquering, should be strong, independent, and macho. At a time when many Americans were reeling from defeat in Vietnam, a Communist takeover in Nicaragua, and devaluation of the dollar on money markets, Ronald Reagan was able to link increased defense spending and a stern posture vis-a-vis Russia's "evil empire" to this widely held idea.

A third basic belief, dating back largely to the New Deal days of the 1930s, holds that Americans are, by virtue of their citizenship, entitled to substantial social welfare benefits. This belief presumably is salient partly because people emphasize security. In a 1988 Gallup Survey, 62% of a nation-wide sample rated job security as an essential element in a good job. (Public Opinion Report, September/October 1990, p. 84.)

This "entitlement" belief is especially interesting in its impact on political orientation, because it sometimes conflicts with another belief that taxes are already too high and should not increase. In a 1990 national survey, 79% of all respondents opposed raising taxes even to meet an unspecified government need (Public Opinion Report, July/August 1991, p. 82). Many people accept when told—but then conveniently forget—that increased social services cost money. Further, given the growing elderly population with a strong need for social services, costs are in danger of going through the roof.

How do politicians attempt to deal with this problem? Oxford Analytica (1986, pp. 182–183) noted four tactics, none apparently very successful to date:

1. Reduce federal expenditures by turning social-welfare programs over to state and local governments. This approach is linked to the rural ethic and the related idea that local governments, small and close to their constituents, avoid the evils of bigness and remoteness. However, it doesn't take a genius to see that this approach often fails to cut costs; it simply relocates them in a way that liberals see as an abdication of responsibility. Further, town and county governments are often viewed as tainted with "redneck" ineptness and corruption.

2. Save money by reducing graft, corruption, and waste. Politicians often sing this tune. But constituents tend to regard it as illusory partly because of a basic belief that politicians generally are self-centered and concerned far more with re-election than with serving the public. It's hard for many Americans to trust their leaders (Yankelovich, 1981, pp. 184–186).

3. Educate the public that hard choices have to be made and some programs—even good ones—cut back or abolished if one wishes to avoid higher taxes. Former Gov. Bruce Babbitt of Arizona took this tack, linking it to the public desire for political candor, during a candidate forum or debate in the 1988 Democratic presidential-primary race. He called for a tax increase, suggested any candidate who refused to do so was trying to fool voters, and challenged his opponents to stand up and join him. Although it earned short-term media play, this gambit failed to ignite much popular support. As noted by Yankelovich (1981, pp. 50–62), many American voters are rather self-centered.

4. Hope that economic growth will generate enough revenue to bail out welfare programs in the near future. Although rather painless for politicians—and for voters

who believe it—this expectation flies in the face of many trends limiting American business growth and industrial domination (Yankelovich, 1981, pp. 163–164).

In another realm, Americans apparently tend to accept the proposition that Blacks and other minorities should be seated at the same lunch counters, should be permitted to attend the same schools, and should be given the same job opportunities as Whites. However, such equivalent *treatment* often does not translate into equal *attainment* in light of a long history of racial and ethnic discrimination. And many Whites do not approve of racial-ethnic quotas and other moves designed to insure equal educational and income attainment (Oxford Analytica, 1986, pp. 184–186).

The moral: programs linked to equal treatment are likely to gain widespread approval. However, those couched in terms of actual attainment by minority groups have a tough row to hoe.

Such discussions of social and ethical priorities in modern America must reckon with recent growth of the moral majority, a loose-knit, conservative coalition with a religious base. Growth of this movement hinges largely on two key beliefs. First, traditional puritanical values are important in America. And second, the nation has largely abandoned these values.

Oxford Analytica (1986, pp. 186–187) suggested that any organization or candidate seeking approval from this segment of rural and small-town America needs to link itself in people's minds with a resurgence of traditional values.

In a related area, Americans favor getting tough in dealing with crime. In a 1991 national survey, 80% of all respondents said they favored expediting the death-penalty appeals process to reduce the current delay between conviction and execution, as long as defendants' rights are protected. That delay often reaches 8–10 years at present. (Public Opinion Report, July/August 1991, p. 79).

When looking at their nation's brief history, many Americans view their Constitution as nearly perfect. They see it as the product of brilliant, idealistic people who initiated a bold experiment in democracy that still stands as a model for the whole world.

When government goes awry as in the Watergate scandal of the early and mid-1970s, Americans assume the system of government, as constructed by the founding fathers, cannot be at fault. Consequently, the problem must stem from the incompetency, laziness, greed, and dishonesty of those who run things.

Further, given the importance of the Constitution, those who err in applying it are seen as violating a sacred trust. Thus they truly deserve the wrath of God (Ladd, 1981). Small wonder, then, that Americans come down hard on politicians who commit deeds that other countries might view as almost routine.

Cultural beliefs become especially crucial in cross-cultural communication, because obviously people of different cultures have different and often conflicting perspectives. Failure to understand and take these factors into account can wreak havoc in public relations efforts.

For instance, British people tend to be reserved and a bit aloof. Americans, on the other hand, are often assertive and gregarious. When people from the two societies interact, the American may seem intrusive and presumptuous to the Britisher. And Brits may come across as stuffy and unfriendly to their Yankee companions (Hall, 1969, pp. 138–143).

Also, Germans place great emphasis on order and hierarchy, which seem stiff and unfriendly to Americans, in both physical and social arrangements. To the German, however, American spontaneity and egalitarianism seem careless and indicative of disrespect or apathy. Small wonder, then, that business people in either nation have trouble functioning in the other with high credibility (Hall, 1969, pp. 131–138).

Finally, marked contrasts between Western and Chinese cultures have recently made it difficult for western corporations and local officials to operate joint-venture firms in the People's Republic of China. Western managers and personnel generally subscribe (albeit imperfectly) to an ethic that stresses individual effort, speed, and rational, linear thinking. Such approaches leave little time for building close relationships and bonds of trust.

Chinese people, on the other hand, prefer to work only with those whom they have taken the time to know and trust. Networks of friendship called *guanxi* play a big part in Chinese dealings and relationship building. Also, joint ventures must take into account a swing from patriarchal to collective decision making in Chinese society (*Manufacturing Equity Joint Ventures in China*, 1987, pp. 54–55).

We now turn to a second broad category of beliefs.

2. Cultural Beliefs Dealing With Oneself and Appropriate Personal Standards of Thinking and Conduct.   In a book entitled *New Rules,* pollster Daniel Yankelovich (1981) traced implications of a basic belief, widespread in the 1970s and 1980s, that we Americans have a right—indeed, almost a duty—to fulfill ourselves as individuals. The basic premise apparently leads some people to leave marriages, change (or simply quit) jobs, and sometimes drift into lives of aimlessness and despair.

In part, this premise resulted from the welfare state and the belief, mentioned earlier, that all Americans are entitled to and can count on having their material needs met (Yankelovich, 1981, p. 170). In light of these factors, past self-sacrifice and saving of money by one's Depression-era parents or grandparents often seem stupid and unnecessary. Other contributing factors are the decline of religion, with its emphasis on self-sacrifice, as a major force in society (Yankelovich, 1981, p. 88) and the alleged thinking of social scientists such as Abraham Maslow (1962) that only self-fulfillment brings one full development as a human.

Maslow and his followers went astray, Yankelovich asserted, because they assumed self-fulfillment results largely from looking inward. On the contrary, philosophers and sociologists such as George Herbert Mead (1955) argued persuasively that we become truly human largely by serving, sharing with and relating to others (Yankelovich, 1981, pp. 239–242).

Despite these drawbacks, the drive for self-fulfillment has had immense impact on modern lives. Further, it has helped challenge some cherished beliefs and re-shape others. For example:

1. It has made people unreceptive to saving money, scaling back lifestyles, and working hard at a time when natural resources appear to be limited, the Germans and Japanese are beating America badly in the automobile and other industries, and personal relationships are declining. Self-denial, not self-fulfillment, is needed to meet these challenges (Yankelovich, 1981, p. 23).

2. Emphasis on marriage as needed to make oneself a "whole person" has declined. In the late 1950s, a majority of Americans criticized those who chose to remain single as somewhat sick, neurotic, or immoral. By the late 1970s, that figure had shrunk to a mere 25%. Also, surveys show that, over the past 30 years, fewer and fewer Americans regard a family with at least four children as ideal (Public Opinion Report, May/June 1990, p. 100). Such changes surely have some bearing on people's tendencies to seek divorces on what previous generations saw as rela-tively weak grounds and on the alleged decline of families as stable socializing institutions (Yankelovich, 1981, p. 97).

3. Also relating to the family, parents of the 1970s and 1980s made fewer sacrifices for their children than earlier parents had. In addition, today's parents demand less of their own offspring in the form of future obligations (Yankelovich, 1981, p. 104). Parental suffering and loneliness sometimes result from all this.

4. Partly in light of modern self-fulfillment goals, Americans generally do not favor redistribution of wealth that can be interpreted as taking away from successful people that which they have earned. This, of course, stands in the way of human-itarian projects and support for social welfare in general (Yankelovich, 1981, p. 141).

5. Some evidence suggests that Americans place less emphasis than they once did on occupation as a determinant of one's worth for living in a given neigh-borhood and joining exclusive organizations (Yankelovich, 1981, p. 144). Perhaps this fact helps explain why young people often do not seek college education as a move toward work that enhances upward mobility.

We now turn to beliefs that help shape one's interpretation of news events as a journalist and that deal with society as a whole, people, institutions, and their interrelationships. We focus on journalists as a vocational group here partly because they are an important public for public relations practitioners (albeit often as a means to an end of reaching another public) and partly because they, but not public relations people, have been objects of recent beliefs research.

3. News-Shaping Beliefs of Journalists, Shared With Many Others Within Soci-ety, That Deal With Institutions and How People Relate to Them.   American jour-nalists supposedly are trained to write in a fair and balanced way, keeping their own biases and preferences from coloring the news. However, news people share certain enduring values with most other Americans. And these values do color the news. Journalists simply cannot hang their citizenship and background in the closet when entering the news room. Partly because they are viewed as obvious and beyond question, such enduring values are seldom considered critically. Yet, often unbeknownst to the reporter or editor, they serve as a frame of reference in evaluating and interpreting events (Gans, 1980, pp. 182–213).

Following are several enduring values that Gans found, in a study of elite American journalists, to be widely held and apt to color the news.

First, *ethnocentrism*—the belief that America is a great country and a standard for the world. Gans said this comes through most clearly in foreign news where developments are often viewed in terms of whether they deviate from or imitate American practice. Also, although many domestic stories are critical, their treatment of problems as deviant cases implies that American ideals are, at the very least, viable (Gans, 1980, p. 42).

Second, *altruistic democracy*—the belief that American democracy, designed to serve the people as a whole, stands as a model for the world. Here again, the news provides tacit support for democracy through frequent attention to deviations from it as an unstated ideal. Nepotism, financial corruption, log rolling, and patronage appointments are reported so as to stress their deviant status. Also, the very concept of a political machine is treated pejoratively with no mention that machines build roads, feed needy people, and do other constructive things (Gans, 1980, pp. 43–45).

Third, *responsible capitalism*—"an optimistic faith that in the good society, businessmen and women will compete with each other to create increased prosperity for all, but that they will refrain from unreasonable profits and gross exploitation of workers or customers" (Gans, 1980, p. 46). Against this backdrop, economic growth is viewed by most people quoted in the American media as a blessing, so long as it doesn't lead to undue bigness of and monopoly by one or a few firms. Entrepreneurial risk and technological innovation are also covered uncritically. Domestic news tends to play down socialism as a force in American society, seldom noting socialist critiques of the nation (Gans, 1980, p. 46–48).

Fourth, *small town pastoralism*—idealizing of small town and rural life and values. Earlier, we noted that this view continues to have a great impact on American thinking and behavior. It shows up in the news most clearly, according to Gans, in coverage reflecting the virtue of smallness and faults of bigness (Gans, 1980, pp. 48–50).

Fifth, *individualism*—the preservation of individual freedoms against encroachment by nation and society. Charles Kuralt's pastoral features on the Columbia Broadcasting System news tended to celebrate self-made men and women. On the other hand, computers and data banks, accused of reducing privacy, are the objects of critical coverage or very little of any kind as are communes and other phenomena that emphasize the group or collectivity.

Sixth, *moderatism*—celebration of moderation in most things. Neither the atheists nor religious extremists are framed very favorably in the news. The same goes for the high-brown or low-brow, the political radical and ultra-conservative, etc. (Gans, 1980, pp. 51–2).

In a related and controversial book, *The Media Elite,* Lichter, Rothman, and Lichter (1986) contended that most journalists working in the elite American media hold liberal beliefs about social and moral issues. This cluster of beliefs may help explain positive news portrayal of school busing to provide quality education for minority children. The authors claim to have found frequent quoting of pro-busing sources in news but little attention to a substantial body of expert opinion and evidence questioning whether busing actually improves school performance (Lichter, Rothman, & Lichter, 1986, pp. 220–253).

Most claims of media bias are controversial. They focus largely on the so-called elite media, *The New York Times, Washington Post,* and a few other prestigious papers, along with the three major commercial networks and the three news weeklies. Also, bias is a slippery concept.

Critics such as Michael Parenti (1986) professed to find a conservative bias, whereas Edith Efron (1971) and others reported a liberal slant. Some journalists contend that, because they are catching it from both sides, they must really be in the middle. However, this argument does not negate the possibility of off-setting biases or the basic point that subjective choice can't be eliminated.

Journalists presumably hold certain beliefs by virtue of being citizens of a given nation or identifying with certain groups. However, another type of socialization affecting journalists—a key public relations public—occurs on the job and in educational experiences leading up to journalistic careers. We now turn to recent work on these conceptions.

4. Beliefs Learned and Practiced by Those Within a Given Vocational Subgroup and Presumed to Affect Job Performance and Evaluation. In a nation-wide study of journalists, Johnstone, Slawski, and Bowman (1976, pp. 114–116) found two viewpoints or belief clusters—the *neutral* and the *participant*—that appear to stem largely from newsroom socialization and experience on the job.

Proponents of the neutral school see news as emerging naturally from events. From this perspective, responsible journalism involves heavy emphasis on objectivity and factual accuracy. Neutral journalists object strongly to biased, sensational, or excessive coverage, to sins of commission that might get in the way of telling nothing but the truth.

The participant school presumably shares with the neutralists a concept of fairness. However, participants see the reporter as actively involved in defining truth, not simply in discovering what is already there. These journalists feel they have to report news in context, sifting through available information to find implications, causes, and meaning. To them, primary sins include news suppression, irrelevance, and superficiality, sins of omission that stand in the way of revealing the whole truth.

In a near-replication of the study by Johnstone, Slawski and Bowman (1976), Weaver and Wilhoit (1986, pp. 112–124) found three belief clusters rather than two. Their *disseminator* concept resembles the earlier neutral perspective. However, the participant concept reported 10 years earlier separated by the mid-1980s into two notions labeled *interpreter–investigative* and *adversarial*.

In a third study, involving 258 journalists on 17 varied newspapers, Culbertson (1983, pp. 10–13) found three clusters roughly comparable to those of Weaver and Wilhoit (1986, pp. 112–124). He called these perspectives *traditional, interpreters, and activists*. In his study, the three clusters focus on the following specific beliefs:

Traditionalists emphasize timeliness and other news elements such as consequence, novelty, and human interest in judging news. Also, they stress objectivity and factual accuracy as key elements in good journalism. Furthermore, they subscribe to journalistic traditions as a general concept. And they place high emphasis on studying the audience.

Interpreters show idealism as reflected in a stated willingness to avoid going on junkets paid for by news sources and to do time in jail if needed to protect a confidential news source. Also, interpretation involves a strong need to clarify causes and implications and to rely on libraries, surveys, and other scholarly tools in collecting and making sense out of news.

Activists see at least some need for more crusaders and social reformers in news rooms around the country, apparently seeing the news columns, and not just the editorial page, as potential contributors to social justice. Also, activists feel more uncomfortable than other journalists with limitations imposed by front-office dictates. They worry a great deal about space and time pressures that often prevent telling a story fully and completely.

Having defined these belief clusters, Culbertson (1983, pp. 16–26) measured their association with perspectives on actual news judgment. Although correlations are moderate at best, the belief clusters differ largely as predicted in four areas.

First, traditionalists place high emphasis on local news, the traditional focus of newspapers in this country. Interpreters, however, stress national news (after all, the federal government and coverage of it are at the vanguard of interpretative journalism in this country). Acceptance of activism correlates with heavy emphasis on international stories. This latter finding makes sense, because the literature (Hampden-Turner, 1971, pp. 50–60; Hoffer, 1951, p. 50) suggests that crusaders define their causes in cosmic terms as a means of enhancing perceived importance and possible social support.

Second, traditional reporters stress spot news whereas belief in the other two schools focuses on interpretation. However, activists and interpreters place interpretation in somewhat different contexts. Activists downgrade spot news but not feature or human-interest coverage, perhaps viewing the latter as a means of gaining attention for their causes. Interpreters, on the other hand, downgrade human interest material, apparently seeing facts as grist for interpretation.

Third, traditionalists show an inclination to follow their audiences in judging news, whereas interpreters and activists mildly avoid doing so. Also, traditionalists tend more than the other two schools to see themselves as similar to or congruent with their publics as to news priorities. In sum, the interpreters' inclination toward careful study of topics covered and the activists' cause orientation apparently give them personal perspectives as an alternative to the audiences' perspectives in judging news.

In a fourth and final area, interpreters tend to score high on what Grunig (1976) called *problem recognition*—a belief that news work involves rather complex decisions about which the journalist has considerable uncertainty. High problem recognition has been shown to correlate with a felt need to seek information actively and analyze it carefully (Grunig, 1976, 1983). And it stands to reason that interpretative journalists see their task as quite complex and demanding.

Two additional points deserve emphasis regarding studies of journalists' professional beliefs.

First, all studies to date suggest that most journalists subscribe somewhat to both the traditional and interpretative views. Whereas senior editors tend to turn thumbs down on activism, young journalists often express some belief in that perspective without rejecting the other two (Culbertson, 1981). Few journalists are pure representatives of any given type.

Second, little evidence has been provided that such professional beliefs translate often into actual news-judgment behavior. Obviously newsroom constraints often force a human-interest oriented editor to play up spot news, an internationally minded reporter to write mostly local stories, and so on.

Lichter, Rothman, and Lichter (1986, pp. 166–219) attempted to establish a connection between editor beliefs and actual news play. They provided an interesting analysis of ways in which such beliefs play a role.

The authors alleged that journalists are socialized to emphasize the political and management aspects of even a technical area such as nuclear power. They regard the human side of the nuclear story as understandable and interesting to media consumers.

Furthermore, antinuclear protesters tend to be nontechnical whereas many nuclear advocates are scientists. Thus, because of a tendency to steer clear of science and other technical matters, the anti side of the nuclear-safety question received more play than the pro side in elite media during the 1970s and early 1980s.

We conclude this section by noting that many of the subcultural and cultural beliefs discussed here are shared by most but not all members of society or a given subgroup. Also, such beliefs change rather quickly in this age of high-tech communication and shifting lifestyle. All of which means a practitioner needs to study his or her publics carefully and explicitly. It's dangerous to rely on broad national surveys conducted some years ago.

We now turn to a different category of beliefs that tell how a given individual defines his or her relationship to a particular situation.

Beliefs About One's Situation

Research cited in the previous section suggests or assumes that powerful beliefs are those that are deeply rooted in one's character or sociocultural setting and that tend to be uniform across time and persons. That this doesn't always hold is suggested by a theory explained in broad outline in this section: James and Larissa Grunig's (1976, 1983) *information systems formulation*.

At base, the Grunigs sought to explain conditions under which those within a public operate in either of two modes relating to information seeking and use.

First, *information processing* denotes a passive mode in which people attend to pieces of information that come their way and grab their attention. Little special effort is made to seek new information, to rationally select what one will attend to, or to integrate disparate pieces of information for meaningful interpretation.

Second, *information seeking* denotes a more active mode that involves information seeking, purposive selection, integration, and interpretation.

The Grunigs believed applied communicators must use layout, writing style, and other message-production techniques to grab and keep attention of those in the information-processing mode. Information seekers, on the other hand, respond strongly to message content and organization. In general, seekers are more eager to learn and more reachable than are processors.

Some previous researchers looked upon openness to new information as a personality trait. The Grunigs took issue with the assumption implicit in the study of such traits that behavior is usually quite consistent for a given person across situational contexts, substantive problems, and significant others attended to. These scholars believed people may shift modes often, depending on how they define a given situation.

Four independent variables played roles in the evolution of information systems theory. Grunig believed these variables interact in ways beyond the scope of this volume and in ways not yet clearly spelled out. These variables include:

1. Problem recognition refers to the degree of uncertainty that one experiences in characterizing a situation. Consider, for example, a race for sheriff in a citizen's home community. Problem recognition regarding the race is high for the citizen who feels the outcome is uncertain—that each candidate has a good chance of winning. In general, problem recognition correlates with active information seeking. After all, if one candidate's victory seems assured (i.e., problem recognition is low), the citizen is likely to feel he or she has a handle on defining the race with little felt need to seek and process further information.

2. Constraints to defining and using information have a bearing on the kind of effort one puts forth in dealing with information. Returning to the sheriff's race, a

person may pay little attention to candidates and issues if understanding is seen as constrained. Such would be true if the citizen lacks a frame of reference to interpret what is said or if the complexity of issues is overwhelming. Also, use of information may seem constrained, as where the citizen is not eligible to vote. Behavior may seem useless even if possible. If one feels the sheriff owns the town and has squelched all meaningful opposition, why bother to build an information base for a meaningless vote?

Constraint recognition can lead one to a passive mode of information processing. However, where involvement and problem recognition are high, perception of constraints can motivate one to focus actively on information about defining, assessing, and overcoming the constraints.

3. Decision rules are used in characterizing information. In evaluating the sheriff's race, one such rule might be the generalization that incumbents usually win. Another might be that, in the local area, Republicans almost always come out on top.

The Grunigs' assessment of the role of decision rules has changed somewhat over the years. Initially, they saw such rules as simplifying devices that reduce the perceived need for seeking, integrating, and interpreting information. After all, if Republicans always win, one can safely predict the winner simply by finding out who is Republican. Other, more in-depth information is superfluous.

Recently, however, data suggest that decision rules aren't always simple or easy to apply. Different rules conflict or interact. And a given rule can require consideration of many factors or attributes in its application. In such cases, a decision stimulates and directs information seeking rather than inhibiting it.

4. A person's involvement in a situation may bear on information seeking and using. Involvement means the perceived closeness of a decision to oneself—the extent to which a person sees success or failure in a decision or in drawing a conclusion, as related to his or her overall feeling of self-confidence and satisfaction. For one to have high ego-involvement, one must perceive many "bridging experiences" linking himself or herself to the topic or object of concern.

In conclusion, it is important to make three points about the Grunigs' theory:

It calls attention to the *process* of information attainment and use. The authors felt that process has too often been overlooked as people have focused on the *end product*.

The Grunigs were critical of attitude concepts on much the same grounds as they were of personality traits. That is, attitudes are often assumed to hold across situations, roles played, significant others attended to, etc. But the evidence casts doubt on the existence of such consistency.

They felt their theory can and does hold across levels on a micro–macro continuum. Openness to new information—and factors affecting it—are important in explaining the behavior of individuals, but also of small groups, complex organizations, and perhaps even larger regions. Much of the Grunigs' recent work is centered on the level of complex organizations (see Grunig & Grunig, 1989, pp. 27–63).

We now turn to a third area of theory and research relating to social context.

Frames of Reference

Some beliefs that frame the way people think and act do not necessarily have the force of culture and custom behind them. Such beliefs stem from an individual's personal experience and socialization. Although many people may come to share them as a result of similar learning and circumstances, belief holders act as individuals. Sociologist Herbert Blumer's (1966) classic definition of the *mass* recognizes this. The mass is an ideal-type group or collectivity in which each individual thinks and acts alone. (To be sure, when people think and act alike, a mass is a powerful force in storming a prison, supporting a political leader, etc.)

The discussion here focuses on *standard-of-comparison* and *schema* theories. Developed within psychology, these theories focus on individual perspectives and experiences. Of course, some beliefs discussed have the force of "sharedness" behind them.

Standard-of-comparison theory stems from a simple but powerful notion. When one judges a quantity, one compares it with some standard (Helson, 1964). For example, a basketball player who is 6 feet 7 inches tall may look very short if one has just watched Kareem Abdul-Jabbar, at 7 feet 3 inches, play. However, the same player may look gigantic if one has just watched a point guard who is 5 feet 4 inches tall. Also, in the realm of social judgment, a speaker of average forcefulness seems timid if one has just heard a very loud and bombastic speaker but quite forceful if she or he speaks right after a shy, soft-spoken individual.

Standard-of-comparison theories postulate that both or either of two factors often influence assessment of quantities. First, people assess a given quantity by comparing it with a weighted average of contextual quantities encountered in one's past experience and present stimulus field (Helson, 1964). Second, Upshaw (1962) and others proposed that extreme values or end points among the stimuli that one has encountered provide the most salient standards of comparison or anchors.

It stands to reason that sometimes extreme anchors are conspicuous and thus used as standards of comparisons. Abdul-Jabbar, for example, was a graceful player and an all-star for many years. Even though he has retired, basketball centers will undoubtedly be compared with him for years. At the other extreme, prominent and widely publicized small men such as the Atlanta Hawks' Spud Webb tend to set the standard for guards.

However, in the absence of such prominent extreme anchors, one may very well—probably unconsciously—develop an average of all players he or she has seen at a given position and use that as a standard of comparison. Also, training to analyze players carefully—or a situation-specific demand that one do so—may contribute to an averaging rather than extreme-anchor approach.

Clearly some contexts or standards of comparison are seen as more relevant and useful than others (Brown, 1953; Perry, 1985). For example, Culbertson (1970) found in an experiment that varying crime-rate data about Detroit influenced people's ratings, on a 7-point scale, of a given crime statistic for Cleveland. On the other hand, similar manipulation of data about Denver had little impact on how people interpreted the same statistic vis-a-vis Cleveland.

Why did Detroit appear to be a more relevant context than Denver when interpreting data about Cleveland? Culbertson (1970) suggested three reasons:

Proximity. Detroit and Cleveland are quite close, both bordering on the Great Lakes. Denver and Cleveland, however, are half a continent apart.

Similarity as to salient physical traits. Detroit and Cleveland were roughly the same size—both much larger than Denver—when the study was done. Also, both were reputed to be rather grimy, rough industrial towns in contrast to Denver, an attractive agribusiness and tourist center. In the same vein, Brown (1953) found greater context effects when both a contextual object and that being judged were brass weights than when one was a brass weight and the other a tray.

Judgment conventions. People divide the nation into regions in their thinking and see themselves as close to cities within their own regions (Carter & Mitofsky, 1961). Thus many no doubt lump Detroit and Cleveland together as part of the industrial Midwest whereas Denver seems far removed from both as part of the Rocky Mountain region. Also, Detroit and Cleveland have long considered themselves rivals in sports and other areas, whereas neither has been a traditional rival of Denver.

We now turn to a second body of theory useful in defining frame of reference, the *schema theory*. Taylor and Crocker (1981) defined schemata pyramidal belief structures that are "hierarchically organized with more abstract or general information at the top and categories of more specific information nested within the general categories." Graber (1984, p. 24) noted that schemata perform four major functions:

1. They determine what information is noticed, processed, and stored. For example, one who believes strongly that political leaders around the world are treacherous tends to call for a strong national defense and a tough, aggressive foreign policy. Thus such an individual is apt to seek information about candidate stands and records in defense and foreign policy.

2. They help one organize and evaluate new information so it fits into their established perceptions. One who believes that governments in capitalist societies

are militaristic is likely to interpret the calling up of a state National Guard unit in America as an aggressive act. (Schemata sometimes lead one astray. The Guard unit may be called up in anticipation of a possible hurricane or flood. But the basic schema about capitalist societies could lead one to achieve premature closure without checking further.)

3. They permit one to go beyond information that is immediately available and fill in missing links. A physician who diagnoses a patient's ailment as a heart problem may conclude, without bothering to check, that certain symptoms such as shortness of breath have been experienced. After all, these symptoms normally accompany heart problems. (Of course, such an inference may be wrong. It rests on the validity of the diagnosis.)

4. Schemata help one solve problems because they contain information about likely scenarios and ways to cope with them. In the example just given, a physician surely would have in mind a plan for treatment of heart problems.

Schemata help one manage the flood tide of information. In fact, such belief structures are essential to bring the complexity of information search and planning down to manageable levels (Graber, 1984, pp. 125–127). Of course, as the previous examples suggest, schemata can involve error and oversimplification. Also, unless they accord with reality, they can lead one to ignore needed information or dwell on irrelevant facts and arguments. Such mistakes, called *bad closing* and *bad opening,* respectively, by sociologist Orrin Klapp (1978, pp. 159–167), can entail inefficiency, confusion, and even mental illness.

In a study of how people process political information, Graber (1984, pp. 154–173) found that schemata revolve around six dimensions:

1. Definitions of situations. For example, most people have in mind stock scenarios about what happens with a familiar event such as a strike. Picketing, late-night negotiating, possible violence, calls for support from other unions, and euphoria at the strike's end are among the elements. News stories tend to be interpreted in terms of whether and how they portray these elements.

2. Cause-and-effect sequences. Consumers tend to approach news with the assumption that high auto traffic and industrialization lead to pollution and that rigidity inherent in bureaucracy causes government inefficiency. Sometimes cause–effect linkages are quite complex with several links in a causal chain.

3. Person judgments. For example, people assume that union leaders mellow with age as they tire of confrontation and learn that negotiations sometimes yield more lasting results. This leads them to interpret news about particular union leaders such as Cesar Chavez, noted leader of farm workers in the western United States, partly in terms of how faithfully they follow this pattern. On the down side, it also contributes to stereotyping, assuming that leaders follow such a pattern without bothering to check the facts in a particular case.

4. Judgments about institutions. Many people feel police are corrupt. Also, the Central Intelligence Agency is widely regarded as nonresponsive to public demands for openness and honesty. And the United States Senate is said to be just a debating society unable to accomplish much of anything. In a related vein, people have normative expectations of organizations. Officials are expected to be fair and behave in a consistent manner. People often interpret the news partly in terms of how fully government bodies appear to meet these expectations.

5. Cultural norms. While in school, Americans learn to value free expression, equality of opportunity, and fair play. They look for news suggesting adherence, or lack of it, to these norms or ideals.

6. Human interest and empathy. People expect officials and organizations to act humanely and with respect for human rights. On the other hand, they are often resigned to the fact that America glorifies competition, holds assertive, self-made people in high regard, and has little compassion for the reticent or lazy.

Belief and plan structures also order actions that people might or do take. For example, Altman and Taylor's (1973) *social-penetration theory* holds that people progress from superficial areas of exchange to more intimate, deep layers involving individual personalities. In a study of college students, Honeycutt, Cantrill, and Greene (1989) found widespread agreement that boy–girl relationships should progress in an orderly sequence from first meeting and asking for a partner's phone number through small talk, kissing, having a formal date, spending informal time together, meeting parents, and giving gifts through living together, sexual intercourse, and eventually marriage. Such perceived scenes form a "memory organized packet" and fall within five global stages such as initiation, experimentation, intensification, self-disclosure, and integration.

Berger, Karol, and Jordan (1989) reported that people who have complex, well-formed plans for persuading others tend to speak fluently and with little delay, when asked to indicate what they would actually say to those others.

In sum, schemata and action plans are needed for simplicity and efficiency in a complex, fast-changing world. Unfortunately, they can be dangerous if their simplicity makes them inaccurate or ineffective and their use shortcuts reality testing. Perhaps the most destructive schemata are stereotypes such as "Blacks are lazy" or "Jews are cliquish." Given the tremendous variety of Blacks and Jews, such stereotypes are bound to be inaccurate. And they serve as justification for insensitivity, discrimination, and even murder.

We now turn to another set of concepts useful in defining the social context of a public relations client or problem.

The Nature and Number of Personal Contacts

Rensis Likert (1961, pp. 46–56) proposed that managers of complex organizations study messages flowing among their members to maximize the overall effectiveness of their most important resource—humans. He and other management scholars called for careful study of communication, with special attention to such variables as:

1. The accuracy and completeness of information transmitted.

2. The extent to which information gets to the right people at the right time for use in decision making.

3. Who initiates contacts, especially between superiors and subordinates. In some organizations, lower-level employees seldom speak unless they are spoken to by their bosses. Such asymmetry limits management understanding of how employees define issues.

4. How formal or informal communication and the climate that it creates are. When people address each other only through channels at specified times and places, grievances and other sensitive matters tend to be hidden or reported inaccurately. Informal conversation around the water cooler and at company picnics, etc., are then useful. In part, that's because the spoken word tends to be less formal and more flexible than the written word.

5. To what extent is communication planned or spontaneous? As just noted, this has a great deal to do with formality.

The literature identifies at least six barriers to interpersonal communication that is adequate in achieving certain goals:

1. The number of people who are available to interact. Rogers (1983, pp. 67–68) noted that interpersonal contact is often needed to sell people on adopting new ideas. And unless a substantial force of sales persons or other change agents are at work in the field, such contact can hardly occur on a large scale.

2. A competitive or cooperative organizational climate. Argyris (1974, pp. 1–33) found that intense competition limits communication. Organization members who aspire to gain in status are often reluctant to divulge information that might give others an advantage or antagonize those who control one's fate.

3. Group size. In a large group, people vary in motives, outlook, and background. That, in turn, leads to a lack of felt togetherness, shared purpose, and intimacy (Cartwright & Zander, 1960, pp. 80–81). Further, in a small group, all members probably have time to express themselves quite fully. In a larger organization, however, not everyone has time to "take the floor" during a meeting. Intimacy and spontaneity of communication may suffer as a result.

4. Organizational structure. A steep, hierarchical arrangement—with several layers of bosses, bosses' bosses, and bosses' bosses' bosses—may lead to incomplete, inaccurate communication. At least two forces operate here. First, subordinates are often reluctant to convey bad news to their superiors, because the latter may "kill the messenger" who brings such tidings. Second, Snodgrass (1985)

reported evidence that superiors take their underlings for granted, perhaps partly because they seldom depend on subordinates, day in and day out, for approval and possible promotion. Such laxity can lead to inaccurate perceptions of what's happening "down below."

5. Space–time relationships. In *The Kingdom and the Power*, Gay Talese (1969) told how communication changed in 1951 when the United Nations moved from small, informal settings on a Bronx campus, and later at a place called Lake Success, to its current skyscraper on the East River in New York:

> The United Nations populace seemed much more united on the Bronx campus, and later at Lake Success on Long Island, than it would (after the move) . . . The skyscraper would bring verticality to the U.N., would divide it into a thousand tiny compartments, would section off these people who had come to New York from all sections of the world seeking unity. But in the Bronx and Long Island, before the Manhattan structures were opened, the U.N. was horizontally spread through several smaller buildings and the delegates, their aides and the press were forced to do a great deal of walking from place to place—and there was much more mingling and meeting along the paths, streets and steps, and the U.N. seemed to (Editor Abe) Rosenthal to be a spontaneous and convivial place. (p. 334)

6. Bureaucratization within an organization. Allegedly developed to control increasingly large numbers of people who had to do just the right things at the right times in industrial plants, bureaucratization involves clear specification of what a person can or cannot do. Also, industrialization and modern organization encourage routinization—a tendency to react in the same way, over and over, without much regard to people's changing needs, capabilities, and circumstances. Such factors limit communication but also give it structure needed for relevance, accuracy, and completeness (Faunce, 1968, pp. 135–175).

We now turn to a theoretical perspective that bears on how individuals and small groups relate to each other and take each other into account. Social contact is one of several factors that bear on relating.

Coorientation Processes

Practitioner, client, and audience may think alike or agree on matters of common concern. But they may behave as adversaries or avoid each other completely, if either party believes the other thinks in ways opposed to his or hers.

In a North Carolina study many years ago (Carter, 1958), medical reporters and doctors agreed that accuracy is of paramount importance in deciding whether a given news story merits substantial play. However, physicians assumed reporters stress timeliness and audience appeal more than accuracy. This belief implies that reporters are sensation mongers.

In light of prevailing professional norms, such beliefs set the stage for possible poor press coverage. Under these circumstances, physicians probably would not talk to reporters if they could help it. After all, a sensational story is apt to exaggerate and contain inaccuracies. That, in turn, could endanger a physician's reputation. But refusal to talk to reporters often leads the press to ignore or distort the refuser's point of view.

This study illustrates an important point. We humans constantly take each other into account, organizing our behavior in light of each other's predicted reactions (Mead, 1955). And one behaves toward another on the basis of how one believes that other does or would react, not on the basis of how God or some objective researcher defines or predicts that reaction.

Such prediction of another's belief or reaction is called *role taking* by sociologists. And in recent years, study of that process has gained clarity because of the Chaffee–McLeod (1968) coorientation model. The model assumes that, when any person P takes another person O into account, three sets of reactions are involved:

The predictor's (P's) own set of reactions or priorities within a given setting.

P's perception or prediction of how the other person (O) would react.

O's actual reactions as defined by himself or herself or some third party such as a researcher.

As shown in Fig. 4.1, the coorientation model focuses on three measures of similarity or difference between these sets of reactions:

Agreement between P's and O's own responses.

Congruency or similarity between P's own reaction and that which he or she attributes to O. High congruency—assuming another behaves as you do—amounts to *ethnocentrism* (when role taking with people as representatives of a

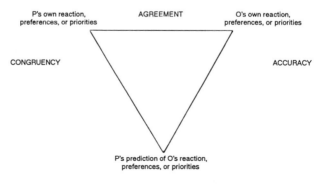

FIG. 4.1.

society or total culture) or *egocentrism* (when role taking with someone as an individual). Such reactions often entail insensitivity and prejudice (Hartley & Hartley, 1952, pp. 302–303). At the other extreme, very low congruency amounts to *polarization,* which often implies a lack of any common ground so as to discourage understanding and dialogue (Turner, 1962).

Accuracy—the level of similarity between P's prediction of O's response and O's actual behavior. This index is often the real bottom line in human relationships. P cannot take O's reactions into account effectively unless P understands or predicts what O's reactions are likely to be.

How can P gauge O's reactions? The literature suggests three basic approaches:

Projection—attributing P's own beliefs or intentions to O. As noted earlier, this entails ethnocentrism or egocentrism (very high congruency) that fails to take into account differences among individuals. However, the technique is easy to use if one buys the debatable assumption that one knows oneself better than one knows others. Gans (1980, p. 230) found that journalists sometimes project their own priorities to news consumers, because the latter seem too numerous and diverse to analyze.

Studying rules that govern O's behavior when O plays a particular role in a given situation. This seems workable where O's role is tightly defined with clearly specified rules governing behavior in detail. An example is a United States Marine in close-order drill who slavishly follows detailed instructions in a manual (Steiner, 1963).

Personal interaction with O. One can get to know another's idiosyncrasies by frequent association, careful observation, and even formal research involving projective tests or in-depth interviews.

Two propositions about the viability of projection or high congruency as a role-taking approach follow logically from the previous definitions.

First, given high agreement, high congruency yields high accuracy. This translates into the truism that P can accurately predict O's thoughts or behavior by assuming P resembles O only if, in fact, the resemblance is present.

In practice, this suggests that a practitioner who grew up among members of a particular public, sharing members' learning experiences and basic goals, has reason to believe that high congruency (projecting his or her own views to that public) may yield high accuracy. (Of course, even with similar backgrounds, practitioner and audience member may have differing current goals and contexts, encouraging different perceptions that may lower accuracy.)

Second, given low agreement, fairly low congruency is a necessary but not sufficient condition for high accuracy.

Take, for example, some "Boston Brahmin" practitioners and sidekicks of the

Kennedy family who open an office in Abilene, Kansas. These Brahmins could hardly use their own perceptions as a guide to those of Kansas wheat farmers. They'd need to put forth special effort in studying local publics.

Bowes and Stamm (1975) suggested that accuracy is often a more realistic communication goal than agreement. Persuasive communicators often seek to bring a public around to agreeing with their points of view. Unfortunately, attitudes to which the holder is highly committed often resist change stubbornly. But the audience member can learn the communicator's point of view without accepting it as his or her own.

High accuracy coupled with low agreement entails understanding of views quite different from one's own. Such "opening" contributes to breadth of perspective, recently defined by Culbertson (1989) as an important concept for public relations. This, in turn, contributes to tolerance of another's views, some doubt (high problem recognition in information-systems theory) about one's own position, and resultant active information seeking (Grunig, 1976, 1983). Western philosophers dating back at least to Milton (see Peterson, Jensen, & Rivers, 1966, pp. 89–91) suggested that even erroneous arguments contain elements of or a stimulus to seek the truth. As a result, well-informed decisions tend to be superior to poorly informed ones.

A final point deserves emphasis when applying the coorientation model. When a person P accurately perceives O's behavior or priorities, P need not (and often probably should not) slavishly follow O's views in making decisions.

When P perceives a difference between his or her own and O's views (i.e., when congruency is at least moderately low), P can do either or both of two things:

Follow O's preferences when evaluating goals and messages.

Follow P's own set of preferences. This is called *high autonomy* (Culbertson, 1983).

Extremely high followership to the exclusion of autonomy, or visa versa, is questionable in most situations. High followership leads to a lack of innovativeness and poor adjustment to changing public opinion (unless, of course, one keeps careful track of opinion change over time) (Murphy, 1991). At the other extreme, very high autonomy can entail arrogance and loss of touch with one's audience.

Clearly some blend is called for. The nature of that blend is a challenging question with important ethical implications for contemporary communicators (Culbertson, 1983).

One final point deserves emphasis. If congruency is very high, autonomy and followership do not yield different decision-making outcomes. Following self and audience give nearly the same result. And no tug of war between the two perspectives seems likely.

We now take a further look at the five viewpoints used to define social context as they relate to the two attributes of social science theories mentioned earlier in this chapter. These are structure vs. function and macro vs. micro.

More on the Two Dimensions

Content. Because of their content, cultural and subcultural beliefs, as well as schemata, shape information seeking, interpretation, and behavior. For example, a schema that the nation is threatened by evil outside forces might lead prospective voters to seek information about a presidential candidate's personal toughness and views on national defense. Also, the same underlying concept could help set a high standard when interpreting the candidate's comments about the national defense budget. And belief holders might very well vote—behave—on the basis of how they assess what the candidate says about military development.

Structure. One's frame of reference is basically structural, however, because its role derives from how it relates to something that one uses it to define or assess.

Assume, for example, that you are a die-hard fan of that infamous automobile of yesteryear, the Ford Edsel. You might then use the Edsel as a standard of comparison in assessing a modern car, say the Chevrolet Corvette. You evaluate the Corvette by comparing it with the Edsel as to design, length, miles per gallon of gasoline, etc. The point is that the Edsel's role in the whole process hinges not on its length or mileage viewed in isolation, but on how these things compare with the car that's now being defined, the Corvette.

Also, coorientation is inherently relational and, thus, structural. Regardless of what he or she believes (i.e., belief content), any person P can agree or disagree with another. Also, P can predict or perceive that other's view accurately or inaccurately. And P can see the other as like or unlike herself or himself, yielding high or low congruency. Each of the three basic coorientation concepts consists of a relationship between two beliefs or sets of beliefs held by or attributed to one or more persons.

Turning to situational-belief theory, two individuals can face ostensibly identical situations as to content but see them in vastly different lights. One person may feel she has the resources and ability to cope with an attacker and a supportive environment for coping, whereas another may express only fear and trepidation in what appears to be an identical situation. The first experiences low uncertainty regarding what to think and do—low problem recognition. She may also see few barriers to effective functioning, creating low constraint recognition. On the other hand, lady number 2 may score high on both of these variables. The point is, both ladies relate differently to what is, on the surface, the same situation as to content.

Finally, social contacts have to do with the manner in which people relate to each other. Formal or informal? Accurate or inaccurate messages conveyed? One-way or two-way communication? Does information get to the right people when they need it? These are among the questions asked in analysis of social contacts. All focus on how and with what behaviors people relate to others and take them into account.

We now turn to the second dimension used to compare and contrast these theories: macro vs. micro level. Studies here fall at four distinct levels: societal, subcultural, personal-relational, and individual.

Societal Level.   As noted earlier, cultural beliefs have great force partly because all or most people within a society hold them and see them as relating to societal well-being. Thus, these notions gain wide acceptance as an important basis for shaping thoughts and behavior.

For example, a deep-seated and widely shared belief in freedom from dictatorial control forms a basis for American views of many heads of state. Sometimes such shaping even leads the nation to war. In 1991, for example, the Persian Gulf War was justified partly to weaken Iraqi President Saddam Hussein.

Subcultural Level.   Assumptions at this level are held by a somewhat smaller group than are cultural ones. However, subcultural beliefs also play a shaping role and have great force partly because they are emphasized in socialization within a vocational, ethnic, religious, or other group. It's especially important to note that people's jobs and careers tend to hinge on accepting and adhering to vocation-based beliefs. Making a living is central within a materialistic, individualistic society such as the United States.

Social-Relational Level.   Social-contact analysis focuses on the nature of interaction among people who actually talk and communicate, one-on-one, with each other. Such communication occurs among a few dozen or hundred people, for example, say CEOs of Fortune 500 corporations who tend to encounter each other because of shared membership in groups such as the Chamber of Commerce and the Business Round Table or 535 United States Congress persons who often share gyms, recording studios, cloakrooms, and committee assignments.

However, personal interaction is not possible among all of the tens or hundreds of thousands of schoolteachers or plumbers all over the country. When dealing with these groups, the more abstract subcultural level of analysis is needed.

Chaffee and McLeod (1968) developed their coorientation model to aid the study of how two individuals relate to each other. Some scholars analyzed one person's or group's perception of a large collectivity in coorientation terms. However, this requires averaging or otherwise aggregating data from the group's many members. Such an exercise, in turn, involves *reification*—creating in the perceiver's mind an estimate that is more or less bogus, because it would not even exist in the absence of the data-collection procedure! Thus coorientation scholars are most at home with the social-relational level.

Individual Level.   Of course, those within a society or subgroup no doubt have similar beliefs about problem recognition, involvement, and constraints. However,

TABLE 4.2
Characterization of Theoretical Viewpoints on Basis of Content Vs. Structure and
Micro-Macro Level

| | Object of Study | |
Micro-Macro Level	Content	Structure
Society	Cultural beliefs	
Large group with shared problems, socialization	Subcultural beliefs	
Social-relational		Social-contact, coorientation
Individual	Schemata	Standard-of-comparison, Situational beliefs

each person in a complex, pluralistic society has her or his own set of significant others, reference groups, goals, and problem situations. These variations help determine how one thinks and behaves in any given case, suggesting a need to study each individual separately when using information-systems theory. No two people have precisely the same situational beliefs.

Furthermore, in such a society, differing experiences lead to differing frames of reference. For instance, one of the authors watches a great many National Basketball Association games, whereas the reader may not. Because he sees quite a few people like 7 foot 7 inch-Manute Bol, an NBA player, one author of this book views a 6 foot 9 inch-advisee who comes to his office quite frequently as being of medium height. The reader, on the other hand, could very well see the same guy as a giant!

Such differences in day-to-day experience, coupled with differing schemata that affect interpretation of experience, almost force the study of frames of reference at the individual level.

Finally, as noted earlier, schemata operate within the individual's mental processes and do not assume sharedness or group-level functioning. Of course, some schemata are shared widely.

Tab. 4.2 summarizes the theoretical views noted here in relation to the two underlying criteria discussed.

SUMMARY AND CONCLUSIONS

We conclude this chapter by noting that concepts useful in defining the social context relate closely to the political and economic realms. In fact, it is difficult if not impossible to separate the three sets of ideas. We now try to suggest the extent and nature of these relationships by noting at least five specific "tie-ins" between this chapter and the ones to follow.

First, political context cannot be understood without a close look at social contacts that bear on who wields power and how. In a typical city, for example, the mayor may have a great deal of formal power based on his or her position as chief executive. Yet a persuasive city council member may turn out to be a well-connected mover and shaker, an informal leader commanding respect and a following that makes him or her a significant person when it comes to gaining appropriations for a city agency. The informal vs. formal distinction is treated in chapter 5.

Second, study of the political context surely requires analysis of opinion leaders and who they contact regularly and with influence. Katz and Lazarsfeld (1964) suggested long ago that opinion leaders often do not have great fame or formal power. Rather they tend to have role-centered expertise gained in the course of day-to-day living (Katz & Lazarsfeld, 1964, pp. 321–334). Also, they tend to be heavy consumers of relevant media output (Katz & Lazarsfeld, 1964, pp. 309–320). At the same time, Troldahl and Van Dam (1965) found that in the realm of public affairs, people who converse tend to reinforce each other rather than have one person change the other consistently as the distinction between leadership and followership implies.

Turning to the economic context, we find at least three parallels between the socio-psychological concepts developed in this chapter and the analysis of resources going into and coming out of a client organization.

First, the concept of frame of reference or adaptation level seems central to full understanding of the basic economic notions of *marginal utility* and *diminishing marginal returns*. These latter ideas imply, for example, that a community with no total-care facility for the elderly has a low adaptation level with regard to the value of such an institution. Local residents might then find it easy to drum up support for growth in this particular area of social welfare. However, once one or two facilities have been built, value attached to still further health care centers might decline.

In a related vein, school boards surely must reckon with the public belief that any given tax levy in behalf of education should meet a school's most urgent needs. Consequently, people naturally tend to see declining value in levies where they are placed on the ballot annually for several years. School boards, like athletic coaches, can "go to the well once too often" within their game plans.

Second, audience involvement, a key notion in information systems theory, surely has much in common with the economist's notion of *demand inelasticity*. Demand for a product is inelastic where people buy about as much of it when prices are high as when they aren't. Such behavior suggests intense, loyal commitment—hence involvement—with respect to the product.

Third, schema theory focuses on beliefs that tend to influence and set the stage for other beliefs—to shape one's overall world view regarding news, job behavior, or some other substantial aspect of life. Such beliefs have much in common with basic corporate values that, according to Peters and Waterman (1982, pp. 279–291), shape successful corporations and their economic plights. These associations are developed further in the chapters to come.

REFERENCES

Altman, I., & Taylor, D. A. (1973). *Social penetration: the development of interpersonal relationships.* New York: Holt, Rinehart & Winston.

Anderson, N. H. (1981). Integration theory applied to cognitive responses and attitudes. In R. E. Petty, T. M. Ostrom, & T. C. Brock (Eds.), *Cognitive responses in persuasion* (pp. 361–397). Hillsdale, NJ: Lawrence Erlbaum Associates.

Argyris, C. (1974). *Behind the front page.* San Francisco: Jossey-Bass.

Berger, C. R., Karol, S. H., & Jordan, J. M. (1989). When a lot of knowledge is a dangerous thing: The debilitating effects of plan complexity on verbal fluency. *Human Communication Research, 16,* 91–119.

Blumer, H. (1966). The mass, the public and public opinion. In B. Berelson & M. Janowitz (Eds.), *Reader in public opinion and communication* (pp. 43–50). New York: The Free Press.

Bowes, J. E., & Stamm, K. R. (1975). Evaluating communication with public agencies. *Public Relations Review, 1,* 23–37.

Brown, D. R. (1953). Stimulus similarity and anchoring of subjectives scales. *American Journal of Psychology, 66,* 199–214.

Carter, R., Jr. (1958). Newspaper "gatekeepers" and the sources of news. *Public Opinion Quarterly, 22,* 133–144.

Carter, R. E., Jr., & Mitofsky, W. (1961). Actual and perceived distances in the news. *Journalism Quarterly, 38,* 223–225.

Cartwright, D., & Zander, A. (1960). *Group dynamics: Research and theory.* New York: Harper & Row.

Chaffee, S. H., & McLeod, J. M. (1968). Sensitization in panel design: A coorientational experiment. *Journalism Quarterly, 45,* 661–669.

Culbertson, H. M. (1970). The interpretation of a message in light of contextual magnitude and relevance. *Journal of Communication, 20,* 32–50.

Culbertson, H. M. (1981). Reporters and editors: Some differences in perspectives. *Newspaper Research Journal, 2,* 17–27.

Culbertson, H. M. (1983). Three perspectives on American journalism. *Journalism Monographs, 83.*

Culbertson, H. M. (1989). Breadth of perspective: An important concept in public relations. In J. E. Grunig & L. A. Grunig (Eds.), *Public Relations Research Annual* (Vol. 1, pp. 3–25). Hillsdale, NJ: Lawrence Erlbaum Associates.

Culbertson, H. M. (1991). Role-taking and sensitivity: Keys to playing and making public relations roles. In L. A. Grunig & J. E. Grunig, (Eds.), *Public Relations Research Annual,* (Vol. 3, pp. 37–65). Hillsdale, NJ: Lawrence Erlbaum Associates.

Culbertson, H. M., & Stempel, G. H., III (1985). Linking beliefs and public relations effects. *Public Relations Research & Education, 2,* 23–35.

Efron, E. (1971). *The news twisters.* Los Angeles: Nash.

Faunce, W. A. (1968). *Problems of an industrial society.* New York: McGraw-Hill.

Fishbein, M., & Ajzen, I. (1981). Acceptance, yielding and impact: Cognitive processes in persuasion. In R. E. Petty, T. M. Ostrom, & T. C. Brock (Eds.), *Cognitive response in persuasion* (pp. 339–369). Hillsdale, NJ: Lawrence Erlbaum Associates.

Gans, H. J. (1980). *Deciding what's news.* New York: Vintage.

Graber, D. A. (1984). *Processing the news.* New York: Longman.

Grunig, J. E. (1976). Organizations and public relations: Testing a communication theory. *Journalism Monographs, 46.*

Grunig, J. E. (1983). Communication behaviors and attitudes of environmental publics: Two studies. *Journalism Monographs, 81.*

Grunig, J. E., & Grunig, L. A. (1989). Toward a theory of the public relations behavior of organizations: Review of a program of research. In J. E. Grunig & L. A. Grunig (Eds.), *Public Relations Research Annual*, (Vol. 1, pp. 27–63). Hillsdale, NJ: Lawrence Erlbaum Associates.

Grunig, J. E., & Hunt, T. (1984). *Managing public relations*. New York: Holt, Rinehart & Winston.

Hall, E. T. (1969). *The hidden dimension*. New York: Doubleday Anchor.

Hampden-Turner, C. (1971). *Radical man*. Garden City, NY: Anchor.

Hartley, E. L., & Hartley, R. E. (1952). *Fundamentals of social psychology*. New York: Knopf.

Helson, H. (1964). *Adaption level theory*. New York: Harper & Row.

Hoffer, E. (1951). *The true believer*. New York: New American Library Mentor Books.

Honeycutt, J. M., Cantrill, J. G., & Greene, R. W. (1989). Memory structures for relational escalation: A cognitive test of the sequencing of relational actions and stages. *Human Communication Research*, *16*, 62–90.

Johnstone, J. W. C., Slawski, E. J., & Bowman, W. W. (1976). *The news people*. Urbana, IL: University of Illinois Press.

Katz, E., & Lazarsfeld, P. F. (1964). *Personal influence*. New York: The Free Press.

Klapp, O. (1978). *Opening and closing: Strategies of information adaptation in society*. New York: Columbia University Press.

Ladd, E. C. (1981). 205 and going strong. *Public Opinion, 43*, 126–134.

Lichter, S. R., Rothman, S., & Lichter, L. S. (1986). *The media elite: America's new power brokers*. Bethesda, MD: Adler & Adler.

Likert, R. (1961). *New patterns of management*. New York: McGraw-Hill.

Lipset, S. M., & Raab, E. (1973). *The politics of unreason: Right-wing extremism in America, 1790–1970*. New York: Harper Torchbooks.

Manufacturing joint ventures in China: A progress report and experience guide. (1987). Chicago: A. T. Kearney Management Consultants.

Maslow, A. (1962). *Toward a psychology of being*. Princeton, NJ: Van Nostrand.

Mead, G. H. (1955). *Mind, self & society*. Chicago: University of Chicago Press.

Murphy, P. (1991). The limits of symmetry: A game theory approach to symmetric and asymmetric public relations. In L. A. Grunig & J. E. Grunig (Eds.), *Public Relations Research Annual*, (Vol. 3, pp. 115–131). Hillsdale, NJ: Lawrence Erlbaum Associates.

Oxford Analytica (1986). *American perspective*. Boston: Houghton Mifflin.

Parenti, M. (1986). *Inventing reality: The politics of the mass media*. New York: St. Martin's Press.

Perry, D. K. (1985). The mass media and inferences about other nations. *Communication Research, 12*, 595–614.

Peters, T. J., & Waterman, R. H. (1982). *In search of excellence*. New York: The Free Press.

Peterson, T., Jensen, J. W., & Rivers, W. L. (1966). *The mass media and modern society*. New York: Holt, Rinehart & Winston.

Public opinion report. (1990, May/June). Values: Stability and change. *The American Enterprise*, p. 100.

Public opinion report (1990, September/October). What's important at work? *The American Enterprise*, p. 84.

Public opinion report (1991, July/August). Get tough across the board. *The American Enterprise*, p. 79.

Public opinion report (1991, July/August). The truth about taxes. *The American Enterprise*, p. 82.

Rogers, E. M. (1983). *Diffusion of innovations*. New York: The Free Press.

Rosenberg, M. J. (1960). A structural theory of attitude dynamics. *Public Opinion Quarterly, 24*, 319–340.

Snodgrass, S. E. (1985). Women's intuition: The effect of subordinate role on inter-personal sensitivity. *Journal of Personality and Social Psychology, 49*, 146–155.

Steiner, I. D. (1963). Interpersonal behavior as influenced by accuracy of social perception. In E. P. Hollander & R. G. Hunt (Eds.), *Current perspectives in social psychology* (pp. 263–268). New York: Oxford University Press.

Talese, G. (1969). *The kingdom and the power*. New York: Bantam.

Taylor, S. E., & Crocker, J. (1981). Schematic bases of social information processing. In E. T. Higgins, C. P. Herman, & M. P. Zanna (Eds.), *Social cognition: The Ontario symposium* (Vol. 1, pp. 89–134). Hillsdale, NJ: Lawrence Erlbaum Associates.

Troldahl, V. C., & Van Dam, R. (1965). Face-to-face communication among major topics in the news. *Public Opinion Quarterly, 29,* 626–634.

Turner, R. H. (1962). Role-taking: Process vs. conformity. In A. M. Rose (Ed.), *Human behavior and social processes* (pp. 20–40). Boston: Houghton-Mifflin.

Upshaw, H. (1962). Own attitude and scale judgment. *Journal of Abnormal and Social Psychology, 64,* 85–96.

Weaver, D. H., & Wilhoit, G. C. (1986). *The American journalist.* Bloomington, IN: Indiana University Press.

Woelfel, J., Cody, M. J., Gillham, J., & Holmes, R. A. (1980). Basic premises of multidimensional attitude change theory: An experimental analysis. *Human Communication Research, 6,* 154–167.

Yankelovich, D. (1981). *New rules.* New York: Random House.

5 The Political Context in Public Relations: Getting Things Done

This program to build a new recreation center will surely fly if we can just sell Mayor Glotz and Jody Smathers on it.

Public relations practitioners often talk in this way. In doing so, they recognize that few worthwhile efforts just happen. Someone must take the lead. And the statement above recognizes the importance of **formal** leadership (exercised by Mayor Glotz by virtue of his position in the community and the authority that goes along with it) and the **informal** variety (Ms. Smathers leads largely because of her persuasive powers and the respect that she commands as an individual).

Webster's Third New World Dictionary (1988) defines politics in part as "the relations between leaders and non-leaders in any social grouping (as a political community, church, club or trade union)." This definition—the broadest of eight provided by Webster—fits our discussion of political context. We deal only in passing with campaigning that helps government officials get elected. That area is of central concern, day in and day out, to only a few specialized public relations practitioners. We focus instead on leadership and persuasion—cores of politics more broadly defined.

To begin, leadership is the process wherein some people change or shape the behavior of others. Leading is a two-way street; one cannot do it well without good followers. Leadership results from the relationship between leader and follower and not from the behavior of any one person.

In discussing leadership, it is helpful to focus on two broad areas: (a) the roles that people play and how they play them in leading, and (b) strategies that leaders employ in gaining and using power or influence. This chapter addresses these domains.

LEADERSHIP ROLES

To expand on the first two paragraphs, leadership has two aspects—formal and informal. In any given situation, a leader usually relies to some extent on both.

Formal leadership hinges on sanctions—rewards and punishments—that a leader gives, or at least could threaten to impose, in exchange for the followers behaving (or not behaving) in a particular way. The leader is granted the authority, as a corollary to his or her leadership role, to impose sanctions. The granting is done by the institution or social system of which that role is a part.

In days gone by, many managers subscribed to a so-called *X theory* (Hersey & Blanchard, 1969, pp. 40–42) that asserts that people respond mostly to external rewards (bonuses, raises, promotions, pats on the back, etc.) and punishments (threatened or actual firings, demotions, and scoldings). Thus formal leadership was assumed to be important.

On the other hand, **informal** leaders get people to do or not do things through persuasion, charm, praise, and recognition. Also, such people exert influence by acting as attractive role models. In recent years, Argyris (1974, p. 42), Fromm (1970, p. 164) and other scholars argued that many, if not most, Westerners respond to such intangible rewards more than to dollars and cents or material goods. This theory, called *Y* (McGregor, 1960), implies that informal leadership is important.

Public relations practitioners must often lead informally, if they are to lead at all. In dealing with clients and publics, they are seldom in a position to back up demands with formal threats or tangible, dollars-and-cents rewards. They must often activate volunteer workers and others who are not their subordinates within an organization. Thus, the study of informal leadership is central to the political context of public relations. We now turn to some constructs important in defining and improving that type of leadership.

Group Maintenance Vs. Task Achievement

Bales and Strodtbeck (1951) long ago noted that leaders need to accomplish at least two kinds of things.

First, they must provide direction in completing a group task. Many, if not most, groups have goals—building a hospital, winning an athletic contest, earning money, and so on. Leaders must map strategy and point the way. And they must lead— either by personal example or by giving advice and orders—in reaching those goals.

Second, they must build and keep group morale and support. This involves settling disputes, selling members on the group's importance, coordinating member activities so the left hand knows what the right hand is doing, and other human relations efforts.

In studying problem-solving groups, Bales and Strodtbeck (1951) found that leaders swing back and forth between **group-maintenance** and **task-achievement** concerns as time passes. The process often goes something like this:

1. A group forms to carry out some task (e.g., raise money). For a time, members work with great singleness of purpose on that job. In short, attention focuses mainly on task-oriented concerns.

2. ‘As a plan of action takes shape, a few people begin giving orders and making suggestions. That's done largely to coordinate member efforts, synthesize arguments and plans offered, and achieve efficiency.

3. Before too long, some people become unhappy. They may not like those who emerge as leaders. Or they may disagree with the leaders' suggestions and orders. Jealousies arise. Tempers flare. The group may even fall apart unless someone takes the lead in group maintenance—soothing feelings, promoting understanding, and just plain letting off steam (perhaps by telling a joke or, unfortunately, berating an outsider).

4. Emphasis swings back to the task when group-maintenance problems appear to be under control. This completes a full cycle (task orientation to group maintenance and back to task orientation). Another cycle begins, and so on and on.

It's important to remember that Bales developed and tested his theory largely while working with new, unstructured problem-solving groups. Members often were strangers facing a strange task usually without any group history or time-tested approach to either group relations or task achievement.

Community-action leaders, on the other hand, typically deal with established groups that have developed role and power structures, patterns of personal interaction, and often pretty definite ways of approaching problems. Such groups might not follow the neat cyclical pattern just described. Still, leaders in most settings must deal with both task achievement and group maintenance.

Hersey and Blanchard (1969, pp. 101–102) pointed out that groups and situations differ as to relative need for group-maintenance and task-oriented leadership. Consider, for example, a group of workers trapped in a burning building. They would follow almost anyone who knows where still-functioning elevators and stairways some distance from the fire are located. Group morale and jealousies would be forgotten because of the urgent task of escape. At the other extreme, consider a Friday-night social club that has no goal or task other than to meet and have an enjoyable experience. The leader's main concern in such a case would focus on group maintenance—drumming up enthusiasm, insuring that well-liked individuals get invited to meetings, and avoiding unpleasant arguments so members continue to meet.

Of course, most public relations clients become involved in group activities that are designed to achieve certain goals. In analyzing any program, one clearly must look at both kinds of leadership. What are the needs? And are leaders meeting them?

We now turn to another typology useful in describing and assessing leadership activity. This system defines three ways of exercising leadership, each relating both to task achievement and group maintenance.

Institutional Leaders, Effectors, and Activists

Freeman, Farraro, Bloomberg, and Sunshine (1963) tried several methods of identifying leaders in Syracuse, New York. Their study reveals three distinct leader groups that overlapped very little. In brief, these groups are described as follows:

> Institutional leaders. Sometimes called legitimizers, these people have a great deal of prestige in the community, group, or society where they lead. Ex-presidents of the United States are a good example. They have no formal power and may do little day-to-day work in support of a program. However, assuming they are highly respected as individuals, their blessing encourages others to work hard. Also, their long-term vision of the future may carry much weight as program leaders develop long-term goals and global strategies.
>
> Effectors. These are the take-charge people who make many day-to-day decisions about how to get things done. Also, they ride herd to complete tasks well and on time. Freeman et al. (1963) noted that an effector is often an ambitious young professional or junior executive on the way up.
>
> Activists. These folks do the hard, nitty gritty work, such things as serving on committees, stuffing envelopes, soliciting funds door-to-door, and so on. They lead by example, putting in long hours, faithfully and effectively, in a way that others can admire and imitate.

Freeman did his analysis in a good-sized city, Syracuse, New York. In a smaller community or organization, specialization as to leadership role might be less marked. There a given person may often exercise two, or even all three, types of leadership.

Clearly a leader can operate in more than one of these areas at a given time. For example, a mayor may remark during a televised press conference that she would like to see a new public swimming pool in town next year. Then she is acting as both an institutional leader (seeking support for a new idea because of her prestige) and an effector (making a hard-headed, practical decision, in line with her formally defined job, to move on the pool project during the coming year).

A further look at institutional, effector, and activist leaders suggests that each has a group-maintenance as well as a task-oriented mission (Culbertson, 1968). We now pursue this further, discussing Tab. 5.1.

TABLE 5.1
A Typology of Leadership Characteristics

	Group Maintenance	Task Achievement
Institutional leaders	Prestige, Trustworthiness	Forsight and vision, Resources
Effectors	Diplomatic dynamism	Organization ability and instrumental skill
Activists	Enthusiastic, genuine dedication	Ability to communicate and sell

Note. Reprinted with permission from "On the Many Sides of Leadership" by H. M. Culbertson (1968). *Public Relations Quarterly, 13,* 25-30.

First, consider the group-maintenance role of institutional leaders. As well-known people, they make use of the respect that they have already earned. When such figures become identified with a project in the public mind, their prestige can "rub off" on the effort itself (Culbertson & Stempel, 1985; Fishbein & Ajzen, 1981). Of course, institutional leaders need not simply accept the prestige accorded them at any one point. Their public relations executives or counselors can advise them to enhance their images by supporting foundations, underwriting television programs, advancing projects to improve life in the Third World, and so on.

The leader's expertise (foresight, vision, know-how), a primary factor in his or her task-achievement role, may help here, too. For example, people admire former President Jimmy Carter, partly because of the role he played in moving Egypt and Israel toward the so-called Camp David Accords in the late 1970s. Carter is widely credited with demonstrating considerable skill as a mediator at Camp David. Also, he had a vision that, for decades to come, the Middle East would remain at the center of world conflict and the search for peace (Powell, 1984, p. 77). Such an image surely makes him a potential sponsor who can help gain support for varied projects in the 1990s.

Second, we look at the institutional leader's task-achievement role. An important element here is the leader's foresight and vision as just described with Jimmy Carter. To cite another example, automotive executive Henry Ford II supported construction of the Renaissance Center and Cobo Arena in downtown Detroit several years ago, partly because he saw potential gains (new industry, hosting of national political conventions, etc.) 10 or 50 years down the road. He apparently looked at short-term costs in light of these potential long-term benefits. Such "feet on the ground" dreaming, with an eye toward feasibility and cost/benefit considerations, is hard to define, but it doubtless contributes to executive success.

Third, we now turn to the effector's group-maintenance role. The term *diplomatic dynamism* captures the basic idea here. Effectors must ride herd. They must give orders and get action without offending people. Although perhaps not revered as are institutional leaders, effectors must be respected. They must work hard, setting an example for others. They must keep after activists and followers to avoid complacency and backsliding. And they must:

1. Organize efficiently, setting up committees on which members can work well together.

2. Encourage personal contacts to make sure communication within and between cliques, committees, and other groups does not break down. A relevant task here is creation of *linking pins* between departments and groupings within organizations, so those who make a given decision have the appropriate knowledge, expertise, and social support at just the right time (Likert, 1961).

3. Delegate responsibility effectively. Often old-timers within a modernizing organization err by insisting on keeping their "hands in" at every turn. One must trust subordinates and take some risks in delegating authority. Otherwise, middle- and lower-level leadership may be undermined, and followers may become demoralized. Also, one must understand thoroughly the strengths and weaknesses of those who are led in order to delegate wisely.

4. Remind all leaders as well as rank-and-file members in contact with external publics that they must **look at any task from the point of view of the person who carries it out.** Most people are at least a bit self-centered. Thus, they support an organization or client only when they decide "there's something in it for me."

Fourth, the effector plays a central part in task achievement by making many of the difficult decisions in day-to-day implementation. This takes more know-how and skill, perhaps, than either the institutional leader or activist needs. One must often raise money, check public reaction to a new project before it's too late to make changes that the public demands, and clear away or wade through red tape. And countless other kinds of decisions and activity fall into this realm.

Also, the effector must make assignments and name committees so people work effectively and complement each other in getting the job done. Such task-related concerns, of course, are weighed against possible group-maintenance problems. Two individuals who are in constant conflict will not work well together, even though their task-oriented abilities may complement each other perfectly.

Fifth comes the activist's group-maintenance role. A key here is enthusiastic dedication to the program one is working to sell or implement. Enthusiasm must be genuine, not forced (Seymour, 1966, pp. 118). Activists such as personal solicitors in a fund drive also need tact and diplomacy. They must bridge the gap between a program's dedicated supporters and the ordinary citizens whose time, money, and votes are being sought.

Sixth and last is the activist's task-achievement function. In roles that require frequent interpersonal contact with outsiders whose support is important, the activist is often a sales person. This requires understanding the product and being able to view that item from the prospective customer's standpoint. Simple, persuasive communication is crucial.

In other contexts, activists carry out a variety of jobs such as envelope stuffing, typing, and acting as chauffeurs. These tasks often seem routine, boring, and tedious. This, in turn, makes it easy to take them for granted and ignore the skill and dedication that they require. Yet those who watch a group closely—often insiders—appreciate their importance and find inspiration in their successful execution.

We only touch the surface in this brief treatment. Specific execution of the six leadership roles obviously varies from group to group and project to project. Yet all six cells of the Bales-Freeman Model seem important in leadership. Drastic failure in any one cell may be fatal.

We now turn to another distinction among types of leadership presented by a management scholar, Joseph Bower (1983).

Politicians Vs. Technocrats

According to Bower (1983, pp. 11–39), governments, large corporations, and other complex bureaucracies require leadership of different types from two kinds of people—politicians and technocrats. The two types differ dramatically in their goals, ways of operating, and definitions of success or failure. Each group sometimes looks upon the other as corrupt, incompetent, or venal. Yet the two often must work together toward common ends in a highly politicized, advanced, technically sophisticated society such as the United States.

Politicians are exemplified by elected executives such as presidents, governors, and mayors. Technocrats, on the other hand, often work as tenured civil servants in government and as staff personnel in corporations.

Theoretically, politicians represent the will of the people who elect them. They develop and assume responsibility for implementing policies calculated to serve the public. Technocrats, on the other hand, use their specialized expertise in identifying and surmounting barriers to implementation of these policies, in working out the details and implications of tactics and strategies, and in measuring success or failure in implementation (Altheide & Johnson, 1980, pp. 23–26).

Although both are important, the two types of jobs require people who differ in ways that often put them in conflict as shown in Tab. 5.2.

First, technocrats are oriented toward narrow, clearly defined goals (getting people off the welfare roles, producing pistons at lower cost and with few rejections at the quality-control center, etc.). In this sense, they resemble the effectors of Freeman et al. (1963) who deal with day-to-day specifics. Politicians, on the other hand, resemble the institutional leader in having rather diffuse goals and constituencies. In supporting the construction of a nuclear facility, for example, politicians must deal with environmentalists who worry about pollution, with anti-war or pacifist groups, and with others external to the organizations who actually help make the project a success.

Second, technocrats emphasize rational calculation and efficiency. Politicians, on the other hand, often deal with value-laden, often emotional human concerns

TABLE 5.2
Contrasting Perspectives: Politicians and Technocrats

	Politicians	Technocrats
Basic purposes	Establish policies, representing constituents	Implement policies, devise ways to measure success or failure in implementation
Basic focus of thought	Articulate, value-laden, often emotional concerns	Rational calculation, seeking efficiency
Time orientation	Short term	Long term
Scope of expertise	Generalists	Specialists
Scope of focus within organization	Each and every part	Entire organization

Note. Synthesized from *The Two Faces of Management* (pp. 11-13) by J. L. Bower (1983). New York: Mentor Books.

such as wages, affirmative action, and general equality of treatment. On the surface, at least, these factors have little to do with efficiency in getting a job done. From the standpoint of Bales and Strodtbeck (1951), clearly, technocrats are inclined to focus largely (though not entirely) on task achievement. And politicians stress group maintenance—approval and cohesion needed for continuing external as well as internal support.

Third, technocrats think long term. Having studied programs upon which they work in a thorough, sophisticated way, they recognize that short-term solutions may be illusory. Further, they usually expect to keep their jobs for some time, particularly when they work as civil servants. Politicians, on the other hand, must justify support for a program each year in most political and corporate contexts. And they usually look toward re-election in a few short months or years. Thus, they are often forced to think short term.

Fourth, technocrats are normally specialists, trained in academic knowledge and skills needed to achieve a given goal as well as to define and measure results. However, politicians tend to be people-oriented generalists skilled at promoting ideas and programs so they will "play in Peoria."

Fifth and last, technocrats often advocate centralized control for the good of the entire organizations for which they work. At a crucial point in the history of Texas Instruments, for example, successful computer lines (and groups that had developed them) were dropped so the firm as a whole could concentrate on a particular, super-successful computer. Such calculation, of course, seems ruthless to the politician who feels compelled to seek support by minimizing pain and sacrifice for each part of the organization viewed separately.

A key to success, according to Bower (1983, pp. 98–142), is to get politicians and technocrats to respect and understand each other so they can work together effectively. Also, it is crucial to have the right person play the role for which he or she is trained and qualified. Technocrats, such as former Secretary of State Henry Kissinger, seem ill-equipped to gain public support through appeals to the masses. And at the opposite extreme, problems arise when technical, day-to-day decisions are made by politicians. Decisions then become unsystematic, short term, and not based on careful analysis to insure efficient use of resources. Such role switching happened, for example, when corporations such as Chrysler and Lockheed faced possible bankruptcy due largely to inefficiency and failure to meet market needs. The United States government saved these firms, thanks largely to politicians' effort concerned primarily with selling the American people on the importance of keeping jobs and reducing Japanese auto imports to America. Improved quality in technical production and sales was not demonstrated clearly.

Viewed in light of the Freeman et al. (1963) model, Bower's typology suggests a need for institutional leaders to operate as both politicians and technocrats, something that Bower (1983) suggested may not be easy. Institutional leaders play a key role in gaining broad public and group-membership support, a major function of Bower's politician. Yet institutional leaders seemingly also must take the long-term view in setting goals and planning to achieve them, fundamental concerns of the technocrat.

Also, Bower's definition of the technocrat role implies an almost exclusive concern with task achievement. Yet Freeman's effector, as noted previously, must use technocratic skills to achieve group maintenance as well as get the job done.

In sum, existing leadership theory suggests there's seldom a clear line between technocrats and politicians. The good leader must usually play both roles to a degree. And if Bower (1983) and Culbertson (1992) were correct in suggesting that the technocratic and politicians world views are actually distinct, good and well-coordinated leadership within complex, bureaucratic organizations becomes difficult indeed to achieve. That's because people with different world views must understand each other and work together.

In the field of university relations, the politician and technocrat perspectives sometimes clash. This surely occurred quite often in the 1980s and 1990s as post-World War II "baby boomers" became adults and the pool of prospective college freshmen at age 17–18 began to decline. Universities suddenly had to compete aggressively, even ruthlessly, for students.

One admissions director argued that his institution should "position" itself carefully, publicizing strong programs with little nearby competition while placing little emphasis on other academic departments and colleges. Trained as a marketing specialist, the director took a hard-headed technocrat's view of attracting new students.

Although seeing merit in this approach, the admissions director's boss worried that the strategy might not fly politically with senior faculty and administrators. For years, the institution had stressed liberal arts education, though recent budget constraints had weakened such programs. The university's president believed strongly that, for example, any school worth its salt would have to offer a high-quality sequence in Latin. Thus, the idea of talking mostly about vocational–professional programs in addressing high school counselors, parents, and 17-year-olds would encounter high-level resistance.

What to do? Well, the university promoted its professional programs by emphasizing: (a) the high degree to which they integrated humanities, social sciences, and other liberal arts content into their own flexible curricula, and (b) the importance of a combined professional and liberal arts background.

In support of the latter point, university spokespersons noted that we live in a fast-changing world. Today's skills and knowledge will be outdated tomorrow or next year. As a result, the future belongs to those who think about professional concerns (running a newspaper, developing plans for a chemical plant, etc.) with information provided by and intellects nourished by the liberal arts. In this view, neither professional nor liberal arts component could go it alone. Each depends on the other. And key publics need to grasp that.

When presented with this view, both the admissions-director technician and the politically oriented president applauded. Admissions policy at the university took on a new flavor, one that helped increase enrollment substantially, despite a declining pool of prospective students, in the years that followed.

In the corporate and government spheres, also, public relations people must be sensitive to political considerations of what gains broad support among legislators or in the board room. Yet they cannot lose sight, either, of the "bean counters" and other technicians who demand hard-and-fast proof of success and bang for the buck. Such balancing acts surely require great insight and skill in public relations.

The political and technocratic perspectives both have great importance for people who work in government relations, often called lobbying.

In seeking legislators' support for or opposition to proposed laws, the lobbyist must often provide technical arguments in support of specific language that she or he may suggest. Most local, state and, even federal legislators lack the expertise and staff to write specialized laws on their own. Consequently, lobbyists often do much of the writing, thereby providing an important service. Such activity is, at base, technocratic.

At the same time, however, lobbyists must often convince legislators that a given law will either please or raise the ire of significant groups of people. (In some cases, the focus is on a few actual or would-be constituents who feel especially strongly about legislation. At other times, a law's appeal to a large number of citizens is emphasized.) Particularly when focusing on a broad, general audience, the lobbyist must think as politicians do.

To sum up here, public relations people must often deal with three groups having somewhat different perspectives. Legislators are elected politicians. Civil servants act largely as technocrats. And government-relations people must be at home in both realms, recognizing when and where each holds center stage.

We now turn to the second of two sets of concepts useful in studying the political context—strategies for exerting influence.

INFLUENCE STRATEGIES

The first set of strategies was proposed by social psychologist Herbert Kelman (1961). He spelled out three approaches to influencing others, each involving a distinct process and requiring its own set of prior conditions.

Compliance, Identification, and Internalization

As shown in Tab. 5.3, *compliance* occurs when the follower or person influenced seeks social approval from the leader or influencer. By offering such approval, leaders often can get followers to do their bidding. Typically, of course, acceptance is important to the follower, partly because leaders have the ability and inclination to offer rewards or withhold punishment from those of whom they approve.

Prerequisites for compliance include:

A primary concern by followers with the presumed social effects—approval or disapproval—of what they do.

TABLE 5.3
Summary of Distinctions Among Three Processes of Opinion Change

	Compliance	Identification	Internalization
Antecedents:			
1. Basis for the importance of the induction	Concern with social effect of behavior	Concern with social anchorage of behavior	Concern with value congruence of behavior
2. Source of power of the influencing agent	Means control	Attractiveness	Credibility
3. Manner of achieving prepotency of the induced response	Limitation of choice behavior	Delineation of role requirements	Reorganization of means-ends framework
Consequents:			
1. Conditions of performance of induced response	Surveillance by influencing agent	Salience of relationship to agent	Relevance of values to issue
2. Conditions of change and extinction of induced response	Changed perception of conditions for social rewards	Changed perception of conditions for satisfying self-defining relationships	Changed perception of conditions for value maximization
3. Type of behavior system in which induced response is embedded	External demands of a specific setting	Expectations defining a specific role	Person's value system

Note. Reprinted with permission from The University of Chicago Press. "Processes of Opinion Change" by H. C. Kelman (1961), *Public Opinion Quarterly, 25,* 57-78.

Control by the leader over means that followers believe they can pursue to achieve desired ends.

Leader surveillance of the follower. Unless leaders are watching, they can hardly grant approval or dispense rewards for follower behavior. Obviously influence exercised through compliance is specific to one or a few situations for at least two reasons. First, the leader or influencer must watch or become aware of what the follower is doing—a condition not met all of the time even with classic followers such as valets and presidential bodyguards! And second, behavior that seems appropriate and worthy of approval varies from situation to situation.

In light of this, leadership by *compliance* is rather fragile. It's likely to hold only when the leader is watching. Because it rests on external means–ends control, it does not rely on or necessarily create lasting changes within followers. Also, it does not lead to behavior that, as with other kinds of activity, remains fairly constant over time because of the relative stability of underlying personality traits and predispositions.

Compliance does encompass to some extent formal leadership (involving means–ends control) as well as informal (with emphasis on social approval). Still, the follower whose behavior is so determined probably cannot be relied upon to carry on "as led" once the leader departs or the context changes.

The second influence strategy, *identification,* occurs when followers behave as they presume significant others (Mead, 1955, pp. 135–150) would admire them for doing. In identifying, people seek to define themselves as approved others might wish. Influence via identification has three prerequisites:

A concern with what Kelman called the *social anchorage* of behavior. That is, do significant others seem apt to define the behavior as appropriate and laudatory, whether or not they happen to be present to grant overt approval?

Leader attractiveness to the follower. Without this, presumably, followers would not give much weight to leader preferences in defining their (the followers') selves.

Salience of the leader–follower relationship. This may or may not hold over time. For example, an auto enthusiast may have had great admiration in the early 1980s for Chrysler CEO Lee Iacocca, who had recently assumed a high profile and gotten much credit for rescuing Chrysler from impending bankruptcy. By 1990, however, many things would probably have removed this particular hero from center stage in the auto fan's mind. The latter may have purchased a Cadillac. The Chrysler Corporation eventually encountered additional hard times that made Iacocca seem less than omnipotent. Talk of an Iacocca run at the American presidency made him seem less attractive when viewed in this new light. Iacocca simply ceased to be front-page news. And the auto fan may have changed jobs and lifestyles, leading her or him to focus on new significant others. All of these factors may have reduced the Chrysler CEO's salience to the fan.

If identification is to be an effective influence strategy, the leader must make it clear what expectations are for followers who play a particular role. Obviously these expectations must square with those of the followers' other significant others and of society as a whole.

As defined by Kelman (1961), identification clearly falls within the realm of informal leadership. No sanctions or immediate means–ends considerations—the focal points of formal leaders—are involved. Also, with this process, leadership and followership are somewhat fickle, but perhaps a bit less so than in the case of compliance. The leader need not be present in the flesh, exercising surveillance, as with compliance. However, he or she must be on the follower's mind as a valued significant other.

The third of Kelman's influence processes, *internalization,* requires leaders to show that behavior that they seek to bring about helps further the achievement of follower values. For example, a politician may become identified as a promoter of wealth, peace, or strength if he or she finds that constituents value these life goals. Associationist theorists such as Anderson (1981), Culbertson and Stempel (1985), Fishbein and Ajzen (1981), and Rosenberg (1960) supported this point. Preconditions for internalization include:

A concern by the follower with the furtherance of values and the need to behave so as to realize them. This suggests several possible lines of argument that leaders and public relations people may advance. They may establish that the values in question are not being realized at present—or may not be in the future in light of various threats or barriers—unless action is taken. Also, they may suggest that changing conditions (e.g., the conservative atmosphere in America during the 1980s and 1990s as contrasted with liberalism of 10–20 years earlier) require new approaches to achieve a particular important goal (e.g., social justice). Third, they may even call for a reordering of value priorities in the face of changing conditions (national defense and strength may seem less important today than even a few years ago in the wake of the near collapse of Communism).

Leader credibility in the follower's eyes. Here, unlike with the first two modes of influence, the leader is calling for a reordering or changing of the follower's thoughts, attitudes, and intentions. Messages must be evaluated for their believability and not simply for efficacy in gaining approval or defining oneself. It is argued later that, under some but not all conditions, leader credibility is central to such influence.

Perceived value relevance to the issues considered and the behaviors or beliefs sought. Culbertson and Stempel (1985) and Culbertson (1992) suggested that such linkage results from frequent association, at one time and place, between mention of a value and objects presumed relevant to its realization. Also, a behavior or belief is viewed as a cause, effect, or implication of values to which it is linked.

The three influence modes differ on at least two important dimensions: external vs. internal and short term vs. long term.

First, compliance is external to followers, resting on approval and other rewards and punishments offered by those who lead. Internalization focuses on processes internal to followers—specifically, the values to which followers attach priority and beliefs linking those values to particular behaviors and beliefs. Finally, identification stands between the other two modes on the internal–external dimension. This third influence mode rests on self-defining relationships with leaders as viewed by followers. Thus, identification is relational, not internal or external, in that it focuses on the follower in relation to one or more other people.

Second, compliance is most apt to be short term and situation specific. It holds only when leaders watch or become aware of follower behavior, followers believe leaders have means–ends control over them, and followers attach value to rewards that leaders are in a position to give. Such value may decline where followers shift attention to other concerns or find alternative means of goal attainment. In fact, all listed preconditions for compliance are subject to change.

Internalization is likely to be long term if one assumes that: (a) values tend to be lasting and deeply held (Rokeach, 1969, p. 160), and (b) beliefs about how to fulfill or realize values become fairly firmly established and are not subject to constant challenge. Because internalization rests on beliefs within the follower, these beliefs do not generally shift dramatically in the short term in the face of changing external conditions.

Finally, identification is intermediate, in most cases, as to stability over time. The leader need not be present, exercising surveillance and providing overt rewards as with compliance, for identification to occur. However, changes in how followers prioritize relationships and in how they assess people with whom they relate can lead to rather sudden decline in identification-based influence.

How might public relations practitioners view and use these influence strategies? Several generalizations are warranted.

First, public relations people themselves seldom count on compliance by key publics. Practitioners often don't have formal power to give concrete rewards or administer sanctions (except, perhaps, in dealing with their own staffs!). Further, maintaining surveillance over publics is usually very difficult if not impossible.

At times, of course, clients may make threats or stress negative consequences. For example, corporate management sometimes emphasizes ominous consequences to employees of a hostile takeover. Sell your stock to the "invaders," executives warn, and you invite union busting, absentee ownership, and insensitivity to local needs.

Although sometimes warranted, such negative charges may backfire, particularly if one winds up seeking support in the future from those who are charged today! Further, when one threatens someone in order to gain compliance, one in effect tells that person that one can't trust him or her to do the right thing. Goffman (1956) called this an expression of *negative deference*. Such tactics seldom lead to lasting, mutually productive relationships. Even if one does win a battle in such a case, one may wind up losing the war.

Second, identification is a feasible strategy where practitioner and client can point to a respected hero as an advocate or actor in the project being promoted. However, this works only where audience members feel some kinship with, and hence identify with, the hero.

President George Bush took this tack in a speech to the United States Congress on March 6, 1991. He had just led a coalition of some 28 nations in an amazing "100-hour" ground war that expelled Iraq's soldiers from the nation of Kuwait. He was basking in the glory of 90% approval ratings by the American people. And, striking while the iron was hot, he announced a "100-day" crusade to tackle America's domestic problems.

As noted earlier, heroes can fall out of favor. People's needs and goals change, as do the persons with whom they seek what Kelman called self-defining relationships. Also, Boorstin (1971) noted that modern celebrities are part of our "throw-away culture"—famous only for a short time and largely because they are promoted skillfully. Where the identification target is a celebrity, support may be short lived.

In a related vein, Kruckeberg and Starck (1988, pp. 111–119) suggested that public relations people strive more often than they now do for a sense of community—of shared meaning and goals. That implies a need to promote and "hitch one's wagon to" genuine heroes who make contributions of lasting value. This, in turn, enhances the kind of stability in associations and dialogue that creates genuine understanding among varied groups in a complex society.

Third, internalization works only where those in the audience have substantial interest and involvement in what is happening. Only then do people really consider and reach conclusions about how the organization, person, or candidate contributes to value realization and goal attainment.

We now turn to a second typology of strategies for influence exertion.

Central and Peripheral Persuasion

Petty and Cacioppo (1986) proposed two ways of dealing with messages in deciding whether and how they might change one's own beliefs and behavior. The key element in distinguishing between these two approaches is **involvement:** the extent to which one feels beliefs and behaviors relating to the topic in question are important and the level of effort that he or she exerts or is inclined to put forth as a result.

Central processes occur under conditions of high involvement, according to the theory. Here people evaluate arguments carefully, weigh them on their own merits in light of other available information, and reach rather personal, cognitively based conclusions. Because appropriate conclusions are important to them, followers strive to consider all relevant information. They do not select only arguments that appear to support previously existing attitudes and beliefs. Such open-mindedness creates the possibility of attitude or behavior change.

Peripheral processes, on the other hand, require little involvement. Lacking a tendency to seek information actively, analyze or synthesize it, and assess its implications fully, followers here often turn to message, source, and contextual attributes in deciding whether they will accept a message's conclusions and implications. Source credibility, message organization, and social pressure or approval, among other things, come into play.

This analysis has at least two implications for the public relations practitioner.

First, where involvement is low, attributing messages and arguments to highly credible sources becomes crucial. This requires perceived **competency** and **trustworthiness,** among other things (Lemert, 1969; Bradac, Tardy, & Hosman, 1980). Also, it hinges on at least some **prominence** of the communication source. One may not put much stock in what a person says unless one has at least heard of him or her (Culbertson, 1973).

Second, where involvement is high, one needs to present well-reasoned messages that stand up under critical analysis. Recent research suggests high involvement exists where: (a) a person has accomplished something, while connected with the project or organization commanding the involvement, which he or she can take personal pride in, or (b) a person has at least thought of many concrete ways of contributing to the organization or project (Culbertson, 1992). This view squares with the definition of involvement in terms of "bridging experiences" by Grunig and Hunt (1984). Also, theoretical discussions of involvement hinging on actual behavior date back at least to Sherif, Sherif, and Nebergall (1965, p. 65).

We now look at the Kelman (1961) model in light of the typologies of leadership behavior by Freeman et al. (1963) discussed earlier, along with the central–peripheral distinction of Petty and Cacioppo (1986).

Some Context for Kelman

To begin, internalization occurs with all three types of leadership proposed by Freeman et al. (1963). The institutional leader presumably links a project to rather global values. The activist stresses minute, specific behaviors and purposes. And the effector provides concrete strategies and tactics for implementation. All three processes involve encouraging followers to link behaviors as means with overall goals or values as internalization requires.

Second, identification is especially salient for institutional leaders and activists. The former serve as inspiring role models—hence, likely objects of identification— because of their foresight, vision, and prestige. Activists set examples for dedication and nitty gritty skill that followers find attractive, at least in part, because emulation of these attributes helps them strengthen their self-definitions. As described by Freeman et al. (1963), activists are apt to qualify as significant others for people who follow their lead.

Third, unlike the other leader types, effectors often have the clout to lead by compliance. They alone have formal power that affords means–ends control on which compliance hinges. And they can often assign jobs so as to reward or punish. (Of course, the truly accomplished effector leads by example (identification) and explanation (internalization) as well.) However, compliance is available as a leadership approach for effectors, because they typically have at least some means–ends control over their followers.

Turning to the Petty-Cacioppo (1986) model, only internalization requires central processing. That is, only the internalizer needs to change beliefs, values, and the relations among them. Identification and compliance, on the other hand, both involve behaviors designed to bring rewards from external sources. Such rewards qualify as source, message, and contextual factors that Petty and Cacioppo (1986) viewed as important with peripheral processing.

We now turn to specific strategies that informal leaders employ, drawing on theory discussed previously as well as additional constructs.

Some Specific Strategies

Coalition Formation.   Numbers and votes count in most political processes. As noted in chapter 12, osteopathic physicians have long struggled to gain stature within mainstream American medicine and have resisted collaboration with medical doctors, partly because the latter outnumber them by about 20–1. Thus doctors of osteopathy fear that, given highly visible cooperative effort, medical doctors will swallow them up politically. As a result, some health care consumers might lose things such as manipulative therapy and a focus on the whole person that are central to osteopathy.

How can one gain numbers? A common strategy is to make common cause with others, perhaps even people generally seen as foes, so they'll join forces in achieving a particular objective. This, in turn, involves:

Articulating what you and your potential allies have in common. What do you all stand to gain from joint effort? What values and goals do you share, as organizing schemata, with these individuals or groups?

For example, osteopathic physicians profit from working with allopathic (medical doctor) physicians in setting up internships and residencies, in making referrals to cardiologists, many of whom are medical doctors and so on. This, in turn, requires spelling out why you and these others stand, at least temporarily, in a relationship of mutual interdependence. In plain English, that means "When I win, you win." My winning does not contribute to your defeat or vice versa.

Argyris (1974, pp. 11–15) argued that only under such conditions can many groups or individuals achieve the frank, open communication and dedication needed for effective joint effort.

Making frequent deposits in what Dilenschneider (1990, pp. 11–18) called your favor bank. Savvy executives constantly look for ways to help government officials, stock brokers, heads of interest groups, and countless other sorts of people. Such managers realize that, at some unforeseen time, they may need help in lobbying for a law, getting a price break, obtaining a loan extension, etc. Of course, such favors sometimes get labeled as corruption. But Gouldner (1960) noted a pervasive norm that, when people do a favor for one today, one is obliged to return that favor tomorrow. And Thibaut and Kelly (1961, pp. 31–49) suggested that, in more general terms, people tend to do something only if they feel the rewards for doing it are at least roughly in line with the effort put forth and expenses incurred. Thus, favor banks are tools that leaders can ill afford to ignore.

Public Relations people make deposits in their favor banks by taking part in countless civic activities not tied to their clients or bosses in any obvious way. One may volunteer to speak in schools, head the local United Appeal, or help organize a fund drive to remodel her or his church. Also, volunteer work on political campaigns eventually pays dividends. That's true partly because candidates are influential, active citizens well equipped to return favors eventually.

One warning is important here. Make deposits in your favor bank gradually. By all means avoid a big burst of generosity just before you expect to withdraw assistance by your benefactor from the bank. Support a Congressional person just before you lobby for a certain bill, and someone will surely allege that you expect a quid pro quo. That, in turn, can paint you and the official as cynical opportunists. And it may even lead to charges of corruption!

Establishing Behavioral Involvement.   Petty and Cacioppo (1986) indicated that involvement contributes to active, open-minded message processing. Also, there is reason to believe that involvement enhances genuine, long-term behavioral support (Roser, 1990).

According to Cutlip (1965, pp. 271–280), Episcopal church leaders recognized this when raising money to build the famous Cathedral of St. John the Divine in New York City. Early fund raising was disappointing until the leaders realized people would give only if they saw themselves as part of the project and not as outsiders. Thus, an ecumenical theme was adopted so people other than Episcopalians (who, after all, had finite numbers and wealth) could truly be part of the project. Some critics accused the church of opportunism and insincerity, but the cathedral eventually went up!

Membership in a collegiate sports hall of fame. Naming a building after someone who contributes to its construction. Putting up a plaque that identifies a hospital room as "Constructed with a generous gift from Jody Smathers, 1900–1986." Naming someone to an advisory board that defines goals and philosophies for a government agency, a charitable organization, or a school of journalism. These and countless other strategies help build behavioral involvement. One can scarcely help feeling involved in the face of widespread recognition and/or "immortalization" in bronze.

One practical problem arises here. Genuine involvement exists only where the audience member feels he or she has done or at least can do things useful to the organization or project in question. Simply enhancing the presumed general prestige of the organization or project, without a feeling of active personal involvement with it, has little impact on one's supportive behavior (Culbertson, 1992).

Furthermore, giving someone an award of which he or she does not seem worthy reeks of opportunism. Halls of fame recognize prowess on the athletic court or playing field. Other factors enter in, of course. However, administrators surely agonize at times over nominating an alumnus for a university's athletic hall of fame where that person is now a multimillionaire but was only a third-string tackle with an accumulative average of 2.1 on the 1949 team that won two games and lost seven!

Identify Leaders Who Count.   Some have **formal** power. For instance, heads of legislative committees decide whether a law that bears on a public relations client gets on to the Senate or House of Representatives floor for a vote. Heads of regulatory agencies can make life difficult or easy when it comes to enforcing environmental and occupational-safety laws.

Other leaders operate in the **informal** realm. Lobbyists have connections that lead them to exercise influence in subtle ways. Also Congressperson A, although not personally interested (or aware of constituents who are interested) in a particular bill of concern to a public relations practitioner's client, may have done favors for Congressperson B, who does support or oppose that bill strongly. In such a case, A may vote for or against the bill largely to return a favor to B, thereby helping to balance accounts in A's favor bank.

Considerable influence is also exerted these days by interest or pressure groups such as the Sierra Club (promoting conservation of wildlife and natural resources), the American Rifle Association (opposed to certain types of gun control), the National Organization for Women (supporting women's rights), and the American Civil Liberties Union (opposed to developments that limit freedom of expression) (Ball, 1971, pp. 103–120).

Interest groups have substantial government-relations (i.e., lobbying) programs in Washington, DC, and in key state capitals. They also have dedicated—though not always huge—memberships. Their publications and direct mail can activate members to flood legislators with letters, or even phone calls, very quickly. Sometimes, of course, officials dismiss such barrages with a shrug when hundreds of letters have almost the same wording. Such uniformity suggests national headquarters is orchestrating the campaign, perhaps without much spontaneous, heartfelt, grass-roots support.

It certainly helps to have certain interest groups on one's side. They have organized, motivated members in place to help with petition drives, door-to-door solicitation for funds, and other grass-roots efforts. However, many such groups have reputations of being extremely liberal (the ACLU) or conservative (the John Birch Society). Identifying oneself and one's organization or program with such a group can alienate moderates as well as foes of the interest group involved.

It takes long experience and careful study to learn of such arrangements and to develop contacts so as to make use of them.

SUMMARY AND CONCLUSIONS

This chapter focuses on several concepts useful in defining and studying the political contexts of public relations clients. Included are:

1. The distinction between formal and informal leadership.
2. The Bales-Strodtbeck (1951) model of task-achievement and group-maintenance leadership.
3. A distinction among three types of informal community leadership: institutional (or legitimizer), effector, and activist. Freeman et al. (1963) proposed these.
4. The technocrat and politician leadership roles as defined by Bower (1983).
5. The high- and low-involvement modes of message consumption as proposed by Petty and Cacioppo (1986).
6. Three modes of influence as defined by Kelman (1961). These are compliance, identification, and internalization.

We attempt to show relationships among these concepts so as to articulate and clarify practitioner efforts to define clients' political contexts.

These concepts are emphasized, because they shed light on defining public relations audiences and **communicating with them.** This volume deals, at base, with **communication** efforts.

In adopting such a focus, we give little attention to many political concepts relating closely to the law. Also, we steer clear of many issues of organizational structure and function that interest political scientists. For example, we ignore studies of class formation and struggle and of how elites grow, change, and decline. These research traditions no doubt relate to certain public relations problems. However, they play little or no part in our own SPE-context research reported in the next section of this volume. Thus, we have put them on the shelf in writing this volume.

REFERENCES

Altheide, D. L., & Johnson, J. M. (1980). *Bureaucratic propaganda*. Boston: Allyn & Bacon.

Anderson, N. H. (1981). Integration theory applied to cognitive responses and attitudes. In R. E. Petty, T. M. Ostrom, & T. C. Brock (Eds.), *Cognitive responses in persuasion* (pp. 361–397). Hillsdale, NJ: Lawrence Erlbaum Associates.

Argyris, C. (1974). *Behind the front page*. San Francisco: Jossey-Bass.

Bales, R., & Strodtbeck, F. (1951). Phases in group problem solving. *Journal of Abnormal and Social Psychology, 46,* 485–495.

Ball, A. R. (1971). *Modern politics and government*. London, England: Macmillan.

Boorstin, D. J. (1971). From news-gathering to news-making: a flood of pseudo-events. In W. Schramm & D. F. Roberts (Eds.), *The process and effects of mass communication* (pp. 116–150). Urbana, IL: University of Illinois Press.

Bower, J. L. (1983). *The two faces of management*. New York: Mentor.

Bradac, J. J., Tardy, C. H., & Hosman, L. A. (1980). Disclosure styles and a hint at their genesis. *Human Communication Research, 6,* 228–238.

Culbertson, H. M. (1968). On the many sides of leadership. *Public Relations Quarterly, 13,* 25–30.

Culbertson, H. M. (1973). Public relations ethics: A new look. *Public Relations Quarterly, 17,* 15–17, 23–25.

Culbertson, H. M. (1992). Linking Beliefs: What Are The Links? *Public Relations Review, 18,* 335–347.

Culbertson, H. M., & Stempel, G. H., III, (1985). Linkage beliefs and public relations effects. *Public Relations Research and Education, 2,* 23–35.

Cutlip, S. M. (1965). *Fund raising in the United States: Its role in America's philanthropy*. New Brunswick, NJ: Rutgers University Press.

Dilenschneider, R. L. (1990). *Power and influence: Mastering the art of persuasion*. New York: Prentice-Hall.

Fishbein, M., & Ajzen, I. (1981). Acceptance, yielding and impact: Cognitive processes in persuasion. In R. E. Petty, T. M. Ostrom, & T. C. Brock (Eds.), *Cognitive responses in persuasion* (pp. 339–359). Hillsdale, NJ: Lawrence Erlbaum Associates.

Freeman, L., Farraro, T., Bloomberg, W., & Sunshine, M. (1963). Locating leaders in local communities: A comparison of some alternative approaches. *American Sociological Review, 28,* 291–298.

Fromm, E. (1970). Values, psychology and human existence. In A. H. Maslow (Ed.), *New knowledge in human values* (pp. 151–164). Chicago: Regnery.

Goffman, E. (1956). The nature of deference and demeanor. *American Anthropologist, 58,* 473–502.

Gouldner, A. W. (1960). The norm of reciprocity: A preliminary statement. *American Sociological Review, 25,* 161–179.

Grunig, J. E., & Hunt, T. (1984). *Managing public relations*. New York: Holt, Rinehart & Winston.

Hersey, P., & Blanchard, K. H. (1969). *Management of organizational behavior: Utilizing human resources*. Englewood Cliffs, NJ: Prentice-Hall.

Kelman, H. C. (1961). Processes of opinion change. *Public Opinion Quarterly, 25,* 57–78.

Kruckeberg, D., & Starck, K. (1988). *Public relations and community: A reconstructed theory*. New York: Praeger.

Lemert, J. (1969). Components of source "image": Hong Kong, Brazil, North America. *Journalism Quarterly, 46,* 306–313, 418.

Likert, R. (1961). *New patterns of management*. New York: McGraw-Hill.

McGregor, D. (1960). *Human side of enterprise*. New York: McGraw-Hill.

Mead, G. H. (1955). *Mind, self and society*. Chicago: University of Chicago Press.

Petty, R. E., & Cacioppo, J. T. (1986). *Communication and persuasion: Central and peripheral routes to attitude change*. New York: Springer-Verlag.

Powell, J. (1984). *The other side of the story*. New York: Morrow.

Rokeach, M. (1969). *Beliefs, attitudes and values*. San Francisco: Jossey-Bass.
Roser, C. (1990). Involvement, attention and perceptions of message relevance in the response to persuasive appeals. *Communication Research, 17,* 571–600.
Rosenberg, M. J. (1960). A structural theory of attitude dynamics. *Public Opinion Quarterly, 24,* 319–340.
Seymour, H. J. (1966). *Designs for fund-raising*. New York: McGraw-Hill.
Sherif, C. W., Sherif, M., & Nebergall, R. E. (1965). *Attitude and attitude change: The social judgment-involvement approach*. Philadelphia: Saunders.
Thibaut, J., & Kelly, H. (1961). *The social psychology of groups*. New York: Wiley.
Webster's Third New York Dictionary. (1988). Springfield, MA: Merriam Webster.

6 The Economic Context of Public Relations: Footing the Bill

The economic context is the third perspective offered as part of our analysis of important conceptual orientations for public relations practitioners. We believe public relations persons should adopt and adapt economic ways of thinking for several reasons.

First, an understanding of economics and economic concepts is inherently valuable. Reading a daily newspaper or scanning the evening television news shows clearly that economic principles affect our everyday lives. These concepts help us make informed decisions and, in turn, be more effective citizens.

Second, public relations practitioners operate within an economic milieu that directly affects public relations programming and decision making. Economists point out that all of us, as individuals, organizations and societies, operate within an "Economic Circular Flow" of four major realms: the household sector, the business sector, the government sector, and the foreign sector (Chang, 1990, pp. 17–22). Public relations practitioners need to understand this environment well if they are to be effective.

Third, economic terms and an economic way of thinking can be applied directly to the practice of public relations. As is demonstrated later, economic concepts have utility in the public relations management process. Also, it is certainly easier for the practitioner to construct a budget when she has an understanding of the larger economic context.

ECONOMIC WAYS OF THINKING

The importance of economics to public relations practitioners is apparent when definitions of this social science are examined. Wilson and Clark (1984, p. 6) said

103

economics "deals with how society allocates its scarce resources among its un-limited wants and needs" (p. 6). They added that, as a social science, economics is concerned with economic interactions within society.

Chang (1990) focused on individuals within society and the decisions they are forced to make when he said economics is "used to study aspects of human behavior that deal with the relationship" between "scarce resources that have alternative uses" (p. 4).

Moffat (1976, p. 94) took a broader view. He said that, although most definitions of economics refer to allocating scarce resources to satisfy unlimited human wants, there is really no one definition. A few economists believe this social science should be restricted to whatever concerns money, according to Moffat. However, he noted that others feel everything (such as "individual happiness, international wars and morals") should be considered when examining the allocation of scarce resources. And he added that most economists prefer a compromise between these extremes when determining what should be included in the study of economics.

Consistent with the SPE theme of this volume, Moffat stressed that economics draws on all other fields of study. He believed psychology, sociology, physics, mathematics, political science, and other disciplines play an essential role.

Micro Vs. Macro

When applying economic principles to the practice of public relations, it is useful to keep in mind how economic theory is divided. *Microeconomics* is the "theory of economics that examines the choices and interaction of individuals concerning one product, one firm, or one industry." *Macroeconomics* is the "theory of economics that examines the behavior of the whole economy at once" (Wilson & Clark, 1984, p. 11).

Chang (1990) illustrated why it is important to be familiar with both branches of economic theory. Macroeconomic knowledge helps those in business avoid stockpil-ing large inventories when the economy is about to enter a recession or avoid borrowing large amounts of money when interest rates are about to fall. Micro-economic knowledge helps the same business persons decide what prices to charge and how much to produce to maximize profit.

Practitioners apply the same micro and macro concepts to public relations ac-tivities. On the micro level, the unit of analysis may be specific public relations decisions, specific public relations programs, or the public relations implications for specific publics or organizations. In the macro area, the unit of analysis may be public relations decisions and programs that have implications for a larger organiza-tional or societal context.

It is difficult to draw a sharp or definitive line separating micro from macro public relations analyses and applications. Instead, it is useful to view these notions as concentric rings in a circle, moving outward from micro to macro. That is exactly what Grunig and Hunt did when they placed organizational responsibilities in three categories (Grunig & Hunt, 1984, p. 55). The first level deals with the performance of the organization's basic tasks. The second level encompasses the organization's concern with the consequences of those activities for external groups. And the third level denotes the organization's concern with solving general social problems not directly connected to the client organization.

As a practical matter, Grunig and Hunt suggested that the public relations manager focus on the first two, or more micro, rings in the circle. At the same time, they did not suggest practitioners should ignore the more macro concept of "public responsibility." They believed public responsibility should be of concern to all types of organizations, not just large business corporations.

For businesses, the most micro organizational concerns are economic, but social spillovers from these activities produce macro secondary involvements. For non-business organizations, the more micro concerns are social, but these primary involvements produce secondary economic consequences (Grunig & Hunt, 1984, p. 59).

Cutlip, Center, and Broom (1985, p. 116) suggested it is impossible for the contemporary public relations practitioner *not* to think in these macro terms. These authors said the basic trends of current society have brought everything from Big Business to Big Government to Big Special Interest Groups. Therefore, it is incumbent on the public relations practitioner to assume a greater share of the social burden of the long-term consequences of organizational behavior (Cutlip et al., 1985, p. 497). Further, while the budgetary implications of applying an economic way of thinking to public relations is discussed later, Newsom, Scott, and Turk (1989) remarked that dollar costs are associated with these macro activities, and public relations managers need to account for them.

Scarcity

It comes as no surprise to public relations managers, who constantly face demands to do more with fewer resources, that economists consider the basic economic problem to be one of scarcity. Wilson and Clark (1984) said, "Scarcity is the condition that occurs because people's wants and needs are unlimited, and the resources needed to produce goods and services to meet these wants and needs are limited" (p. 6).

Chang (1990, p. 5) cautioned that scarcity is a relative term. He said the absolute quantity of a resource does not have to be small for the resource to be scarce. The resource becomes scarce if the quantity available is not sufficient to satisfy the demands for competing uses of it. Moffat (1976, p. 167) noted that some economists prefer to say resources are limited rather than scarce because resources may be around us in abundance, yet choices must be made among their alternative uses.

What are these resources? Traditionally, economists refer to them as factors of production:

Factors of production include (1) *land,* referring to land in its literal sense and minerals not yet excavated, (2) *labor,* meaning the time and effort of human beings exerted in the process of production activities, (3) *capital,* consisting of machines, producers of durable equipment and buildings, and (4) *entrepreneurship* for the organization of the business enterprise and the assumption of the risk. (Chang, 1990, p. 17)

Although all factors of production are important, the role of the public relations practitioner in managing scarce resources is most apparent when examining entrepreneurial ability. Moffat (1976, p. 94) said entrepreneurship includes management, innovation, risk taking, applications analysis, etc. He added that, all other things being equal, an economy with a larger amount of entrepreneurial ability has the potential to be more productive than an economy with less of this crucial factor.

Optimization

Although economists consider scarcity the major economic problem, they regard optimization or economizing as the primary method of dealing with the problem. Chang (1990, p. 7) said scarcity makes the rationing of resources unavoidable. The process of rationing to achieve some well-defined objective is optimization.

As examples, he cited the plant manager who seeks to produce maximum output with a minimum amount of resources and the consumer who tries within a given budget to purchase a combination of goods and services that provide the greatest satisfaction.

Opportunity Costs and Benefits

However, economists quickly point out that optimization involves more than allocating dollar costs to activities. In the optimization process, public relations practitioners need to consider the *opportunity costs* and *opportunity benefits* of specific choices.

Wilson and Clark (1984, p. 8) said the opportunity cost is the "value of any alternative that you must give up when you make a choice. In short, the opportunity cost is the value of opportunity lost" (p. 8). They defined opportunity benefits as that which is gained by making a particular choice. Chang (1990, p. 5) noted that sometimes the dollar costs of decision are a good measure of the opportunity costs of that decision, but sometimes they are not.

When implementing the economic and management concept of optimization, public relations practitioners benefit by keeping in mind some of the "Frame of Reference" concepts discussed in chapter 4. Remember, Helson (1964) and others suggested that, when making decisions, standards of comparison are used. In this process, either or both of two factors influence the assessments: (a) a weighted average of past experiences, or (b) extreme values or ends of any continuum of such experiences.

By keeping these in mind when assessing the opportunity costs and benefits of any public relations decision, practitioners can avoid several pitfalls. The first relates to using the dollar costs at the extreme ends as the measure of the opportunity cost of any decision. Although estimating the *high* and *low* as part of a range of costs is standard budgeting practice for many practitioners, this may be short sighted in that it focuses only on dollars. As noted previously, sometimes the actual dollar costs are a good measure of opportunity costs, sometimes they aren't.

The second pitfall relates to the propensity to use the weighted average of past experiences as the standard of comparison by which public relations decisions are evaluated. Here the trap is relying on conventional wisdom ("we've always done it this way before") to help decide what the real opportunity costs/benefits are. This weighted average approach may stifle creative or innovating thinking.

Obviously, it is impossible to develop an iron-clad procedure for determining the real opportunity costs/benefits of any public relations decision. Instead, it's more important for the public relations person to remember that, as explained in chapter 4, some standards are more relevant than others. The practitioner needs to develop procedures to help determine which standards are relevant. Sometimes the standard of comparison should be the weighted average, but sometimes it might be related to the extremes that one discerns on the basis of current information and past experience.

Economic Models

As public relations practitioners begin to implement economic thinking in the decision making process, it is important to understand the economic models that describe how resources are allocated among competing uses.

Chang (1990, p. 29), like most economists, said that basically two institutions, the market and the government, allocate resources. He said that, although all societies use both government and the market, various economic systems are classified on the basis of the relative importance of these institutions in allocating resources.

In a related vein, Wilson and Clark (1984, pp. 20, 35) defined a *market economy* as one in which the economic questions of what, how, and for whom to produce are decided mostly by individuals. In a *social economy,* on the other hand, the major economic questions are defined and answered primarily by the government, theoretically representing the best interests of the entire society.

Regardless of the prevalent model operating in any given economy, a combination of individual and social decisions is used to answer three basic economic questions (Wilson & Clark, 1984, p. 12): (a) What will be produced with the limited resources? (b) How will the goods and services be produced? and (c) For whom will the goods be produced?

The previous discussion has many parallels in the practice of public relations. Organizationally, public relations decision making may be highly centralized (as in a social economy) or in the hands of specific practitioners or departments (as in a market economy).

Decision Making

The public relations practitioner needs to answer three fundamental questions that parallel Wilson and Clark's basic economic questions:

What will be the content of any public relations program? Or, in economic terms, what will be produced with limited resources?

What public relations techniques should be used? The parallel economic question asks, how will it be produced?

What public should be targeted? In economic terms, this is asking for whom to produce.

Answering these kinds of questions is not easy. Along with deciding which goods and services a society must produce (food, shelter, national defense, roads, etc.), decisions must be made about the proper mix of goods and services. Remember that an opportunity cost is associated with every good and service. Producing more food may mean less shelter, for instance.

The decisions about how to produce the agreed-upon mix of goods and services are complex, because there are different ways to produce the same goods and services. The opportunity costs associated with each factor of production are different for each society. In some economies it may be less expensive to use high-tech equipment, whereas in others the same tasks can be achieved less expensively by using labor.

To help answer the basic economic questions, both as individuals and societies, economists suggest theory and systematic decision-making processes. For instance, Chang (1990, p. 7) encouraged learning the distinctions and relationships among *positive science, positive economics, normative science,* and *normative economics* drawn by John Neville Keynes (father of the more famous John Maynard Keynes):

. . . a positive science is a body of systematized knowledge concerning what *is,* whereas a normative science is a body of knowledge discussing criteria of what *ought* to be. In other words, positive economics is, in principle, independent of value judgments of scientists and is an objective study of economics. The primary task of positive economics is to provide useful hypotheses or theories in order to make predictions. Normative economics is an art. Statements that arise from normative economics are based on subjective value judgments as well as findings of positive economics. (p. 7)

Chang hastened to add that it is tough to make distinctions between positive and normative economics in real life. The study of positive economics is always influenced by the value judgments of individual economists. The real value of positive economics is its help in building consensus in normative economics regarding controversial economic issues. Furthermore, he suggested applying the scientific method to the study of economics. Doing so allows hypotheses testing to build economic theory (1990, p. 8–12).

Wilson and Clark (1984, pp. 25–32, 41–49) suggested that both individuals and societies follow a 5-step process (fundamentally similar to the scientific method) to make economic decisions:

1. Define the problem
   A. Be objective
   B. Clarify the focus
2. List the alternatives
   A. Limit the alternatives
   B. Be realistic
3. List the criteria used to evaluate the alternatives
   A. Be objective
   B. Be realistic
4. Evaluate the alternatives
   A. Develop a decision matrix
   B. Keep in mind the concept of utility
5. Choose the best alternative
   A. Keep in mind the opportunity cost of your decision

Notice the previous discussion on economic techniques for allocating scarce resources is similar to public relations discussions about the same fundamental issue.

A frequently advocated procedure for making the best of scarce public relations resources requires application of the *Management by Objectives* (MBO) approach to public relations. Nager and Allen (1984, p. 10) defined Management by Objectives as a total management system that focuses on results rather than activities:

> PR-MBO is similar to the business concept of zero-based budgeting in that it requires each public relations activity to be evaluated against results that demonstrate the *return on investment of resources.* Because something has been done in the past is not sufficient reason for doing it now, according to both zero-based budgeting and MBO principles.
>
> In zero-based budgeting, managers literally start with a zero budget, rather than pick up from where the last budget left off. The value to the organization of proposed expenditures must be demonstrated anew and not taken for granted. (p. 11)

The MBO process as outlined by Wilcox, Ault, and Agee (1989, pp. 167–182) is strikingly similar to the 5-step economic decision-making procedure outlined by Wilson and Clark. Wilcox et al. (1989) said the first step is to define the problem, which they suggested, often falls into one of three categories: (a) overcoming a negative perception of an organization or product, (b) conducting a specific, one-time project, or (c) developing or expanding a continuing program.

Wilcox et al. (1989) said the second step is to set objectives. These are either informational (communication related) or motivational (behavioral in nature). In this second step, the public relations practitioner should assign a dollar figure to alternatives. A specific budget and a time frame for accomplishing the objectives should be established.

The third step is to define the audience. Wilcox et al. (1989) said a target public generally falls into one of three categories: (a) a broad general audience, (b) an external target audience, or (c) an internal audience.

The fourth, fifth, and sixth program steps are, respectively: plan, execute, and assess.

Grunig and Hunt (1984) advocated an even more economic way of thinking in their advice to public relations professionals struggling to make public relations decisions with scarce resources:

> Nearly always you will have found more publics and devised more programs to reach those publics than your public relations department has the money and time to implement. You will want to choose public relations programs that maximize the use of resources and contribute most toward organizational goals. (p. 171)

Grunig and Hunt offered three techniques to optimize scarce resources for public relations programs. The first is *Cost-Benefit Analysis*. Here the practitioner adds up the costs of a program and then determines the monetary value of the benefits. If the benefits exceed the costs, it seems wise to implement the program.

Consistent with Chang's observations that a monetary measure is not always the best measure of opportunity costs-benefits, Grunig and Hunt (1984) said:

> You will find it extremely difficult, and probably impossible, however, to make reasonably accurate monetary estimates of benefits. You'll be on more solid ground if you use the idea of cost-benefit analysis to choose the programs that maximize the benefits for the resources spent without trying to estimate the exact dollar value of the benefits. (p. 172)

Second, Grunig and Hunt advocated the use of *Expected Value Analysis* to estimate the expected value of public relations programs for different publics. They believed that, even when the expected value can be calculated for various programs, the practitioner needs a decision-making procedure that allows for maximization of those expected values within the constraints of tight resources.

Third, to do this, Grunig and Hunt urged practitioners to adopt *simplified programming*. This procedure is a variation of linear programming that helps determine which programs make the best use of available resources.

SELECTED ECONOMIC CONCEPTS

We now turn to a discussion of selected economic concepts particularly relevant to public relations. Clustered into three groups, these concepts relate to public relations: (a) goals of individuals and organizations, (b) climate in which individuals and organizations operate, and (c) programmatic decision making.

Public Relations Goal-Related Concepts

Self-Interest.   This notion, central to understanding many economic and public relations activities, has philosophical and practical implications.

Wilson and Clark (1984, pp. 21–24) were not alone when they said the power of self-interest as an economic force cannot be overstated. As an economic concept, self-interest has a long history. Over 200 years ago, Adam Smith conceived of it as more than just a type of calculations by individuals. Indeed, he saw self-interest as the key factor in the efficient operation of a market economy.

This efficiency is due to the reciprocal nature of the concept in an economic context. As Wilson and Clark noted, economists believe that individuals making choices in their own self-interest also do the greatest good for society. The producer and consumer meet in the marketplace with each pursuing his or her own self-interest by trying to maximize profits and minimize costs. Consequently, the bargain that is struck must benefit both the producer and consumer, and this is ultimately best for society.

The *invisible hand* is the name economists give the incentive that guides individuals to make choices in the best interest of society by pursuing their own self-interest. This concept underlies much political thinking as well. Conservatives tend to believe the invisible hand always works in the best interest of society, whereas liberals feel it needs to be guided by government action.

Many public relations practitioners argue that implementing the economic self-interest for an individual or organization is the same as implementing the public relations self-interest. In fact, public relations historians link the development of public relations with economic perspectives that place varying degrees of emphasis on self-interest.

In his analysis of Capitalist, Marxist, New Left and New Right perspectives on public relations history, Pearson (1990, pp. 27–38) illustrated how the same events in public relations history are interpreted differently depending upon the economic/political/historical framework the historian brings to the analysis.

According to Pearson, some public relations historians argue public relations has flourished because business and industry have used techniques of the field to pro-mote their own self-interest at the expense of society. Other historians contend that public relations has flourished as a management practice because practitioners have persuaded organizations to act in society's interest. As discussed earlier in this chapter, these micro–macro questions are not mutually exclusive. If one buys the economic theory of the invisible hand, it seems reasonable that acting in a socially responsible manner *is* in the best interest of the organization and vice versa.

Also, this economic discussion of self-interest builds on the presentation in chapter 4 on Grunig's (Grunig & Hunt, 1984) theory of information seeking. Clear-ly, it is in the self-interest of the public relations practitioner's organization to have members of target publics enjoy bridging experiences that link the public's self-interest to that of the organization. According to Grunig's theory, increasing the public's sense of involvement with organizational goals and objectives should in-crease active seeking for related information by the public. This, in turn, enhances the organization's opportunity to communicate with members of the public.

Efficiency.   An important construct in light of resource scarcity is efficiency. Wilson and Clark (1984, p. 54) said efficiency is using a given amount and com-bination of resources to get the maximum amount of benefit. Historically, the private sector operates to maximize benefits and minimize costs. Consequently, efficiency is the primary concern of the private sector.

Profit.   Although public relations practitioners expect to profit from their effi-cient efforts, an examination of this term from an economic standpoint demonstrates its complexity. Moffat (1976, p. 222) said it is too simplistic to say a business's goal is to reduce costs to a minimum and raise prices to the maximum to earn maximum profit. Other motivations also influence business decisions. These include growth, stability, prestige, security, safety, and convenience.

Further, Chang (1990, p. 241) remarked that profit is more than having a positive balance after accounting for costs. Indeed, the concept of cost includes a normal rate of return on the resources allocated to a given effort. A practical definition of the normal rate of return is the average rate of return on investment in all industries. According to this view, an organization profits only when its profits are greater than this average rate of return.

Equity.   Although efficiency and profit are not related exclusively to a market economy, they are certainly linked to that type of economy. However, equity is relevant to public relations and is one of the goals of a social economy. Wilson and Clark (1984, p. 38) defined equity as "equality of opportunity." The fruits of a social economy's labors are intended to give all members a fair share.

The difficulty lies in deciding what's fair. As a practical matter, social economies provide equitable output by restricting the production of goods and services re-gardless of whether or not citizens want them.

Although the concepts related to efficiency, profit and equity are useful to the practitioner in their own right, they have the greatest use as measures of outcomes of public relations programs. For instance, a given program is efficient and profitable only if it produces more positive results than the average public relations program. Further, there may be times when a practitioner decides to allocate resources in an equitable, albeit inefficient and nonprofitable, manner.

When using these economic concepts as measures of how well specific public relations programs have achieved goals, practitioners may want to draw on socio-psychological theories as well. Leventhal (1976) suggested that persons have several ways of deciding whether outcomes are fair. In some situations people apply the *contributions rule* that holds that an individual's outcomes (profit, so to speak) should be directly proportional to his or her contribution to the process that produced the outcomes.

In other cases, theorists apply the *equality rule* that holds that each individual should receive an equal part of any outcome regardless of the amount of his or her input.

Sherrod (1982) said there is evidence to suggest both of these fairness rules are part of a person's social-norm structure. However, when a person is placed in an interdependent situation (where two or more persons must cooperate in order to achieve a goal), each person initially applies the fairness rule that is in her or his best self-interest.

Thibaut and Kelly (1959), in developing exchange theory, said it is necessary to examine the structure of a relationship between any two persons or organizations when evaluating the nature of that relationship. They argued that it is important to know the specific outcomes or payoffs associated with specific combinations of behaviors on the part of the two individuals and/or groups. Further, these can be described in a matrix of all possible combinations of outcomes.

Using exchange theory, it is possible to demonstrate that, in the short run, one always maximizes gains and minimizes losses by not cooperating in an interdependent situation. However, in the long run, cooperation increases gains. Sherrod (1982) reported that, over time, 75% of those placed in interdependent situations adopt a cooperative stance in order to maximize long-term gains.

Of particular interest to the public relations practitioner is the research finding that, in an interdependent situation, cooperation is enhanced by and enhances trust between the two parties and that trust can be fostered by communication (Sherrod, 1982).

Concepts Related to the Public Relations Climate

These concepts are useful to public relations by providing an understanding of practitioner–public relationships in terms of: (a) economics and (b) environment or climate.

Competition.   Practitioners must compete for attention of an organization's publics. Moffat (1976, p. 51) defined competition as the simultaneous attempt by two or more entities to achieve a goal, which to a certain extent, is mutually exclusive among those parties. Wilson and Clark (1984, p. 56) characterized competition as the rivalry between two or more parties to gain benefits from a third party.

There are two dimensions to the economic concept of competition. Certainly, producers are competing for the consumer's attention. However, at the same time, there is competition among consumers for the favors of the producers. If everyone wanted to consume the same thing, the price would rise in response to demand and only those able to afford higher costs would participate.

Economists classify markets as belonging to one of two categories: (a) perfect competition or (b) imperfect competition. However, there is no real example of a perfectly competitive market. Chang (1990, p. 141) said an important characteristic of an imperfectly competitive market is that prices are not determined in the market but are set by sellers to give them maximum profit. This economic discussion of competition parallels an argument often raised by critics of public relations. That is, a perfectly competitive marketplace of ideas does not exist in our society because of the oligopolistic nature of the information sources and channels. These critics argue minority viewpoints of all persuasions are seldom expressed, because they lack resources to get on the public's agenda.

Management scholars (Argyris, 1974, pp. 1–33) and group dynamicists (Cartwright & Zander, 1960, pp. 80–81) noted two distinctly different types of competition:

A *win–lose* arrangement wherein success by one person or group reduces the chance of success by another. Argyris (1974, pp. 1–33) noted that such competition often reduces candor and completeness of communication within organizations. That reduction occurs, because a participant frequently feels a need to horde or monopolize information and suggestions that give him or her a competitive advantage.

A *win–win* situation. Here two people (for example, a shortstop and a second baseman in baseball) compete in that each tries to outdo the other as to batting average, salary earned, etc. However, the two players must work together, with each contributing to the success of the other, in turning a double play or executing a hit-and-run maneuver.

Clearly, the win–win type of competition often leads to better group functioning than does the win–lose situation. And, public relations practitioners often improve matters by pointing out shared goals and interdependencies among a client's stakeholders. In any event, the nature and intensity of competition influences organizational climate in ways not fully accounted for by the studies of exchange theory noted earlier.

Concepts Related to Public Relations
Program Decision Making

We now turn to a set of economic concepts useful in making program decisions. The thinking that underlies these concepts, in conjunction with other public relations management principles, helps the practitioner make the best choices.

Exchange and Value.   These two concepts have utility when public relations practitioners evaluate the nature of their organizations' relationships with various publics. Wilson and Clark (1984, p. 53–54) said all individual economic choices are guided by one important principle: persons will make choices that provide maximum benefit or minimum cost to them. Central to these choices is the concept of an *exchange:* giving one thing in return for something else.

However, these same economists remarked that persons only participate in a voluntary exchange or relationship (typical in most public relations programs) when both parties benefit or assign value to what is exchanged. Value has two dimensions. Some items have value in use but no economic value. We benefit from consuming air, but there is no economic value to air because so much is available for free. Other items have value in use as well as an economic value or price.

The public relations practitioner influences the economic value of an organization by developing what Althiede and Johnson (1980) called *bureaucratic propaganda.* As noted in chapter 12, organizations and individuals need resources to operate. Consequently, practitioners need to argue persuasively that what their organization offers is of value and, therefore, its products and services are worth the price.

In economics and public relations, things seldom remain constant. Hence, the importance of understanding what economists mean by the term *marginal* and how it is applied to other concepts.

Marginal.   Moffat (1976, p. 175) said it is important to recognize that the word marginal, used in economic terms, refers to a change in some value and not the absolute value itself. Further, it is a concept often linked to other economic terms. For example, a *marginal buyer* is a person who will purchase the product at the current price but will no longer be a willing participant in the exchange if the price rises.

Perhaps the most salient marginal economic concepts public relations practitioners use to explain the behavior of parties in an exchange (or relationship) deal with productivity and satisfaction or utility.

Marginal Productivity.   Economists say almost all production (including production related to public relations) is subject to what is called *diminishing marginal productivity* (Wilson & Clark, 1984, pp. 147–148). This means that, as the use of one factor (such as labor) increases, output of the product increases at a decreasing rate. Further, a point can be reached where the rate of this one factor increases so much that its use becomes counterproductive and output declines.

Economists warn that both explicit costs and opportunity costs are associated with production, and because of diminishing marginal productivity, these costs associated with each unit of production increase in the short run. That doesn't mean a firm or organization can't grow. If all factors of production are increased at the same time, production may become more efficient due to increasing returns to scale.

This latter point is synergistic in nature. That is, expansion or operation within one realm may enhance the efficiency and effectiveness of production in a separate but related realm. And, given the negative public reaction to much business activity in the 1980s, such an argument may sometimes be used to defend a merger of two organizations or the acquisition by one organization of another.

Marginal Utility.   Just as productivity is subject to diminishing returns, so is satisfaction or utility. Wilson and Clark (1984, p. 103) said diminishing marginal utility is the principle that less and less satisfaction is obtained from each additional item consumed in a given time period. (That first slice of a large pizza for dinner tastes pretty good, but the last slice doesn't provide quite as much satisfaction.)

Moffat (1976, p. 178) said economists presume persons will spend their first dollar on necessities such as food, shelter, etc. that have large marginal utility. After those needs have been met, buyers purchase what satisfies the next strongest desire. Therefore, each dollar spent buys less utility or satisfaction than the previous dollar.

Wilson and Clark (1984, p. 103) explained that economists use this concept to support the idea that people only buy more of a product when it costs less. However, two other factors affect the relationship between price and quantity purchased: the income effect and the substitution effect.

The income effect describes the relationship between increasing or decreasing prices and the buying power of income. Simply put, as the price drops one can buy more. Consequently, one's income appears to be greater, because one can buy more with the same amount of dollars.

The substitution effect describes the relationship between increasing or decreasing prices and the mix of goods purchased. If the price of beef goes up, consumers may substitute chicken. However, the substitution effect works both ways. If the price of beef goes down, consumers may substitute beef for chicken again.

Elasticity.   This is the term used by economists to measure the changes in concepts related to productivity and satisfaction. In essence, elasticity is a measure of responsiveness. Elasticity of satisfaction is measured by what economists call the *Demand Curve* (showing the quantities that people are willing and able to purchase at various prices). Elasticity of productivity is measured by the *Supply Curve* (showing the quantities that producers are willing and able to make available for sale at various prices).

One of the most useful ways for the public relations person to implement these marginal economic concepts is to evaluate the nature of any relationship (or exchange) the practitioner's organization has with relevant publics.

From the organization's viewpoint, the concept of diminishing marginal productivity suggests the practitioner will reach a point where the effort to communicate or win over all members of a specific public will no longer be worth the investment. The cost of obtaining favorable evaluations by the last member of the public is substantially greater than the cost of gaining acceptance by the first member.

This is particularly true given the personality structure and communication behavior of what Rogers (1983) called a *laggard* in the process of adopting ideas or innovations. These late adopters tend to be isolated traditionalists who are best reached with personal, rather than media, communication channels. An organization may decide it is not worth the cost to develop a public relations campaign that could win over these types of people.

The same reasoning applies to efforts designed to communicate with different publics. The process of reaching all relevant publics becomes subject to decreasing marginal productivity. This suggests the practitioner should assign a priority to publics and be willing to halt expenditures before they cease to be cost effective. This process is directly related to the concept of marginal utility. Because each dollar buys less satisfaction than the previous dollar, practitioners should do research designed to help them spend first and foremost on publics likely to give the greatest satisfaction.

Further, the practitioner uses the substitution principle to develop an overall public relations program flexible enough to accommodate switching emphasis from one public to another. All things being equal, one public may be more appealing than another. However, if the cost of reaching one public becomes too great, the practitioner may have to substitute a second or third public.

Perhaps an even more fruitful way of implementing these concepts related to marginality is to evaluate how members of specific publics relate to the practitioner's organization.

As outlined by Grunig and Hunt (1984, pp. 129–131, 147–160), one should consider attitudes as situational and specific to identifiable problems and issues, not to some broad, abstract concept. Further, these authors saw attitudes as "mental conclusions" that are part of conscious thinking. Consequently, attitudes and specific behaviors are changed to fit specific situations. Clearly, people invest mental and physical energy, as well as money, in support of organizations that succeed or fail in dealing with specific issues or problems rather than with abstractions.

It is easy to see that members of publics experience a degree of diminishing marginal productivity regarding this type of investment in a relationship with an organization. At some point, the public member may bail out of the relationship, because the cost is too high for the return on investment. When this happens, the public members may substitute other, more profitable relationships with other organizations for those that are too costly.

The public relations practitioner may be able to prevent such desertion of important stakeholders by fostering a degree of brand loyalty to the organization. As Russell and Lane (1990) remarked, the value of the brand goes beyond the value of the product with which it is linked. The public relations practitioner seeking to maintain beneficial relationships with target publics should develop campaigns to enhance the organization's brand equity. That is, public relations efforts can promote positive attitudes and feelings about the organization apart from specific issues or topics associated with it.

Demand and supply curves suggest there are always going to be buyers and sellers in the relationship marketplace. But, the practitioner has to operate in the market to provide a relationship to target publics that have the greatest payoff with the least cost.

Concepts Related to the Consequences of Organizational Behavior

This last section deals with economic concepts that describe what often preoccupies public relations practitioners: dealing with the consequences of both positive and negative organizational behavior.

Externalities.   Economists call these consequences *externalities,* or spillovers, and define them as positive or negative effects of a trade between sellers and buyers on a third party who is not part of the trade (Chang, 1990: 173). Chang cited as an example of a positive externality the societal effects of immunizing citizens against disease (flu shots, polio vaccine, etc.). When person A avoids contracting a disease because of getting a shot, she or he becomes less likely to give that disease to person B who has had no shot. On the other hand, a negative externality would be the societal effects of pollution in water or air.

But Moffat (1976) noted difficulty in assessing spillover costs and benefits of any particular action:

> The cost and benefits referred to include utility units as well as monetary units and therefore it is usually difficult to assess the overall effect of an economic action. For example, just consider the first-order effects when a city exercises its right of eminent domain and builds a public park: it is said that this action is justified if the cumulative happiness of those who use the park is larger than the cumulative unhappiness of those who lost their private property plus those whose payment of taxes made the park possible. But there are also second and further order costs and benefits: appearance of the neighborhood may be changed, someone may be injured during construction, local businesses may benefit from people coming to use the park, and air pollution may result from people driving to use the park. (pp. 256–257)

It is apparent to public relations practitioners that any discussion of externalities involves the role of the government and consumers. Economists also recognize this.

Chang (1990, pp. 249–251) said the government has several options when dealing with positive and negative externalities. When an organization is involved in the production of goods and services that benefit society (such as flu shots), the government may provide a subsidy for research and development. This subsidy helps the firm recover costs of producing the benefits that go to the general public. For negative externalities like air and water pollution, Chang said the government can force firms to absorb the costs through the levy of a pollution fee or by directly regulating company activity through the Environmental Protection Agency.

Wilson and Clark (1984, pp. 72–73) said the control of negative externalities is really an application of property rights that the government can deal with more effectively than the private sector. Only the public sector has the power to pass laws that protect the air, water, and private property.

Consumers are not without some say regarding externalities. Wilson and Clark noted that, although the public sector can legislatively force companies to pay for damages caused by negative externalities, these costs will be paid for through higher market prices. Consequently, consumers express their opinions by buying or not buying at various prices. Second, consumers express their opinions regarding externalities in the voting booth. By supporting or not supporting specific candidates and legislation, consumers signal their reaction to positive and negative externalities.

It is beyond the scope of this chapter to develop complete public relations strategies for dealing with these organizational spillovers. However, two points can be made. First, the astute public relations practitioner should be able to recognize the positive and negative externalities associated with an organization's economic activity. Keep in mind that these are effects on third parties (publics) not directly involved in the economic activity. Second, the practitioner should encourage activities that result in positive externalities and discourage those that result in negative spillovers.

REFERENCES

Althiede, D. L., & Johnson, J. M. (1980). *Bureaucratic propaganda*. Boston: Allyn & Bacon.

Argyris, C. (1974). *Behind the front page*. San Francisco: Jossey-Bass.

Cartwright, D., & Zander, A. (1960). *Group dynamics: research and theory*. New York: Harper & Row.

Chang, S. (1990). *Modern economics*. Boston: Allyn & Bacon.

Cutlip, S. M., Center, A. H., & Broom, G. M. (1985). *Effective public relations*. Englewood Cliffs, NJ: Prentice-Hall.

Grunig, J. E., & Hunt, T. (1984). *Managing public relations*. New York: Holt, Rinehart & Winston.

Helson, H. (1964). *Adaption level theory*. New York: Harper & Row.

Leventhal, G. S. (1976). Fairness in social relationships. In J. W. Thibaut, J. T. Spence, & R. C. Carson, (Eds.), *Contemporary topics in social psychology* (pp. 211–239). Morristown, NJ: General Learning Press.

Moffat, D. W. (1976). *Economics dictionary*. New York: Elsevier.

Nager, N. R., & Allen, T. H. (1984). *Public relations: Management by objectives*. New York: Longman.

Newsom, D., Scott, A., & Turk, J. V. (1989). *This is PR: The realities of public relations.* Belmont, CA: Wadsworth.

Pearson, R. (1990). Perspectives on public relations history. *Public Relations Review, 16,* 27–28.

Rogers, E. M. (1983). *Diffusion of innovations* (3rd ed.). New York: The Free Press.

Russell, J. T., & Lane, W. R. (1990). *Kleppner's advertising procedure* (11th ed.). Englewood Cliffs, NJ: Prentice Hall.

Sherrod, D. (1982). *Social psychology.* New York: Random House.

Thibaut, J. W., & Kelly, H. H. (1959). *The social psychology of groups.* New York: Wiley.

Wilcox, D. L., Ault, P. H., & Agee, W. K. (1989). *Public relations: Strategies and tactics.* New York: Harper & Row.

Wilson, J. H., & Clark, J. R. (1984). *Economics: The science of cost, benefit and choice.* Cincinnati: South-Western.

III SIX VARIED CASES

7 Police in America: Catching Bad Guys and Doing Much, Much More

As police chief in a small midwestern town, Joe Glotz worked hard to enhance relations between his department and local citizens. For years he gradually added new programs far removed, on the surface, from the traditional police role of catching heavies and bringing them to justice. Nowadays, police personnel spend more than half their time unlocking car doors, telling school kids about police work, putting on programs in drug education, patrolling residential streets in the daytime, operating a booth at a local craft festival to inform citizens about crime-related matters, escorting floats through town during the annual homecoming parade of the large state university in town, and so on.

Suddenly, following a local election, Glotz faced a city council that attempted to institute zero-based budgeting. This means each and every city project must be justified on the basis of real benefits per dollar spent. The chief can no longer add or keep programs primarily because they have been around for a long time or because they are in line with current state and national trends.

Glotz commissioned a comprehensive study of local police work and its public relations posture. He hired a public relations professor at a local university to tackle the project. The professor insisted on proceeding slowly and carefully, in four steps:

1. Reviewing the literature on police community relations, defining the social, political, and economic contexts at the national level.

2. Talking at some length with local citizens and leaders to get a handle on contextual matters that are quite unique to the local scene.

3. Talking with the police chief and other department personnel to describe local police–community relations efforts with some precision. The effort here was to determine what was being done and why.

4. Surveying local citizens to find out what they regard as the most and least important police activities.

Within about 4 months, the public relations professor, working with the police chief, completed the study. Findings are listed below, followed by possible implications for policy and action.

BASIC BACKGROUND

The National Context

Across the nation, police chiefs like Glotz face an interesting public relations dilemma. Historically, and even at present, people who define police roles emphasize crime detection and apprehension as core, high-status activities. Training, awards, and recognition focus largely on these areas, not on peace keeping, crime prevention, and service activities.

Public opinion across the country supports this view. In a 1981 nationwide survey, 57% of those answering said police should respond only to calls that, according to the caller, involve an actual or suspected crime (Flanagan, 1985).

Despite this, American police men and women spend about 80 to 90% of their time maintaining order in a broad sense, not in enforcing the law (Bard, 1973). There are at least four fundamental reasons for this: One is economic and three have to do with cultural beliefs (held by large segments of the population as a whole and inclined to help shape diverse specific beliefs and behaviors).

In the economic sphere, tight budgets call attention to the idea that it's less expensive to prevent crime than to catch crooks after crimes have been committed. Police departments often feel overwhelmed, not staffed and funded to make enough arrests to stem a rising tide of crime.

In such a setting, public service helps build support, partly because it permits police to relate to citizens in helpful, nonpunitive ways. Clearly people feel good about the local police department when cops start their cars, help them across streets, and rescue their cats from window ledges (Pugh, 1986). In a recent national survey, those who support police most strongly tend to value such activity (Flanagan, 1985).

Turning to citizen beliefs, thinking seems to have changed in at least three areas:

Widespread recognition that crime brings great cost and suffering to its victims. Such costs are often seen as justifying a hard-line approach to law enforcement and sentencing (Erskine, 1974, 1982). Yet the deterrent value of harsh punishment is far from unanimously accepted. And surely victim suffering is reduced only in a rather brief, superficial way by hanging crooks or "locking them up and throwing the key away."

Growing realization that, to do its job, a law-enforcement agency must be respected and seen as legitimate by diverse racial, ethnic, and socioeconomic groups. Such acceptance, in turn, requires ongoing two-way communication between police and their constituencies. Citizens must feel that cops are present to serve them and not simply to write parking tickets and catch an occasional heavy (Cain, 1973).

A widespread belief that society as a whole—and not just criminals—bears some responsibility for crime. Broken homes, unemployment, and other societal problems are thought to pave the way for lawbreaking (Erskine, 1974). In light of this, many contend that punishing crooks deals primarily with symptoms of crime and only tangentially with its root causes (Walthier, McCune, & Trojanowicz, 1973).

Although these ideas carry great weight, police personnel playing a community service role must overcome several barriers:

1. Widespread operation in patrol cars, not on foot as in days gone by. This change is for the sake of efficiency, permitting one or a few police men and women to protect large areas. However, a patrol car cannot easily help an old lady cross the street! In general, such personal contact with ordinary citizens in friendly, supportive settings has been reduced. As a result, cop and citizen often meet primarily where there is fear and suspicion—a real or potential adversary relationship. Such encounters do not foster mutual understanding, liking, and trust (Cain, 1973). Within our theoretical scheme, this development has to do with the nature of social contacts between police and the public.

2. Professionalization that supposedly leads police to behave in line with bureaucratic rules and abstract calculations. On the positive side, this presumably reduces the chance of prejudice and miscalculation leading to conflicts with citizens and abuse of police power. However, it also contributes to beliefs that cops are not attentive to unique local needs (Fink & Sealy, 1974). Here subcultural beliefs and related practices contribute to some possible deterioration in police–citizen contact.

Barriers 3 and 4 have to do with socialization and related subcultural beliefs presumably held within the law-enforcement field.

3. Lack of social science and humanities training helpful in human relationships. Apparently there has been some improvement here. Forty-six percent of all American cops reportedly had completed at least some college training by the late 1970s ("Police under Fire," 1978). However, in the police science curriculum at a technical college near Glotz's town, only 4 of 30 courses focus on traditional social science disciplines.

4. Police perspectives that differ from those of other human service providers to whom police often refer troubled people. For instance, Walthier et al. (1973) reported that police are trained to value bureaucratic activities and formal standards along with competitiveness and assertiveness. Also, they are expected to protect themselves and society from "bad guys" (Baker, 1985, p. 140). Social workers, on the other hand, tend to place low priority on rugged individualism (Walthier et al., 1973). They often look hard for societal causes of crime in seeking to rehabilitate criminals.

Such divergence may make cooperation between the two groups difficult and ineffective. Yet cops are the only people on duty 24 hours a day to observe and catch someone about to jump off a building or crash a car. They must often decide when a person has mental problems that warrant turning him or her over to a mental health agency for definite diagnosis. That, in turn, helps determine a case's possible disposition.

Barriers 5 and 6 have to do with role and power relationships involving police. Also, number 5 focuses on the closely related question of available economic and personnel resources.

5. Low status and few resources for work in police–community relations (PCR). Too often, PCR personnel have little training for or clear definition of their jobs. Further, they tend to view such assignments as demotions. As a result, police public relations often emphasizes hype and surface appearance rather than real two-way communication needed for truly effective public relations (Grunig & Hunt, 1984, pp. 30–37, 40–42; Trojanowicz, 1973).

6. Lack of status and respect for police in general. Cops tend to come from lower socioeconomic strata. Yet they are seen by citizens with whom they deal most often—also from lower strata—as representing powerful elites. In a real sense, then, they are caught in the middle, with little or no direct base of social or political support (Whittington, 1971).

Despite such constraints, police departments have made substantial strides in community relations. Neighborhood Watch programs have brought police and citizens together in cities such as Detroit (Viviano, 1981) and New York ("The 'blues'," 1985). To cite one outstanding PCR example, the New York Police Department has involved nearly 200,000 civilians in projects ranging from senior escort services to precinct youth councils ("Billy Holiday," 1985).

To sum up, national developments, trends, and research suggest that Chief Glotz has good reason, and lots of expert opinion behind him, when he emphasizes community relations activity in his town. However, he faces additional reasons for and barriers to such activity in light of factors unique to his town and others like it on the edge of the rather economically depressed region known as Appalachia.

These factors bear on cultural and subcultural beliefs, role and power relationships, and available resources in the area.

The Local Context

Glotz's police force faced difficult challenges, partly because a state university in town had grown from a small college that trained primarily school teachers through the 1930s and 1940s to a cosmopolitan university that enrolled almost 19,000 students by 1971. These students came from all over the world, bringing diverse foreign and "big-city" ways with them.

Of course, as on most large American campuses, many students became involved in the drug subculture symbolized nationally by the Woodstock rock concert and the famous rock group, The Grateful Dead. No doubt people from all over the state assumed a small-town police force such as the one now headed by Glotz could not prevent drug consumption. Partly as a result, a rather riotous spring concert became an annual event in town for some years—much to the chagrin of local citizens.

Other elements of the political and social contexts contributed to a sense of alienation and separation between townspeople and students. Because students eventually equaled or surpassed townspeople in numbers, conflict between the two groups became troublesome and potentially explosive (though the likelihood of an explosion may have been reduced by widespread student apathy with respect to local government). Developments included:

Anti-Vietnam War protesting in the late 1960s and early 1970s. As with other state universities in the region, rioting forced early closure of school after the May 1970 killing of four Kent State University students by members of the Ohio National Guard. Stones thrown through local merchants' windows became commonplace in those days.

Academic liberalization of that period that, according to critics such as Bloom (1987, pp. 313–335), lowered academic and admissions standards. Many felt this permitted some students who were destined to become law-enforcement problems to enroll.

Formation of Centers for Women's and Afro-American Studies. Presumably designed to enhance study and appreciation of the heritage and culture of Blacks and women, these centers became bastions of social protest not viewed with great favor by the many conservative citizens of the area.

Growth of the university, with its increased faculty as well as students, helped create three rather distinct groups of people in the area with different priorities as to government service. Splits among these groups became especially salient in the mid-1960s when consolidation of the local school system with nearby rural systems threw kids with dramatically different kinds of parents together, at least through the sixth grade. Predictably, parents became concerned and emotional when their children—often viewed as impressionable, vulnerable extensions of themselves—became subject to what they regarded as threatening, unwholesome influences.

The three groups were often referred to with the following labels:

Gownies—faculty and staff at the university. These people generally have lots of education and fairly high socioeconomic status. Many want strong college-preparatory curricula along with rigorous, stimulating academic environments for their children.

Townies—those living in or near the town but not serving as university faculty members. People here tend to fall between the other two groups in terms of socioeconomic status and level of concern with schools.

Hilljacks—residents of isolated rural areas outside the town but within the consolidated school district. These people tend to be of low socioeconomic status. Many are on welfare. Most are said to have low regard for learning and to view schools primarily as babysitting aids. (Such impressions, although widely held, may be inaccurate. Further research is needed to test them.)

Such divisions showed up prominently in varying approaches to raising children and enforcing the law as related to them. Of course, gownies emphasize serious academic pursuits for their children, and they seek a supportive school and broad social environment. However, hilljacks (and to some extent townies) place less emphasis on academic work, particularly that focusing on preparation for college.

Viewed from the perspective of university people, residents of outlying communities provide a puzzling contrast in looking at education and child rearing.

At one level, many of these people are rather devout members of fundamentalist religious groups that take conservative (hence, ostensibly propolice) stands on moral issues. However, some appear to have almost given up the fight in the wake of apparent failure to keep their children away from the seductive influences of peers, television, and the central town's "joints" or bars.

Town residents, on the other hand, appear to feel that their daughters and sons go astray upon coming under the macho spell of hilljacks when entering middle school. Rural kids often define studying as "sissy behavior" and use high-pressure tactics—sometimes even beatings—to bring town as well as rural kids into line with their behavioral norms. Youthful rebellion results often from such an explosive mixture, sometimes leading to crime.

In the political sphere, Glotz's police department has a somewhat checkered past stemming in part from its own members' behavior and in part from laws passed and actions taken by city government.

For one thing, almost 20 years ago, the acting police chief took unusual measures to quell anti-Vietnam War rioting by university students. For example, a patrolman drove a police cruiser down the crowded main street of town on one occasion as the chief lay on the rear floorboard and heaved smoke or tear-gas grenades out a car window. And several years later, this same individual was reported by the media to have used a cruiser to run down his wife's car and crash into it while she was driving. Justly or not, such reports created rather vivid memories that have probably lasted for some time.

Also, the city council passed a law making it illegal to simply carry an open beer can at certain times when walking down the main street. And the council established an active meter maid program to dish out parking tickets. Although justified in many ways, these moves are apt to create a widespread impression that the city's government—including its enforcement arm—have used a "Mickey Mouse" approach designed to serve the city rather than its individual citizens.

After uncovering these aspects, the researcher conducted a study to discern current citizen priorities in town regarding police education and service activities. We now turn to the methodology and findings of that study, followed by an analysis of possible action implications.

METHODOLOGY

To begin, Glotz and his colleagues developed a list of programs carried out by the city's police department. In several meetings with him, the researcher and university Public Relations Student Society of America (PRSSA) students became familiar with needs presumably addressed by and the philosophy behind these programs. Questionnaire items were developed to gauge public reaction in two areas:

Overall importance. In all, 24 departmental activities and programs were described with enough detail so even uninformed citizens would have an idea of objectives and types of effort involved. Respondents then indicated whether they felt a given program or activity was *very important, fairly important,* or *not important.*

Level of department activity. Here seven types of activities and programs were described. Interviewers asked for assessments of whether the department was doing *about the right amount* in each area, *should do more,* or *should do less.*

In addition, questions dealt with age, occupation (defined in the respondent's own words and placed in several categories as noted later), and overall importance attached to education for crime prevention. Responses to the latter item were *very important, fairly important, not very important,* and *not important at all.*

Also, respondents were asked what they felt was the most serious crime problem in town. Responses were quite varied, but most fell into nine categories defined by the researchers after data were collected. Further, interviewers asked for guesstimates of how many police officers should be on duty, ideally, during an average 8-

hour shift. The average number actually on duty, four, was used as a benchmark in interpreting estimates.

An initial questionnaire required about 15 minutes to answer—long enough to discourage many prospective respondents. After initial pretesting, items were pruned and combined so administration required only about 5 minutes.

Phone interviews were completed by 13 members of the PRSSA chapter. Most were juniors and seniors who had completed at least one course in social science research methods. Also, all crew members practiced interviewing on each other, as well as on friends and roommates. And all underwent a training session of more than 1 hour just prior to interviewing.

Random digit dialing was used, with numbers chosen from three residential exchanges in the community. Only off-campus students were covered, as freshmen and sophomores who lived in dorms had minimal participation and interest in city politics and government.

About 62% of all attempted interviews were completed, yielding 213 usable interview schedules. This response rate was seen as adequate, because comparison of the sample with the city's population as described in recent census data on income, sex, and other demographic traits indicated the sample was quite representative.

More detailed discussion of methodology is found in Culbertson and Shin (1989). We now turn to survey results.

SURVEY RESULTS

Most data are reported in percentages. It's important to keep in mind that, with a sample size of slightly over 200, the data provide a sampling error of about 5% to 6%. For example, a sample percentage of 55% permits one to conclude with 95% confidence (that is, with 19–1 odds in favor of being accurate) that the population value falls between 49% and 61%. Where percentages are far removed from 50, the sampling error declines.

To begin, the data support the general concept that police should be involved in educating the public to reduce crime prevention. To get at this we asked the following question:

> Police departments have long focused on tracking down and apprehending law offenders. However, recently, many policemen have become active in educating the public in order to reduce victimization. How important or unimportant would you say such educational activities should be for the police department here in Athens? Would you say these are very important? Fairly important? Not very important? Or not important at all?

Almost half (47%) of the 213 persons answering said *very important*. An equal number said *fairly important*. Only 10 people (5%) said *not very important*, where-

TABLE 7.1
Ratings of Crime Prevention Activities Involving Education and Consultation as to Importance
and Activity Level

| | Importance | | | |
Activity	Very Important	Fairly Important	Not Important	No. of Ratings
The Neighborhood Watch Program, which helps prevent crime by training private citizens to be alert for suspicious activities and to watch each other's property	63%	33%	4%	212
Visits and consultations by police to help reduce theft from homes and businesses	33%	49%	17%	212
School liaison programs in which a police officer spends 2 hours a week in each of 8 local schools to interact with students	37%	39%	24%	210
Stranger Awareness Program, designed to teach children what to be aware of and how to react when approached by strangers	79%	19%	2%	214
Police Department's sexual assault program, which works in connection with Careline and My Sister's Place	74%	26%	–	207

| | Level of Need | | | |
	More is Needed	Current Level About Right	Less is Needed	No. of Ratings
Free theft-prevention surveys for homes and businesses	24%	62%	14%	186
Stranger-awareness program in local schools	62%	33%	3%	182
Sexual-assault prevention programs	68%	31%	1%	188

as just 2 said *not important at all.* Overall, then, an overwhelming majority of people bought the basic notion of police as educator.

Approaching the same question in another way, we summed ratings across the 24 specific activities rated as to importance. Results here are very much the same as with the single global rating noted previously. In total, 48% of all activity ratings were *very important,* whereas 37% fell into the *fairly important* category and just 15% were *not important.*

Looking at the data from still another angle, we summed ratings as to appropriate activity level across the seven categories of activity covered (see Tab. 7.1, 7.2, and 7.3 for the specific wording involved). Almost half (48%) of these ratings indicated satisfaction with current levels of activity in service and education. Forty-six percent

TABLE 7.2
Ratings of Drug Education Activities as to Importance and Activity Level

Activity	Importance			
	Very Important	Fairly Important	Not Important	No. of Ratings
Drug education programs held annually in elementary schools	72%	23%	5%	211
Drug education programs in middle school presented at teachers' request	69%	25%	6%	211
High school drug education programs stressing the impact of drug-related arrests, especially on careers	73%	24%	3%	212
Lectures and literature that alert parents and other adults to signs of drug use among kids and teens	58%	37%	5%	211

	Level of Activity Needed			
	More is Needed	Current Level About Right	Less is Needed	
Drug education programs for students in local schools	60%	38%	2%	169
Drug education programs for adults and parents	51%	41%	7%	187

called for increased activity, whereas only 5% preferred a reduction. Obviously, then, votes for more activity exceed those for less by about 9 to 1, indicating rather strong endorsement of educational and service activity.

Specific activity ratings are presented in Tab. 7.1–7.5. It's important to remember that ratings of importance and quantity of these services do not get at their quality.

Tab. 7.1 reveals strong endorsement of the Neighborhood Watch, Stranger Awareness, and Sexual Assault programs. *Very important* ratings in these areas range from 63% for Neighborhood Watch to 79% for Stranger Awareness. Furthermore, with respect to the latter two projects, about two thirds of all respondents said *more is needed,* and most others endorsed current levels of programming.

In Table 7.2, high priority is obviously shown for drug education. About 70% of all citizens interviewed rated drug education as very important at each of the three school levels (elementary, middle, and high school). Furthermore, 60% expressed the view that more drug education is needed in local schools. Drug education programs for parents also received strong endorsement, albeit somewhat less so than with children. About 58% of all respondents said lectures and literature in this area

TABLE 7.3
Ratings of Patrol Activities as to Importance and Activity Level

Importance

Activity	Very Important	Fairly Important	Not Important	No. of Ratings
Patrolmen on foot in the residential sections during the daytime	20%	37%	43%	214
Patrolling the residential sections on foot during the evening	44%	29%	27%	212
Police officers patrolling the mall and business sections of town	33%	47%	20%	214
Police patrolling the uptown area during the evening	57%	39%	4%	214
Police officers patrolling the uptown area during the day	16%	48%	36%	214

Level of Activity Needed

	More is Needed	Current Level About Right	Less is Needed	
Police patrols in residential areas	40%	57%	3%	189
Police patrols in business sections of town	23%	70%	6%	203

TABLE 7.4
Ratings of General Service Activities as to Importance

Importance

Activity	Very Important	Fairly Important	Not Important	No. of Ratings
Public speaking on police-related topics at local civic organizations or events	17%	59%	29%	212
Police escorts during funeral processionals	22%	35%	43%	214
Bicycle safety lectures given annually in elementary schools	31%	53%	16%	213
Unlocking automobiles for those who can't find a locksmith	41%	34%	25%	214
Routine checks of vacant homes and businesses when residents are away	42%	50%	8%	214
Investigation of auto accidents	60%	35%	5%	214

TABLE 7.5
Ratings of Activities Connected With Specific Events as to Importance

Activity	Importance			
	Very Important	Fairly Important	Not Important	No. of Ratings
Operating a booth for crime prevention literature at the annual Fall Festival in the city Parking Garage	12%	52%	36%	209
Providing traffic control at the Indian Summer Run, city's Marathon, Walk-a-thon, Bike-a-thon, Bicycle Criterium, and other such events	43%	51%	6%	213
Providing traffic control at University Homecoming Parade, other parades, and street demonstrations	46%	45%	9%	212
Providing child finger-printing done annually in schools and during Crime Prevention Week at the city Mall	58%	29%	13%	211

were very important for parents, whereas 51% called for increased activity with that sector of the population.

Turning to Tab. 7.3, it appears that police patrols did not have great appeal in some times and places. Seven questionnaire items dealt with this area, and responses present a mixed picture. Tab. 7.3 gives some support for these conclusions:

The importance accorded to daytime patrols wasn't very high. In fact, only 20% rated daytime patrolling in residential areas as very important, whereas 43% said this activity was not important. Like figures for uptown daytime patrolling were 16% and 36%. Perhaps people reason that few crimes are committed in daytime—at least, in locations where policeman on patrol could do much good. Also, people may associate daytime patrols with parking or speeding tickets— doubtless an unpopular byproduct of police activity!

Evening and night patrols were much more important to people. In fact, 57% said evening patrols uptown were very important, whereas 44% gave a comparable response with evening residential locations in mind.

On the whole, most people felt current levels of patrolling were about right. However, a significant number (40% with residential patrols and 23% in talking about the business sections of town) called for more patrolling. Very few people favored reductions in this area.

General satisfaction with current levels of patrolling is especially interesting in view of another piece of our data. We asked the following question:

What would you say is the minimum number of police officers necessary to staff an 8-hour shift? You may not know, but give your best estimate.

Guestimates given here range all the way from 3 to 85 (the latter from an international student at the local university who spoke in terms of a cop at every corner, perhaps suggesting an association with martial law!). The mean estimate given, however, by the 191 people who ventured a response, is 13. That figure exceeds by more than 3–1 the actual size of the average shift within the department, 4!

Of course, these findings must be viewed with some skepticism. Many people gave estimates reluctantly, after suggesting they really didn't know. Furthermore, doubtless few people had much awareness of sophisticated communication equipment that permits policemen to respond rather quickly where problems arise and cuts down, to some extent, the needed size of staff. Given these caveats, however, people who become aware that only four police officers are on duty during an average shift may be receptive to appeals for greater public support. Most see the ideal shift as being much larger.

Taken together, Tab. 7.4 and Tab. 7.5 support at least two conclusions about public perceptions of police service in the area:

High priority is accorded to those programs that deal with crime prevention and serving people in emergencies. Sixty percent of all respondents attributed high importance to investigation of auto accidents (see Tab. 7.4). About 58% responded similarly with child fingerprinting during crime prevention week (note Tab. 7.5), and almost half (42%) gave very important ratings with routine checks of homes and businesses that are vacant.

Low importance was accorded to what people saw as public relations or ceremonial activity. Only 12% of all respondents attributed high importance to a Fall Festival crime prevention booth (see Tab. 7.5), whereas just 17% endorsed fully the need for public speaking at local civic meetings and events. In the same vein, referring to Tab. 7.1, just 37% of all ratings on the school liaison program fell into the very important category. And Tab. 7.4 shows the score for funeral escorts was but 22%.

Obviously such data do not tell us that public relations types of activities are unimportant. These programs may indeed have much greater impact than is apparent to a layperson who'd given little thought to police operations. Also, it should be noted that, although firm endorsement of such activity was rare, strong objections were also few and far between.

Such services as bicycle safety training in schools, traffic control at special events, and unlocking of automobiles gained intermediate levels of public emphasis well above purely ceremonial or public relations activity but below programs connected with emergency and crime. Obviously these services are appreciated by substantial numbers of local residents. Further, those who do need something like unlocking of a car door, although perhaps few in number, have intense needs that are likely to lead them to feel grateful toward the police department.

Comparison of Subgroups—Ramifications
for Political Context

In an attempt to find differences across subgroups, comparisons were made on the basis of sex, age, and job. In analyzing age, the sample was divided into four groups of roughly equal size: college age (18–22), young adult (23–29), adult (30–42), and older people (43–88).

When looking at occupation, we coded people's reported jobs into seven groups: blue-collar, white-collar, university faculty/staff, nonuniversity professional and management people, unemployed and housewives (combined because they responded similarly overall and did not show up in the sample often enough to permit separate analysis), retired persons, and university students.

Conventional wisdom suggests that women, older folks, retirees, and sometimes blue-collar workers tend to be conservative on questions of law and order. We expected and found that these groups tend to place high priority on police activities. However, such relationships are small and are not found with all activities rated. Overall, the similarities outweigh the differences. In sum, most subgroups place fairly high priority on most police activities except those seen as purely ceremonial.

There is a consistent tendency for women to attach greater importance than men to police activities in two areas: protection of children (including that from drugs) and patrolling of residential areas. As shown in Tab. 7.6, women tend more often than men to regard drug education activities as very important. This holds at statistically significant levels with elementary school, middle school, high school, and adult drug education efforts. Also, women place special emphasis on child fingerprinting and (by a nearly significant amount) on bicycle safety lectures.

Again in Tab. 7.6, women tend more than men to place strong emphasis on residential patrols both in daytime and in the evening.

Encouragingly from the department's point of view, women do not show substantially greater feelings than men that more police department activity is needed in these areas.

There is also a very slight but consistent tendency for those 43 and older to attach great importance to police department activities. This holds for ceremonial and public relations activities as well as drug and crime prevention matters.

Finally, the 21 retired folks in the sample tend to regard most every police activity as very important, registering stronger support than any other vocational subgroup. The small sample size prevents definite conclusions here. But the tendency for this subgroup to support police efforts in all areas is consistent enough to suggest that retirees are potential allies of the local police department.

It also is of interest to compare subgroups with regard to naming certain types of crime as the "most serious crime problem" in town. To begin, Tab. 7.7 presents the frequency with which nine types of crime were mentioned in response to this item. (Incidentally, 200 people provided answers here. Only 14 couldn't or wouldn't do so.)

TABLE 7.6
Percentages of Men and Women Who Rate Selected Department Activities as Very Important

Activity	Men's Rating	Women's Rating	Probability of Difference Occurring by Chance
Activities Relating to Children			
Drug education programs held annually in elementary schools	61%	80%	.01
Drug education programs held annually in middle shcool presented at teacher's request	59%	77%	.02
High school drug education programs stressing the impact of drug-related arrests, especially on careers	64%	81%	.02
Lectures and literature that alert parents and other adults to signs of drug use among kids and teens	46%	67%	.01
Bicycle safety lectures given annually in elementary schools	26%	36%	.07
Providing child fingerprinting, done annually in schools and during crime prevention week at the Mall	47%	66%	.01
Patrols in Residential Areas			
Patrolmen on foot in the residential sections during the daytime	15%	23%	.01
Patrolling the residential sections on foot during the evening	33%	51%	.03

Note. Men responding to each item ranged from 91 to 92. Women responding ranged from 117 to 119. These figures are used as bases in computing the above percentages. Probabilities of chance occurrence are determined by chi-square, with 2 degrees of freedom, reflecting differences in proportions giving three responses: very important, fairly important, and not important.

Theft, including burglary and breaking and entering, was named by almost one fourth of all persons answering. Drugs and drug related crimes finished second with 21%, followed closely by vandalism at 19.5%.

The fourth most oft-mentioned type of crime in town, rape, showed up in 14% of all responses. Several rape cases had gained widespread publicity in the city over a period of 2 or 3 months prior to the survey. Also, apparent frequent talk about rape—especially so-called date rape—among university students may have helped raise this figure. (Although most responses placed in this category mentioned rape explicitly, a few dealt with sexual abuse and sexual harassment.)

About 8.5% of all responses touched on assault, 5.5% on murder. These figures

TABLE 7.7
Percentages of Respondents Naming Nine Types of Crime as "Most Serious Crime Problem" in the City

Type of Crime	Percentage Naming as Most Serious
Vandalism	19.5%
Drugs (including alcohol, drunk driving)	21.0%
Theft (including burglary, breaking and entering)	24.5%
Assault	8.5%
Murder	5.5%
Rape (including sexual abuse, harassment)	14.0%
Arson	1.0%
Disorderly conduct	2.0%
Miscellaneous (including shoplifting)	4.5%
	100.5%

Note. The base figure for computing all percentages is 200, that being the number of respondents who provided an answer on this item. Some respondents mentioned more than one type of crime, so the percentages sum to slightly more than 100.

may have been raised by several rather sensational murders in the area over a period of about 2 years.

Somewhat surprisingly, subgroups within the population differ very little in emphasis placed on various types of crime. None of the three predictor variables used here—sex, age, and vocation—correlate significantly, overall, with frequency of mention for various types of crime.

Some clusters of responses show up in ways that make sense:

Twenty-nine percent of white-collar workers and 34% of university students nominated vandalism as the most serious crime problem in the city. Presumably most white-collar people work in stores and offices. And police reports in the local newspaper suggest that vandalism occurs quite often in stores and on the university campus.

Three groups frequently named theft as the top crime problem. Thirty-six percent of all blue-collar workers, 44% of the university's faculty and staff people, and 35% of the retired folk gave this response. These nominations make sense if one assumes that theft is especially common in poorer residential areas and in university buildings such as the library (where theft had become something of a scandal). Also, it's often said that retired folks who travel a great deal or are physically infirm feel vulnerable to thievery.

Thirty-one percent of all university students, and 33% of all women surveyed, mentioned either rape or assault as the top crime problem. Women are especially apt to be victimized by such crimes. And as noted earlier, a good deal of concern about rape had shown up on campus in recent years.

Taken as a whole, the previous results suggest that people look at crime in rather personal terms. That is, each individual worries most about types of crime to which she or he feels most vulnerable.

Overall, however, citizens seemed to agree that theft, drugs, vandalism, and rape are the city's most serious crime problems. The data here on drugs certainly square with the high importance ascribed to drug education at all levels as reported earlier.

The literature review provides substantial evidence that Americans regard control of crime as the primary function of police. They expect that special importance would be accorded to types of crime identified in recent publicity as common and menacing both locally and nationwide. Further, it is reasonable to hypothesize that community service activities such as unlocking car doors and giving bicycle safety classes, not being tied to crime control in a clear way, would get lower priority.

In general, the findings reported previously support this line of reasoning. In Tab. 7.8, data provide a more explicit test. And, as expected, importance ratings fall in the following declining order of importance:

1. Education activities relating to drug, child, and sexual abuse. These problems had gained extensive recent publicity at the time of the survey. First, regarding child abuse, a television movie about the death of a boy named Adam, first shown in the mid-1980s, presumably helped move this topic onto the public agenda. Missing children signs had since shown up on gas station walls and cereal boxes, and in many other places. Second, drug and substance abuse had been the object of frequent news coverage in the mid-1980s, much of it about athletes and other prominent people. And third, sexual abuse included rape and sexual harassment in the work place—topics that had gotten much attention, nationally and locally, over several years. Athens had witnessed several highly publicized rape trials—along with widespread discussion of date rape on campus—during several months prior to the survey.

2. The general concept of crime detection and apprehension of criminals. As noted earlier, American police and citizens have long regarded this area as the core responsibility of police.

3. General service to the public. Despite their call for a primary focus on crime, the American people do view this realm with some favor. For example, in a 1982 national survey, 57% of all respondents advocated restricting police response almost entirely to alleged crimes. However, 41% of those who said they'd limit police response to crime calls still felt that cops should assist heart attack victims. And 69% believed cops should break up a noisy family argument late at night (Flanagan, 1985).

4. General communication activities such as speaking to service clubs and setting up a booth at an annual fall craft festival. Such efforts are apt to be of low priority, because they do not link up clearly with any aspect of the police role described in the literature as receiving high priority.

As shown in Tab. 7.8, results are as expected. Police department activities on drug, sexual, and child abuse (type 1) received the highest importance ratings, followed in order by general crime prevention (type 2), community service (type 3),

TABLE 7.8
Mean Importance Ratings for Four Types of Police Activity

Activity	Mean	Standard Deviation
Type 1--Education relating to drug, child, and sexual abuse		
Sexual assault (1 item dealing with department's sexual assault program run with two social service agencies)	2.73	0.443
Drug education (4 items focusing on high, middle, and elementary school children as well as parents)	2.62	0.422
Child safety (2 items, one on teaching children to react when approached by strangers and one on an annual project to obtain children's fingerprints)	2.61	0.486
Type 2--General crime prevention		
Theft prevention (3 items on a neighborhood watch program, consultation to crime-proof homes and businesses, and routine checks of vacant homes and businesses)	2.35	0.453
Business-section patrols (2 items dealing with regular patrols in general, and in the evening, for the city's business district)	2.33	0.525
Type 3--Community service		
Traffic control (2 items on traffic control at university events and at several local athletic contests)	2.35	0.555
Unlocking (1 item on unlocking car doors for motorists)	2.16	0.797
Transportation (2 items on escorting funeral processions and giving bicycle safety lectures in elementary schools)	1.96	0.562
Type 4--Communication and image building		
Public relations (2 items on operating a booth at a local craft festival and speaking at local events)	1.85	0.522

Note. All items involved 3 choices, with a value of 3 assigned to *very important,* 2 to *fairly important,*
and 1 to *not important.* Means given are averaged means for all items within a given index.

and image building (type 4). In fact, only one index, for traffic control, has a mean
that is equal to or greater than any mean within a lower-numbered type.

Further analysis revealed that these four types of items represented different
points on a single underlying dimension of police support. That is, most people who
supported type 4 activities (communication and image building) are strong fans in
that they attach high importance to all other types of police activity. A second group
downgraded type 4 but favored strong emphasis on both community support and
crime prevention. A third group emphasized only crime-related efforts (types 1 and
2). A fourth set emphasized only type 1 (highly publicized crime).

And finally, a fifth group of what might be called diehard foes of modern police
efforts turned thumbs down on all types of educational and service activities studied.

These data suggest a building block theory of police support. Only those who
favor crime prevention efforts are receptive to arguments in favor of community

service. Only those who accept a need for service efforts are apt to see a need for police communication efforts, and so on. A chief such as Glotz must gain appreciation for the importance (and probably merit, though we did not study that here) of police work at one level before moving on to the next step.

On the down side, of course, a kind of domino theory might apply. Widespread perception that local police are doing a bad job in crime control and prevention, especially on highly publicized, salient crimes, may lead to resentment of emphasis on other areas of police activity.

Further detail on this analysis is found in Culbertson and Shin (1989). We now consider some strategy and policy implications of the data taken as a whole.

IMPLICATIONS

We now summarize three key points from the literature review and local survey. We discuss 14 specific plans of action, as well as the reasoning behind them, which are linked to these points.

Please read each action plan. Then, drawing on the research and literature reported earlier, provide your own reasoning in support of or opposition to them. Only after that should you examine our reasoning.

Point 1—Citizens place high priority on crime prevention and protection, especially with regard to highly publicized problems of drug use, sexual abuse, and child safety.

In light of this finding, it is important to address key publics about the department's recent crime prevention, apprehension and conviction record, innovative crime prevention projects, and types of crime that are more important than is generally realized. This, in turn, suggests at least four courses of action.

Action 1—Prepare a press release at the beginning of the year emphasizing progress made to date in combating crime. Present this release to local reporters in person, using every opportunity to call it to their attention and answer their follow-up questions.

The release might report number of arrests made, number of convictions obtained, and number of reported crimes committed. Special emphasis would be placed on serious crimes, especially relating to drugs, child abuse, and sexual abuse.

Reasoning.   Research shows that people define crime fighting as the primary mission of law enforcement agencies. Also, they regard education and prevention in this area as very important. Thus, linking local police efforts to crime fighting and prevention should gain support for the department.

One related point merits attention. The story is apt to get good play if local media people follow up by calling and interviewing Chief Glotz to gain detail beyond that in the release. People tend to see something as important when they commit effort to it. Journalists are no exception. (Of course, such further contact is likely only if the police chief and relevant reporters know and respect each other. Fortunately, such respect has developed over time. It would not appear magically for one event or story.)

Also, exposure to this information may be enhanced if the police chief and his colleagues utilize channels other than straight news. For instance, they might convince a local semi-weekly paper to do a feature on a day in the life of a person on patrol, with pertinent statistics and interpretation inserted. They might appear on local radio and television talk shows to tell the crime prevention story, with emphasis on citizen input, where the department goes from here, and how.

Action 2—Fairly late in the program year, the department might tell in like manner how it serves the community in noncrime related ways.

Involvement in boy and girl scouting, supervision of bicycle races, escorting of parades, and other service activities might be stressed in releases, interviews, and brochures, but only after the crime-fighting story has been told emphatically.

Reasoning.   Research shows that people attach importance to service and public relations activities of the department **only if they believe it works hard and effectively in crime control and prevention.** If ratings in the latter areas are low, people might well see general service activities as wasteful and misdirected.

Action 3—Examine crime reports in the area to identify types of crime that are serious and fairly common but that are not seen as important by most local citizens.

Tab. 7.7 shows that very few people regard shoplifting or disorderly contact as the most serious crime problem. Yet merchants could doubtless testify that shoplifting costs them many thousands of dollars each year. Also, disorderly conduct often entails drinking and crowd behavior that can lead to more serious crimes such as murder and rape. Talk shows and press coverage could help gain appreciation for these points.

Reasoning.   The survey shows that people are somewhat self-centered in assessing the importance of police activities. For example, retired folks worry a lot about thievery, because they often travel, and their homes tend to be vacant.

Given this perspective, correct assessment of crime prevalence and importance to individual citizens, linked to department programs, should help build a foundation for public understanding and support.

Action 4—Promote and support fully the Drug Abuse Resistance Education (D.A.R.E.) program in Glotz's town and county.

This 5-year-old program, begun in Los Angeles, had been adopted in 49 states by the time of the study. Under it, a trained member of the local police department teaches a class on drug-related matters once each week for over 4 months in elementary schools. In addition, the D.A.R.E. officer visits other classrooms in school through the fifth grade to encourage young people to see police officers as friends, not as a threat.

Reasoning.   Survey results indicate local support for drug education efforts such as this is very strong. Also, D.A.R.E. offers national resources and training for a local officer at little or no expense to the city. The program provides a valuable opportunity for personal contact with impressionable children. All in all, D.A.R.E. seems to be a no-lose effort.

We now turn to a second major point gleaned from past research—this one stemming largely from studies throughout the nation that were reviewed earlier.

Point 2—Good police–community relations hinge largely on supportive, friendly, continuous two-way communication and personal contact between police and citizens. Several trends have detracted from such contact in recent years. Thus, special efforts are needed to rebuild it.

We now consider seven courses of action supported by this basic finding.

Action 5—Do what you can to promote academic work in human relations at nearby colleges and police academies that train police personnel. Encourage, or even require, the officers to take such training.

Reasoning.   As noted earlier, police curricula emphasize such training very little. Further, trends toward bureaucratization, professionalization, and widespread use of patrol cars limit friendly, supportive police–citizen contact. Yet such communication is very important in developing broadbased community support. Officers must seize every opportunity in this area. (Unfortunately, the department's most recent annual report indicates officers were completing very few hours of such training.)

Action 6—Provide pay and human relations training for auxiliary police personnel.

These volunteers are community members with some interest and experience in law enforcement. They help the department during major parades and other episodes requiring an unusually large officer force.

Reasoning.   Unfortunately, auxiliary personnel are sometimes portrayed locally as tough, macho individuals with little training or restraint. Such charges seem largely unfounded, but auxiliary personnel surely need continuous training. When they are on duty, volunteers represent the department. Their errors are every bit as harmful as mistakes by full-time officers.

At about the time of this study, Glotz recommended that the city pay auxiliary personnel who had put in at least 10 hours of volunteer service during the previous month. He reasoned that pay could enhance morale as well as willingness to under-go training.

Action 7—Encourage police involvement in community activities.

Such efforts range from folding bandages for cancer patients to regular participation in the school system's Parent-Teacher Organization, membership in service clubs such as Kiwanis and Rotary, and coaching of summer or after-school athletic teams.

Reasoning.   Such off-the-job contacts enhance police–community relations by showing that police are genuinely interested in the community's overall welfare. Appropriate civic involvement also shows that cops can be kind and humane without sacrificing their toughness and effectiveness as law enforcers.

Because police obviously are not being paid for volunteer work, such activities reflect sincere, genuine concern for local citizens. Of course, coercing personnel to volunteer might be counter-productive. People are not effective community volunteers unless they really put their "hearts" into it.

Action 8—Hold forums in which current and potential participants in Neighborhood Watch can dialogue with police officers about the need for and role of that program.

Free refreshments, Neighborhood Watch posters, promotion through church bulletins and Sunday Schools, and other techniques using support of local opinion leaders might encourage participation.

Reasoning.   The local survey shows widespread approval of and public emphasis on **Neighborhood Watch.** However, this approval had not translated into much real activity in recent years. It's not clear where the problem lay. But the potential is there given effective organizing by the department along with strong attempts to show why **Neighborhood Watch** is important and just what it can accomplish.

Action 9—Explore carefully with fellow police officials, the mayor, city council, and other local leaders the possibility of increasing foot patrols.

Such patrols, especially in the daytime, may need some selling to the public. The local survey shows rather lukewarm support for—though little real opposition to—such patrols. And patrolling on foot would require more personnel and dollars than does patrolling in cars.

However, Chief Glotz has often stationed officers on foot in certain crowded areas to enhance their visibility and discourage potentially unruly behavior. Perhaps selective foot patrolling at other times and places, as the budget allows, would provide supportive, informal, friendly contact with citizens.

Furthermore, survey findings suggest public willingness to at least listen when the department asks for more money to do patrolling. After all, only 4 patrol persons now operate on an average shift. Yet the public estimates, on the average, that 13 people are needed! Furthermore, the department's strongest supporters—older folk and women—see particular value in patrols. It seems imperative to cultivate these "fans."

Action 10—Recruit heavily through local senior centers and organizations with lots of older members for police volunteers in the Retired Senior Volunteer Program (RSVP).

At the time of the study, a handful of senior citizens were already working at such things as maintaining a list of cars that had been towed and sending notices related to speeding tickets.

Reasoning. This core of **RSVP** workers can help recruit fellow seniors, holding down departmental costs in the process. And of course, cost cutting is a popular theme among local media and citizens. Furthermore, the survey suggests that older citizens are staunch supporters of a wide variety of police activities. This, coupled with the time that retirees have on their hands, suggests that many might be honored to serve as volunteers.

Action 11—Examine carefully the feasibility of a Boy Scout Explorer Post within the department.

In this program, senior Scouts ages 15 to 20, explore career opportunities in law enforcement. Also, they are trained to help the department in nonthreatening activities such as escorting parades and supervising bicycle races.

Reasoning. This program provides direct day-to-day behavioral involvement—**bridging experiences** with the department—for an important segment of the community. Such direct involvement could create stronger, more loyal support than would even admiring attention from the outside.

To be sure, some effort and cost are involved. One could not expect to recruit a large number of **Explorers,** as high-school age kids apt to find police work attractive doubtless are often busy with school and other activities. However, **Explorers** should make the program cost effective by providing some volunteer help. As with **D.A.R.E.,** this program seems to be a can't-miss proposition.

We now turn to a third basic point supported by research and arguments given earlier.

Point 3—Certain cultural beliefs (held by most people within the society about the role of government and police) and subcultural beliefs (held by those in law enforcement work as well as in other local groups) affect people's views of any police department. Such beliefs deserve close attention in police–community relations.

Proposed action 12 relates to local subcultures, whereas numbers 13 and 14 derive from a belief held widely throughout the United States that government should be altruistic, serving the public rather than itself.

Action 12—Make a special effort to talk informally, regularly, and in depth with members of and personnel who have frequent contact with the area's three subcultural groups.

As described earlier, these groups include residents of nearby farms and villages (hilljacks), nonuniversity people in town (townies), and university students as well as faculty members (gownies).

Informal contacts at barber shops, churches, stores, and other gathering places help police tap into local networks. Also, fairly regular, planned visits might occur with school principals, township and village officials, welfare workers, ministers, and others in service-oriented work. Conversations can focus on ways in which the police department might meet area needs and on ways to enhance understanding of one segment by another.

Reasoning.   As noted earlier, the three segments appear to have different perspectives on laws, education, and other matters. Intermingling of the three sets of school children at an early age apparently creates problems in family relations and school performance as well as crime. Mutual understanding among the three groups coupled with separate programming for them may help.

For example, police programs might focus on police-related vocational training in outlying areas but on more academic analysis of drugs and other matters (causes and solutions at a societal level) in city schools, especially in more advanced, academically oriented courses.

Of course, the police department's jurisdiction does not extend into outlying rural areas, though some of its problems undoubtedly originate there. Cooperation with the local sheriff's department and nearby organizations is crucial.

Action 13—Respond with great care and some skepticism when area locksmiths and wrecker companies urge or pressure the department to quit unlocking car doors when citizens call.

Groups in the private sector have lobbied recently to prohibit police department opening of car doors. Chief Glotz reports that his personnel do this, on average, about five times each day.

Reasoning.   To be sure, Glotz may be tempted to cut back on this activity given his tight budget. A patrol person who unlocks a car door could use that time to enforce the law.

However, the local survey indicates widespread approval of and high emphasis on this particular police service. People who need to unlock car doors are often in a hurry, and **effective public relations requires that one look at the issue from their point of view.** They are apt to resent being told by police that they must call and wait on a locksmith or wrecker company. Receiving a bill from that entrepreneur would not reduce their resentment, especially because they have become accustomed to free service from police. Explanations that police are required to refrain from such activities by law might seem hard to swallow, as people assume the police themselves enforce that law!

Also, as noted earlier, cutting back such services runs counter to the basic belief of most Americans that government should **serve them.**

Action 14—Recommend strongly that the city council at least think twice before toughening its policy on releasing impounded autos only upon payment by owners of all their fines.

At the time of the study, city law required that the police department return impounded cars as soon as owners pay their towing bills. Some council members favored a change here to help the city collect fines so as to gain badly needed revenue. And, prior to the survey, Chief Glotz had spoken in favor of such a move.

Reasoning.   However, more than a few survey respondents suggested such a move would prove to some that the police serve city government, not citizens.

Further, in depressed areas such as this one, some people may need their cars and trucks to earn money needed to pay fines! Thus great care is in order here.

This concludes Glotz's basic list of action plans building on the research and literature review. Please develop other ideas and show how the study provides a rationale for or against each of them.

We now turn to a more detailed look at how the analysis thus far has used specific points analyzed earlier in the chapters outlining the social, political, and economic contexts.

ELEMENTS OF THE SPE CONTEXT—A LOOK BACK

Thus far we have mentioned contextual elements only in passing as we looked at prospective actions. A brief concluding discussion of these elements may now help organize the analysis and suggest avenues for future research.

First, consider the basic belief, documented in previous research as well as indirectly in our own, that American police should focus primarily on catching crooks and bringing them to justice.

As held by members of the public at large, this belief qualifies as Type 1 (dealing with institutions and how people relate to them) cultural and subcultural beliefs as defined in chapter 4. However, when we focus on the acceptance of this priority within the police vocation, we are dealing with a Type 4 belief (held by those within the vocation to define their own behavior). It is reasonable to conjecture that police hold this belief more intensely and firmly than does the public at large. That's because police have undergone intense socialization vis-a-vis police behavior whereas most citizens have not. Such a difference in what Grunig (1983) called *involvement* causes problems in public understanding and support. Police personnel may place high priority on achieving convictions, whereas citizens do not.

Second, we have also discussed a widely held belief, called altruistic democracy by Gans (1980, pp. 43–45), that government should seek to serve society and not primarily themselves or government. This qualifies as a Type 1 belief when viewed as being held by most members of the public at large and as Type 3 when studied in terms of police themselves as belief holders.

Such possible moves as cutting back on unlocking of car doors and impounding cars until all of the owners' fines are paid were questioned, because in many eyes, they run counter to this belief. Once again, police must consider a possible divergence between their own interpretations and those of the public at large. Chief Glotz may not see rigorous impounding as failing to serve the public at large. But some citizens are apt to hold such a view.

Third is the expectation that police be empathic and understanding in dealing with people. We conjecture that within society as a whole, many people accept this belief (Type 1, as it deals with institutions and how people relate to them). Yet many police trained in rigorous, tough law enforcement reject such an expectation as unrealistic; after all, crooks can shoot police when police try to reason with and understand them. Viewed in that light, Type 4 beliefs on this matter differ from Type 1, causing potential public relations problems.

Fourth, it has been suggested that police and social workers differ on such basic societal values as rugged individualism and the question of whether it's more important to protect society or a suspect. Such beliefs fall into Type 3 (cultural beliefs regarding proper standards of conduct and goals) and affect occupational behavior much as cultural beliefs spelled out in chapter 4 affect the thinking of journalists.

Clearly such beliefs serve as schemata, affecting which information people attend to and how they interpret it. Also, they are viewed as standards of comparison. For example, someone expecting a cop to be understanding may have a high *adaptation level* on "understandingness" so even a minor act of misunderstanding seems important and major.

Attributes such as bravery, courage, and manliness hold different levels of importance or salience for police and for citizens as a whole. Such contrasts in frame of reference also tend to hamper police–community relations.

Grunig's (1983) situational-beliefs theory is also useful as Chief Glotz attempts to plan programs and evaluate their acceptance or impact. Specifically:

> Genuine dialogue with local citizens, as advocated in our discussion of townies, gownies, and hilljacks, would undoubtedly raise questions about public needs and ways to solve them. Answers to such questions are often vague and unclear. As that becomes apparent, problem recognition increases, leading to active information seeking. Such a result is healthy in the long run.
>
> Such projects as RSVP, Explorer Scouts, and Neighborhood Watch should increase citizen involvement in police department activities, yielding greater information seeking, understanding, and loyal support. Also, these citizen activities lead people to feel they have some impact on police affairs and law enforcement, thus reducing constraint recognition and enhancing information seeking.

The matter of social contacts also showed up in our analysis. In particular, activities were evaluated on two bases. First, did they encourage police–citizen interaction in an informal, spontaneous way without formal rules or any implication that cops have great status and power over citizens or vice versa? Second, did the contacts occur in an atmosphere free of threat and coercion? A yes answer in each case should ultimately enhance mutual understanding.

Heavy emphasis has been placed here on the social context, perhaps most important to the chief as he seeks to define local needs and formulate or evaluate programs that meet them. However, in the economic realm, Glotz's departmental annual report for the year following the survey reveals several points that, with a little addition and long division, suggest some points apt to make citizens and city officials unlikely to cut funding and be somewhat receptive to small proposed increases:

1. As with most service agencies, human resources bulk large. In fact, salaries for the 26 paid personnel in the department accounted for 87% of the general funds available to the police department. This points up the importance of credibility assigned to police personnel. If employees are thought to be doing a good job, most money in the department budget is likely to be seen as well spent.

2. In all, police protection in the area costs about $1.05 million per year for roughly 15,000 citizens. This figures out to about $70 per person, which is not a lot in this dangerous, crime-ridden era.

3. The department's operational budget, covering all expenses other than salaries and benefits for personnel, totalled only about $142,000 for the year. The department recovered about 80% of that, $112,000, in stolen property. Because this property presumably went back to its owners, citizens as a whole really had to kick in only 20% of the operational budget, about $30,000, without "repayment."

4. Average salary for the department's 26-person work force was only $26,000, which is fairly low for skilled people working in a high-risk, dangerous occupation.

5. Since Ronald Reagan assumed the presidency in 1981, state and federal funds and grant monies for local law enforcement have largely dried up. The concept of revenue sharing by Washington has gone out of favor. Thus local police departments seeking expanded resources must "help themselves."

Political Maneuvers: A Process View

Turning to the political context, Chief Glotz must deal with his department chairman (called the city service director) and the mayor in formulating annual budget requests. Glotz first outlines a proposed budget, item by item, with justifications spelled out. The city service director then revises and shapes requests in light of what he believes the mayor and city council are apt to accept.

Next, both of these officials huddle with the mayor and hammer out a version that all three can live with. After this, the executive branch presents a single, unified request to a three-person finance committee of the city council. Finally, after negotiations within the finance committee and between that committee and the mayor, the annual budget goes before the seven-person council for a vote.

An articulate young councilman and finance committee member had this to say about the process:

> As is almost universal in such cases, Chief Glotz enters negotiations realizing that compromise will be essential. Thus he may ask for $15,000 for a given program knowing that he can and probably will have to live with, say, $12,000.

Such "over-shooting" in anticipation of later trimming tends to be done primarily by the three executive-branch officials—the chief, safety-service director and mayor. Line items rarely change much after the budget reaches council. The mayor usually insists that her department chairs work out firm requests among themselves and with her—and that they not go over her head to council members. (The mayor's predecessor had permitted some departmental appeals to council, sometimes creating a rather chaotic, unpredictable budgetary process.)

Council does occasionally question specific line items, seeking justifications from Chief Glotz. However, such questions are rarely pointed or very detailed. In fact, council has usually passed line items on service and educational programming in recent years by votes of 7–0 or 6–1.

The young councilman emphasized three favorable aspects of recent police department planning and relations with council.

First, Glotz, a fine administrator, has done very well in keeping track of federal, state, and other possible grants that might improve programs and ease strain on the city budget. The D.A.R.E. program, mentioned earlier, is a prime example. The council respects this effort and tends to regard budget requests as prudent, partly because it feels Glotz has explored all avenues for funding.

Second, D.A.R.E. and other programs require long-term planning. Educational efforts need that and patience, because they seldom yield tangible results immediately. Improved planning has helped the department become more proactive and not spend most of its time, as in the past, responding to crises as they arise.

Third, the department received a vote of confidence several years prior to the current study. At that time, a charter commission looking into possible changes in the form of city government considered and rejected a proposal for a civilian review board. Such boards exist in many cities to hear citizen complaints about the police, and they generally come into being where complaints are numerous.

"Some of us now on council were part of that process," the previously mentioned young councilman recalled. "I opposed the review board because I saw no need for it. There simply were not enough complaints to warrant such action. That conclusion, apparently shared by others, helped build a positive feeling about our town's police–community relations."

In conclusion, Glotz can count on a supportive though sometimes skeptical legislature (council). He has both a need and an opportunity, therefore, to concentrate heavily on developing good rapport with the mayor. And he obviously commands her respect and admiration.

REFERENCES

Baker, M. (1985). Cops: Their lives in their own words. New York: Simon & Schuster.

Bard, M. (1973). The role of law enforcement in the helping system. In J. R. Snibbe & H. M. Snibbe (Eds.), *The urban policeman in transition: A psychological and sociological review* (pp. 407–20). Springfield, IL: Thomas.

Billy Holliday of the NYPD. (1985, September). *Ebony*, pp. 46–50.

Bloom, A. (1987). *The closing of the American mind*. New York: Simon & Schuster.

The "blues" on beat street. (1985, January 29). *Newsweek*, p. 49.

Cain, M. E. (1973). *Society and the policeman's role*. London: Routledge & Kegan Paul.

Culbertson, H. M., & Shin, H. (1989). Police in America: a study of changing institutional roles as viewed by constituents. In J. E. Grunig & L. A. Grunig (Eds.), *Public Relations Research Annual*, (Vol. 1, pp. 155–174). Hillsdale, NJ: Lawrence Erlbaum Associates.

Erskine, H. (1974). The polls: Fear of violence and crime. *Public Opinion Quarterly, 38*, 131–145.

Erskine, H. (1982, September). Opinion Roundup. *Public Opinion Quarterly, 5*, 26.

Fink, J., & Sealy, G. (1974). *The community and the police: Conflict or cooperation?* New York: Wiley.

Flanagan, T. J. (1985). Consumer perspectives on police operational strategy. *Journal of Police Science and Administration, 13*, 10–21.

Gans, H. J. (1980). *Deciding what's news*. New York: Vintage.

Grunig, J. E. (1983). Communication behavior and attitudes of environmental publics: Two studies. *Journalism Monographs, 81*.

Grunig, J. E., & Hunt, T. (1984). *Managing public relations*. New York: Holt, Rinehart & Winston.

Police under fire: Fighting back. (1978, April 3). *U.S. News and World Report*, pp. 37–40.

Pugh, G. M. (1986). The good police officer: Qualities, roles & concepts. *Journal of Police Science and Administration, 14*, 1–5.

Trojanowicz, R. C. (1973). Police community relations: Problems and process. In J. R. Snibbe & H. M. Snibbe (Eds.), *The urban policeman in transition: A psychological and sociological review* (pp. 119–138). Springfield, IL: Thomas.

Viviano, F. (1981, September). What's happening in murder city? *The Progressive*, pp. 38–42.

Walthier, R. H., McCune, S. D., & Trojanowicz, R. C. (1973). The contrasting occupational cultures of policemen and social workers. In J. R. Snibbe & H. M. Snibbe (Eds.), *The urban policeman in transition: A psychological and sociological review* (pp. 260–280). Springfield, IL: Thomas.

Whittington, H. G. (1971). The police: Ally or enemy of the comprehensive community health center? *Mental Hygiene, 55*, 55–59.

8 Livestock Association Magazines: A Tie That Binds, Informs, and Promotes

As the decade of the 1980s began, magazines and newspapers serving the beef, swine, and sheep producing portions of the North American livestock industry faced a series of social, political, and economic challenges that mirror those faced by other segments of public relations and the media.

First, these magazines and newspapers need to improve their writing, editing, and layout/design as technological changes continued to sweep through the communications industry. Conover (1990) detailed these dramatic changes along with the difficult decision of whether to adopt desktop publishing. Watkins (1991) offered evidence that the 1980s saw widespread adoption of new technology by public relations, trade/association, and consumer/newsstand magazines. Over 80% of the magazines responding to her survey in 1990 used desktop publishing for various editorial, design, and production functions, compared with relatively few adopters in 1985.

Second, these publications have to reconcile the sometimes conflicting perceptions of their staffs on two topics frequently discussed throughout the public relations and mass communication industries. The first topic is external and focuses on the role these publications play for readers in the livestock industry. Understandably, organizations are continually evaluating their purposes or reasons for being. Livestock publications are no exception, and again understandably, staff members of a given magazine often differ as to what their purposes are. As with other segments of public relations, the livestock publication industry serves varied needs in varied ways. The next section of this chapter outlines several structural dimensions of this field.

The other major topic is internal and centers on the changing demographic and psychographic characteristics of livestock publication staffers, particularly in terms

152

of gender. Specifically, an increasing number of women are entering agricultural journalism, and livestock editors differ as to the potential impact of this trend.

Finally, the editors and publishers face the challenge of meeting the needs of readers and advertisers as the dynamics of communication in an increasingly fragmented society change rapidly. These agricultural communicators have to become more "audience oriented" at a time when the audience increasingly tunes in and out, pays attention at differing levels of intensity, and demonstrates different capabilities for understanding (Vivian, 1991).

To help those in the livestock publishing industry meet these challenges, a multifaceted research and consulting program was initiated in the early 1980s to answer questions related to these challenges. This chapter reports many findings of this effort and demonstrates the usefulness of examining public relations issues as to their social, political, and economic contexts.

THE LARGER CONTEXT

Although all segments of agricultural communication are important to the economy, specialized livestock magazines have received particular research attention because of their pivotal role in the diffusion of agricultural information. Drawing on previous research that indicates farmers' sources of information vary from topic to topic, Adams and Parkhurst (1984) asked Nebraska farmers and ranchers which kinds of information they consider to be important and where they get it.

The study shows that farmers and ranchers saw clear differences among communication channels. Further, they rated farm magazines as significantly more important than all other channels as information sources. This held with respect to the many specific information needs about which the researchers asked. Thus Adams and Parkhurst concluded that land-grant universities (which have large agricultural components) should expand their use of farm magazines in public relations efforts.

These specialized publications can also be looked at from an industrial publication viewpoint. The livestock industry is a multibillion dollar segment of the agricultural industry and is responsible for the breeding and marketing of cattle, hogs, sheep, and horses. As with other important industrial segments, an active press covers the livestock industry. For the most part, this press includes magazines, although some publications use a tabloid or *maga-paper* format. Also, as with other industrial publications, some are horizontal in that they cover wide segments of the industry whereas others are vertical and cover only narrow segments.

Many livestock publications function within independent firms and rely exclusively on advertising and circulation revenue. However, many others are sponsored by state cattle associations, breed organizations, etc. This latter group of periodicals resemble many other "house organs" in providing association members with information and ideas designed to increase their involvement in association-sanctioned activities (Cutlip, Center, & Broom, 1985, pp. 500–507).

The editors of these publications serve many masters. As Cutlip et al. (1985) put it, "The association . . . serves membership interests that may differ widely, shaped by regional influences, particular specialties within a craft, or varying political, ethnic, or proprietary predispositions" (p. 501).

Grunig and Hunt (1984, p. 254) suggested this can put a lot of pressure on the association public relations person responsible for designing the overall communications program. These authors pointed out that members are highly autonomous and can join or drop out of an association at will. They recommended that the communication program be designed to get helpful information to members when they need it.

However, this is easier said than done. Cutlip et al. (1985) noted that it is a lengthy process, because the needs of all association members must be represented in the decision-making process. Unfortunately, because of circumstances common to all associations, it is hard for the editor of a livestock association magazine to resist pressure from members who consider themselves more "equal" than others. That is, often those who serve as association officers and leaders may not be representative of the total membership. But because of their service to the association, they believe their concerns should receive much attention in association publications.

Finally, livestock publications—as public relations magazines or independent media—can be looked upon as performing a service journalism function for readers. This orientation requires editors to feature technical and educational information in the hope that members will read it and then take specific action to adopt "new and improved" methods or techniques. Reed (1990) made the case that service journalism often must provide a great deal of what Lemert (1981) called *mobilizing information*. Such content tells readers how to act given an existing preference or attitude.

Reed correctly noted that service journalism is only one of several strategies that an editor uses to attract readers. Furthermore, the strategy is often easier to articulate than to accomplish. The editor who uses it must decide which type of service information should be published, which readers it should be directed to, and how large its role should be in the overall editorial mix.

The framework for the research and consulting effort reported in this chapter involved two organizations: the Livestock Publications Council (LPC) and the *Angus Journal,* a magazine published by the American Angus Association. As the name implies, LPC is a collection of over 100 publications covering the livestock industry. The Council is headquartered in Encinitas, California, and its members include publications focusing on single breeds of livestock and multibreed publications serving various segments of the industry, as well as state, regional, and national livestock-related association magazines.

A major purpose of the Livestock Publications Council is to provide continuing education for the editorial and advertising staffs of its member publications. One step toward this end is an annual contest that provides editors with an independent evaluation of the "General Excellence" of their publications in relation to their purposes and circulation size. In addition, editors submit entries in over 30 writing, design, and advertising categories for additional evaluation.

The judging and evaluation are conducted by magazine, public relations, and advertising professionals who are independent of the livestock industry, as well as journalism educators who specialize in these areas. The process culminates in a series of annual meetings and seminars where the evaluations are discussed and winners receive awards. Coordinating this project gave the author an opportunity to develop a comprehensive research program.

Part of this research effort was an in-depth study of the public relations and communication program of the American Angus Association. With more than 30,000 members, it is the largest beef-registry association in the world. Founded over 100 years ago, the association serves the Angus cattle breeder by maintaining breeding records as well as marketing and advertising Angus beef. In addition, the association assists individual breeders in managing their farm and ranch operations. A key vehicle for providing such assistance is the *Angus Journal,* a monthly four-color magazine containing articles, editorial comment, and advertising.

The researcher sought answers to four basic research questions in his decade-long consulting and research program. We now discuss the methods used in regard to each of these questions, along with major findings.

IMPROVING MAGAZINES IN A HIGH-TECH ERA

1. How Can Editors Improve the Writing, Editing, and Design of Publications While Adopting Desktop Publishing Technology?

This question was defined and preliminary answers sought through a detailed literature review and thoughtful dialogue during meetings and training sessions with editors. A summary of this analysis follows.

Beginning in the early 1980s, the question was raised formally as part of the Livestock Publications Council's annual meetings and informally among editors and their staff. For instance, as the decade progressed, a growing number of annual meeting sessions were devoted to this topic, and exhibits of new hardware and software increased dramatically in number.

Notice that the question is not, "Will the new technology improve the writing, editing, and design of publications?," although that question was voiced as well. Basically, editors saw the new technology as potentially useful in mechanical production (typesetting, paste-up, printing, etc.) but not in writing, editing, and designing their publications.

Second, for many editors in this group, the question was not "if" but "when" they would employ the new technology. Consequently, they focused on maintaining and enhancing editorial quality in the face of what many recognized would be dramatic changes in noneditorial areas.

A comprehensive answer to this question is beyond the scope of this chapter. However, we can summarize two major themes that emerged regularly when consultants, vendors, and other editors who had adopted desktop publishing spoke about this issue. These themes are consistent with those detected by Watkins (1991) in her evaluation of other public relations and trade association magazines.

First, early adopters of the new technology found it did not reduce the need for thorough grounding in the fundamentals of writing, editing, and design. Even as the new technology was adopted by member publications, evaluators in the annual publications contest saw a need for LPC member staffers to improve their fundamental skills and techniques. Consequently, the LPC continuing education effort focused heavily on these fundamentals.

Watkins (1991) also reported that the most effective magazine designers who use desktop publishing understand the principles of design and use the computer to implement those principles. The computer has limitations, and good designers cannot simply turn over control of the design process to a machine.

The second major theme in discussions of desktop publishing centered on the need for realistic expectations of what the new technology can do. Here, Watkins' (1991) retrospective was particularly relevant. Early in the decade, vendors, in particular, touted desktop publishing as a revolutionary force in livestock publishing. These early presentations sometimes implied that all you need to do is tap a computer key and your publication will magically appear. However, experience soon showed LPC members that the new technology did not match these early expectations.

Again, Watkins' study (1991) supports this finding. For instance, she reported that many magazine editors and art directors made the move to desktop publishing, because they believed it would save time and money as well as provide more control over their publications. She reported, however, that although magazines have saved time and added flexibility, they have not saved money.

Furthermore, she reported there were major changes in the staff structure and assignment of responsibilities for design and production of the magazines. New computers and software allow one person to accomplish tasks formerly requiring several staffers. Consequently, there was a reduction in staff or a reassignment of duties that, in many cases, increased the workload of designers. For instance, many are not only designing the magazine but are serving as the typesetters as well.

We now turn to a second question to which we applied a two-pronged research strategy. First, we conducted open-ended interviews with a small sample of livestock editors to define issues that they defined as salient for the industry that they served. And second, 29 veteran livestock magazine editors filled out a structured questionnaire indicating their perceptions of audience members' situational beliefs, defined below on the issues identified in step 1.

2. What Perceptions do Livestock Publication Staff Members Have of the Role Their Publication Plays for Readers?

Although this question is of particular interest to those in the livestock publishing industry, it is also important to the public relations practitioner seeking to communicate with audiences of specialized publications. Obviously one cannot really reach readers of a magazine with information important to them unless one convinces editors that their readers perceive such importance. Awareness of perceptions held by one group of editors provides an understanding of the processes that generate these beliefs among other types of editors.

Further, members of specialized magazine audiences are bound together by common interests and activities. They need to communicate about specific topics, and the communication often results in specific behavior. Thus public relations practitioners need to consider such audiences as publics.

Consequently, Grunigs' (1984) situational theory for explaining the communication behavior of publics is particularly helpful. As detailed in several other chapters of this volume (see especially chapter 4), Grunig suggested that four independent variables help explain when and how people communicate about specific issues or topics, and when they have thoughts about these issues. These variables are problem recognition (whether a person has a need for information and stops to think about an issue), level of involvement (whether the person connects with the issue), constraint recognition (whether the person thinks substantial personal control can be exerted to help resolve the issue), and the presence of a referent criterion (whether the person thinks there is a solution for the issue or problem).

Grunigs' (1984) theory has utility for explaining the communication behavior of specialized magazine publics. Given that overall readers have a degree of involvement with the general subject matter of the specialized publication, they should be concerned about specific issues or topics within the framework of the general subject matter. Further, it is reasonable to assume that the readers' level of involvement and perceived constraint will vary from topic to topic, just as will the readers' perceptions of problem solutions.

As for determining how this relates to the editorial process in specialized magazines (and the chance for the public relations person to convey a message to the magazines' readers), Culbertson's research (1983) on the role an editor's perceptions of audience preferences play in editing behavior is relevant. (This research is discussed in chapter 4.)

Using a large sample of newspaper reporters and editors, he tested a News-Orientation Model that has three elements: the journalist's own interests, the journalist's perception of audience interests, and then the journalist's news judgment decisions. Culbertson's model allows for three measures: *congruency* (similarity between the journalist's interests and those attributed to the audience), *followership* (the extent to which the journalist's actual news judgment decisions resemble perceived audience interests), and *autonomy* (degree of similarity between items selected and the journalist's own interests).

Culbertson (1983) noted that traditional news decision making involves high followership on the part of editors. Indeed, he found that overall followership scores exceeded autonomy among newspaper reporters and editors.

Combining the issue-oriented thinking of Grunig and the followership notions of Culbertson, we believe it valid to assume that specialized magazine editors are deeply concerned about which issues or topics are of concern to readers. In part, such concern entails editor interest in identifying: (a) issues over which readers feel they have some control, (b) issues in which readers are likely to have high involvement, and (c) topics/problems for which readers feel they have solutions.

Further, it is reasonable to speculate that, if publications really serve, they should almost always help readers develop solutions to their problems. Furthermore, editors are likely to claim some credit for helping readers find these solutions. In other words, editors of specialized magazines believe their publications play an important role in this process for the readers.

There is a certain functional logic in this interpretation. The more a magazine meets needs and serves a function for the readers, the more likely it is to succeed as a business venture.

STUDIES OF EDITOR BELIEFS

Identifying Salient Issues

To test these assumptions, we surveyed a sample of editors, who were members of the Livestock Publications Council, regarding their perceptions associated with specific social, political, and economic issues identified by the Council and government officials as being important to livestock ranchers.

Although each issue is associated primarily with one social, political, or economic context, the issues are multifaceted and are related to the other contexts as well. The selected issues were:

Federal and State Regulation of the Livestock Industry.   As with other industries, all segments of the livestock industry (individual ranchers, feedlot operators, meat packers, etc.) have to deal with increased governmental regulation.

Although many individual ranchers are opposed to governmental intervention for philosophical and political reasons, the negative economic impact of such regulations is cited most often as the primary reason for opposition to most such regulation. For instance, individual ranchers believed rules and regulations associated with the use of pesticides, herbicides, and other chemicals used in their daily operations increase the total cost of producing their product. Resulting high costs, in turn, result in lower demand by consumers.

The Marketing of Surplus Dairy Cattle for Beef.   For many reasons, including an oversupply of dairy products and the difficulties associated with running a small dairy farm in an age of big agricultural operations, the federal government developed a dairy herd buy-out policy in the early 1980s. This program allows for controlled dispersal of dairy herds across the nation. Beef cattle ranchers were not happy with this program, because most surplus dairy cattle were processed for beef, thereby depressing the price the rancher could get for his product.

A Growing Emphasis on Nonred Meat Sources of Protein.   Many in the livestock industry viewed this as a social and political issue with severe economic implications. For a variety of reasons (including a concern for animal rights and the growing awareness of the link between red meat and harmful cholesterol), Americans began to decrease their consumption of beef during the 1980s. Naturally, beef ranchers were concerned about this.

The Increase in Meat Imports.   This issue was viewed as being primarily political but with economic consequences. The 1980s may be remembered as the decade when the interdependence of nations within a global economy became apparent to the average United States citizen. In the case of beef farmers, the free trade agreements that made it possible for them to choose from a wide variety of imported consumer goods also made it possible for beef to be imported from Latin America and Australia along with other parts of the world. Again, beef producers worried about the effect on prices for domestic beef.

Herd Improvement Techniques.   Although there is a degree of romanticism associated with the "bucolic life down on the farm," today's cattle ranch is a high-tech operation that requires skillfully trained, knowledgeable personnel. Ranchers recognize that they need to implement the latest herd-improvement techniques, such as those associated with genetic engineering, if their individual operations are to remain competitive in the marketplace.

Breed Promotional Activities.   As with other animals, there is a variety of beef-cattle breeds. Each breed has distinct, if sometimes subtle, characteristics that make it more or less profitable for a specific size of ranch, geographic location, or type of beef product. Breeders, who in essence continually develop the seed stock for these specific breeds, depend on their breed associations to develop and promote a brand loyalty for their products. Increased promotion of their breed often results in increased demand for their products and consequently a higher price.

Further, there is a social and cultural dimension to breed public relations. In addition to promoting product differences among breeds, breed associations also serve as cheerleaders for those raising each breed by identifying and promoting the product differentiation of ranchers and producers. For instance, one breed association may promote the willingness to experiment of its ranchers whereas another may focus on adherence to traditional values among its members.

Also, breed associations promote local, regional, and national meetings and gatherings that have social and educational purposes. The associations offer scholarships for ranchers' children, have divisions for subsets of their members (teenagers and women, for instance), and in general, promote ranching and farming as a way of life as well as a profitable occupation.

Animal Rights and Animal Health.   Many ranchers see this as another social issue with drastic economic implications for beef producers. Animal rights activists, those opposed to the consumption of red meat, some medical and nutritional researchers, and many beef consumers oppose regular use of antibiotics, growth hormones, and other drugs in beef production. However, beef producers argue these supplements are necessary to maintain animal health and increase marketable weight.

High Interest Rates and Other Costs of Credit.   Obviously, this is an economic issue. However, like the other issues, it is multifaceted. At times in the 1980s, interest rates were so high that ranchers could not purchase new equipment or land in order to maintain or expand their operations. Many small family farms and the way of life associated with them were threatened when ranchers found it impossible to make principal and interest payments on the tractors and pick-up trucks needed to carry out their operation.

Meat Grading.   This issue, which related to how the federal government rated beef (good, choice, prime, etc.), seems at first glance to be straightforward. However, it was viewed by the beef industry as an economic issue with highly political overtones. The process through which the government decided how to rate beef was seen as subject to political pressure. This political process had economic consequences, because beef producers are paid more for prime than for choice beef.

The meat-grading issue was complicated by its social context dimension: many nutritionists began to advocate the consumption of the leaner, less expensive cuts of beef. Although beef producers responded to this new demand by breeding cattle with less fat in their meat, these new consumer demands (which many ranchers considered to be based on scare tactics) disrupted traditional marketing methods.

Trade Association Activities.   The previous discussion makes it clear that the livestock industry faced many difficulties at the time of this research and consulting project. Like other industries, the livestock business has a number of trade associations (such as the Beef Council) whose purpose is to develop advertising, marketing, public relations, and lobbying programs for the industry in general. These trade associations are supported financially by those at all levels in the livestock industry.

As might be expected, the complexity of the problems facing the livestock industry do not allow for easy solutions. Also as might be expected, there are differing opinions about how to go about developing procedures to solve the problems. Consequently, livestock industry personnel engage in much formal and informal discussion about trade association activities.

Studying Editor Assumptions About Readers' Situational Beliefs

Methodology.   Using these social, political, and economic issues as a base, we adapted a procedure proposed to measure situational variables (Grunig & Hunt, 1984). As Grunig noted, past research involving gatekeepers relied primarily on attitudinal variables. However, his work and situational theory suggest that perceptions related to specific issues are better predictors of communicator behavior.

The sample for this exploratory and descriptive study consisted of 34 editors of single-breed livestock magazines. Twenty-nine, or 85% of these editors participated by completing and returning a mail questionnaire. Nearly 83% of all respondents had attended college, with the largest percentage majoring in animal science (24.1%). Other majors included agricultural journalism (17.2%) and journalism (13.8%).

The respondents were veterans in the livestock publishing business, having worked in this area for an average of nearly 12 years and in a management position at their publication for an average of more than 7 years.

To get at problem recognition, editors were asked how often they thought their readers stopped to think about each of the 10 issues. To indicate constraint recognition, editors told whether they thought their readers could do anything personally that would make a difference on handling of issues. For level of involvement, editors were asked to what extent they saw a connection between each issue and the personal situations of their readers. Finally, to detect the presence of referent criteria, editors were asked how definite an idea readers had about what should be done in these areas.

In a related effort, editors were asked what role they thought their publications had played or were playing in helping readers develop solutions to problems related to the specified issues.

Results.   As we expected, editors felt their readers differed as to level of problem recognition, constraint recognition, involvement, and access to referent criteria on each issue or topic.

Furthermore, editors believed their publications had differing degrees of influence on readers for different issues. Specifically, the more editors perceived readers as recognizing an issue/topic, being involved, having a solution, and/or being able to implement the solution, the more likely the editors were to believe their publications helped develop solutions for readers.

We also found that editors perceived their readers as being most concerned with issues and topics that were "close by" and "personally manageable." Issues and topics (like herd improvement techniques) that readers deal with on their ranches or farms ranked high on the theoretical dimensions. Issues and topics that were distant and difficult for the reader to control (like governmental regulation) ranked low on the theoretical dimensions.

GENDER-RELATED BELIEFS

We now turn to a third research question central to the analysis.

3. What is the distribution of males and females employed in the livestock publishing field, and what are staff perceptions of the impact of gender on such work-related variables as employment status, work environment, and job satisfaction?

In a comprehensive analysis of women in the media, Lynch-Paley (1991) explained why questions like these are important. By the early 1980s, nearly two thirds of all journalism graduates were female. As these people found employment, the workplace changed and researchers began looking closely at the roles women play in public relations and other mass communication-related professions.

For the most part, results of these studies are disturbing. For instance, Broom and Dozier (1986) found that, even with many other variables held constant, gender predicted income in the public relations profession. That is, men earned more than women performing the same job. Further, Broom and Dozier refined understanding of the two apparent roles in the communications field: managers and technicians. They found that managers earn higher salaries partly because they are usually males, whereas technical roles tend to be held by low-earning females.

In another study funded by the International Association of Business Communicators (IABC), Cline et al. (1986) substantiated Broom and Dozier's findings and confirmed other assumptions as well. They expressed concern that if the public relations profession becomes female dominated, salary and status will decrease just as they have in other female-dominated professions such as nursing and teaching.

Further, as Lynch-Paley (1991) reported, researchers began to investigate the impact of gender on the professional activities and daily functions of journalists. She concluded that it is legitimate to ask whether a journalist's sex affects such factors as relationships with peers and access to professional contacts and sources.

Those involved in livestock publishing soon came to feel that gender-related questions should be asked about their field. For one thing, these publications are linked to a traditionally male industry (women are seen as playing very narrow and specific roles in the livestock industry). Also, livestock magazines are structured similarly to publications in other areas, play a key role in covering an industry, and are attracting recent journalism graduates.

A two-part study of gender-related variables in the livestock publishing workplace was undertaken in light of these concerns.

Methodology.   First, to obtain an indication of the formal roles males and females play in livestock publishing, the mastheads of 59 livestock publications were examined to determine how many people of each sex work in managerial and technical areas. Although there are always exceptions, at the time of this study the managerial positions in livestock publishing were editorial in nature. That is, the boss most likely had the title of editor. Because these publications staffs were small, assistant managers had the title of assistant editor, writer, or reporter.

The technical areas were those associated with production (layout, paste-up, design, art, graphics, typesetting, etc.) and advertising (primarily sales).

Traditionally in the livestock publishing field, the complete listing of all staff members is included on the masthead of each publication. Consequently, coding and classifying gender names with job titles gives a picture of the gender distribution for managerial–technical positions.

Second, a two-part questionnaire was administered to nearly 70 livestock publication staffers attending an annual meeting of the Livestock Publications Council. The first part of the questionnaire contained questions with forced-choice responses, and the second part featured open-ended questions for which respondents gave their own answers.

Results.   Nearly 60% of the respondents were female. In spite of the fact that respondents averaged over 7 years experience working for livestock publications, they were clustered at the lower end of the age scale with 71.6% between 18 and 39.

The respondents' primary areas of responsibility were: editorial 30.9%, production 16.2%, and advertising 14.7%. Just over 38% reported they work in all three areas—not an uncommon situation on smaller magazines of all types. A little more than half (56.7%) worked for association publications.

Consistent with the results of other studies, 80% of these staffers believed more women than men were entering livestock publishing. However, both the questionnaire data and the masthead analysis show that men are usually managers, whereas women are technicians. Women are underrepresented in editorial positions (36.4%) but are employed about equally in production (53.7%) and advertising (50.9%).

Nearly two thirds of respondents to the questionnaire believed the livestock industry prefers to work with male staffers on livestock publications. However, virtually the same percentage believed that, when it comes to evaluating a journalistic dimension like credibility, gender does not make a difference.

Nevertheless, a number of respondents indicated women have a tough time with industry sources. One said, "I think the prejudices are not as strong as in the past, but are still there. However, changes are happening as people are accepted for what they can do, regardless of gender or position."

Some of our most interesting findings relate to the environment of livestock publications as a place for men and women to work. Male and female respondents differed significantly on the question of whether men and women are promoted equally. Whereas nearly 80% of men believed promotions were equally attainable for both sexes, only half that percentage of female respondents felt the same way.

That pattern of responses also held for two important economic variables. Significantly more women than men believed men earn more than women for the same job in the livestock magazine field. The same was true when respondents were asked if men get raises faster than women. Female respondents believed they did, male respondents that they did not.

In spite of these response patterns, more than two thirds of all respondents did not believe overt bias against women exists within livestock publications. However, consistent with the studies cited earlier, over 70% of all respondents agreed that subtle factors work against women in the livestock field.

Finally, however, the overwhelming majority of respondents saw the increase in the number of women in livestock publishing as a positive factor. Also, virtually all respondents of either sex agreed they were personally satisfied with their jobs.

STUDY OF READER PERCEPTIONS

We now turn to a fourth and final research question on reader perceptions of livestock magazines.

4. What are readers' perceptions of the role of a livestock association magazine?

To help answer this question, the American Angus Association commissioned a study to "take the pulse" of its members on a wide range of items and issues related to its communication program.

Methodology.   The framework of the study called for both qualitative and quantitative research methods. The first qualitative effort was a systematic, but non-theoretical, content analysis of the *Angus Journal,* the association's four-color magazine containing articles and editorial comment as well as breed and livestock advertising.

A second qualitative component involved personal interviews with key staff of the association and magazine, major advertisers in the *Angus Journal,* and association members. Notes from these sessions were distilled and served as the basis for a focus-group script. Then, in a third and final qualitative phase, a group of representative association members were assembled and asked about how and when they read the *Angus Journal*. Further, they discussed readership patterns for different content categories, as well as advertising effectiveness, association leadership, and communication with members.

The issues that surfaced in the personal interviews and focus-group session, as well as issues of concern to the *Angus Journal* staff, were analyzed in the concluding quantitative phase of the study: the distribution of a mail questionnaire to a national sample of readers. In total, data were collected on over 150 different variables at this stage.

As detailed earlier in this chapter, livestock publications are multidimensional and need comprehensive strategies to meet the information needs of readers. The *Angus Journal* adopted several content tactics designed to help meet these needs:

> As an association magazine, it provides news and information about the association to its members. Representative content for this category includes news about association-sponsored activities, listings of new members, and minutes of the board of directors.

> The *Angus Journal* uses a service-journalism approach to provide content designed to improve readers' ranch or farm management skills. Examples of such content include columns on how to use genetic information to improve herd characteristics, how to use specific techniques to market and advertise cattle, and how to improve pasture land. In most every case, readers are urged to take specific actions to implement these improved methods.

> Assuming that association members want to read about other members, the *Angus Journal* provides human interest and personality-profile feature stories. These include columns and stories on farm and ranch life, features on young people, and profiles of individual breeders and the way they live.

Investigating these strategies was designed to help answer a major question in the mind of every association magazine editor: How can I satisfy the diverse information needs of my readers? Clearly, some read the magazine primarily for its service content. Yet, the editor feels that, in order to maintain readership, some human interest material must be presented. But how much? Further, as implied in the analysis by Cutlip et al. (1985), some members (not to mention the association staff) put a premium on news and information about the workings of the association itself.

Results.   We found a definite hierarchy of content preferred by readers. Survey respondents gave the highest priority to service content in the form of management information.

Human interest content, such as feature stories and personality profiles often used by editors to enhance readership, were not viewed as salient by the majority of

Angus Journal readers. Also, perhaps to the chagrin of the association staff, reports on association activities took a back seat to the other two types of content.

Interestingly, regardless of the content format—service article, human interest feature, or association report—association members wanted the *Angus Journal* to deal with all sides of controversial issues. These issues could relate to the association or the livestock industry in general.

To a certain extent, airing all sides of controversial issues in the association magazine is in keeping with a traditional political function of an association: develop a process that leads to membership consensus on issues and then articulate that consensus position (or positions) within the political arena.

However, this process can lead to all kinds of perceived public relations problems for the association staff. Who decides how many sides there are to an issue and who should speak for each side? Will the full airing of all sides diminish the perception of member consensus and, thereby, reduce political clout? These are political-context questions that the association and *Angus Journal* staff need to consider.

Another finding is that content preferences and actual readership varied according to age and size of ranching operation. The older readers, with larger ranches and herds, emphasized association and human interest content. But, the younger association members, with smaller ranches, preferred and read more of the service management information.

We speculated that the older, more established readers with larger operations saw little need for service information in the *Angus Journal,* because they had many other management resources at their disposal. The younger members, with less extensive operations and resources, may rely on the *Angus Journal* as a primary source of management information.

We now turn to implications of our entire program of research, taken as a whole.

IMPLICATIONS

The results of this research effort have implications for those working in the agricultural communication field as well as for public relations practitioners in other specialized areas. A number of action plans for these persons grow out of two major points.

Point 1—Communication managers need to recognize that structural factors associated with changes in technology and employee demographics are potent forces that influence the final products of any organization.

This is true for managers operating within media organizations associated with a particular industry (such as livestock publications), as well as for public relations persons working for organizations seeking to establish effective relationships with these media organizations.

As discussed earlier in this chapter, changes in technology and employee demographics are occurring throughout the public relations and communication field.

Although several of the action plans associated with this first point state what may seem obvious, there is ample evidence to suggest the information needs to be emphasized.

Action 1—In this time of transition, publication managers should continue to hire those with solid fundamental writing, editing, and design skills to staff their publications.

Reasoning.   As Watkins (1991) noted, experimentation with new technology creates a blurring of job responsibilities among current employees. In general, it is the professionally trained editor, writer, or designer who is asked to perform production tasks formerly handled by a typesetter, not the other way around. Watkins (1991) said the new technology gives the publication staff greater control over the final product. However, this control carries with it a price for individual staff members: increased responsibility and workload.

This conclusion is echoed by others who have investigated the impact of new technology in the newspaper industry. In a literature review, Izard, Culbertson, and Lambert (1990, pp. 15–17) found that in the long run, the new technology appears to be a good thing for overall accuracy and quality within this segment of the mass media. However, information overload, less opportunity to think about complex issues and provide context because of the increased speed in the production flow, as well as less professional proofreading are negatives associated with the adoption of the new technology in the newspaper business.

All of this means it is more important than ever to have staff grounded in fundamental communication skills.

Action 2—Public relations practitioners seeking to place messages in specific publications should accommodate the technological requirements of those publications.

Reasoning.   This is another way to state what has been traditional practice in public relations. For instance, the standard format for press releases derived from the technological requirements of the newspaper copy desk. Today, the technological requirements of a specialized publication often dictate that press releases be distributed in a package containing both hard copy and a computer disk. Our study and Watkins' suggest staffers struggling with new duties as a result of technological change would welcome such an accommodation.

Action 3—Publication managers should develop strategies to minimize the real and perceptual differences between male and female staff members regarding promotions, salaries, and pay raises. At base, this means providing equal pay for equal work and providing equal opportunities for advancement. Also, it is important to demonstrate that such equality exists.

Reasoning.   Such differences represent a ticking time bomb that needs to be defused by publication managers in order to maintain the long-term health of their publications. Our research with livestock publication personnel suggests managers need to become aware of both subtle and overt forms of discrimination between males and females in the communication field. For one thing, this means recognizing that women are most likely to be a "hired hand" (serving as a production technician) at a livestock publication rather than the "ranch boss" (serving in the role of editor). Resentment generated by this condition is detrimental to the organization.

Further, livestock publication managers can begin to make structural changes in this area by working with journalism and agricultural communication programs at colleges and universities to create an awareness among female students of the need to train for management positions. Support for such training might take the form of scholarships for female students majoring in journalism or agricultural communication but minoring in management, finance, or marketing.

Action 4—Public relations practitioners should develop strategies for interacting with journalists that minimize source-reporter conflicts due to gender.

Reasoning.   This is particularly true when the practitioner is working in a traditionally male-dominated field like the livestock industry. Although livestock publication staffers acknowledged that industry sources prefer to work with males, the staffers believed that important journalistic dimensions, such as perceived credibility, were not affected by gender.

However, as Lynch-Paley (1991) detailed, this perception is not shared by female journalists in other fields. Her study of female congressional correspondents in Washington, DC reveals that being female often has a negative effect on relationships with their industry sources. Consequently, social concerns aside, both female and male public relations practitioners can enhance important relationships with journalists by being sensitive to gender issues.

Point 2—Public relations practitioners *can* use public relations theory to help develop effective communication campaigns.

Academic researchers often lament the fact that practitioners have little regard for public relations theory (Hamilton & Shipman, 1991). It seems practitioners appreciate theory for academic reasons but see little use for it outside of the classroom.

This rings hollow when practitioners examine public relations practices in light of what is taking place in other communication programs. Marketing experts rely on theoretical concepts (developed as a result of research programs) to identify target market segments and position products or organizations. Many practitioners bristle at equating public relations with marketing. However, success in the latter field should spur public relations practitioners to adopt theoretical approaches. Hamilton and Shipman (1991) did just that by demonstrating that the Grunigs' situational-theoretical variables can be linked to traditional media demographics used by marketers.

In the extensive livestock communication research effort reported in this chapter, concepts from situational theory as well as concepts underlying current definitions of "service journalism" were applied in very practical and useful ways. The results of this effort suggest the following action plans.

Action 5—Use theory and research to identify issues and topics that are most likely to be of interest to media gatekeepers, thereby enhancing the chance of success for any media relations effort involving press releases, press conferences, interviews, etc.

Reasoning. Our work with livestock magazine editors demonstrates the usefulness of situational-belief theory in identifying gatekeeper agendas. Editors believed readers of their publications were most concerned about issues or activities that they deal with personally on their ranches or farms. These issues and topics have a "situational-theory profile" that dictates high readership: high relevance, high involvement, and high control or opportunity to make a difference.

In essence, our research demonstrates that editors have the ability to segment a relatively homogeneous group (livestock breeders) as to how persons within that group relate to issues on theoretical dimensions. Further, a good deal of research suggests that a segment of readers who score high on situational-belief variables (that is, high in problem recognition, involvement, and the absence of perceived constraints) with regard to a given issue will seek and process information about that issue actively. In providing content for that segment, the editor might logically focus on these active issues. Therefore, it behooves the public relations person to identify such issues and craft media messages accordingly.

Action 6—Use theory and research to determine the appropriate form for messages and package these forms so that members of target publics can readily use them.

Reasoning. Our research with readers of a specialized association magazine reveals a definite hierarchy of preferred content. These readers preferred service journalism content in the form of management information over human interest and association content. As noted earlier in this chapter, researchers such as Reed (1990) linked specific service-journalism content to Lemert's concepts of mobilizing messages (1981).

However, even for the American Angus Association, *not all* members prefer mobilizing messages over other types of content. Further, association magazines (such as the *Angus Journal*) do need to provide news and information about the association. Consequently, we suggested that the *Angus Journal* staff package the magazine to give service-journalism content the most prominent display, with association news being readily available but not featured.

As for human interest content, we suggested that the *Angus Journal* staff develop some hybrid stories. That is, feature or personality-profile items can include management or association information. In this way, the staff can use the human interest content as a bridge to reach those readers primarily interested in it but also in need of association or service information.

To a large extent, we suggest that public relations practitioners adopt a common sense approach to communicating with members of target publics. That is, the practitioner should know the characteristics of the audience, understand what issues and topics are of interest to it, and provide information about those topics in a format that enhances attention. However, as community newspaper editors who receive countless press releases with no local angle can attest, this is a common sense approach that many practitioners ignore.

REFERENCES

Adams, J. L., & Parkhurst, A. M. (1984). *Farmer/rancher perceptions of channels and sources of change information* (Tech. Rep. No. 9). Lincoln, University of Nebraska, Department of Agricultural Communications.

Broom, G. M., & Dozier, D. M. (1986). Advancement for public relations role models. *Public Relations Review, 12,* 37–56.

Cline, C. G., Toth, E. L., Turk, J. V., Walters, L. M., Johnson, N., & Smith, H. (1986). *The velvet ghetto: The impact of the increasing percentage of women in public relations and business communication.* San Francisco: International Association of Business Communicators.

Conover, T. E. (1990). *Graphics communications today* (2nd ed.). St. Paul, MN: West.

Culbertson, H. M. (1983). Three perspectives on American journalism. *Journalism Monographs, No. 83.*

Cutlip, S., Center, A., & Broom, G. (1985). *Effective Public relations* (6th ed.). Englewood Cliffs, NJ: Prentice-Hall.

Grunig, J. E., & Hunt, T. (1984). *Managing public relations.* New York: Holt, Rinehart & Winston.

Hamilton, P. K., & Shipman, K. (1991). *Grunig's situational theory: A replication, application and extension.* Paper presented at the meeting of the Association for Education in Journalism and Mass Communication, Boston, MA.

Izard, R. S., Culbertson, H. M., & Lambert, D. A. (1990). *Fundamentals of news reporting* (5th Ed.). Dubuque, IA: Kendal-Hunt.

Lemert, J. B. (1981). *Does mass communication change public opinion after all?* Chicago: Nelson-Hall.

Lynch-Paley, D. (1991). *Covering the capital: Is gender an issue?* Paper presented at the meeting of the Association for Education in Journalism and Mass Communication, Boston, MA.

Reed, B. S. (1990). *The link between mobilizing information and service journalism as applied to women's magazine coverage of eating disorders.* Paper presented at the meeting of the Association for Education in Journalism and Mass Communication, Minneapolis, MN.

Vivian, J. (1991). *The media of mass communication.* Boston: Allyn & Bacon.

Watkins, P. G. (1991). *Assessing the impact of microcomputers on magazine design.* Paper presented at the meeting of the Association for Education in journalism and Mass Communication, Boston, MA.

9 Motel Inn, Inc., Corporate Franchise Relations: A Giant on the Move

Since the early 1960s the United States has experienced proactive citizens forcing change in government and business. Much of that activity originated in and was fruitfully executed through appropriate interpersonal and mass communications.

For diverse strategies and accomplishments, we may look to Ralph Nader, Gloria Steinem, Norman Mailer, Martin Luther King, perhaps even Lee Iacocca. Their communication campaigns—designed to inform, influence, persuade—raised consciousness levels, if not eyebrows, of Americans about numerous subjects and causes dealing with safety, quality, and freedom of life.

Rice and Paisley (1981, p. 3) explained that effective campaigns are based on five principles:

1. Assessment of the needs, goals, and capabilities of target audience
1. Systematic campaign planning and production
3. Continuous evaluation
4. Complementary roles of mass media and interpersonal communication
5. Selection of appropriate media for target audiences

Yet, one seldom considers how a corporate organization becomes proactive within its own ranks. All too often the right hand has little if any knowledge of what the left hand is doing! Only a few organizations watch the hand, feed the hand, and in fact, closely monitor the pulse of employees and customers.

Not surprisingly, that kind of vigilant decision making over long periods of time provides certain organizations with incredible media prominence and cultural recognition. These companies enjoy the exhilaration of communication success to the

171

extent their names are often mistakenly viewed as generic terms signifying their particular industries. Excellent examples include Kleenex, Coca Cola, and Xerox. Surely the longevity and protracted profitability of these firms point to something, perhaps a lot of things, being done properly!

Indeed, such was the case at Motel Inn, Inc., a maturing and innovative organization that has come of age and set the standard of medium-range travel accommodations in this country and throughout the world for several decades. This study of the motel chain's Franchise Relations Department is a model for transformation leadership and issues management.

Top-level executives of Motel Inn, Inc. affected no less than a role-making coup de grace in the hotel–motel industry. They identified a need for better interactive communications among their hotel–motel managers and owners. Then, they created and used new corporate roles that removed the need for managers in certain areas. Their communication and interaction with owners, operators, and general managers of franchised Motel Inns throughout the United States fostered the corporate–franchisee alliance, motivated managers, and boosted the bottom line for corporate headquarters and individually owned motel operations.

As growth goals were met and local ownership eliminated many corporate-level managerial positions, something unusual occurred. Although specific corporate positions did become extinct, those managers moved up (not off) that proverbial corporate ladder to perform innovative role-making activities in other departments, divisions, and even in newly formed companies. Achievement stories shed light on winning relationships gained through management by communication.

In the early 1980s, Motel Inn executives, including Senior Vice-President Daniel James of the Hotel Services Division (HSD), established the Franchise Relations Department. The overall mission was to position Motel Inn, Inc. as the dominant brand of the 1990s. James confidently stated that information was the key word during the decade of the 1980s, but in the 1990s the word would be service (Personal Communication, May 1990).

The services provided by Motel Inn, Inc. headquarters must be the appropriate information and tools to facilitate franchise operations. James said he is a firm believer in the ripple effect. Providing those services meant reaching beyond those who were licensed to operate a hotel under the auspices of Motel Inn to communicate with general managers and staff—sales representatives, clerks, food and beverage personnel, and housekeeping—the total staff at each unit.

"And that brought about the Franchise Relations Department; to find ways to communicate and recognize our people who are doing work on a day-to-day basis," James said. The problem was the extent to which the organization had grown. "How do we handle that huge battleship?" was James' primary concern.

This chapter, then, offers a microcosm of one department—newly formed, breaking industry ground—in a division of an international corporation that benefitted from understanding social, political, and economic contexts.

The objective was to improve awareness among Hotel Services Division (HSD) customers and employees about the products and services available from HSD. The general strategy was to develop and implement an external-awareness program for franchisees and major independent customers who publicize newsworthy activities of the division.

METHODS

Informal Research

To comprehend concepts and problems peculiar to the industry, for several months in mid-1987 the third author of this volume started regularly monitoring media for any mention of Motel Inn and related data in local daily and business weekly newspapers, spot checking national publications such as *The Wall Street Journal* and *The New York Times,* plus the *Los Angeles Times* (California infamously sets trends). Also, notice was taken of television broadcasts (local, network, and cable news), famous films (e.g., White Christmas, Holiday Inn) depicting hotel–motel industry, and trade journals (e.g., *Broadcasting, Advertising Age*) and magazines salient to travel-vacation customers and travel agents (e.g., *Key* magazine).

Further, all previously published internal brochures were examined to determine overall organizational marketing strategy for identified target markets such as traveling sales people, senior citizens, newlyweds, or families. Considerable attention was paid to: (a) local and national economies (encompassing amount of public discretionary income, costs, access, and demand), (b) media visibility and portrayal of Motel Inn, and (c) internal and external perception of Motel Inn's place in the hotel–motel industry hierarchy.

Informal research was carried out to clarify the jargon, special character, and routines of the industry. Past and current Motel Inn employees who worked in communication and graphics outside the new Franchise Relations Department were interviewed.

At the request of Jane Kinai, head of Franchise Relations (FR), several initial meetings were held with her and FR staff members. Although no formal interview guide was used, general nondirective questions were followed by items that probed broadly and deeply. The purpose was to gain varied information that might prove useful in strengthening franchisee commitment to Motel Inn. Other goals were positive, frequent involvement (particularly hassle-free payment of fees to headquarters), purchase of furniture and ancillary merchandise manufactured by other divisions within the corporation, increased awareness of major corporate services, and enhanced motivation at headquarters and field units (Personal Communications, June 1987).

Fees, of course, serve as the organizational headquarters' life blood. Frequent infusion was a key goal. Attainment of that and other goals required knowledge and interpretation by long-time employees of their new responsibilities, department, and constituencies. Also, it was crucial to grasp words and phrases used to describe salient circumstances and people—the jargon of Motel Inn and the industry. Such knowledge was essential to communicate effectively.

Further, we probed during interviews to identify symbols meaningful in both the corporate and field (specific-unit) environments. This pinpointed concepts relevant to personnel ranging from owners and managers to clerks and housekeepers. Also, interviewers asked for detailed explanations of missions and goals as well as departmental infrastructure and employee responsibilities.

Formal Research

Franchise Relations began pulling together demographic information about owners, general managers, and other personnel across the United States. Most of the franchisees were male, second-generation owners of more than one Motel Inn or a Motel Inn and another brand motel. They were college-educated (with at least a bachelor's degree, and some having earned a master's) and fairly wealthy. From their rather comfortable vantage points, they leaned toward conservative management and communication policies.

These profiles, along with historical data, formed a good basis for planning strategies and campaigns. In addition, formal in-depth interviews were held with Daniel James, Senior Vice-President of the Hotel Services Division, and Don Lewin, Corporate Executive of DML Enterprises in Ft. Lauderdale, Florida, owner of several brand motel–hotel franchises including a Motel Inn unit (Personal Communication, July 1990).

Unfortunately, quantitative data was very limited. There was no documentation of interaction with franchise owners or operators. Hence, before-and-after data were unavailable.

Franchise Relations sought to establish ways of measuring communication with specific publics. Truly, the department sought to build a Motel Inn Franchise data bank.

Previously, Motel Inn had shown evidence of sophisticated thinking. James, recognizing the equally sophisticated operations of franchisees, spoke quarterly with board members and owners. His objective was to build trust through open communication, now and in the future.

For example, each year Motel Inn, Inc. sponsored a franchisee conference, offering varied workshops on management techniques and marketing tools. When asked, 45% of the general managers said their owners, for a variety of reasons, failed to pass on instructional or marketing data from Motel Inn headquarters!

Perplexed by the lack of owner participation and communication with on-site managers, James went to franchise owners. He said, "We ran a conference and spent money. We wanted to bring the general managers together so they'd implement!"

He also visited with managers and asked them to identify Motel Inn problems and to propose improvements. He explained, "Programs galore are still in place and need to be reevaluated. My ability to meet with managers in individual sessions turned out to be important."

Kinai suggested that the main thrust was getting people united. "Everybody has to go after the same cause," she said.

The approach was to build competitiveness, especially for general managers, and help get their troops enthused so they would make a solid commitment to the Motel Inn concept and their individual units. Kinai said that essentially, "We bring people together." Coordination of those people and projects included a variety of communication campaigns.

FRANCHISE RELATIONS CAMPAIGNS

Idea Campaign

Across the United States, some 2,500 Motel Inn hotel and motel owners were operating successfully in the mid-1980s. These were prosperous entrepreneurs who had shown enough courage and foresight during the past 25 years to buy one or more franchises by the name Motel Inn and thus, to share in the rewards that accrued from having the glowing purple sign that travelers had come to trust. Incontrovertibly, many people recognized the corporate position statement and preferred to "Stay with someone you trust."

The Motel Inn story is one of the world's great recent business success stories. The company sprang from a single motel in Tennessee, in the early 1950s to one of the most respected names in travel accommodations in less than a generation. Henry K. Williams, the family man who established his empire on clean, no-frills rooms for middle-class American travelers where "kids stay free," was no longer at the Motel Inn helm in the mid-1980s. The corporation then belonged to stockholders and was operated by a board of directors headed by CEO Michael Rone, a Harvard business graduate.

The company had changed with the economic environment and by virtually all standards had flourished. Motel Inn was a premier brand, a logo that was worth the progressively rising franchise price and monthly percentage of gross revenue franchisees paid to the corporation. The firm now owned several casinos and had an international group of hotels. It was branching into up-scale hotels with the Tiara Plaza line, down-scale motels with the Hamilton Inn line, and business travelers' residence motels with Ambassador Suites.

The firm was manufacturing and selling motel furniture, had one of the most sophisticated telecommunications reservation systems in the world, and had been an innovator in satellite entertainment, food and beverage service, and real estate management. Motel Inn, Inc. was doing so well, in fact, that it became a target for corporate raiders in the heyday of leveraged buy-outs in 1986 and 1987.

The prospect of being bought, fractured, and sold off in parts, was the catalyst that forced Motel Inn to do some introspective soul searching. The corporation's success could be attributed to two aspects of its enterprise: (a) the current market value of hotel properties was far greater than what appeared on the books as assets and (b) the casinos and monthly franchisee fees were cash cows that provided a steady stream of revenue.

As part of the strategy to avoid an unfriendly takeover attempt, Motel Inn divested itself of many international properties and sold some of the corporate-owned hotels and motels in the United States. The organization took on debt and paid a tidy dividend to investors as sound protection from a raid, at least for the short term.

By selling corporate-owned properties, the company became much leaner. The move emphasized that Motel Inn's business was concentrated in the lucrative casino operations and in the 2,500 franchisees who paid for the privilege of using the name. Actually, more than half of the corporation's revenue came from franchise operations.

This aspect of the organization had not been ignored in the past. Corporate headquarters did, after all, have a vice-president in charge of Franchise Relations, but the franchisees gained attention when the board realized that Motel Inn's future success would be measured in terms of how well headquarters managed the franchisees.

What's in a Name?

In fact, the prospect of holding and building the franchisee base was not at all certain. Many of Motel Inn's competitors had flourished during the "motel generation." Best West, Ramada, Travel Lodge, Econolodge, Motel 6, Motel 8, and Scottish Inns were only a few of the national brands eager to convert a franchisee to their stables.

There was pressure also to keep the Motel Inn name untarnished. For instance, if a franchisee refused to invest in repair and maintenance of a property, travelers would have an unpleasant experience that would reflect badly on the Motel Inn name. In cases where headquarters couldn't convince an owner that upkeep makes good business sense, the corporation's only option was to take back the name and delete that owner from the franchisee list. After nearly 30 years of operation, many of the original franchisees might question whether another renovation investment would pay off during their "watches."

Investments in renovation had become expensive as construction materials led inflationary prices throughout the 1970s and 1980s. The materials and supplies services that Motel Inn had been selling to franchisees were a greater percentage of the cost of business than had been the case previously, and these costs might be seen as prohibitive in a market where competitors use such prices to their advantage.

Finally, the hotel and motel market had become fragmented. Motel Inn was still a dominant brand at the middle of the market, but competition was increasing with names such as Hyatt, Marriott, and Hilton at the plush end of the scale and Red Roof, Comfort, and Budgetel at the no-frills end. There was diversity as well in market segments geared to business, to vacationers, to resort-area travelers, and conventions.

For Motel Inn, the question became: What should the corporation be doing to insure that the Motel Inn name retains strong value for a franchisee? Of course, a franchisee is interested primarily in the degree of profitability obtained from keeping the name Motel Inn rather than from other brands that come courting.

The corporation recognized all along that franchisees expect these "me" benefits, so one level of internal communications was aimed at the 2,500 hotel owners through headquarters' Franchise Relations office. But now that the franchisees had been identified as the major income providers and the competitive market had become quite formidable, the time had come to take a closer look at how well the company was holding the franchisees.

The Value of an Idea

Franchise Relations Department was a relatively small branch of total operations geared to communication with the 2,500 hotel owners. The Department ran contests to stimulate hotel employees' interest in customer service and cleanliness as well as competitions for recipes that could be used in restaurants. Also important was coordination of national events such as school and health related programs that franchisees could sponsor.

Additionally, the office was the focus of communication between headquarters and franchisees for dissemination of new policies or innovations, for printed material such as directories and newsletters, and for queries from franchisees to headquarters. If a franchisee visited headquarters, Franchise Relations sent a limousine to the airport. The office also arranged the annual conference for hotel owners. In every respect, Franchise Relations was the public relations office specializing in headquarters–franchisee communications.

When Motel Inn's focus turned to the franchise operations, an important undertaking was a year-long idea-generating program. This project was designed to allow franchisees to share money making and savings ideas. For instance, a member of the management team of a Motel Inn restaurant began advertising free lunches for senior citizens on their birthdays. The owner discovered that on the average, three people escorted a senior to the prize luncheon, dramatically increasing the restaurant's business and profit.

This idea was sent to Franchise Relations and entered into a quarterly idea contest. Judges selected the best ideas each quarter, and those appeared in a quarterly newsletter sent to all franchisees. Twenty of the year's best ideas were selected for the grand prize, usually a vacation trip for the management team submitting the idea and their spouses.

However, this contest was languishing. The entry process required paperwork detailing cost and returns. The prize was equivocal, and the contest had not been well publicized. Fewer than 75 entries had been received in the previous year, and good ideas were so rare that the deadline for publishing the quarterly newsletter was missed twice.

Management questioned the value of the idea contest and raised this concern with Franchise Relations. However, after some discussion, all agreed that a good idea was invaluable. The stark reality was that no other service offered by headquarters to franchisees was worth the potential value of one good idea that had worked for one owner and seemed worthy of emulation by others. Instead of canceling the contest, Motel Inn instructed Franchise Relations to insure its success.

Idea Contest Restructured

Informal research consisted of person-to-person or telephone conversations with hotel owners to determine why those who submitted ideas had decided to participate and to find out what had prevented many from participating. The chief reason given for not submitting ideas was lack of incentive. Thus, management concluded: (a) The contest had to be relatively easy to enter, (b) the prize had to be dramatic enough to distinguish this event from all the other contests, and (c) busy franchisees had to be reminded constantly.

Ease of entering the contest was enhanced by reducing the entry form to a half-page document that emphasized the management team's names and the scope of the idea itself rather than extensive documentation of hotel costs and income benefits. A paragraph in narrative form was sought, and contestants were told they might be contacted by telephone if more details were needed.

In addition, several of the prize winners were called for more information, and Franchise Relations learned that excellent ideas often are buried in garbled prose. If interviewed by phone, most of the owners could explain their ideas with confidence and exuberance.

Making the prize extraordinary required more imagination. The franchisees, after all, were prosperous hotel owners who were accustomed to first-class accommodations and special treatment. But Franchise Relations soon identified the most alluring prize Motel Inn ever offered. Each winning hotel's management team of five and their spouses would be flown to the Caribbean for a week's cruise aboard the Wind Star, the largest sailing ship in existence. Of course, all expenses were paid, and the ship was reserved entirely for the Motel Inn contest winners.

Designing the contest as on-going was merely a matter of devising a continuing, year-long campaign to generate ideas that would culminate in contest winners being whisked away for their Caribbean sailing venture. We now can trace these campaigns over 2 years with a quantitative evaluation of their effects.

Passport to Paradise

Introduction of the idea contest featured several new twists beginning with a mock passport printed as a four-page brochure with a green cover. The passport copy described the ship: NAME: Wind Star; AGE: 2 Years; BIRTHPLACE: France. Center facing pages of the brochure provided the new, revised idea contest rules. The back pages contained color pictures of cabins and entertainment areas on the Wind Star and descriptions of the trip the sailing ship makes through the Caribbean Islands.

By the first quarter's deadline, the number of idea entries generated in the new contest nearly equaled the total number received during the previous year's contest. The first year saw four idea newsletters published on schedule, with the last two adding insert pages to handle the overflow.

Two reminders were sent to franchisees at regular intervals: (a) a 5-by-7-inch postcard printed with a full-color photograph of the Wind Star under sail on the front and the contest's remaining quarterly deadlines on the back and (b) a specialty advertising piece consisting of a heavy plastic bag, about 3-by-4 inches filled with sand, blue water, and a few sea shells, similar to the clear toy globes children shake to see snow falling on a scene. A note was attached to each plastic bag reminding franchisees about the final deadline.

In the first year of the revised contest, about 275 ideas were generated. A 16-page brochure was published to feature the winning ideas, and 2,500 copies were printed for distribution at the annual franchisees' convention. The year's better ideas became a conference seminar topic, drawing full-house attendance at repeated sessions. All copies of the idea book were gone after the first 2 days of the conference.

Winning teams were notified of their victory, and first-class arrangements were made to whisk the champions to the Wind Star. The Caribbean sailing trip was as spectacular as touted in Franchise Relations' promotionals during the year. In fact, these seasoned international travelers rated the cruise one of their finest excursions and the best prize they had ever won through Motel Inn or elsewhere (every team from the first trip entered the idea contest the next year). Franchise Relations managers who enjoyed the trip as hosts decided on the spot to book the Wind Star for the next year's prize, and this set the tone of the second idea contest.

For the evaluation of the first year's contest, there was no question about the communication and motivation breakthroughs. Generating and sharing ideas that might increase profitability had been identified as an important part of the company's communication with its franchisees. The previous year's contest produced too few good entries to share in the form of a quarterly newsletter. To insure program success, the formula had three parts: (a) ease of entry, (b) a dramatic prize, and (c) constant reminders.

The project was a great success statistically. Also, qualitative evaluation through telephone inquiries, personal comments, and communiques suggested numerous hotel owners had adapted contest-generated ideas to their own properties. Many grateful managers thanked Franchise Relations for sharing the suggestions.

Promotionals that succeeded as well as the Passport to Paradise idea contest presented a dilemma: What do you do to cultivate additional interest and advance the program for the next year? That was a very serious question, as it is for public relations efforts in virtually every annual event from fund raisers to anniversaries. In the case of Franchise Relations' idea contest, the problem was compounded by the accomplishments of the first coordinated effort. Also, there was built-in redundancy in selecting the Wind Star sailing cruise as the second year's prize. What year-long theme would continue the sensational results?

Treasure Hunt

After several weeks of debating whether to abandon the contest's focus on the prize, a decision was made to build on the first year's success with a slight twist. When people think of the Caribbean and sailing ships, the images that stir their imagination are tropical islands, soft breezes, the sea, and pirates—yes, pirates!

Sunny beaches may be the modern city dweller's idea of rest and relaxation, but sailing ships mean pirates and pirates mean adventure. That was the excitement Franchise Relations decided to build in promoting the second-year idea contest. Naturally, the department would use a treasure hunt theme to sustain interest. The idea contest entry form was designed as part of the theme using a captain, the hotel owner or manager, and mates, the four-person management team that would qualify for the trip.

The first promotional piece was a treasure map designed on a large piece of parchment paper. When opened to its full measure, the large, intricate, and seductive graphic guide was designed to simulate a board game with a winding track along which color drawings were painted: a pirate captain, a spy glass, blue water, a sailing ship, sea gulls, palm trees, islands, a spade for digging, and other friendly symbols of the pirate era.

Each stop on the map indicated one phase of the contest: identify your shipmate team, come up with a money-making idea, complete the entry form, etc. At the end of the map's game board track, "X" marked the spot. Feedback from the franchisees was good. They understood that the map was the kick-off piece for the contest, and entries began flowing in for the second idea contest.

A plastic toy shovel was used as the next reminder. The dark blue spade contained a printed message tied to the handle with a prod to "keep digging for those winning ideas." The next piece was even more compelling. Franchise Relations ordered 2,500 clear plastic bottles with corks. A label for the bottle featured an island with a sailing ship on distant water and a man in a dinghy rowing toward the boat.

The label was "Float a Note—Don't Miss the Boat." A scrap of parchment with rough edges was printed with Old English typeface lettering as a reminder that the idea treasure hunt was continuing. This slip of paper was rolled up and stuffed into the bottle and sealed by the cork. Who could receive such a promotional piece through the mail and ignore it?

Feedback from the bottle message was phenomenal. Many of the franchisees called simply to say they thought the bottle was a great idea. One hotel owner wrote he had put a free dinner coupon in the bottle and had dropped it off a bridge into a local stream. Later that week, a family came to his hotel restaurant and claimed the free dinner from the bottled coupon. His management team entered the bottle idea in the contest. (Motel Inn did not publicize the incident because of the potential backlash from polluting local tributaries with bottles.) Still, the bottle generated more idea entries than any other promotional piece used.

The last reminder was a 10-inch old-fashioned wooden skeleton key. The design was such that managers could at least use the key as a paper weight or simply as a desk or table object. Attached to the key with a string was a note to "unlock your creativity" and enter the idea contest.

EVALUATION

By the end of the second year, more than 450 ideas had been entered in the contest. The quarterly newsletters, all with extra pages, came out on schedule, and Franchise Relations had a scrapbook of letters from hotel managers who wrote to compliment Motel Inn and express their satisfaction and achievement shown by having adopted a franchise idea. The ideas generated the second year were far-ranging:

1. A beach hotel submitted its success with a weekly outdoor barbecue on a luau theme.

2. Several hotels offered their monthly calendars of events designed to promote restaurant and bar activities.

3. Sales departments shared ideas about generating new business and meeting clients.

4. Among the most innovative and worthy ideas were those that combined hotel promotions with civic group fund raisers and charities.

5. Senior citizens as well as disadvantaged and physically handicapped populations were the beneficiaries of many other ideas.

6. Hotel managers submitted their policies for hiring teens, for working with summer college interns, and for providing educational scholarships.

7. Ideas included room cleanliness contests for the hotel's maid staff, clever twists on bed turn-down service, a lights-off program to conserve electricity, and 10-minute room service on late-night pizza orders.

For the annual franchisee convention, 4,000 copies of a 32-page magazine were printed to highlight the year's best ideas. The full-color cover was a blazing sunburst yellow fading into red. In the center was a huge, open treasure chest loaded with jewels and a bright yellow light bulb. The caption was "A Treasure Trove of Ideas," indicating that this magazine was everyone's prize from the second year's treasure hunt idea contest.

That year's winners enjoyed an equally exciting cruise on the Wind Star, and Franchise Relations again set new records in communication with its internal public, with the congratulations of an appreciative Motel Inn corporation.

Communication Plan

To complement the array of programs, communications were synchronized between internal-headquarters audiences and managers in the field. The last thing Motel Inn executives wanted was a motivated franchisee group relying heavily on corporate divisions that were unprepared or unwilling to cooperate with associates or customers in the field. Detailed programs went into effect.

First, Franchise Relations developed a direct marketing program to recognize new customers and major purchases by existing customers. For example, thank you letters were sent to each customer, regardless of account size; 6 months after an order was placed, the customer received a short questionnaire on the Hotel Service Division's level of service and product quality. Finally, brass-framed "before" and "after" photographs were given to customers who had completed major refurbishment of their units.

Franchisees and other important visitors were given appropriate attention at the Tennessee Motel Inn, Inc. headquarters beginning usually with a limousine at the airport. A system had been created to ensure a prepared agenda for each dignitary. There was a bulletin board to display photographs of franchisees and major visitors. The coordinated Showroom tours were led specifically by Showroom personnel. First-time visitors to the remodeled Showroom received jackets or other gifts and favors, then later a thank you letter for expressing interest.

Samples and brochures helped the customer make buying decisions. To communicate the value of those sales tools, an HSD Message Card accompanied each sample and brochure mailed from the Catalog Department.

Additionally, an archive was created to house the many artifacts of Motel Inn. Donations were made from local citizens, previous owners, and Henry K. Williams, including photographs, brochures, posters, books, furniture, and signs.

To further communicate HSD's story through positive news coverage, lending credibility to available services, Franchise Relations offered two key articles for internal publications, *Operations Overview* and *Number One Magazine*. The articles were reprinted and distributed with a cover letter to franchisees within a month after original publication.

Also for internal audiences at the headquarters, there were programs to develop and implement awareness to educate, motivate, and create feelings of pride. The first was a series of job seminars for numerous departments. Each seminar was targeted to a specific HSD department or job function and featured a well-known, influential speaker in the particular topic areas.

Monthly activities were planned for a "turned-on" employee-motivated environment within HSD that emphasized superior customer service. For example, in February a heart-shaped sticker placed near each employee's phone emphasized service with the slogan, "Don't promise more than you deliver; Deliver more than you promise." In July a message card with a lion theme was placed on each desk. The card indicated, "The customer is king." In November a note from Hotel Services Vice-President James to HSD personnel said, *"Thanks* for *giving* me your best all year." Numerous other programs were implemented to carry through and document the open communications James believed vital to any organization.

By 1989, the Franchise Relations Department administered six major programs for franchise domestic Motel Inns. These included the idea contest discussed earlier, a *Directory of Services,* and a Superior Hotel Award. Also, the Department played a leading role in creating and distributing *Tip Offs,* a publication for motel personnel; *Housekeeper's Dust Off,* directed at housekeepers; and kits with materials designed to help motels minimize complaints and problems during renovation.

Random Sample Survey of General Managers

In October of that year, franchise general managers across the country received mail questionnaires entitled, "What's Your Opinion?" to determine the effectiveness of these programs. The single-sheet $8\frac{1}{2}'' \times 14''$ double-sided instrument contained 20 questions. Sixteen items were structured (either–or, Likert-type agree–disagree, and rating items), whereas four were open ended.

Questioning progressed from general to specific involvement with the 6 individual programs to measure concept understanding, perceived support from headquarters, internal and external acceptance, and profitability.

For example, specific items included: "Did you use the *HouseKeeper's Dust Off* materials (yes/no) and "How useful would you say the publication of ideas (in *Tip Offs* and the annual idea booklet) has been in developing your program?" (rating scale from *very useful* to *not useful at all*). Much space was provided to allow respondents to articulate their opinions in their own words. Also, it asked how the idea contest could be improved.

From the random sample of slightly less than 1,300, by November 15, the Franchise Relations Department received 325 completed questionnaires, representing a 25% response rate. The data were coded and tabulated by Motel Inn computer services, then sent back to Franchise Relations. The 25% response, although low, was considered adequate here in that it probably covered a large number of general managers with strong commitment and involvement. That premise follows from the well-known maxim that 20% of the people in many organizations do 80% of the work.

From his Florida franchise headquarters, owner Don Lewin articulated the views of many managers, as reflected in the survey. He agreed that Franchise Relations programs were valuable, particularly to the employees. However, Lewin questioned their potential for owners. He said, "*Dust-Off* was a good motivational tool, but any company could do the same *if it chose to stimulate the employees*. Fortunately for us, not all do. Within the right context, a variety of techniques are appropriate."

Overall, the general managers indicated that the programs helped generate team spirit and improve employee-management relations at individual units. However, there was some doubt as to whether they contributed to the bottom line.

Survey Results

The managers replied that programs administered by the Franchise Relations Department were "somewhat" or "extremely valuable," particularly the *Directory of Services* (89%), *Tip Offs* newsletter (87%), Idea Contest (87%), and Superior Hotel Award (86%). Rated slightly lower were the *Housekeeper's Dust Off* (69%) and the Renovation and Signage Kits (63%).

Although few general managers said they felt Franchise Relations programs "improved bottom line" (28%), almost two thirds said the programs "generated team spirit" (66%), "improved employee–manager relations" (57%), and helped increase "employee–management communication" in both amount and quality (56%).

Managers did indicate areas they believed called for improvement such as more "equitable distribution" of recognition, especially with the Superior Hotel Awards. A few said "no follow-up system is in place" for some of the programs. This suggests hotel managers require more feedback on program or contest outcomes, such as the *Housekeeper's Dust Off* (27%) and the Idea Contest (8%). Although fewer than 5% of general managers mentioned it, some hotels do need materials in languages other than English, probably Spanish, but no specifics were provided.

Other Measurements

Criteria for a different type of evaluation are also available. James and Lewin (Personal communications, May 1989 and February 1990) were quick to admit there is a cost associated with enthusiasm. Certainly, people were paying more attention to business, repairs were up, turnover was down, guest complaints were fewer, and the bottom line looked much brighter in units that historically did not interact with headquarters. Importantly, communications increased throughout the organization. James said:

> We had to serve our customer. My customers were the franchise and shareholders. And each year the system improved. Operators wanted to be part of the bigger team, and loathed their unit not making a cut at the top of the list. General managers brought in

sales, engineers, housekeepers to work together. We automatically had to focus on line organization—and that worked!

James' explanation was the change in synergism within the hotels. He said, "Headquarters pushed. Friendly intimidating." People come over to the ranks because that's where the masses are. As people {customers} became more informed, their loyalty to brand increased, and Motel Inn became stronger internally.

"The level of competitiveness was the key. All forces intertwine and weave a nice product to motivate, reward people in a system you don't have direct control over." James concluded, "License rules, not controls."

IMPLICATIONS

Clearly, top management at Motel Inn, Inc. had a firm grasp of the social, political, and economic contexts in which the organization operated. Several activities were put in place, some translating into on-going actions within the corporate structure and among individual franchise units. For example, franchisees came to appreciate the importance of sharing information with each other directly, as well as with headquarters. Such sharing became a hallmark of the firm.

Management by communication—a wide-open system—became highly valued. As a result, the franchise owners and their general managers, a prime target for headquarters, had increasingly frequent dialogue with executives, communication and marketing managers, and production employees. Such openness became contagious, spreading through all levels of the organization.

SPE Context: A Brief Review

Through envisioning perspectives of various publics, the Franchise Relations Department acted as advisor, then conduit, for all manner of communication within and among levels. The department provided a set of mechanisms whereby corporate Motel Inn spoke, listened, and acted. *Social contacts* became more and more frequent, disseminating information and ideas accurately, completely, and widely among management and staff. Lower-level personnel took the initiative increasingly, speaking with candor. And all this happened, at base, because *management listened.*

Over time, Franchise Relations came to learn about *schemata* used by various groups within the firm. One such basic belief was that the franchises and corporate headquarters operate in a win–win *competitive* situation. Creativity was spurred as franchisees realized that sharing and cooperation served their best interests and those of Motel Inn, Inc. Competition for vacation trips and other prizes was intense. However, contests were structured to encourage sharing of ideas and learning from each other.

Intrinsic to this trickle-down effect were the costs and benefits of *group mainte-nance*. Through compelling communication, management nurtured, informed, and motivated. Rapport within the firm grew as a result.

Constant *personal contact* by corporate executives with franchise owners and general managers stimulated system-wide interaction throughout Motel Inn, Inc. The result was an environment literally charged with trail-blazing vitality. The obvious message to internal and external audiences from maintenance to managers was, "You belong, we care about you, and we depend on you." Such openness maximized synergy.

Importantly, the atmosphere of success permeated individual units, building spirited, cohesive teams, embracing the oft-neglected housekeeping departments. At some motels, personnel really began, for the first time, sharing information and ideas. Employees started to understand departments *other than their own* and to suggest ways of improving productivity in those units. Greater personal commit-ment enhanced *involvement* (Cacioppo, Harkins, & Petty, 1981) and *problem rec-ognition* (Grunig, 1983). This, coupled with help from various sources in *recogniz-ing and surmounting constraints*, led to more active, varied, analytical *information seeking and processing*.

Results included smoother internal relations at specific units and marketing cam-paigns reaching further and further out for community-service based activities. To be sure, Motel Inn still looked for a positive bottom line. However, programs also profited customers in unanticipated, intangible ways—*externalities* as defined in chapter 6. A variety of techniques celebrated life, marking human events in unusual ways. As a result, communities became better places in which to live.

For example, one motel set up a mini-mall for engaged couples. Areas businesses put up "stores" displaying tuxedos, wedding gowns, flowers, jewelry, honeymoon travel opportunities, etc. Another motel provided free space for a nonprofit organi-zation working on behalf of a local family in need. Motel expenses sometimes reached rather high levels in such projects. Furthermore, employees who caught the community spirit often donated time and cash, thereby making deposits in their *favor banks* so as to enhance their long-term leadership potential.

Benefits of such generosity were great. Recognition by civic leaders, the media, and others helped propel those numerous motels into the hearts of their commu-nities. In some areas, Motel Inn became the town meeting place. Business increased along with motel prestige. *Exchange* relationships and results suggested that, in-deed, it is sometimes more profitable, not to mention blessed, to give than to receive.

In conclusion, the Franchise Relations Department clearly fulfilled its mission in facilitating communication and augmenting marketing. Improved understanding and *coorientation* occurred as corporate managers used two-way *social contacts* to understand themselves and the firm more fully through the looking glass provided for them by many and varied others.

Cultural and situational beliefs relating to community involvement and service were validated and *internalized. Group maintenance* within Motel Inns was enhanced. Some new *coalitions* within and across organizational boundaries improved performance. *Power-gaining strategies* were recognized and managed. Customer loyalty may have translated into *inelastic demand* for motel services and rooms. And personnel at all levels came to appreciate that the *utility of good service was anything but marginal or diminishing*! Furthermore, *opportunity costs* attached to any alternative other than good service were high indeed.

With open management policies and appropriate follow-through, an organization can come to view various internal and external publics as co-owners of itself. This may help move toward the ideal of *two-way symmetric* public relations as many factors converge to create not just a big picture, but a living piece of art.

REFERENCES

Cacioppo, J. T., Harkins, S. G., & Petty, R. E. (1981). The nature of attitude and cognitive responses and their relationships to behavior. In R. E. Petty, T. M. Ostrom, & T. C. Brock (Eds.), *Cognitive responses in persuasion.* Hillsdale, NJ: Lawrence Erlbaum Associates.

Grunig, J. (1983). Communication behaviors and attitudes of environmental publics: Two studies. *Journalism Monograph, 3*(81).

Rice, R. E., & Paisley, W. J. (Eds.). (1981). *Public communication campaigns.* Beverly Hills, CA: Sage.

10 Black Studies in Transition: A Discipline in Search of its Key Publics

You are American, not African . . . We can't even trace our blood back only to Africa because most of us are part Indian, Spanish, Irish, part any and every damn thing. But culturally, we represent a synthesis of any number of these elements. . . . Yes, we have a special awareness because our experience has, in certain ways, been uniquely different from that of white people; but it was not absolutely different. A poor man is a poor man whether he's black or white.

Ralph Ellison, 1970

THE LARGER CONTEXT

In response to the social and political turmoil of the late 1960s and early 1970s, many American universities were under pressure from Black students to introduce Black studies courses into their curricula. Courses were hastily developed sometimes before qualified instructors could be found to teach them. Consequently, many Black studies departments were developed as full-fledged schools within their universities. Unfortunately, many of their curricula were better developed in the minds of those who demanded their existence than they ever were on paper. As time passed, these departments or schools, variously labeled Black Studies or Afro-American Studies, developed a questionable academic reputation. This reputation resulted in a loss of respect among other university professionals and a lack of meaning to the student body at large.

Some of these departments were formed to hastily quiet student protests and to take advantage of the flood of government funds being poured into the new discipline for political reasons. Consequently, staffing of the new departments was often an emergency venture. Anyone with a degree and black skin was viewed as an asset, even though his or her academic experience may have been nominal or in an unrelated field.

The key to the success of those early Black studies departments lay in their high visibility. Though the term *political correctness* was not being used then, it became a major determinant in staffing decisions. Blackness, not scholarship, was the criterion for staffing these new departments, and the darker the applicant's skin, the more politically correct he or she appeared. Although not all Black studies departments were assembled and staffed with untested professionals, those that were created an image that was imposed on all of them. Whether true or not, that common legacy left an image of unprofessionalism that many Black studies departments are still grappling with today.

Founded in 1969 as the Black Studies Institute, Midwestern University's Black studies program wages a continuous uphill battle against the legacy of its beginnings. Starting out as an autonomous unit with its own dean, it was incorporated into the College of Arts and Sciences in 1980. Its loss of autonomy was viewed as a demotion by many students and staff. Having its status changed to that of a department and losing its dean undoubtedly meant a reduction in the institute's power as a political entity on campus. On the other hand, being part of the university's largest college was interpreted by some as a very favorable move. By having the former Black Studies Institute, now the Center for Afro-American Studies (AAS), placed within the College of Arts and Sciences, it was hoped that Black studies courses would receive a wider acceptance and greater legitimacy (Barnes, 1992). In addition to making Black Studies courses part of general education requirements for all Midwestern University students, the change was also seen as giving White students greater access to those courses.

Losing its status as an independent unit was viewed by many as a consequence of the Center's overall loss of influence with Black students, the same group that years earlier had been responsible for its birth. Others, more concerned about making Black studies courses a legitimate part of the total university experience, saw the change as an opportunity to give Black studies courses a status equal with that of other disciplines. This duality of objectives, wanting to be separate and autonomous on one hand and needing to be part of the established academic community on the other, contributes to the Center's ambiguous image.

Black studies departments at Midwestern and other universities were born largely because of image problems: the lack of positive Black images in the American educational system. They exist today hobbled by images of unprofessionalism and provincialism. Having had such image problems and poor definitions of its publics, today's Black studies departments are having a difficult time adjusting to changing social and political climates of today's universities. Many programs are viewed as irrelevant by Black students and the black community, as well as by White students and faculty.

METHODOLOGY

Research in public relations or any discipline is as varied as the backgrounds of the practitioners. This chapter reflects the qualitative approach. Through structured reading and interviews with informed people, the background for this study evolved. The next stage of development, formal planning, helped define the scope and length of the study. The historical analysis helped define the broader issues involved and provided an essential bridge between yesterday and today to help understand the full significance of the Institute's evolution.

The genesis of this study emerged during a 6-month period while the primary author of this chapter was a graduate student coordinator at the Center for Afro-American Studies' Cultural Arts Center. During that period data was gathered on the frequency and use of the Cultural Center by various student groups. A preliminary study of the Center's publications was also conducted during that time. Issues of the *Black Bull, Sauti, Afro-American Affairs,* and their successors were examined from 1972 to the present. Further study was conducted over the next year in the university archives.

Phone and personal interviews of past and current students, faculty, and staff were conducted over that same period. Additional material was gleaned from published interviews in the university and in the local press. Much of the comparative student data was extracted from the 1974 Black Student Questionnaire, a university-sponsored survey of Black students.

Books and magazine articles written during and about the student movement during the late 1960s and early 1970s were also helpful.

Probably the most useful in providing insight into the turbulence at Midwestern during the Black Studies Institute's founding was a doctoral dissertation written by the Institute's second dean (Sutton, 1972). That study, although not representing the full spectrum of Black student opposition to the group eventually given control of the Institute, nonetheless gives a fairly accurate account of the conflict from the administration's perspective.

ORIGINS OF BLACK STUDIES AT MIDWESTERN UNIVERSITY

To understand what has happened to those programs whose very existence once spelled relevancy to Black students, we must examine their key publics and determine how well they are being reached. We proceed by studying the genesis and development of a Black studies center at a medium-sized liberal arts university in the Midwest. For purposes of our study, the university is known as Midwestern. Nearly 200 years old, Midwestern University is noted for its beautiful and historic residential campus, its proximity to three state parks, and its small town Appalachian atmosphere.

Most of the 18,000 students at Midwestern come from in-state. Nearly 7%, the largest percentage of any university in the state, come from abroad. Less than 5% of Midwestern's students are Black.

In 1969, the Black students at Midwestern confronted the university administration and demanded that $200,000 be allocated to establish a Black studies program (Sutton, 1972, p. 69). Furthermore, they insisted that it be established in all haste, that it be staffed with Black instructors, and that they, the Black students, be given the power to determine who those professors would be. In return, the students agreed not to riot and close the university down. All of their demands were met, and the Institute for Black Studies was established with a hastily approved curriculum and little understanding of what the program's goals were or of how they would be achieved.

Historical Development of Black Studies Programs

Before examining the evolution of the Black studies program at Midwestern University, we briefly examine the climate that led to the growth of similar programs throughout the United States during the middle and late 1960s.

The Issues.   As part of a nationwide protest against segregation and discrimination, students in all-Black institutions organized the Student Non-Violent Coordination Committee (S.N.C.C.) in 1961. When liberal and concerned White students joined, S.N.C.C.'s influence was broadened considerably. However, when Stokely Carmichael replaced James Forman as head of S.N.C.C. in 1965, things began to change. Carmichael declared that from that point on, S.N.C.C. would be all Black. This dictum gradually spread to other civil rights groups, such as the Congress of Racial Equality (CORE) and local branches of the Black Students Union (Redding, 1970, p. 584).

The assumption of a need for separation became a kind of self-defeating extremism. This resulted, in the rhetoric of the revolution, in such phrases as "cultural identity," "cultural nationalism," "ethnic monism," and the all-too familiar "Black power" (Redding, 1970, p. 585). Student leaders used these phrases to shape an ideology that railed against Western tradition as racist, corrupt, and irrelevant.

Given the conditions defined by the students—White-controlled institutions that foster racist beliefs of Whites toward Blacks through the learning process, social irrelevance, and the cultural alienation of Black people in response to the racist learning environment—the demand for Black studies programs to which only Blacks would be admitted was naive. Meeting the demand would perpetuate the very racist conditions that Black students said they opposed.

The fact that activists did not speak for all Black students is illustrated by Black students at Yale. These young people did not speak of Black studies courses. They argued instead that any course in American history that slighted or ignored the Black man's role was a bad course. They contended that writing by Black Americans was

American writing and that attempts to segregate it from the body of American letters was an exercise in ignorance (Redding, 1970, p. 587).

Similar changes occurred at Harvard. In April 1969, six Black students were named to a committee with the job of designing an Afro-American department in a situation closely paralleling that at Midwestern. Three of the students were elected by the Association of African and Afro-American Students, a student political organization without open membership. All student members voted on tenure and term appointments, and some became members of the executive committee of the new department that they helped create. Thus, Black undergraduate students were given powers previously held only by senior Harvard faculty (Rosovsky, 1972, p. 561).

A key element was ignored in this situation only to become a bone of contention that led to the eventual decline of many Black studies departments. Although students undoubtedly had to play a major role in the development of the new Black studies courses, their level of experience and expertise as teachers and researchers did not qualify them for the responsibilities they were assigned. Learning and research not produced by experienced, trained intellects became viewed as hollow.

Black studies developed as a discipline almost in a vacuum. Some Black students conceived of Afro-American studies largely as a professional field designed primarily to produce community leaders. Undergraduate study seemed destined to be central because many wanted to return to their communities directly after college. Postgraduate work covering a wide range of social science and humanities courses was viewed by many as irrelevant and beyond their reach.

Henry Rosovsky, chair of the economics department and the Faculty Committee on African and Afro-American Studies at Harvard in 1968, said the creation of his and similar committees stemmed directly from two concerns: Afro-American or Black studies and the quality of Black student life (Rosovsky, 1972, p. 564).

Issues relating to the quality of Black student life are hard to define concisely. The real point is that the quality of life is not good because it is difficult to be Black in a predominantly White institution. Along with that feeling comes a sense of guilt among Black college students about being in school when their families are suffering in the ghetto. This guilt led to demands for relevance at Midwestern and other universities, meaning two things. The first was instruction and research specifically directed toward improving the lot of Blacks in this country. The second was an intellectual effort to end racism (Rosovsky, 1972, p. 566).

There was also a strongly stated desire for the possibility of privacy—a privacy into which the Black student could withdraw, be with his or her own ethnic group, and reinforce his or her sense of culture and identity.

Reactions to Student Demands.   As John Blasingame (1969, 1970) observed, the first problem uncovered in surveying Black studies programs around the country was confusion over objectives. Phrases such as "need," "demand," "relevance," and "such programs need no justification" were used in place of goals or objectives. When asked why Black studies programs were established on their campuses, most college professors in the United States said simply that the Black students demanded them.

Reacting to student demands for relevance, a number of colleges combined social service concepts with traditional academic pursuits. In spite of the fact that neither students nor faculty knew what the students meant by relevance, some effort was made to give students some contact with and skills they could ostensibly carry back to the Black community. However, few academics tried to find out what the Black community thought relevant to its needs, as symmetric public relations dictates. Given such an omission, inconsistent, vague goals were inevitable (Blasingame, 1969, p. 551).

A consensus did develop that Black studies programs should instill pride, develop a sense of personal worth, and provide some tools for restructuring society. Attempts to meet the last objective have often helped create the most confusing and contradictory aspects of the programs.

Blasingame (1969, p. 550) stated that many Blacks desperately needed a more sophisticated knowledge of American society. Most Blacks did not have to attend college to learn that Whites were opposing them socially, economically, and politically. Instead, Blacks needed to study business practices, high finance, labor law, judicial procedures, consumer practices, and the communications media. A program lacking academic respectability was of no use to Black students and was certainly irrelevant to the Black community.

In theory, Black studies programs at predominantly White universities were open to all students. However, no consideration was given to the program's relevance to the White community. In a society dominated by Whites, racism and the institutions through which it is enforced are largely products of White control, not Black. Thus, a failure to identify or consider Whites contributed to a loss of influence for most Black studies programs in the United States today.

An Economic Context of the Development of Black Studies

At a time when most traditional departments in state universities had difficulties operating with a million-dollar annual budget, Black studies programs were established with less than $250,000 to be used for teaching personnel and a host of community-action programs. Many colleges did not make a serious commitment to Black studies programs, because they felt the demand would die out shortly. Consequently, rather than setting aside university funds to establish the programs, they turned to foundations for support.

The lack of commitment extended beyond inadequate financial support to even more serious realms. Most damaging was the elimination of any required standards for teachers. Because of the lack of commitment and the urgent demand, many colleges hired all manner of people, including Black preachers, Urban League administrators, even undergraduate Black students, to teach Black-oriented courses. Social workers, graduate students, high school teachers, principals, and practically anyone who looked Black or had mentioned Blacks in an article, book, or seminar paper found themselves teaching (Sutton, 1972, p. 63).

Some Political Considerations

Understanding the political dynamics of the Black studies enigma helps clarify the position of today's Black studies programs. We begin by looking once more at their origins.

Black students demanded not only that Black studies courses be developed but also that only Black instructors be hired to teach them. Blackness in and of itself gave no mystical guarantee of an understanding of the Black man's problems, life, or culture. In their fervor to find Black teachers, however, Black students ignored the possible crippling effects of simply hiring any Black man or woman. They often suggested teachers whom no administrator, regardless of persuasion, could accept.

The term had not yet come into vogue, but Black students opposed the hiring of any Blacks they believed to be *politically incorrect.* More crippling than the Black students' demands to hire only Black teachers was their insistence that those teachers have the "right" political ideology. Black scholars being considered for positions in these programs had to gain the approval of their academic credentials by the faculty, but that wasn't all. They also had to cater to the demands of Black students (Sutton, 1972, pp. 74–79).

Often, when the Black scholar escaped the ideological snare of the Black students, he or she faced the almost equally dangerous trap of being overworked by White colleagues. Frequently, because there were few Blacks on the faculty, presidents and deans used Black studies professors as all-purpose troubleshooters to defang militant Black students (Blasingame, 1969, p. 552).

The Social Dynamics of Activism

Whenever their politics of violent rhetoric resulted in concessions, Black student activists behaved as if they had won a major war though the real power remained invested in the university, which could choose to exercise that power.

Socially, Black students were no different from White students of their time. Black students were alienated and felt neglected within the university, but so did many Whites. The similarities generally revolved around three areas: (a) course offerings and other educational opportunities at the university, (b) the forms and quality of undergraduate social and cultural life, and (c) the relationship of the university to the community (Sutton, 1972, p. 74).

The key group of students who became leaders at Midwestern and other universities in the late 1960s and early 1970s had engaged in S.N.C.C. activities earlier. As S.N.C.C. underwent a metamorphosis under the banner of Black power and the leadership of Stokely Carmichael, students were politicized. Furthermore, involvement with S.N.C.C. brought them nearer the urban center of the wider Black-nationalist politicization of the Black community. In a sense, these students, the bulk of whom were raised in Black ghettos in the Midwest and elsewhere, stood in a special relationship to the general rise of Black militancy (Sutton, 1972, p. 231).

This relationship enabled student leaders to master Black nationalist ideology and tactics and subsequently politicize a highly visible number of Black students. These students, approximately 300, were seen as a necessary base of support if the leaders were to intimidate Midwestern University's power structure into granting a series of demands they were formulating.

GENESIS OF THE BLACK STUDIES INSTITUTE AT MIDWESTERN UNIVERSITY

Most Black studies programs shared the following goals:

1. to correct American history by recognizing the past and present experience of its Black citizens,
2. to hasten integration by improving the understanding of Blacks by non-Blacks,
3. to prepare Black students for taking part in the mainstream of society with pride and self-confidence,
4. to prepare Black students to understand and work for the Black community, and
5. to provide Black students with a sense of power (Sutton, 1972, p. 235).

Begun in 1969 as the Black Studies Institute, Midwestern University's Black studies programs suffers from the same legacies of provincialism and unprofessionalism that plague other Black studies efforts today. As today's Center for Afro-American Studies, the former Institute is viewed in a variety of ways by its key publics. Unfortunately, these perceptions are inconsistent with the goals expressed by the Center's administrators.

The stages of development of Midwestern University's Black Studies Institute paralleled those at other institutions around the country. These stages were: (a) an exploration or deliberative stage, (b) a rallying-of-the-forces stage, (c) a concession or conciliation stage, and (d) a stage of institutionalization. Underlying these stages was a thrust toward Black nationalism, using campus and Black studies programs as a strategy toward achieving a quasi-form of Black nationalism in the United States (Sutton, 1972, p. 283).

The Institute quickly established itself as the mecca for Black pride on campus. Through its support of the Black student newspaper, *The Black Bull,* the Institute became both a cultural haven and a political springboard for the more active Black students and staff.

As the Institute evolved into the Center for Afro-American Studies, changes occurred politically, socially, and economically. These called for redefinition of its key publics and readjustment of recruitment and promotional strategies. However, these changes have failed to keep pace with the changing composition of Midwestern's student body and with that body's academic and social needs relative to the Center.

The Center has two primary responsibilities to its key publics: (a) to provide a useful and meaningful academic experience and (b) to provide needed social experience and support. It addresses social needs through services offered by its cultural component, the Arts and Cultural Center.

The goals of the Cultural Center, as expressed by the Institute's second dean at the Cultural Center's inauguration in 1975, are: (a) to provide a meeting place for Black students, (b) to encourage more Black participation on the social and cultural level at Midwestern, (c) to rejuvenate the movement of the 1960s through various social productions, and (d) to eventually house the offices of all Black student organizations (Afro American Affairs, 1975).

Except for providing a meeting place for Black students—and really for only a few of them—the Cultural Center failed to reach its goals. That failure stems largely from ineffective promotional and educational strategies concerning the Center's availability to its key publics that include Black, international, and women students.

The Center's academic role suffers from the same problems that beset its cultural arts image. Fewer students now enroll in Black studies courses than ever before, and this decline is especially noticeable among Black students, the Center's designated public. In the fall of 1990, only one student registered for a major in Afro-American Studies (AAS). In the previous year, not a single student did so. Black studies courses are viewed by both White and Black students as having little relevance to their goals of academic and professional excellence. Efforts to market the courses as vital and useful are ineffective.

The Political Significance of Being on the Black Studies Faculty

In the winter quarter of 1989, the Center offered 11 courses. Only three full-time faculty were teaching at the Center. The chairman taught 5 courses and a part-time instructor 1. The remaining 5 courses were handled by two full-time faculty.

Joyce Bell, then chairperson, joined the Midwestern University faculty in 1964, 1 year after the first Black faculty member was hired. She served as the second dean of the University's Center for Afro-American Studies from 1972–1977.

Frank Chloe, a member of the faculty since 1974 and past chair of the Department, oversees the programs sponsored by the Arts and Cultural Center.

Because Black faculty are so few in number, Chloe and Bell agree that the pressure on them is great (Estep, 1988). They say Black faculty members live with all the expectations their White counterparts do—teaching, researching, writing grant proposals, meeting with students—plus the additional responsibility of acting as mentors and role models for Black students. Chloe feels there are different sets of expectations for Black and White faculty.

"In every area where there are Black faculty, they're overworked," he explains. "Black faculty spend so much time with students, they're always drained and tired and falling behind on their research."

To Bell, some things have changed for Blacks on the Midwestern University campus over the past 25 years. Other things have not. She explains:

> Housing, in terms of access, has changed, and there's a much better distribution of black students among the colleges than there ever was.
>
> There used to be a predominant emphasis in the social science area, particularly history and sociology. Now kids are in engineering and the medical college that weren't there before. (Estep, 1988, p. 5)

According to Bell, Black students today are confronted by many of the same problems they faced 25 or 30 years ago, particularly those evolving from inadequate preparation. Many schools are products of residential segregation. In terms of equipment and teaching preparation, most Black schools are not as strong as all-White suburban schools.

THE PROBLEM DEFINED

Incongruent Public Image—A Social Context

The present image of the Center for African-American Studies suffers from being perceived as a Black enclave whose interests and goals encompass the needs of only Black students (and indeed only a select minority of them). Its failure to be perceived as an integral part of the broader university community by its essential publics further contributes to its poor image.

Like the Center itself, Black students are trying to achieve and mesh two purposes whose aims often seem to be at odds with each other. Some Blacks are not very cause oriented, are not grounded in the traditional Black church, and feel they have much in common with White and international students. These individuals find themselves labeled as outsiders by students involved with the Center along traditional lines.

Non-Black American and international students usually have little knowledge of the Center for Afro-American Studies and even less of its Cultural Center.

Despite its failure to successfully reach every segment of its diverse public, the Center for Afro-American Studies and the Cultural Center still have an accepted, historic function serving the needs of Black students at a predominantly White university. Black students on predominantly White campuses often need the social and cultural haven of familiarity and acceptance that many find only among a group of others like themselves. In this respect the Cultural Center offers a safe and familiar setting where students can orient to the university environment comfortably. Sitting in classes with other Blacks and being taught by Black professors gives students a sense of acceptance that they may not experience in other classes.

Many Black students on predominantly White campuses do not have a clear understanding or acceptance of themselves. Certainly, Black students today can have White, Hispanic, or Asian friends and aspire to be successful. They must, however, accept themselves for who they truly are. They must accept their culture, literature, music, and heritage. The majority of Black students today do not understand the political issues pertaining to Blacks, nor do they see the need to understand their history as Black people. Instead they focus mostly on whether Afro-American studies courses will lead to better jobs or to more money when they graduate.

A student whose extracurricular life centers around students of one race has little opportunity to learn to interact with people of all races. Such interaction is important in forging lasting friendships and in most professional careers. A segregated life can breed contempt for the very system students want to succeed in after graduation (Nemko, 1988, p. 111).

Most successful minority students consider their ethnicity to be part of who they are but not all of who they are. Such students deal with racism and perceived racism very differently (Sedlecek, 1987, p. 485). Successful people rarely blame their failures on racism. As a minority counselor said, "Racism may be an explanation, but it's not an excuse."

One primary benefit of a university with as many diverse cultural components as Midwestern University is the education one gains from interacting with people from such a wide variety of cultures. Often insulated by her minority lifestyle before attending college, the Black student who further limits her social and cultural interaction to those within her own group, inhibits her development both personally and professionally. Thus, the Center must accurately identify and assess its publics' needs if it doesn't want to fall into the trap of promoting counterproductive cultural isolation.

Fifteen years ago it was fairly easy for Black students to define their needs and goals on the Midwestern University campus. Consequently, the Center for Afro-American Studies could more easily address them.

In the 1960s and 1970s, Black students wanted more power and a voice in decisions made by the university administration (Peterson, 1978, p. 199). Black pride was an integral part of Black students' vocabulary, and they did not just want to "make it" or be Xerox copies of White students.

Circumstances have changed, as have Black students. A few researchers are writing about their concern for this new Black student (Coachman, 1985; Louis, 1985). Even parents are speaking of the changes they see in their sons and daughters (Gaines-Carter, 1985). Other changes that have been discussed about changing

Black students include changes in attitude, perception, and expectations of those on predominantly White campuses.

The prevailing conclusions state that in general, Black students have little knowledge of their own history and heritage or of Black people's contributions to society. They know little of the sacrifices made by others so they could get an education. Many of today's Black students are very materialistic and clearly want to make a lot of money for themselves.

When asked how they feel about the social climate at Midwestern in a 1974 survey, most Black students readily admitted that they hated it. They looked forward to the weekends when they could get back home to "listen to real music, relax, and have fun" with people who shared their tastes in music and dance. For both men and women, the social wasteland of the area is symbolized by its lack of Black hair-care professionals.

Because the city has no Black barbers or beauticians, Black students cut and style each other's hair rather than experience the anger and embarrassment of being rejected by local barbers who proclaim themselves incapable of cutting Black hair. Some Black students talk about getting away from Midwestern and its surroundings much as soldiers talk of going home on leave. They count the days until breaks and graduation, as if they are combat veterans approaching their mustering-out date.

In the 1974 survey, 500 questionnaires were distributed in residence halls and other locations on campus. In all, 117 questionnaires were completed. Black students agreed that social and cultural activities specifically designed to meet their needs should be increased to reflect more adequately the proportion of minority students at Midwestern University. The attitudes prompting this response helped define the goals of the planned Arts and Cultural Center.

In 1974, as today, the Center for Afro-American Studies struggled to define and take into account the changing characteristics of its key publics. One definition focuses on "non-traditional, mainly black students" (Childs, 1987), a very specific audience. A later, more inclusive definition involves "students either enrolled in courses or majoring or minoring in Afro-American Studies, International Studies, liberal arts, business, education, communication, and health and human services majors." (Childs & Terrell, 1989). These two versions clearly show a need to define more sharply the department's constituency.

The very element that proved to be the earlier Center's greatest asset, its high visibility as a Black "haven or safe house" (Haggerty, Personal Communication, 1991), became its major liability in the 1990s. Although many Black students still need the feeling of social unity derived from taking courses in AAS, others look upon those same courses as "a piece of cake." Black studies courses were once vitally important to Black students because no attention had been given to that area. As the 1974 Black Student Questionnaire indicated, most Black students perceived the university setting as hostile and needed the refuge of the Black haven provided by the Center of Afro-American Studies.

The Center's primary purpose as a refuge and source of pride and identity for

Black students is out of date. The psychological, social, and political realities of the 1990s and beyond dictate a fuller understanding and appreciation of the multiethnic and multicultural society America is today instead of a return to the cultural isolation of the 1960s.

Although not listed among the Center's original goals, the need to reach White students has become a key to the unit's survival. Unfortunately, recent attempts to isolate and attract White students have met with little success. The university-supported survey of 1974 failed to address the issue of the Center's White public or even acknowledge the need for wide participation by White students in Black studies courses. Certainly this failure to establish White student involvement as a major goal of the department contributed to the poorly developed relationship that today's White student body has with the Center and its cultural arm.

A major factor contributing to the department's poor image among non-Black students is the experience many White students have while taking Black studies courses. Many White students who take Black studies courses do so because they feel sympathetic to the problems Blacks have with discrimination and second-class citizenship. They enter the class experience with an unbiased and open attitude. Yet, as is often the case, the White student in a Black class is made to feel like the enemy. Black students challenge the White student's motives, discount his or her sympathy, and make the student regret having taken the course.

Consequently, many White students come out of their Black studies' classroom experience feeling worse about the racial issue than when they entered. This results in those students never taking a Black studies course again. Even more important than getting White students in Black studies classrooms, the Center must see that their experiences there are good ones. White students who have satisfying experiences in Black studies courses can do more to promote the Center's image among certain publics than even the best promotional literature.

More Political Context

Founded in 1975 at the height of the Center's power, the Arts and Cultural Center opened to a wave of optimism. The Resource Center for Afro-American Studies published a bimonthly, quality newspaper, the *Afro-American Affairs*. The 1975 spring issue of that paper listed the goals of the new center as: (a) to provide a meeting place for Black students (with pool tables, pin ball, ping pong, cards, television room, dance area, and study halls available), (b) to encourage more Black participation on the social and cultural level at Midwestern, (c) to rejuvenate the movement of the 1960s through various social productions, and (d) to house eventually the offices of all Black student organizations.

Judging by the test of time, the goals originally expressed for the cultural arts center require further assessment. Rekindling the movement of the 1960s among students at a predominantly White university seems to be more rhetorical daydreaming than reality. Black student organizations today are struggling to maintain their existence because of a lack of participation and membership. Some of these organizations, including Black sororities and fraternities, have moved from a stance of political, educational, and social involvement to one that is strictly social. Black organizations can get hundreds of Blacks to a dance but only a handful for a study session or survival workshop, or to hear a guest speaker on Black culture. This reflects the priorities of at least some of today's Black students. Thus, a significant support structure is lost.

On political issues, the majority of today's Black students do not truly understand the Black community or the effects of certain important events. Therefore, today's Black youth cannot understand the uproar over the attacks by the Reagan and Bush administrations on affirmative action and equal opportunity programs. Because of this lack of political awareness, many Black students are disinterested—not upset and not angry.

The civil rights movement helped give birth to the anti-war and women's movements. In the 1980s, it may have been more expedient to merge the activist spirit of the 1960s with the women's movement than to breathe life into what many felt was politically moot. For purposes of funding, image building, and forming power coalitions, a merger with the women's movement would have reaped tremendous benefits for the Center. Overtures have been made to women's groups through offering women's studies seminars and meeting space in the building that houses the Center. However, no concerted, planned effort has yet come about.

The failure to house the offices of the major Black student groups (Black Students Union and Black Students Cultural Programming Board) was an important loss for the Center of Afro-American Studies. Housing those two groups in the Culture Center would put it at the heart of most Black student activity, because most such programs are sponsored in part by those groups. Unfortunately, the offices are located in the university-wide Student Center, as are the offices of the Student Activities Commission (SAC). That venue is more expedient, politically, for the student groups who receive their funding from SAC.

The Cultural Center has also failed to encourage more Black participation, both socially and culturally, in the total university community. In the 1974 survey, race was a dominant influence in 42% of the respondents' choices for friends and activities. Sixteen percent belonged to a sorority or fraternity, and 24% belonged to a predominantly White extra-curricular organization. Those figures today remain nearly the same, according to an informal polling of Black students who attended activities during a recent 6-month period at the Cultural Center.

International students complain of feeling isolated and unwelcome when they wander into the Cultural Center out of curiosity. Although the Center defines all international students as a public, in actual practice that definition embraces primarily people from Africa and the Caribbean. All others, especially Asians and Europeans, are discouraged by the reception they get from black students at the center. Because it has not developed a truly multicultural and multiethnic image, the Center has failed to attract large segments of the international community.

Finally, providing a meeting place for Black students to watch television, play games, host dances, and study is often the only goal that others in the university community can identify when asked about their perception of the Cultural Arts Center. Even as late as 1985, the Center was perceived as a place for Black students to "party hearty." Dances there frequently ended with fights among the participants. The chair has tried to address that image problem by discouraging certain groups from having dances there and by closely monitoring those that are held. Despite her efforts, the legacy of the past still survives among many students, particularly those with no direct involvement in the Cultural Center. The stereotypic image of Blacks being rowdy and violent was reinforced frequently by the conduct of Black students who attended dances at the Center. In contrast, most activities today are church oriented, catering to responsible students. However, the stereotypical image of Blacks as more interested in fun and games than in academics still persists.

Today, with the exception of Black History Month, the Cultural Center is used primarily by a CAAS-sponsored gospel group and a Bible study group. Each of these organizations is scheduled to use the Center four times a month, suggesting to some that the Center is little more than an all-Black Christian-oriented facility. One student's comment sums up the feeling of many when she says, "If I wanted to pray and get preached at, I'd go to church."

Publications Reflect the Center's Changing Fortunes

We have noted the Center's evolution from institute to departmental status. Another graphic illustration of the Center's changing political role is the evolution of its publications. The declining eminence of the Afro-American Studies Center is eloquently illustrated in the changing fortunes of the Center's house organ, the *Afro-American Affairs*.

One clear reflection of the support given to the Center by the university is its support of the Center's publication. From the inception of *Afro-American Affairs* until 1980, the university gave academic credit to students who worked on the paper's staff. Awarding such credit gave the students who worked on the paper a uniquely favorable status. In contrast, none of the students who worked for the predominantly White-run student newspaper, *The Post,* received academic credit.

When the Institute became a department in the College of Arts and Sciences in 1980, its change in political clout was mirrored in the design, staffing, and quality of its publication. The paper changed its name to *Sauti,* a Swahili word meaning "the voice." Also, the format changed from a tabloid size on newsprint to a much smaller page.

Publics often develop their impressions of an organization from its publication. Sometimes a dynamic editorial staff produces a paper that suggests greater energy and competence within the entire organization than really exists. However, if the organization is dynamic and growing, it commonly engages an editorial staff that mirrors that dynamism. And, at the opposite extreme, a lackluster publication usually comes from a lackluster sponsoring organization.

Using four sheets of $8\frac{1}{2}$ by 14 inch mimeograph paper folded into 16 pages, the 1980 edition of *Sauti* was less striking visually than its predecessors. However, its lack of size was compensated by its substance and intensity. The reduction in size and funding of the Center was reflected in the reduction and size of its house organ, but the commitment to fire and excellence remained. Thus, the paper still had a loyal readership, and the center was perceived as strong and vital.

Further Cuts.   By 1983, the staff of the Center for Afro-American Studies had declined from a high of 16 paid employees in 1975 to a subsistence-level of 4 full-time faculty and a secretary (Estep, 1988). Half of its previous office space was given to a homeless sociology/anthropology department in a move that made the Center's staffers feel they "were being evicted without notice."

The political fortunes of the Center were summed up by Frank Chloe's comments in that same editorial. Chloe (Afro American Affair, 1975), past chair of the department and a faculty member since 1973, said, "I have witnessed the decline of the Arts & Cultural Center from a place where Afro-American painters, writers, and musicians of world renown perform into a [place that's a] ghettoish dump" (p. 5).

In 1984, *Sauti* still had real class. Published weekly, it maintained a loyal readership among the Black students. By 1986, however, the paper was reduced to two folded pages of 8½ by 14 mimeograph sheets, with a staff composed of four work-study students. Layout was sloppy and amateurish, reflecting the general image of the Center within the total university community. Though identified on its masthead as a weekly, the paper came out irregularly, about once a month.

As of 1991, one of the Center's better efforts is its quarterly newsletter. Printed on four pages of 8½ by 11 inch paper, it is well designed and written with professional-quality photos and graphics. However it is not the kind of paper that creates a clear image of the Center within the student body. It is primarily an academic publication with information about developments in the field and other material of interest to professionals.

The latest student edition of *Sauti* suggests the Centers fortunes may be rising (*Sauti*, 1991). Reflecting the professional background of its faculty advisor, a former city editor of a major metropolitan newspaper, *Sauti* is published as a slick tabloid with a colorful masthead and black and white photos. Its layout is well organized and pleasing to the eye. Its stories are predictable, such as "Black Men, Black Women," and its writing uneven, but it is a very clear improvement over its immediate predecessor.

Without a viable, well-written and professionally designed publication, the Center for Afro-American Studies will continue to reap the negative benefits of its poorly defined and promoted public image.

ECONOMIC CONTEXT

Without access to past departmental budgets, it is difficult to compare the financial position of today's Center with that of its predecessor. However, we can estimate current allocations by examining the department's present staffing and support services.

Today's staff includes three full-time and two part-time faculty. In addition to three graduate assistants, the Center has a full-time secretary and an undergraduate assistant. Lack of monies for conference attendance and other professional-development activities reflects the department's funding situation. In addition, making funding for new programs and training is difficult to obtain.

The present chair, Dr. Rosewood, assumed his position in July 1990, after Dr. Chloe's term expired. Rosewood, also a long-time employee of the department, was chair prior to Chloe's appointment. Rotating chair responsibilities is commonly practiced by many departments. However, other departments have more than two eligible faculty from which to choose! The practice of rotating department-chair duties between the same two faculty reflects the static condition of the department. Without new faculty to bring fresh approaches and enthusiasm to the position, breaking established patterns that have contributed to the department's poor image is more difficult. Rotating chairs between two faculty members also illustrates the university's lack of commitment to recruiting and hiring new personnel for the department.

Another indicator of the department's standing within the university community is the chairperson's salary. Nor surprisingly, medicine and science chairpersons are among the highest paid at Midwestern. Chairs of family medicine and osteopathy each earn a base salary of more than $93,000. These figures are for 12-month faculty, as is the Center's chair. (Faculty, Administrative Salary Printout, 1990). Physics and mechanical engineering chairs each earn more than $73,000 per year. Average departmental salaries range between $63,000 and $67,000 yearly. The chairs of the civil engineering, journalism, telecommunications, history, and economics departments fall within this category.

Department chairs at the lowest level earn between $51,000 and $59,000 annually. The chair of the Center for Afro-American Studies earns $55,604 a year. Others in that salary range include heads of the English, art, political science, psychology, and nursing departments.

English, political science, and psychology courses are required for all students, as some argue Black studies should be. Others feel the department's inclusion in the College of Arts and Sciences has made great strides toward giving its courses university-wide legitimacy. However, some feel that the department's greater legitimacy is offset by its loss of autonomy.

IMPLICATIONS OF NEEDS AND ASSESSMENTS

The current public image of the Center for African-American Studies and its service component, the Arts and Cultural Center, is poorly defined by the department and poorly understood by its various publics. Black students, its chief public, have conflicting images of the department and the Center based primarily on inaccurate and incomplete information received from other students. Many feel that Black studies courses require less work than traditional courses. Furthermore, it is felt that Black instructors, as "sisters and brothers," should not hold Black students to the same performance standards as are required by White professors.

Other Black faculty do not support the Center and its programs, because they fear being labeled as separatists by their White colleagues. They also fear being trapped in the politically and economically limited role of a Black faculty person, one who is perceived by peers as a Black first and a professional second.

The problems faced by Black students on a predominantly White campus cannot be addressed adequately by a Black studies department that isn't perceived as being an integral part of the total university community. On the other hand, the need for Black students to have a place where they can feel comfortable on a White campus still exists.

Among Black students at Midwestern University, the chief complaint is one of social and recreational isolation. Because the majority of Blacks come from the state's major urban centers, they are not attracted to the entertainment found in the local uptown bars—bars that the White students enter in droves. Television and radio stations also contribute to their feeling of isolation by airing programs that are geared to White rural audiences. Black students recently completed a successful 2-year effort to bring the Black Entertainment Network into the area via cable television.

To service its publics as well as meet its own needs, the Center for Afro-American Studies needs to define its publics clearly and sharply to reposition its image in relation to the total university community.

Redefining and Repositioning its Image

Forming a Clear Definition of Publics.   To encourage more participation in the social and cultural life of the university, the Center needs to broaden its base of support. It must move into a new era of involvement, one that demands different strategies than those recycled from the 1960s. Rather than positioning itself as an island of blackness in a white sea, the Center needs to market itself as a multicultural oasis with tentacles that reach into the greater university.

The Center presently has at least four key publics: (a) Black students, (b) international students, (c) women, and (d) White students. To help define its publics more clearly, the Center could design a questionnaire much like the one used in 1974, though broad enough in scope to include all students. Such a survey would provide feedback to develop the strategies needed to meet its publics' needs.

Action 1—The Center needs to embark upon a full-fledged campaign to promote itself as a legitimate, exciting source of useful knowledge.

Reasoning.   Having its courses listed among the "Third World" Tier II General Education requirements for all students at Midwestern is certainly a step in that direction. However, this greater accessibility produces little benefit in terms of increased enrollment unless the Center's courses are perceived as relevant to today's students' academic and professional goals.

The Center must market itself as a department that offers courses that are relevant for students in the 21st century. It needs to offer courses that are important to those students considering majors in Afro-American Studies but also to those majoring in other disciplines. Such a strategy was initiated when the department began marketing its courses as part of other disciplines, such as politics, economics, and the social sciences. The idea was timely but had limited effectiveness due to inadequate marketing.

The Center's current marketing strategy goes little further than distributing brochures that outline the courses being offered. For the kind of public image desired by the Center, a campaign based largely on brochures is inadequate. To dispell the image of Black studies courses as being easy and nonessential, a full-fledged marketing and image campaign must be conducted by a full-time, public relations professional who may or may not be a member of the faculty.

Action 2—To recruit more Whites, the Center must repudiate its current image of serving only Black interests and undertake an intensive educational effort depicting the Center as a multicultural and multiethnic body.

Reasoning. The Center can co-sponsor events with other schools and departments to show how its courses coalesce with others. Through its cultural arm, the Arts and Cultural Center, it can host activities that are clearly multiracial as well as multicultural.

However, the department can only accomplish so much on its own. In order to incorporate Black studies courses into the academic mainstream, the university must help make those courses available to a wider audience. By making certain Black studies courses are part of the graduation requirements for all students, as are certain English and mathematics courses, the university will have created an environment that encourages students to have a genuine cross-cultural experience.

Action 3—In attracting women, the Center can use many strategies that attract White students as a whole.

Reasoning. The chances of successfully attracting women seem greater than those for attracting some other publics. Because of their struggle against second-class citizenship, women are a natural constituency for the Center. Lecturers from Afro-American Studies and Women's Studies can each address themes that Blacks and women hold in common. For instance, by focusing on their shared need to combat discrimination, the Center could become more appealing to women.

Action 4—Many activities can be coordinated with the university's Center for International Studies.

Reasoning. By virtue of their past colonial history, many international students have a natural affinity for Afro-American Studies. Little is currently being done to channel those common interests other than sponsoring an occasional panel discussion that is attended primarily by Africans. Efforts must be made to increase the Center's attractiveness to international students. At present, many internationals feel isolated from White students and would welcome the opportunity to participate in shared activities at the Cultural Center. But they must be wooed first. The department must identify their needs, before it can intelligently incorporate them into its goals.

Action 5—The Center should continue efforts to develop a sharply targeted, first-rate publication.

Reasoning.   With this tool the Center can redefine its image throughout the total university community. The Black Student Union at Northern State University, a similarly sized institution in the northern part of the state, publishes an exceptionally well-done monthly magazine on slick paper that is distributed statewide. Such a quality publication gives its readers the distinct impression that Northern's Black Studies Department is well funded, vibrant, and vital (Spectrum, 1986).

In sum, if it wants to be perceived as a place of welcome for all students, the Center needs to make an all-out effort to attract female, international, White, and other students. There is little reason to fear that, by broadening its appeal to other groups, the Cultural Center will lose its attractiveness to Blacks.

Action 6—The Center's staff must take a closer look at whether it wants to embark on a campaign to get Black students to "hang out" at its own Cultural Center rather than at the university-wide Student Center, where most of them spend time at the present.

Reasoning.   Many students chose Midwestern's Student Center over the Cultural Center as much for its central location and large-screen television as for anything else.

Currently most student groups, Blacks among them, use the university's Student Center as the location for their group-sponsored events. The Center's staff needs to determine why the university-wide Student Center is more convenient (free access, larger rooms, easier to reserve space, etc.) and address itself to those particular reasons if it wants to become a center of student activities.

On the other hand, the Cultural Center gives students a unique opportunity for interaction by offering itself as a forum for diversity of thought and genuine cultural exchange. By building upon its attraction to its varied publics, the Center can become an interesting and exciting place. With a proper needs assessment to help provide a comprehensive understanding of its publics, today's underutilized Cultural Center can become a vital hub for intercultural exchange and growth.

A LOOK BACK AT THE SPE CONTEXT

SPE contexts were utilized in this chapter to provide an overview of the Black studies phenomenon at the macro or general level as well as the specific or micro level. Although it requires another chapter to discuss the full theoretical implications of the Midwestern study, we pause here to highlight the broader applications of the SPE model.

Some of the social contexts we found useful in our analysis of the Center for Afro-American Studies include: (a) cultural beliefs, (b) beliefs about one's situation, and (c) schemata (Culbertson & Jeffers, 1991, p. 43). For example, the Black student activists demanding a role in the formation of the Black Studies Institute operated primarily from two perspectives: (a) cultural beliefs about institutions such as the predominantly White university and how they related to it and (b) cultural beliefs dealing with themselves and their own personal standards of thinking and conduct.

From their viewpoint, threats of disruption and violence were justified unless a Black studies department was established. Perceiving themselves as aggrieved and abused by the White power structure, they felt justified in proceeding by "any means necessary."

Important social schemata helped determine which information each side used to form its responses to the conflict surrounding the Center. The administration operated from a position of social responsibility and compromise. By relinquishing curriculum control to the students, university leaders met the social need for a Black studies program and kept the school open. The students evaluated the administration's position in light of their own needs and the right to have Black studies available to them. Both groups used their own particular sets of belief structures to define the situation at hand and develop action plans.

Some of the more important political contexts at work from a public relations perspective include influence strategies and leadership roles. Under conditions of high involvement, such as existed during the formation of the Institute, people evaluate arguments carefully and reach cognitively based conclusions. Where involvement is low, however, attributing messages and arguments to highly credible sources becomes crucial (Culbertson & Jeffers, 1991).

The high involvement of Black and White students during the formation of the Black studies program was not adequately exploited. Both sides failed to form coalitions based on shared, accurate information. Later, publications were utilized to articulate an in-house argument to those who already believed rather than as a vehicle to bring other audiences into the fold.

The leadership of the Center for Afro-American Studies contributed to the lack of coalition-building among the university's various populations. Formal leaders, such as the second dean of the Center who was the administration's choice, did not have the influence of the informal leadership exerted among the student body by certain student leaders. Thus, the university's formal leadership was ineffective within the student body. And the student leadership was not interested in forming coalitions with other groups at that time.

From an economic perspective, exchange principles state that persons only participate in a voluntary exchange or relationship when both parties benefit from or assign value to what is exchanged. For example, Midwestern's Black student leaders demanded a voice in determining Black studies curricula and personnel in exchange for not inciting the Black student body to riot in a way that might close down the university. University administrators, wanting to keep Midwestern open and deal responsibly with social demands for Black-oriented courses, agreed to fund the Black Studies Institute demanded by the students.

Both groups voluntarily gave up something of value to achieve their goals. The students relinquished the power of their threat of disruption by accepting the proposals offered by the administration. And university officials surrendered some of their autonomy in designing and establishing curricula in exchange for an open and riot-free university.

From a public relations perspective, the choices to form and staff Black studies departments deal with two economic concepts: self-interest and efficiency. Colleges and universities make choices in their own self-interest (to keep the colleges open and avoid violent disruptions) and for economic efficiency (to use a given amount and combination of resources to get maximum benefits). Poor administrative choices, such as those at Midwestern and other universities, helped develop a legacy of unprofessionalism for Black studies departments that is still prevalent today.

REFERENCES

Barnes, J. (1992). Personal interview, Center for Afro-American Studies, Ohio University, Athens.

Blasingame, J. W. (1969). Black studies: An intellectual crisis. *The American Scholar, 38,* pp. 550–552.

Blasingame, J. W. (1970). "Soul" or scholarship: Choices ahead for Black Studies. *Smithsonian, 1,* p. 58.

Childs, F. (1975, Spring). The quest for survival. *Afro-American Affairs.* Ohio University, Athens, OH, p. 5.

Childs, F. (1987). Afro-American Studies experimental education proposal. Ohio University, Athens, Ohio.

Childs, F., & Terrell, M. J. (1989). Afro-American Studies experimental education proposal. College of Arts and Sciences, Ohio University, Athens, Ohio.

Coachman, W. (1985, May). *Guest in a strange house.* Paper presented to Illinois Committee of Black Concerns in Higher Education, University Park, IL.

Culbertson, H. M., & Jeffers, D. W. (1991). The social, political and economic contexts: Keys to front-end research. *Public Relations Quarterly, 36,* 43–48.

Estep, B. (1988, April). Black faculty worried about declining numbers, *Outlook,* Ohio University, Athens, OH, p. 5.

Gains-Carter, P. (1985, September). Is my "post-integration" daughter Black enough? *Ebony,* pp. 54–56.

Louis, E. T. (1985, August). The life and times of a college buppie. *Essence,* pp. 50–52.

Nemko, M. (1988). *The Black and Hispanic student at State U.: How to get an Ivy League education at a State University.* New York: Avon.

Peterson, M. W. (1978). *Black student on White campuses.* Ann Arbor, MI.: Institute for Social Research.

Redding, D. (1970). The Black youth movement. *The American Scholar, 38,* p. 587.

Rosovsky, H. (1972). Black Studies at Harvard: Personal reflections concerning recent events. *The American Scholar, 38,* p. 561.

Afro American Affairs. (1975, Spring). *Lindley center opens.* Ohio University, Athens, OH, p. 5.

Sauti. (1991, Fall). Ohio University, Athens, Ohio.

Sedlecek, W. E. (1987, November). Black students on white campuses. *Journal of College Student Personnel, 28,* p. 485.

Spectrum. (1986, Fall). Black United Students, Kent State University, Kent, Ohio, p. 3.

Sutton, W. S. (1972). *The evolution of the Black Studies movement with specific reference to the establishment of the Black Studies Institute at Ohio University.* Unpublished doctoral dissertation, Ohio University, Athens, OH.

11 Internal Public Relations in City Government: Serving the Servers

A Midwestern state association formed to assist personnel of municipal governments within its borders has a long-standing commitment to provide specialized training and continuing education to such key personnel as mayors, city managers, finance directors, and commissioners. However, beginning in the early 1980s, the association has also helped train the growing number of municipal personnel responsible for public relations. As a result of this effort, a separate public relations division was formed within the association to meet the special needs of these municipal communicators.

In some instances, these people have titles that identify them as being in charge of public relations for their municipalities. In other cases, public relations duties fall within the portfolios of individuals with other titles such as assistant city manager.

In the mid-1980s, the communicators recognized that all municipal employees could benefit from seminars on public relations. Consequently, beginning in 1985 and continuing toward the end of the decade, a series of workshops was developed in cooperation with a state university's Center of Communication.

One goal of the project, led by faculty members from several communication-related departments at the university, was to provide "frontline" training to municipal employees in communication techniques and principles of public relations. This goal was met because before the workshops were discontinued, hundreds of municipal workers from all over the state received public relations awareness training.

Although the specifics varied slightly from one situation to another, the general framework for the training sessions allowed for two to four instructors to lead small group discussions and provide individual consultations. Two 4-hour sessions were held each day, and employees were given release time to attend one of the sessions. Depending on the size of work forces in various departments, participants ranged from 25 to 100 per session.

A second goal of the project was to develop a mechanism for gathering data that allowed workshop sponsors to close the feedback loop by providing information to help improve training. Thus, a research component was added to the series of workshop presentations allowing for systematic analysis of employee attitudes regarding municipal public relations. This chapter shares some of the insights and knowledge gained through these workshops and the gathering of data.

THE LARGER CONTEXT

A *Time* magazine article published during the seminar highlighted one major reason why municipal communicators were interested in enhancing public relations awareness among employees. The article summed up the frustrations of millions of Americans when it implored: "Pul-eeze! Will somebody help me?" (Pul-eeze!," 1987). The work ethic, it was said, has declined in the service sector in our society. The authors went on to suggest that, if the United States economy is to thrive, the service concept will have to be "serviced."

Many management experts agree with the *Time* article. Consultants James Quinn and Christopher Gagnon (1986) noted that service industries offer even more opportunity for growth—and for mismanagement—than do product-based industries. These authors also believed it is essential to take a hard look at services, how we manage them, and how much they contribute to the nation's economy.

Quinn and Gagnon lamented that many people still equate the service sector with making hamburgers and shining shoes. However, in reality, service organizations are highly complex and sophisticated. They account for more than two thirds of the nation's gross national product and an even larger percentage of all employment.

Fortunately, although the service sector is becoming more complex, so is the thinking about how to improve performance within it. Suggestions range from restructuring large organizations into *co-corps,* which operate for the purpose of benefiting the public instead of making profits (Collier, 1979) to devoting more study to *emotional labor.*

The latter term was coined by Hochschild (1983) to describe a "part of a distinctly patterned, yet invisible, emotional system—a system composed of individual acts of 'emotion work,' social 'feeling rules,' and a great variety of exchanges between people in private and public life" (pp. x–xi). Hochschild's research with flight attendants and bill collectors documents that in a service industry, "the emotional style of offering the service is part of the service itself" (p. 5).

With the problem of poor service perceived as being so pervasive, public relations practitioners throughout society will surely be called upon to help provide remedies. In fact, programs to help organizations improve services may become the new growth area for public relations.

Practitioners venturing into this arena will not find the environment alien. In fact, management concepts designed to improve service within an organization sound similar to principles designed to improve public relations. When describing their *service management concept,* Albrecht and Zemke (1985) said:

> First, as a result of working in and with organizations, we are biased to believe that high-quality service at the front line has to start with a concept of service that exists in the minds of top management. This service concept must find its way into the structure and operation of the organization.
>
> We also believe in the value and importance of measuring service. An intimate and objective knowledge of how you are doing—in the customer's eyes—is critical. Market research, the service audit and a process of measuring service quality and feeding back this information to the frontline people are crucial ingredients in moving an organization to a high level of service orientation. (p. vi)

Albrecht and Zemke's notion of providing employee feedback—and hence, training—is seen by most experts as crucial in improving organizational service. Organizations frequently cited as having outstanding service tend also to be cited for having outstanding employee training and development programs (Branst, 1984). As indicated previously, the public relations practitioner may be the best person within an organization to provide this employee feedback and training.

If the concept of improved public service is important to the business world, it is even more important in the public sector. Government at all levels is increasingly challenged to be more responsive to the public. Often, "responsive" translates into providing more services with less tax dollars.

The pressure to improve service is particularly intense at the local municipal level not only because taxpayers have a greater opportunity to be responsive themselves (by not voting for tax increases or candidates who advocate them) but also because of closer social contact among those who live in the same community. It is reasonable to suppose that citizens expect especially good service from municipal workers who are friends and neighbors.

Nevertheless, public service by municipalities is believed to have declined along with that provided in the private sector. Often, employee unionization is cited as the reason for this decline (Davis & West, 1985; DiTomaso, 1978; Seroka, 1979). In some studies, however, more employee-centered variables (such as job satisfaction) are linked to municipal-worker efficiency (Pintor, 1976).

RESEARCH QUESTIONS, METHODOLOGY, AND RESULTS

Research Questions

The questions investigated in this study were chosen because municipal communicators could benefit from the answers to these questions when developing comprehensive training programs for employees.

The specific questions are:

1. What are some of the components of public service that municipal employees link to an overall municipal public relations program? In other words, what actions and activities do employees themselves consider to be important to an overall public relations effort?

2. What is the underlying structure of city employee attitudes regarding these public service activities? Given that public service actions are important to an overall public relations effort, what is the state of employee attitudes regarding these actions?

3. What is the relationship between that attitudinal structure and other job-related variables, such as job satisfaction? Job satisfaction is an oft-investigated variable in organizational communication research. As noted earlier, other research has linked it to public-employee performance.

4. Finally, are there identifiable municipal-employee communication patterns that might be used by public relations practitioners to improve public-service attitudes and perhaps performance?

It should be apparent that these research questions relate directly to the issues discussed in the social, political, and economic context chapters presented earlier in this volume. As regards the social context, answers to the previous questions help identify cultural and subcultural beliefs shared by municipal employees. Seeking input from municipal workers about what actions and activities they consider to be important to public relations and their attitudes about these matters provides the practitioner with information about three types of beliefs: (a) cultural beliefs about the institution of local government and how employees relate to it, (b) cultural beliefs associated with the personal standards of thinking and conduct for the individual municipal employee, and (c) subcultural beliefs learned and practiced by the subgroup of municipal employees and presumed to affect their job performance.

Turning to the political context, there is clearly a potential for conflict between the elected political city commissioners and the technocratic municipal workers over public relations goals, objectives, and programs. Also, as detailed in chapter 5, any organization's leadership has to struggle with the problem of task achievement while maintaining group morale and support. Those public relations practitioners whose municipality participated in the workshop series made headway on both fronts. The workshop series and its research component provided valuable information necessary to design and implement effective training and public relations programs. Further, the workshops helped improve group morale and support by providing employees with an opportunity to participate in the process.

Focusing on the economic context, municipal public relations practitioners have no choice but to come to grips with the scarcity of resources at their disposal and assess the opportunity costs and benefits associated with various public relations programs. By having their employees participate in this workshop series, municipal communicators received feedback that helped them set priorities, enhance positive externalities, and minimize negative ones.

Methodology and Results

The data needed for the research component of this project were gathered in two ways. First, during the workshops described earlier, municipal employees were asked to write down activities, actions, issues, and topics they considered important to their role as public servants. Further, they described both positive and negative personal experiences that seemed relevant to the municipality's overall public relations effort. These interactions were analyzed to help answer questions 1 and 4 previously stated.

Second, once the activities/actions and issues/topics had been identified, the researchers developed a survey instrument to measure attitudes about the activities/actions, job satisfaction, and communication behavior relating to the issues/topics. This survey form, designed to gather data needed to help answer questions 2, 3 and 4 listed earlier, was administered to employees in one municipality considered to be representative of many others.

Although towns and cities differ, the municipality studied here is typical in many ways of other Midwestern cities of the same size. It has a city-manager form of government with elected city commissioners who appoint a city manager to act as chief administrative officer. The job of mayor is largely ceremonial and is often rotated among the commissioners. At the time of this study, the population was nearly 40,000. Slightly over 100 employees worked in four divisions: Public Works (street and sanitation), Public Safety (fire and police), Finance and Records (taxation, voting, and administration), and Community Affairs (internal and external public relations).

Question 1. What actions and activities do municipal employees consider to be part of a public relations program?   One major category of activities and actions that municipal workers link to public service and an overall public relations campaign relates to contacts by employees with the public. Examples of such activities include:

1. *Providing solutions to citizen problems.* The very label *public servant,* assigned to politicians and technocrats alike, conveys the notion that a key job of municipal employees is to solve citizen problems. Municipal workers accept this and recognize that they must do so effectively if they are to be perceived favorably.

2. *Dealing with a wide range of types of citizens.* Municipal employees come in contact with the whole range of citizen types within their community. These include criminals, the elderly, children, the poor, the rich, the mentally

stable, and the mentally unstable. Workers recognize the need to interact with this wide spectrum.

3. *Promoting citizen understanding of municipal policies.* By virtue of living within a town or city, citizens are subject to its rules and regulations. Many people have contact with a city worker only when they have violated an ordinance or policy. In addition to acting as enforcers, workers see a need to promote awareness and understanding of the municipality's rules and regulations.

4. *Establishing working relationships with citizens.* Municipal employees realize they cannot do their jobs well in the absence of mutually interdependent and beneficial relationships with citizens. Further, workers feel establishing these relationships enhances the overall public relations program of the municipality.

To illustrate such concerns, consider municipal employees completing work in a neighborhood. They are asked by a senior citizen to trim a tree branch in the citizen's backyard. If they abide by policies prohibiting city workers from doing noncity work on private property, they have to tell the citizen to look elsewhere for help.

Yet the citizen views the municipal workers as public servants who should help community members. Trimming the branch (which may only take a few minutes) would generate a good deal of positive feeling about the city. Nevertheless, the employees must decide what to do as well as what to tell the citizen. They may just go ahead and trim the branch in spite of municipal policy or they may tell the citizen "no" for reasons of legal liability.

Employees also linked a second major cluster of actions and activities to the effectiveness of an overall public relations program. Because of the major differences between the two clusters, the researchers decided to focus on the first set as they sought answers to the other research questions. Nevertheless, it is important to briefly describe this second set of actions and activities.

The researchers considered this second set to be an internal or organizational cluster. Some relevant activities include: providing job-related training to employees, implementing effective management techniques, and eliminating overlap among job responsibilities.

An example cited by employees centers on the uneven performance of municipal workers. In one case, Division of Public Safety employees passed on citizen complaints about missing street signs at key intersections to Division of Public Works employees who were responsible for maintaining them. However, due to inefficiency in Public Works, the street signs were not replaced. Feeling frustrated because citizen complaints were not being addressed, Public Safety employees began to go around the Public Works Division and put the signs up themselves.

Rightly or wrongly, Public Safety employees believed they provided better public service and resented the perceived lack of commitment by Public Works employees.

Further, Public Safety people realized that poor performance by one division or department was bound to hamper any public relations effort by the city as a whole.

Question 2. What are the attitudes regarding these public service activities? The researchers found three aspects of municipal-employee attitudes about the public-contact activities described previously.

One set of positive attitudes focused on actual public-contact experiences of employees. For instance, employees did not mind when citizens interrupted their work by requesting information or help.

A second set of attitudes, slightly negative, related to self-perceptions during contact with citizens. For example, employees reported feeling frustrated with their limited authority to solve citizen problems.

A third set of attitudes, which were positive, related to employee perceptions of local citizens. Here, for instance, employees did not believe the public was made up of "cranks, oddballs, and deadbeats."

Question 3. What is the relationship between these attitudes and other job-related variables? The researchers looked for a relationship between the two variables and the public-contact attitudes. First, job satisfaction correlated positively with two of the three sets of attitudes: those dealing with self-perceptions and those related to beliefs about citizens in the community. Apparently, a city employee who has positive internal feelings about contact with citizens and positive attitudes toward community residents is likely to be satisfied on the job.

The second job-related factor investigated was the time that each employee spent with the public each day. In each municipality, some employees had a lot of public contact whereas others had very little. It seemed reasonable to suppose the amount of daily contact may relate to attitudes about that contact. However, the data does not show any such relationship.

Question 4. Are there communication patterns among municipal employees about public service related issues/topics? As noted earlier, the researchers analyzed workshop participants' responses to identify specific issues/topics related to contact with the public. This procedure revealed four major issues:

1. Municipal ordinances and regulations.
2. Handling citizen complaints.
3. The quality of services to citizens.
4. Adequate funding to provide these services.

The rationale for believing these issues were important is not hard to discern. Much of a municipal worker's behavior is governed by ordinances and regulations. In many cases, the ordinances are an employee's "reason for being." Unfortunately, citizens are not always happy with the ordinances or the way they are enforced. Consequently, dealing with complaints is a major part of a municipal worker's job. Although the workshop discussions revealed that most municipal workers are truly concerned about providing quality service to citizens, they believed their efforts to do so are often hampered by lack of an adequate budget.

As noted in chapter 4, there is good reason to believe a person's communication behavior is linked to beliefs about her or his situation. For this project, the Grunigs' situational theory, explained in chapter 4, was used to examine the communication patterns of municipal employees relating to the four issues identified previously. (For further elaboration on this theory, see Grunig, 1976, 1983; Grunig & Grunig, 1989; and Grunig & Hunt, 1984.)

Essentially, the Grunigs said that persons communicate and have attitudes about specific situations, not broad generalizations. Their research shows that at least three variables (sometimes four) are responsible for how often and how much persons communicate about specific issues. These include the degree to which the person considers the issue a problem (problem recognition), whether the person feels capable of doing anything about the issue (constraint recognition), and how involved the person is with the issue (level of involvement).

As explained in chapter 4, the Grunigs considered communication to include both information seeking and information processing. The latter is a passive mode wherein people attend to pieces of information that come their way and capture their attention. Information seeking denotes a more active approach that involves purposive selection, integration, and interpretation.

The procedures used to measure the theoretical and communication variables were recommended or utilized by the Grunigs. For the theoretical variables, municipal employees were asked how often they stop to think about the issues explained previously as a measure of their degree of uncertainty (problem recognition), whether they could do anything personally that would make a difference in the way the issues are handled (constraint recognition), and to what extent they saw a connection between themselves and the issue (level of involvement).

For the communication variables, respondents were asked how they would treat the receipt of a memo about each of the issues (information processing): read it immediately, put it aside to read when time is available, skim it briefly, or not read it at all. In addition, they were asked how likely they would be to attend a voluntary meeting after work hours about each of the issues (information seeking): very likely, somewhat likely, not likely, or not attend.

The survey data confirms that these four issues were important to municipal workers. In general, they thought about the issues frequently (high problem recognition), believed they could do something about the issues (low feelings of constraint), and considered themselves to be involved with the specific issues (high involvement). In addition, the data show them to be active processors and seekers of information about the four issues.

The most active issue turned out to be the one dealing with complaint handling. Employees reported it a great deal and said they were highly involved with it. Fortunately, they also believed they could do something about how complaints were handled. Further, just as the Grunigs' theory predicts, employees were most likely to communicate about this issue.

An issue associated with the greatest degree of constraint had to do with obtaining an adequate budget. Perhaps for a number of reasons, city employees felt that they had less control over this issue than the others. Predictably, they were less likely to process or seek information about budgeting than about other matters studied. However, those most likely to communicate about underlying budget concerns also felt good about their dealings with the public and had positive perceptions of others involved in such dealings.

One of the most interesting findings of this study is the strong relationship of information processing and seeking with job satisfaction. The data show that, the more satisfied an employee is with the job, the more likely she or he is to communicate about the four issues.

IMPLICATIONS

A number of action plans grow out of four major points that can be drawn from this case study.

Point 1—The results support the often-stated notion that "actions speak louder than words" in public relations.

In spite of the fact that public relations techniques are most often communication related, this study demonstrates that noncommunication actions and activities are linked to the overall public relations effort of a municipality by those involved— municipal employees. Of course, this means a public relations program is seen as ineffective by employees if the municipality is providing poor public service to the community.

Action 1—Develop a Quality Assurance Policy and Service Auditing Procedure that provide for the systematic analysis of citizen needs and how they might be met in the most efficient and least costly way.

Reasoning.   Business and industry have learned that to compete in a global economy they must provide consumers with quality products and services. Given the emphasis that employees place on the quality of service and its importance to the overall public relations program, municipalities need to take a page from that book and identify specific procedures for measuring the quality of services provided.

The public and private sectors differ as to specifics. However, quality-assurance policies for business and industry share five underlying concepts that also apply to municipalities. These are:

1. A commitment to maintain a customer focus. Employees must remember that each person's job exists to satisfy customers. Thus, workers must listen to customers to identify ways of improving products and services. And it's crucial to provide customers with advice on how to solve problems with minimal expense.

2. A commitment to maintaining employee involvement in developing the quality-assurance program. Underlying this commitment is a belief that those performing any function are most qualified to identify ways of improving that function.

3. A commitment to employee training. Successful organizations seek to foster an environment where employees look for learning opportunities that provide for personal growth and lead to improvements in the organization's products and services.

4. A commitment to a process of service, not a one-time event. Providing quality products and services requires sustained effort. Thus, an organization must commit itself to an on-going process of continually discovering ways to improve.

5. A commitment to measure improvements and incorporate them into the organization's procedures. A quality-assurance program must allow for standardization of improvements, measurement of improved performance, and evaluation of results in light of potential performance.

Many municipal public relations practitioners regard Quality Assurance Programs as too marketing oriented. After all, there is no real competition; citizens cannot choose to select services from another municipality.

However, in a larger context, there is a great deal of competition. Citizens evaluate city services in light of service offered by business and industry. Because the private sector provides a frame of reference or standard of comparison, as discussed in chapter 4, quality of service in the public sector must keep up to be appreciated.

Point 2—The clusters of relevant municipal-employee actions/activities and communication issues/topics are complex and multifaceted.

This study identifies two major sets of actions/activities that employees believe are linked to public relations. These are an external-public contact cluster and an internal-organizational cluster. Further, employees are active communicators on the four distinct issue/topics identified in this study.

Action 2—Develop a training program that provides employees with knowledge about who in each department is in the best position to solve specific citizen problems. Such training could be required for all employees or simply for those in frequent contact with the public (receptionists, switchboard operators, etc.). One option is to provide all municipal employees with a card or handout that serves as a reference when one is asked who to see about solving a problem.

Reasoning.   In general, the municipal employees surveyed expect to have contact with the public and do not look upon those with problems as people to avoid.

However some respondents admitted to having negative internal feelings about the self-perception aspect of their public-contact experience. This should raise a red flag for municipal officials concerned about improving attitudes toward public service, because this dimension correlates positively with job satisfaction.

Closer examination here reveals that employees are bothered the most about not being able to help solve people's problems. At least, many felt frustrated about being unable to tell citizens who might help. Indeed, some problems may have no good solution. However, employees surely can be trained to identify the specific person or department best suited to seek a solution in a given case.

Action 3—Develop a public-education program for citizens that generates knowledge about which departments, persons, etc., citizens should contact for answers to specific questions or solutions to specific problems.

Reasoning. For many of the reasons cited previously, it is important for citizens to make contact with those best suited to answer questions and solve problems. With a little reflection, each municipal department should be able to develop a list of topics for which it can best be viewed as the primary contact. This information, perhaps coupled with answers to "most frequently asked questions," could be distributed to citizens in order to make the problem-solving process more efficient.

Action 4—Continuously train employees on how best to handle citizen complaints.

Reasoning. As noted earlier, the data show complaint handling to be the most active communication issue among these employees. Fortunately, they don't feel constrained in their ability to deal with the citizen complaints. However, this may not always be the case. As personnel change due to expansion, promotion, attrition, etc., different employees may need training in dealing with this sensitive topic.

Based on this study as well as others using the Grunigs' situational theory, there is every reason to believe employees will seek information about such high-involving, problematic issues as complaint handling. If management does not provide instruction and advice on how to deal with complaints, employees will continue to seek such input anyway. Everyone involved can profit from a systematic plan for providing employees with needed information.

Action 5—Develop an internal communication program to generate knowledge and understanding of the budget situation.

Reasoning. This study reveals that the budget is the communication topic about which employees feel most constrained. Further, views on this issue correlate with many other opinions. Without assigning causality, this suggests that employees most likely to communicate about underlying budgetary concerns also feel good about their dealings with the public and have positive perceptions of others involved in that process.

Consequently, municipal officials clearly must inform workers about the budget.

However, simply providing information is not enough. Internal communication must also promote understanding of budgetary realities and provide employees with chances to have some input into the budgetary process.

Such an approach is consistent with the two-way symmetric model of public relations investigated by the Grunigs (Grunig & Grunig, 1989). Using this model as a guideline, municipal officials can develop ways to engage in a dialogue with employees about the budget. This promotes understanding and also yields new and innovative ways to deal with budget constraints.

Point 3—Municipal public relations practitioners should not overlook job satisfaction as an important variable in any public relations program.

Common sense suggests that employees who are satisfied with their jobs are most likely to enhance the effectiveness of any public relations program. However, this study reveals several specific dimensions of a public relations program that are linked to job satisfaction. First, those employees who are satisfied with their jobs are likely to have positive feelings about themselves as well as about citizens with whom they come in contact. Second, this study confirms the need for employee communication behavior to promote job satisfaction.

Action 6—Establish an Employee Council, with representatives from the various divisions, to serve as a mechanism for obtaining feedback on employee problems and concerns.

Reasoning. It is unrealistic to expect that all employees have high job satisfaction all of the time. However, given the importance of such satisfaction to the overall public relations effort, the municipal public relations practitioner needs to develop early warning detection systems for identifying potential problems that may lead to dissatisfaction.

An employee advisory council that meets regularly with the public relations person can be one part of that detection system. Ground rules must encourage frank and candid discussion by employees so the practitioner becomes aware of potential problems.

Action 7—Develop a program to train supervisors how to communicate effectively with their employees.

Reasoning. As noted earlier, this study confirms the importance of employee communication to job satisfaction and a municipality's overall public relations effort. Based on results here, municipal officials who lament, "If only the dissatisfied employees would read the information we provide them, they would see what we are talking about," need to realize that dissatisfied employees are less likely to process information, much less seek it.

This creates a need for much effort in developing effective communication programs. One extra step involves training supervisors to communicate effectively with their employees. Previous studies show that employees prefer to have their immediate supervisors serve as primary sources of information (Rosenberg, 1985). However, supervisors often gain their management responsibilities despite poor communication skills. Consequently, training programs to improve these skills pay handsome dividends for employee communication.

Point 4—It is important to investigate the relationship between the internal-organizational types of actions/activities and any public service/public relations program.

Although not fully investigated here, such structural variables contribute greatly to organizational communication and effectiveness. Certainly, municipal employees link these kinds of activities to an overall public relations effort.

Action 8—Use the information gathered as part of the Quality Assurance Program and form an Employee Council to review and improve management procedures.

Reasoning. The management activities identified by employees as being related to the overall public relations effort are likely to be scrutinized as part of the Quality Assurance Program and by members of the Employee Council. For instance, these procedures should help uncover inefficient or inadequate employee training, ineffective management techniques, and overlapping job responsibilities: all activities associated with an ineffective overall public relations program.

A LOOK BACK FROM SPE CONTEXT

Social Context

The municipal public relations practitioner needs to be aware of several content vs. structure conflicts that exist in this setting. One conflict involves the perceptual content of employee beliefs about what public servants should do for citizens vs. the structural reality of what services municipal employees can actually provide given the budgetary constraints they face. And a similar conflict exists for citizens. People often interact with municipal employees in ways based on outdated content factors that collide with structural realities.

For example, many citizens in this community are surprised to find that the front desk in the city police station is staffed only from 8 a.m. to 5 p.m., Monday through Friday. At other times, the citizen encounters a pulled window shade at the receptionist's window that bears instructions on how to use an adjacent phone in the lobby if the citizen would like to speak with someone.

For economic reasons (as well as for operational efficiency), the city police participates in a central 911 dispatch system that connects the city police, county sheriff, and state police. Consequently, picking up the phone in the lobby of the city police station connects the citizen with a sheriff's department dispatcher on the other side of town. If the citizen needs to talk with a city police officer, the sheriff's dispatcher relays the message back to the city police station.

This process is disconcerting for the citizen who (based on outdated content factors) drives to the police station and collides with the structural reality of a closed front desk.

The public relations practitioner can reduce such conflicts by articulating them and developing public relations programs that help employees and citizens match expectations with reality. This, in turn, may involve enhanced coorientation between workers and citizens as each understands differences between the two. For instance, a person may feel strongly that a traffic light should go up at a specific corner. Resources may not permit this. But the city can expect the person's continued support only if the person knows why money is in short supply.

A municipal public relations practitioner can also improve the overall public relations program by being sensitive to the micro vs. macro dimension that exists for municipal employees. It is evident that municipal employees interact with citizens on micro (as individuals) as well as macro (department, division, municipal, societal) levels. This study documents that employees have distinct attitudes and perceptions about public relations activities, actions, and issues along this micro-macro continuum. The municipal practitioner can enhance the public relations effort by categorizing existing programs along this continuum. That, in turn, may suggest new programs designed to function at different micro-macro levels.

The municipal public relations person also can develop a better overall program by fleshing out the schemata that municipal employees use as frames of reference for performing their roles. Specifically, the practitioner can provide information directly related to the six dimensions discussed in chapter 4:

1. Definitions of Situations. This study shows that employees have perceptions of how they are supposed to behave in specific situations. If these current perceptions are not accurate, the public relations person can help correct them.

2. Cause and Effect Sequences. The municipal worker is faced with many such sequences that flow directly from a municipality's rules and regulations or budgetary constraints. The public relations person should make sure employees have an accurate understanding of these.

3. Person Judgments. Employees in this study have positive judgments of citizens in their community. The municipal public relations practitioner needs to encourage and enhance these.

4. Judgments About Institutions. The practitioner can provide specific information about the institution of municipal government in general and the specific municipal governmental institution for which the employees work.

5. Cultural Norms. As discussed earlier, municipal workers and citizens hold specific perceptions based on cultural norms regarding the role of public servants in society. It may be that practitioners need to develop programs that begin to alter these cultural norms.

6. Human Interest and Empathy. Although all employees have varying degrees of these characteristics, the public relations practitioner can encourage an environment that fosters these.

The public relations practitioner should also focus on overcoming the barriers to interpersonal communication and social contacts discussed in chapter 4. Three of the six barriers are particularly relevant to this case study:

The number of people who are available to interact. As noted in chapter 4, active interpersonal contacts are needed to sell people on adopting new ideas. With the content and structure of municipal government undergoing change, it is important to have employees who function as informed and persuasive salespersons interacting with others in the community.

A competitive or cooperative organizational climate. At the micro level, the practitioner needs to develop internal programs that minimize competitiveness between departments or divisions within city government. On the macro level, the public relations person needs to recognize the competition for public support and tax dollars that exists within the community. For instance, city, county, regional, and state governmental structures all need citizen support, and there is a reluctance to cooperate for fear of losing any perceived advantages of one municipality's programs over another's.

Bureaucratization within an organization. Although bureaucracy provides a degree of accuracy and completeness to municipal government, it also stifles creativity and responsiveness to citizen needs. Public relations practitioners can develop internal programs that balance the need for employees to "do just the right things at the right times" with a degree of flexibility to make independent judgments that serve the best interests of citizens.

Political Context

This case study provides some guidance for the municipal public relations practitioner as to which leadership and influence strategies are most appropriate. Specifically, results suggest that the internalization strategy described by Kelman (see chapter 5) is most appropriate for developing a municipal public relations program.

Identifiable values associated with being a public servant should be viewed by employees as relevant to their job-related behaviors. Further, this study shows high interest and involvement in specific issues related to a municipality's overall public relations program. Such involvement is one precondition for an influence strategy based on internalization. All of this suggests that the practitioner needs to present well-reasoned messages to employees that stand up under critical analysis.

Economic Context

This study suggests a need to examine the marginal utility of the various public service actions and activities linked to the schema of being a public servant. Some steps recommended earlier in the chapter (such as establishing a Quality Assurance Program and an Employee Council) reveal that many actions and activities need to be re-ordered and prioritized in accordance with their marginal utility.

It may be that public information and education programs can decrease the demand for the least efficient programs and create understanding as to why the supply of these programs has decreased. Or, perhaps public information campaigns can be used to increase the marginal utility of programs by stimulating demand for those that are extremely important but are perceived as being unimportant.

REFERENCES

Albrecht, K., & Zemke, R. (1985). *Service America!: Doing business in the new economy.* Homewood, IL: Dow Jones-Irwin.

Branst, L. (1984). Disneyland—A kingdom of service quality. *Quality, 23,* 16–18.

Collier, A. T. (1979, November–December). The co-corp: Big business can reform itself. *Harvard Business Review,* p. 121.

Davis, C. W., & West J. P. (1985). Adopting personnel productivity innovations in American local governments. *Policy Studies Review, 4,* 541–549.

DiTomaso, N. (1978). Public unions and the urban fiscal crisis. *The Insurgent Sociologist, 8,* 191–205.

Grunig, J. E. (1976). Organizations and public relations: Testing a communication theory. *Journalism Monographs, 46.*

Grunig, J. E. (1983). Communication behaviors and attitudes of environmental publics: Two studies. *Journalism Monographs, 81.*

Grunig, J. E., & Grunig, L. A. (1989). Toward a theory of the public relations behavior of organizations: Review of a program of research. In J. E. Grunig & L. A. Grunig (Eds.), *Public Relations Research Annual* (Vol. 1, pp. 27–63). Hillsdale, NJ: Lawrence Erlbaum Associates.

Grunig, J. E., & Hunt, T. (1984). *Managing public relations.* New York: Holt, Rinehart & Winston.

Hochschild, A. R. (1983). *The managed heart: Commercialization of human feelings.* Berkley: The University of California Press.

Pintor, R. L. (1976). Satisfaction in work and formalism as bureaucratic phenomena: An analysis of attitudes in Chile. *Revista Espanola de la Opinion Publica, 44,* 101–145.

Pul-eeze! Will somebody help me? (1987, February 2). *Time,* pp. 49–57.

Quinn, J. B., & Gagnon, C. E. (1986, November–December). Will services follow manufacturing into decline? *Harvard Business Review,* pp. 95–103.

Rosenberg, K. (1985, May). What employees think of communication: 1984 update. *IABC Communication World,* pp. 46–50.

Seroka, J. H. (1979). Local public employee unionization: Trends and implications for the future. *The Policy Studies Journal, 8,* 430–437.

12 David and Goliath Coexist: The Story of Osteopathic Public Relations

Hugh M. Culbertson
Carl J. Denbow
Guido H. Stempel III
Ohio University

For more than a century, David has been struggling for survival against the mighty Goliath in American health care. And, like his Biblical counterpart, David appears to be winning.

Unlike in the Bible, however, there has been no effort to annihilate Goliath. Rather, David has been content to stay alive, grow, and maintain an identity in the face of efforts by Goliath to wipe him out.

David, in this discussion, is a branch of modern health care called **osteopathic medicine.** Doctors of Osteopathy (hereafter labeled D.O.s) are growing in numbers but still count for little more than 5% of all total-care physicians in the United States. Although D.O.s were always trained to do surgery and from the beginning were well schooled in a variety of diagnostic techniques, they once shunned the use of therapeutic drugs. At that time (circa 1892–1920), their treatment arsenal, in addition to surgery, relied almost exclusively on manual movement of the bones, joints, and muscles, using a group of techniques called osteopathic manipulative treatment (OMT). Today's D.O.s still use OMT, take X-rays, and perform surgery, but they also are fully licensed to prescribe drugs (Denbow, 1977; Gevitz, 1982).

Goliath is the dominant allopathic branch of health care in the United States. Allopathic physicians, called medical doctors or M.D.s, account for well over 90% of American physicians. Also, they make up the powerful American Medical Association that seeks to establish standards of training and performance, define the political posture of American medical care as a whole, and set the tone for health-care public relations.

In the early 1980s, two of the authors of this chapter studied public awareness of and beliefs about osteopathic medicine and its major tenets (Culbertson & Stempel, 1982). In 1991, all three of the present authors extended and repeated that research, looking for changes during a turbulent decade in American health care. The present chapter discusses results and implications of this research viewed as a whole.

First, however, we pause to look at the methodologies employed. We use a plural word here, because as is argued throughout this volume, no one method provides real understanding of the social, political, and economic contexts.

METHODS

In both 1981 and 1991, we began by reviewing numerous trade and popular magazines in the main and medical libraries of our university. We spent several weeks in each year reading about: (a) major concepts and tenets of osteopathy and (b) emerging and changing issues in health care. The latter, in 1991, included such things as costs, insurance, Health Maintenance Organizations, the right to die, care for AIDS victims and their families, and care for the poor and homeless.

Second, we completed hour-long interviews with 12 osteopathic educators in 1981 and with 8 in 1991. Having listed 20–30 topics and issues uncovered in step 1, we asked rather general questions about them. We also turned on a tape recorder and took notes while interviewing. (Recorders run on batteries, which sometimes run down!) Our respondents did most of the talking, but we asked questions where needed to follow up on intriguing but unexpected comments, to get interviews back on track, and to seek added detail. We typed a transcript almost immediately after a given interview, making marginal notes to help us interpret what was said and to relate that respondent's comments to those of the others.

Third, in 1981, we conducted two focus groups, each with about 12 D.O.s, at the annual meeting of a state osteopathic medical association. Here, as in step 2, we asked a few general questions and turned on a tape recorder. Also, we made comments where needed to follow up on important and unclear points and to keep the discussion from wandering too far afield. (However, we had fairly high tolerance for off-the-wall remarks, because they sometimes proved insightful.) Again, we typed transcripts right after the sessions.

After step 3, we felt we had identified most major issues affecting osteopathic medicine. At this point, we had a good grasp of the questions but not the answers! Thus, in step 4 carried out only in 1981, we developed a rather lengthy questionnaire with 35 questions, most of them multiple-choice. We administered this instrument in about 30–35 minutes by telephone to each of 252 D.O.s—a one-third sample drawn randomly from an up-to-date membership list of our state's osteopathic association. The response rate was a very high 85%.

Underlying this step was a basic premise. **A profession's public relations posture depends every bit as much on what professionals believe as on what the public believes.** Good public relations requires listening at least as much as speaking (Grunig & Hunt, 1984) as emphasized in chapter 1 and elsewhere in this volume.

At the conclusion of this survey, we felt confident in preparing a questionnaire to seek general-public reaction about issues of concern to osteopathy. Also, we measured public gripes, suggestions, and beliefs about which D.O.s might have little awareness.

Thus, step 5 was a general-population telephone survey. Once again, the questionnaire was highly structured, taking about 10 minutes in late 1981 and early 1982 and 15–20 minutes in 1991. The increase was to cover numerous issues that had come to fore during the intervening decade. At the conclusion of this phase, we were able to look for changes in belief and in 1981–1982, to compare what the public thought with what D.O.s *believed* they thought.

Samples sizes were 490 in 1981–1982, 390 in 1991. These figures permitted conclusions about all residents of our state with about a 5% margin of error in each survey. That is, where 50% of all respondents gave a certain answer, odds were 99–1 that the population value fell between 45% and 55%. Population estimates much higher or lower than 50% yielded greater precision (Broom & Dozier, 1990, p. 130). Also, some analyses that dealt with fairly small subgroups involved margins of error up to about 10%.

Fortunately, however, 1981–1982 and 1991 percentages differed very little. Thus the level of precision listed in the preceding paragraph is quite conservative. When one repeats a study and gets basically similar results, increased confidence in these findings is warranted.

Where differences between percentages or correlation coefficients are discussed in the text following, all could occur by chance no more than 5% of the time unless otherwise indicated.

Finally, in a sixth step in 1982, we analyzed press coverage of health care issues in Ohio's 11 largest-circulation daily newspapers. Osteopathic medicine was all but invisible in the media (Culbertson & Stempel, 1983b). Thus, although some useful ideas about improved press coverage were suggested, we give little attention in this chapter to the content analysis.

Obviously, in the 1991 replication, we did not start from scratch in learning about osteopathy. This, along with budgetary limitations, led us to complete only a three-phase study. Included were step 1 listed previously (literature review), step 2 (in-depth interviews of experts), and step 5 (a general-population survey).

In the general-population surveys, we used random-digit dialing (Broom & Dozier, 1990, pp. 363–368) in both 1981–1982 and 1991. This involved creating possible phone numbers at random. It permitted us to reach unlisted numbers that range from about 15% to 40% of all residential phones in most communities.

Response rates are hard to determine with random-digit dialing because some nonworking numbers do not have working recordings that clarify their status to callers. However, the rate was about 60% in each of the two surveys.

Advanced communication students served as interviewers after careful training. Further details on methodology can be obtained by writing the senior author.

The research identified seven concepts central to osteopathic medicine. These were holistic medicine, the importance of primary health care (general or family practice plus some other specialties), doctor–patient relations, wellness, the role of the musculoskeletal system (bones, joints, and muscles) as a "window" through which one can diagnose ailments in many parts of the human body, osteopathic manipulative treatment, and the body's self-healing capacity. We now discuss each of these concepts: what they mean, how they relate to osteopathy (and each other), and how both physicians and the general public feel about them.

KEY OSTEOPATHIC CONCEPTS

Holistic Medicine

The concepts behind this rather vague term are central to osteopathic philosophy, and it appears the words "holistic medicine" have at least three meanings for D.O.s:

Different organs and parts of the body are interdependent. A liver ailment is apt to affect the heart and vice versa. A strong, healthy heart helps many body parts fight off or avoid countless ailments. And so on.

Mind, body, and some would add spirit, are interrelated. One's will to live can indeed spur recovery. Without it, a person is apt to make slow progress or none at all.

A person's well-being hinges in large part on his or her social-physical environment. A tense or abusive home situation, constant exposure to smoke and other pollutants, and lack of space or time for relaxation or exercise are among countless environmental factors that harm health.

As noted later, these notions underlie other osteopathic concepts. What's more, most respondents in our samples accept them, at least in the abstract. About 90% of the general-population respondents agreed in 1991, as did 87% in 1981–1982, that "It's generally important for doctors to treat the whole person." In each survey, at least 99% accepted the proposition that "A patient's mental state and morale are very important in recovering from most illnesses" (see Tab. 12.1.).

However, Tab. 12.2 shows an interesting anomaly, one noted elsewhere in this chapter. **Most citizens approved of the health care that they and their families had received, but they took a rather dim view of American health care on the whole.**

On the plus side, 85% of our 1981 respondents (89% of those in 1991) agreed that the doctors whom they themselves see most often care a great deal about patients as people. However, moving to the nation as a whole, 81% in 1982 and 85% by 1991 agreed with the **negative** statement that "In America today, most doctors look only at specific ailments, not at the 'whole person,' when making diagnoses and treatments." This overwhelming agreement supports the widely held

TABLE 12.1
Percentage of Respondents Agreeing and Disagreeing With Statements About
The Importance of Treating the Whole Person

It's generally important for doctors to treat the whole person—not just a specific organ or part of the body that might be ailing at a given time.

	1981-1982		1991	
Agree strongly	61	87%	65	90%
Agree somewhat	26		25	
Disagree somewhat	9		6	
Disagree strongly	4		3	
	100% (n = 471)		99% (n = 374)	

A patient's mental state and morale are very important in recovering from most illnesses.

	1981-1982		1991	
Agree strongly	89	99%	86	100%
Agree somewhat	10		14	
Disagree somewhat	1		0	
Disagree strongly	0		0	
	100% (n = 482)		100% (n = 385)	

view, noted later, that America needs more generalists in an age when the most prestigious and highest paid physicians tend to be specialists. That gets to the heart of our second key osteopathic concept: the central role of primary health care.

Although emphasizing holistic medicine as basic to osteopathy, educator respondents did not advocate a direct focus on it in public relations. At least three pro-

TABLE 12.2
Percentage of Respondents Agreeing and Disagreeing With Statements About the Extent to
Which Doctors Treat the Whole Person

For Society as a Whole

In America today, most doctors look only at specific ailments, and not the "whole person," when making diagnoses and treatments.

	1981-1982		1991	
Agree strongly	42	81%	40	84%
Agree somewhat	39		44	
Disagree somewhat	13		10	
Disagree strongly	6		6	
	100% (n = 455)		100% (n = 362)	

For Respondent and Family

The doctor whom I see most often cares a great deal about his patients as people.

	1981-1982		1991	
Agree strongly	55	85%	56	89%
Agree somewhat	30		33	
Disagree somewhat	11		6	
Disagree strongly	4		5	
	100% (n = 472)		100% (n = 362)	

fessors felt the term had become a catch phrase or fad, perhaps partly to replace manipulative treatment as a hallmark of osteopathy. They also saw the term as unclear; this may be due in large measure, to the increasing tendency of people throughout the world to associate it with the use of mineral water, herbs, yoga, acupuncture, witch doctoring, and other things largely unrelated to osteopathy (Denbow & Feeck, 1988).

However, as noted earlier, the idea that physicians must deal with the whole person lies at the heart of our next basic osteopathic concept: the centrality of primary health care.

Primary Health Care

Until quite recently, the United States was largely a rural society. And in small towns and villages, the local family physician was clearly the person to whom one went with any ailment or health-care question. Such physicians still play an important part in American health care, as one of our 1991 educator respondents noted. Said he:

> I spent 11 years as a solo general practitioner in smaller communities. Then there was no question in the public's mind about what kind of doctor I was supposed to be. I made house calls, delivered babies, set fractures, prepared lacerations, admitted patients to intensive care, scrubbed on surgeries, and did my own minor surgeries. This was in accord with the image of the G.P. In addition, as a D.O., I was expected to provide manipulation a significant percentage of the time.

By mid-20th century, increasing numbers of physicians specialized in the heart, the eye, the skin, and the bones as well as in subspecialties in such rarefied fields as neurological surgery, endocrinology, and clinical immunology. These specialists gained in stature and earnings.

Specialization grew partly because scientific medicine grew and became more complex. No one physician could master more than one or two specialty areas. And, of course, resulting sophistication increased the accuracy of diagnosis and effectiveness of treatment along with, unfortunately, health care costs.

Because they controlled and created most medical schools, internships, and residencies, M.D.s dominated the growing medical specialties. In general, D.O.s saw these specialties as a good thing. However, they had one serious reservation. Specialists tend to focus on particular ailments or parts of the human body. This, in turn, leads them to lose sight, to some degree, of the whole person—central to our first key concept of osteopathy discussed previously.

"This is natural," said one 1991 educator respondent. "Spend five or 10 years studying, say, the pancreas, and you tend to see any patient entering your office as a walking pancreas with a few ancillary appendages!"

Furthermore, the growth of specialized medicine created a subtle public relations problem for general practitioners. Some people began viewing them primarily as doctors who treat only sore throats and other minor ailments.

Actually, effective primary care physicians do much more than that. They act as patients' allies, referring them to appropriate specialists (not an easy task) and coordinating input from various physicians so as to provide an overall program of wellness and treatment. Such coordination and patient support have become more and more important as health care increased in complexity and as numerous bureaucrats and coordinators played a growing role.

"Patients will not get the best possible care," said one professor, "if they simply go to the 'grand palace of healing' in their own or a nearby city when something major comes up."

Many residents of the state we studied appeared to recognize a problem here, however incompletely and intuitively, as shown in Tab. 12.3. On the one hand, they felt more generalists were needed by the nation as a whole. Specifically, although a plurality (43%) said the current balance between general or family practitioners was about right, nearly 2.6 times as many people called for more generalists (41%) as for more specialists (16%). On the other hand, 52% of all respondents reported having gone to specialists who were not their family physicians in the past 3 years. This was up from 43% in 1982. All of which suggests that, as viewed by the general

TABLE 12.3
Percentage of Persons Who Have and Have Not Gone to Specialists in Three Years and Who Call for More Specialists, More Generalists, or Maintaining Current Balance

Have you gone to a specialist who is not your family physician in the past 3 years? (Please exclude here regular eye or hearing examinations.)

	1981-1982	1991
Have gone to specialist	43	52
Have not gone	57	48
	–––––	–––––
	100% (n = 488)	100% (n = 387)

Some physicians, often called *family physicians* or *general practitioners*, provide diagnosis and treatment or referral for a large variety of ailments and conditions. Other doctors are *specialists*, dealing primarily with certain organs or parts of the body such as the eyes, the heart, the kidneys, and the feet.

On the whole, would you say America has about the right balance between general practitioners and specialists, or not? If not, which type of doctor should be trained in greatest numbers over the next few years? *Specialists? Or general practitioners?*

	1991
More specialists needed	16
Right balance between the two	43
More generalists needed	41
	–––––
	100% (n = 339)

public, specialists are playing a gradually increasing role in health care delivery, but that there may be some uneasiness about this phenomenon.

The generalist vs. specialist issue is related to health-care availability. As shown in Tab. 12.4, the latter problem is of concern to 92% of all 1991 respondents, as they agreed that "Not everyone in America who needs health care can get it." This was up from 78% in 1981–1982. The people who felt strongly about their agreement increased from 50% in 1982 to 73% in 1991.

However, those who agree strongly here, those who agree somewhat, and the disagreers did not differ demonstrably in 1991 on the need for more generalists or more specialists in the United States. Apparently, then, people attributed health care availability problems about equally to a lack of generalists and of specialists.

As an aside, Tab. 12.4 shows that once again respondents criticized American health care as a whole. Yet almost all agreed that good care had been available to them when needed.

Clearly, the need for generalists is apparent to many citizens. Educators agreed that this concept, perhaps more than any other, remained a hallmark of osteopathic medicine worthy of emphasis in the profession's public relations.

Few would argue against the idea that osteopathic medicine places greater emphasis than do M.D.s on training primary care doctors, said one professor. He further stated that allopathic schools that turn out 15% family physicians are extremely proud of that. At the same time, schools of osteopathy are turning out at least 50%.

TABLE 12.4
Percentage of Respondents Agreeing and Disagreeing With Statements About
Health Care Availability

For Society as a Whole

Not everyone in America who need medical care can get it.

	1981-1982	1991
Agree strongly	50 ⌉ 78%	73 ⌉ 92%
Agree somewhat	28 ⌋	19 ⌋
Disagree somewhat	12	3
Disagree strongly	11	5
	101% (n = 452)	100% (n = 377)

For Respondent and Family

In general, good health care has been readily available when and where my family and I have needed it.

	1981-1982	1991
Agree strongly	63 ⌉ 95%	62 ⌉ 93%
Agree somewhat	32 ⌋	31 ⌋
Disagree somewhat	4	3
Disagree strongly	1	4
	100% (n = 482)	100% (n = 382)

The dean of the college of osteopathic medicine at our university reported that about 54% of the 427 alumni of his unit were in family practice when we interviewed him in 1991. In addition, about 10% were in two other primary care fields—general internal medicine and general pediatrics. An additional 9% worked in emergency medicine, a form of primary care that generally is not classified as such. Thus, about three fourths of all alums are really in primary care, broadly defined.

Primary care is important partly because the physician practicing this type of medicine sees a patient over and over. Such contact permits sensitivity to individual needs and a caring, close relationship with patients. This leads to our next basic concept in osteopathy, doctor–patient relations.

Doctor–Patient Relations

"Good relationships with patients are about 90% of the battle," one osteopathic educator said. "If you don't get along with them, they are not going to do what you want them to. Thus your efforts as a physician become a waste of your time and theirs."

Another professor noted growing public demand for caring doctors. "People used to expect to be abused," he commented. "They were often willing to wait two hours, then spend five minutes with their physicians. They are not willing to do that any more."

Historically, D.O.s have felt compelled to go the extra mile in serving and keeping their patients partly because they were a minority and were labeled by the American Medical Association as cultists and quacks. This motivated many osteopathic offices to make follow-up calls and find out whether patients were recovering satisfactorily, to send out reminder cards about forthcoming appointments, and to take lots of time answering questions and explaining diagnoses and treatments in a friendly, caring way.

As a result of all this, many D.O.s responding to our 1981 survey said they very seldom lost a patient to another doctor once he or she entered their offices.

However, by 1991, some educator respondents worried that D.O.s had begun to lose that minority feeling partly because their branch of medicine had become accepted more widely. Explained one professor, "I am not sure the doctor–patient relationship is as important to young doctors today as it was to those of us who practiced 30 years ago."

On the plus side, however, the same educator asserted that his college of osteopathic medicine tried hard to show students the importance of this. He felt such efforts were generally successful, especially for those who wind up in family practice.

We noted earlier that specialization has detracted from doctor–patient relations in some cases. For one thing, the specialist sees a patient less often and regarding a smaller variety of concerns than does the generalist. The specialist focuses on a specific ailment or body part, not on the whole person. Clearly the latter view is important in doctor–patient relations.

A more subtle problem also stems from growing specialization and health care sophistication. The doctor is often seen as a solver of problems, a person who uses fancy procedures to treat diseases rather than people. That, in turn, obscures the fact that doctor and patient *share* responsibility for patient health. They must work together with a realization that both doctor and patient are fallible.

Said one D.O. in 1991, If patients are willing to believe there is overwhelming technical sophistication—and if doctors act like the specially charged purveyors of all this sophistication—the fundamental relationship between doctor and patient will lose something. Ideally, one should seek advice and the other provide it. Neither should develop expectations which might fall apart.

One bit of data from our 1991 audience study showed that many people have developed blind faith in health-care measures that might detract from a felt need to cooperate with physicians. As shown in Tab. 12.5, about 42% of all respondents agreed that "Modern medicine can cure most any ailment." (There is one encouraging note here, however. Only 9% agreed strongly with this statement, whereas 33% agreed somewhat. Thus, many agreers appeared to have some doubt.)

Physicians often asserted that bureaucratization associated with increased complexity of care provided plus the need to control skyrocketing costs detracts from doctor–patient relations (Black, 1988). Resulting procedures create tremendous hassles. By one estimate, physicians working in certain clinics and hospitals spend almost one half of their time filling out forms and attending to administrative details.

Also, bureaucratization has led nurses, professional administrators of various types, insurance personnel, and other nonphysicians to get their fingers into the health care pie to an increasing degree.

As one educator put it, "Sometimes it's difficult when you walk into a medical facility to see the essence of the place. It's hard to find doctors and patients interacting. Too many ancillary people have been hired to deal with the system."

About 79% of our respondents reported that they had family physicians in 1991,

TABLE 12.5
Percentages of Respondents Agreeing and Disagreeing With Statement That Modern Medicine Can Cure Most Any Ailment

	1991
Strongly agree	9
Agree somewhat	33
Disagree somewhat	40
Disagree strongly	19
	101% (*n* = 369)

TABLE 12.6
Percentage of People Who Hold Various Beliefs Among Those Who Have Family Physicians and
Those Who Do Not

	Those With Family Physicians	Those Without Family Physicians
Agree strongly that the doctors they see most often care a great deal about patients as people.	60% (n = 285) 59% (n = 378)*	34% (n = 61) 34% (n = 80)*
Agree strongly that the doctors they see most often do a good job of explaining diagnoses and treatment.	66% (n = 293) 58% (n = 384)*	50% (n = 64) 41% (n = 86)*c
Agree that not everyone in America who needs medical care can get it.	94% (n = 288) 75% (n = 375)*	87% (n = 75) 86% (n = 85)*
Agree strongly that, in general, health care has been readily available when and where respondent's own family needs it.	64% (n =293) 66% (n = 389)*	58% (n = 74)a 48% (n = 91)*
Suggest that doctors with whom they have dealt recently tend to prescribe drugs more often than needed.	19% (n = 381)*	37% (n = 88)*
Rate health care of oneself and close relatives over the past 5 years as excellent.	32% (n = 294) 36% (n = 389)*	26% (n = 88)b 20% (n = 94)*

*Denotes results from 1981-1982 general-population survey. Nonasterisked percentages refer to 1991 data.
a p = .09; b p = .07; c p = .02
In all rows without alphabetic superscripts, differences between those with and without family physicians differ at p = .01, based on z - tests of proportion differences.

whereas 81% gave the same response 9 years earlier. Having a family doctor went along with a good feeling by patients about many aspects of health care. In Tab. 12.6:

1. Sixty percent of all 1991 respondents who reported having family physicians, but only 34% of those who did not agreed strongly that doctors whom they see most often care a great deal about their patients as people. In 1982, the ratio was 59% to 34%.

2. Sixty-six percent of 1991 interviewees who had family doctors, but only one half of those who did not, agreed strongly that the doctors whom they saw most often did a good job of explaining diagnoses and treatments. In 1982, this margin was 58% to 41%.

3. Sixty-four percent of the 1991 respondents who had family physicians, compared with 58% of all others, agreed strongly that in general, health care had been readily available when and where the respondent's own family needed it. This

difference was not quite large enough to achieve statistical significance. However, the same difference 9 years earlier (66% vs. 48%) had been.

4. Thirty-seven percent of 1982 respondents without family physicians, but only 19% of those with such doctors, suggested that doctors with whom they have dealt recently tend to prescribe drugs more often than needed. (This question was not asked in 1991.)

5. Thirty-two percent of those with family physicians in 1991, compared with 26% of those without, rated health care for themselves and close relatives as excellent over the past 5 years. This difference narrowly missed conventional significance levels, as it could have occurred by chance seven times in 100. The comparable 1981 difference, 36% vs. 20%, was significant statistically.

In-depth interviews with educators suggest that in a number of areas, a doctor can serve patients well only if she or he has a close, caring relationship with them and the resulting skill and inclination, stressed in coorientation theory, to view problems from patients' points of view. The focus here is on social contacts with continuity and two-way communication as defined in chapter 4.

In a recent survey (Denbow, 1991), alumni of the college of osteopathic medicine at the researchers' university rated health care from the perspective of a patient. Those assessments were then compared with actual general-population responses obtained in a national survey reported in *The New York Times* (Belkin, 1990).

Overall, the young physicians expressed views quite similar to those of the population as a whole. For example, a majority of both groups felt most doctors do not spend enough time with patients or explain diagnoses and treatments well to them. However, on the plus side, both doctors and citizens in general gave physicians credit for being up to date on recent medical advances.

Data also suggest a self-critical attitude by young physicians that might encourage them to consider patient reactions thoughtfully.

Treating Alcohol and Substance Abuse.   In this realm, the physician must look into patients' backgrounds and family situations as well as their current lifestyles. Extended, intimate conversation with patients and their significant others is seen as important.

Continuing contact with addicts' families gives important clues for diagnosis and treatment. Knowing family members socially may help. Physicians obviously do not often develop such contacts unless they take a highly personal interest in their patients.

Doctor–patient relations are especially important in dealing with substance abuse for at least three additional reasons.

First, substance abusers often withdraw into a shell, developing few close relationships. Thus, the physician must make a special effort to find out what their lives are really like (Carlat, 1989).

Second, effective treatment sometimes entails confronting patients and forcing them to face the truth about themselves. That may antagonize people, so they quit confiding in or taking advice from their physicians. It's often difficult for the latter to decide when to risk breaking off a relationship—and thus eliminating the chance to be of further help—by taking a confrontational tack (Katz, 1984).

Third, physicians must often ask embarrassing or obnoxious questions of suspected abusers. The experienced general practitioner learns to do this. But without that skill, it can be a major challenge indeed (Katz, 1984).

Educators noted recent improvement in training young physicians-to-be to deal with substance abuse. Unfortunately, they agreed some older practitioners haven't caught up with recent developments in this area. Substance abuse deserves continuing emphasis with regard to both physicians' enhancing their own work and their speaking to the general public.

Addictionology—A New and Broad Focus?   Drug and alcohol addictions are prime examples of obsessive behavior. Addicts behave in a certain way constantly and with little flexibility. Further, they seemingly have little power to avoid carrying out the behavior in question in light of possible consequences.

Recently, it's become apparent that some people become addicted in some sense to food, work, thinness (as with anorexia), sex, and other things. Some physicians emphasize similarities among diverse addictions. Support groups patterned in varying degrees after Alcoholics Anonymous have sprung up to deal with many such problems.

On the surface, these behavior patterns have much in common. However, educators saw a danger in over-emphasizing the similarities. For example, drug and sex addiction may stem from very different sorts of factors. Perhaps the drug addict needs treatment in a residential treatment center for a number of months whereas the sex addict could best be treated through weekly counseling from a psychiatrist, sex therapist, or pastor. Thus, giving similar treatment across the board can be downright dangerous.

Physicians working in this area need to relate to their patients in a close and understanding way for at least two reasons.

First, they must gain a sense of how social support is developing within a support group and of the implications of that support. Such a sense is needed to decide how fruitful support groups are as well as to improve their functioning.

Second, they must encourage patients to realize that, social support or no, *people must ultimately face and take responsibility for solving their problems as individuals.*

"I have to stop," one must say to himself or herself, "or my life and things I hold dear will go down the tube."

The American Osteopathic Association now has an American Academy of Addictionology that studies a broad range of addictions and educates physicians about them (Fitzgerald, 1989). However, one educator saw real danger in applying the addiction label to such diverse types of behavior as taking drugs, sex, and overeating. And another said the Academy is made up largely of general practitioners who lack sufficient expertise to shed much light on related problems.

In conclusion, D.O.s must work to formulate a coherent story about addictionology. Only then can they communicate it to the public at large. However, one thing does seem certain. Good doctor–patient relations play a crucial role in treating addicts.

Treating AIDS Victims and Their Loved Ones.   The spread of AIDS has created much trauma. Strong emotions come to the fore at the mere mention of this disease, partly because it is fatal and at this writing, has no known cure or preventive vaccine. Also, prejudices associated with homosexuality, drug use, and sexual promiscuity sometimes make it hard to achieve close, understanding doctor–patient relations.

Such relations assume particular prominence in dealing with AIDS for several reasons.

First, physicians surely feel some obligation to comfort and counsel victims' relatives and friends (Bronstein, 1987). Only the caring doctor takes time to understand fully and minister to these people.

Second, a doctor must often help an AIDS patient face death. This requires great compassion and sensitivity, especially where patients lack a religious orientation and social support to provide inner peace and strength.

"When people have a serious illness, how can you be candid about the realities and still give them a reason to live," asked Leonard H. Calabrese (D.O.), a noted AIDS expert in Cleveland, Ohio (Gabe, 1987, p. 12).

"How do you tell someone who is just getting over pneumonia that they may have to start thinking about whether they want life-support systems?" Calabrese continued. "There is no magic formula for this. It doesn't get any easier."

Third, recent, widely publicized cases have helped create a climate in which doctor and patient fear each other as possible sources of AIDS. Fear often detracts from close, caring relationships.

Relating to this latter point, physicians have long exposed themselves to danger when treating contagious ailments. However, certain death has seldom been an expected result of such exposure (Bronstein, 1987).

Physicians are required to treat any patient, one professor who taught surgery told us in 1991. We accept that. But we'd like to know what we are up against in a given case. It is legal to test for syphilis, for example, without the patient's consent. But not so with AIDS. And AIDS can kill you while syphilis generally does not.

Another fairly recent twist on this issue created stress for physicians. Health care professionals allegedly have transmitted AIDS to a few patients. This stimulated a move to require testing of the professionals.

Supporters of that effort want to protect patients by testing health-care personnel but not the converse, one educator noted. He described this as somewhat ironic, because if a physician has AIDS, chances are he or she contracted it from a patient in the first place!

Also, ironically, crusaders on behalf of AIDS victims may have created a public relations problem—doubtlessly inadvertently—for physicians. Such crusaders have told the public often that AIDS cannot be transmitted through casual contact. Thus, it is argued, we can safely go to school with or work alongside victims if we simply take reasonable precautions to avoid the exchange of bodily fluids.

It's reasonable to hypothesize that most people feel this applies to physicians as well. Furthermore, it's a rather small jump beyond that to argue that health-care personnel can protect themselves by wearing gloves, washing hands, sterilizing needles, etc. Not so, said one surgeon whom we interviewed in 1991.

"You frequently complete an operation, take your gloves off, and find blood on your hands," he pointed out. "You have stuck yourself with a needle and have concentrated so intensely on what you were doing that you did not realize this had happened."

Such thorny issues place a strain on doctor–patient relations. Unfortunately, as noted earlier, this is especially challenging in a difficult and ultra-sensitive area such as AIDS treatment. Much the same holds for a related and oft-discussed contemporary issue, the right to die.

The Right to Die.   Recent court cases on turning off life-support systems have spurred a public debate about a person's right to die in the face of grave suffering or affliction (Bronstein, 1987). So has a 1990 case in which a Michigan physician created a device and permitted an Alzheimer's Disease victim to use it in taking her own life.

In 1991, educators told us without exception that in their view, removal of life support systems may be warranted in some cases. However, all agreed that doctors could not take *positive* steps to speed up death without, at the very least, reducing the medical professions' credibility and with it the all-important trust between doctor and patient.

"One goes to a physician expecting help in getting better, not in moving on to the next world," a respondent commented. "If the patient feels the doctor is just biding his or her time and not striving for improved health, the doctor–patient relationship will be destroyed."

Furthermore, all osteopathic educators with whom we talked agreed that physicians can and should play a role in helping patients spell out their wishes and take actions such as preparing a living will where appropriate. It's also important that patients make well informed decisions before they become gravely ill. Clear thinking becomes difficult once a crisis arises or a person is incapacitated.

Physicians themselves are under a lot of stress in dealing with the terminally ill, one professor noted. The doctor can cope with issues relating to death more effectively and easily where a patient has already expressed clear preferences on such things as the use or nonuse of life-support systems when chances of recovery are nil (Katz, 1984, pp. 215–217).

Osteopathic professors told us that, by 1990, students in their college of osteopathic medicine studied this issue carefully in class. Further, young physicians were said to discuss patient rights to avoid extraordinary life-support measures a great deal among themselves, but perhaps not with their patients. Further debate is called for in this area.

We now turn to another realm of health-care practice in which doctor–patient relations are especially important.

Serving the Poor and Homeless.   In recent years, public attention to the homeless and poor has increased. Bag ladies sleeping above grates right next to limousines have appeared quite often on the evening television news. Poverty has gotten extensive media coverage, partly because it seems bizarre in an affluent society.

The poor are hard to treat, and require special compassion and understanding, partly because they have long had little access to sophisticated health care. Further, they often do not have regular check-ups, well-rounded diets, or sound overall wellness programs. Thus, their health problems tend to be numerous, serious, and different from those of the population at large.

The educators' college of osteopathic medicine came into being several years ago with a pledge that it would train doctors to serve nearby depressed rural areas. This mission has proven to be a tremendous challenge.

Students willing and able to work in the inner city or in depressed rural areas are much in demand among medical schools, one professor told us.

Unfortunately, however, the poor have large medical needs but little capacity to pay for them. The government, by and large, does not pay the full freight. Thus, many young doctors seek to serve the poor with great idealism but soon move elsewhere because they simply can't pay debts incurred as a student and still earn a living without such a change.

It all boils down to one thing, educators told us. As a society, America has not yet addressed the question of whether person A should live longer than B, because A has more money.

Our general-population data show a strong linkage between doctor–patient relations and another key osteopathic concept: wellness. We now turn to that area.

Wellness—Physician as Teacher

The old cliche that an ounce of prevention is worth a pound of cure is the cornerstone here. Obviously it's usually less expensive and painful to avoid illness through exercise, diet, plenty of rest and sleep, limited alcohol consumption, avoiding excessive stress, etc., than to endure and treat related ailments once they develop.

In our 1991 study, all educators agreed that wellness squares beautifully with osteopathic philosophy. The word doctor has come to mean teacher in our society. The wellness-oriented physician plays that role a great deal. Such counseling is sound, partly because it places responsibility for good health where it really belongs, on the **patient.** As emphasized later, physicians usually cannot set things straight by themselves.

"In the past, doctors treated diseases," a surgeon told us. "They waited until people got sick and then provided treatment. Now we spend much more time helping folks remain well so as to prevent illness and help the body heal itself."

Having said all that, faculty members felt wellness efforts have enjoyed limited success nationwide. At least four problems apparently have stood in the way.

First, practicing medicine of this type takes time. You must explain and discuss at length. It isn't like a person coming in with a sore throat and getting a shot.

Second, people who follow physician recommendations on wellness often don't give credit where it's due. They seldom know if they'd have gotten sick without dietary or exercise regimens or other preventive measures they may have taken. Thus, doctors have a hard time proving to themselves, as well as to patients, that they have accomplished something concrete.

Third, as one respondent put it, "Most people like to hear about wellness. But they often don't practice it very well, as *it requires changes in their lifestyles* (emphasis added). And many Americans are rather self-indulgent people not inclined to make such changes."

Fourth, as noted earlier, Americans tend to have great faith in technology, and they apparently apply this to scientific medicine. About 42% of our 1991 general-population respondents agreed that "Modern medicine can cure most any ailment." Obviously preventing illness may seem less than urgent to one who assumes modern medicine can cure it anyway.

Our 1991 general-population data paint a somewhat more optimistic picture of wellness behavior and physicians' impact on it than these comments suggest. Seventy percent of all who answered the pertinent question reported making changes in their diet, exercise habits, drinking, etc., within the past year or so. And 29% of the self-reported changers indicated such wellness shifts had involved altering their lifestyles a lot, whereas 44% reported some change and only 27% a little or none at all. Furthermore, 51% of all citizens reported having discussed wellness concerns or practices with a physician during the past year or so.

Do physicians have an impact? Several findings suggest an affirmative response here, at least with regard to family doctors:

1. About 76% of those with a family physician, but only 40% of those without reported that a doctor had played at least some part in recent changes of wellness behavior.

2. About 80% of those who discussed wellness with their physicians in the past year or so reported making wellness changes of some kind during the past

year. This compares with 58% of the respondents who did not report such discussions.

3. Focusing on this group that reported some wellness changes, 34% of people who had discussed wellness with physicians, but only 21% of the nondiscussants, reported making major changes during the past year. Apparently, then, discussion with physicians correlated with making changes and, among the changers, with the magnitude of the shifts involved.

4. About 41% of those who said physicians played a major role in their wellness behavior reported major changes during the past year. This compares with 25% among those who ascribed a minor role or no role at all to physicians.

Taken as a whole, these data support calls by at least three educators for D.O.s to stress wellness when speaking to lay persons one on one and in seeking awareness of osteopathy by the public at large. In fact, one doctor defined keeping people well as "the future of medicine." Several agreed that promoting wellness plays a real part in cutting health-care costs, a challenge discussed later.

We now turn briefly to an osteopathic concept often seen as closely related to wellness.

The Bones Joints, and Muscles:
A Window on the Body?

The basic idea here is that ailments residing in many parts of the human body have some impact on the bones, joints, and muscles, referred to as the musculoskeletal system. It follows that a physician can sometimes diagnose an ailment centered elsewhere by looking closely at that system. Further, he or she can apply treatment by manipulating or applying pressure to the bones, joints, and muscles.

"In the old days, say 40 years ago, this notion was a cornerstone of the profession," one educator told us. It remains important, but only as one of several techniques at the D.O.s disposal. Emphasis on the idea has declined in recent years. Our professor respondents gave several reasons for this.

First, physicians within our sample disagreed as to whether, on the whole, available research supports examination of the bones, joints, and muscles to help diagnose ailments located elsewhere. Part of the problem is that D.O.s have done little research of any kind. And M.D. researchers have shown little interest in the musculoskeletal system, partly because they have seen it as an unlikely focus for saving lives. (In 1982, when we interviewed a few M.D.s, several said this was the one area in which they disagreed fundamentally with D.O.s. They simply felt evidence for the viability of the window-on-the-body approach was rather soft. Apparently, by 1991, at least some osteopathic educators had come to agree with them.)

Second, new technology had provided other means, sometimes faster and more accurate, than examining the musculoskeletal system in diagnosing some ailments.

Third, interpretation of musculoskeletal symptoms as a clue to ailments else-where requires much experience as it involves subtle nuances. Many D.O.s do not have that experience. Realistically, some may not be able to get it in light of the fairly limited role of examining the bones, joints, and muscles compared with modern diagnostic techniques taken as a whole.

Viewing the musculoskeletal system as a window on the body relates closely to manipulative treatment, our next key concept. In fact, some feel the diagnostic and treatment aspects are so closely related they must be viewed as opposite sides of the same coin.

Osteopathic Manipulative Treatment

This term refers to a series of treatment techniques that involve massaging and applying pressure to ones bones, joints, and muscles.

In 1981–1982, 61% of the 252 D.O.s surveyed felt OMT was very important in the practice of medicine. Another 37% chose the *fairly important* response, whereas only 2% said *not important at all*.

By 1991, emphasis on OMT may have declined somewhat in the eyes of D.O.s, as exemplified by osteopathic educators, and it clearly did for the general public. However, research now underway on the effectiveness of OMT might help lead to a turn-around here. At the time of our interviews, no results were yet available from this project.

Educators made these points about OMT as learned and practiced in osteopathy today:

1. Three noted that overall teaching of OMT in osteopathic classrooms has improved in recent years, partly because of better linkage to its roots in many disciplines.

2. However, two educators commented that students who have studied OMT rather thoroughly in class often see it practiced little or not at all when they reach their third or fourth year of training and enter hospital or clinical settings. This may lead some young D.O.s to lose interest in manipulating (though we lack current data about them, and some observers profess to see a recent upturn in interest). A modest downward trend was suggested in our 1981–1982 D.O. survey that reveals a positive correlation (.31 on a scale from 0 to 1.0) between years spent practicing medicine and importance attached to OMT.

3. OMT was said to have lost some ground, partly because it's time consuming in a period where physicians as well as patients are inclined to look for a quick fix.

4. In part, new knowledge and sophistication in modern medicine may have reduced emphasis on OMT simply by making it one element on a huge array of health care concepts and techniques. After all, no doctor can master every-thing.

It should be noted that as early as the 1950s, some D.O.s were questioning the uniquely osteopathic aspects of health care, partly for scientific and partly for political reasons. This was in a period when to secure equal recognition from state and federal governments the osteopathic profession was stressing its similarities with allopathy, not the differences.

That battle being won, some osteopathic educators now feel that traditional osteopathic concepts like OMT and the window on the body are of greater interest to osteopathic students today than they were in the recent past. Time will tell whether this will continue when today's students become tomorrow's practitioners.

Following is a summary of our general-population data on OMT.

First, Tab. 12.7 shows that less than one third of all respondents (32% in 1981–1982, 31% in 1991) answered affirmatively when asked if they had ever heard of OMT. (We asked this question to avoid follow-up queries that might lead respondents to manufacture opinions on the spot, even if they had none. Researchers call this reification and regard it as a major problem.)

Second, as noted in Tab. 12.8, just two thirds of our 1981–1982 respondents who'd heard of OMT gave the correct answer (something suggesting manipulation of or applying pressure to the bones, joints, and/or muscles) when asked what manipulative treatment meant to them. That figure declined slightly to 54% by 1991. Interestingly, definition of manipulation basically as something connected with chiropractic practice jumped from 6% in 1981 to 30% in 1991! Chiropractors are another school of health-care professionals who manipulate, but differently from the approach used by D.O.s. We have more to say on this later when discussing the identity of osteopathy in the public mind.

TABLE 12.7
Percentage of Respondents Who Report Having Heard of Manipulative Treatment and Who Regard it as Good or Bad

Have you heard of the term manipulative treatment?

	1981-1982	1991
Yes	32	31
No	64	65
Unsure	4	4
	100% (n = 486)	100% (n = 388)

In general, would you regard manipulative treatment as a good thing for medical practice? As a bad thing? Or does it seem neither good nor bad?[a]

Good	62	56
Neither good nor bad	33	37
Bad	5	8
	100% (n = 150)	101% (n = 117)

[a]This question was asked only of those who reported having heard of manipulative treatment.

TABLE 12.8
Responses to the Question, "What Does Manipulative Treatment Mean to You?"[a]

	1981-1982	1991
Persuasion by doctor	2%	2%
Persuasion by doctor to seek unnecessary care	2%	3%
Psychosomatic illness	2%	–
Manipulate bones, joints, muscles	67%	54%
Part of chiropractic care	6%	30%
Part of osteopathy and chiropractic	2%	4%
Psychological manipulation	2%	–
Miscellaneous	18%	7%
	101% (n = 150)	100% (n = 117)

[a]This question was asked only of those who reported having heard of manipulative treatment.

Third, Tab. 12.7 shows that of those professing to know about manipulation, well over one half (62% in 1982, 56% in 1991) regarded it as a good thing overall for medical practice.

Fourth, in 1981–1982, we asked D.O. respondents to estimate what percentage of their patients had been manipulated in their offices during the past year. There was great variation, with some veteran D.O.s manipulating 70%–80% of their patients and others, primarily specialists and younger doctors, manipulating none at all. However, the average for all respondents was 32%.

Fifth, in that same time frame, lay respondents guesstimated how many patients were manipulated by D.O.s in their state. Response options were *all, most, some, very few,* and *none.* A total of 38% said either *all* or *most,* as shown in Tab. 12.9. This substantial minority overestimated the use of manipulation by D.O.s, as *all* and *most* clearly are greater than 32%.

Sixth, Tab. 12.9 also suggests somewhat more accurate perceptions about the frequency with which D.O.s administer OMT in 1991 than in 1981–1982. *Some*—a word that equates roughly with 32%—increased during the 9-year interim from

TABLE 12.9
Percentage of Respondents Giving Various Estimates of How Many Patients Ohio Osteopathic Physicians Manipulate[a]

	1981-1982	1991
All of their patients	6	4
Most of their patients	32	30
Some of their patients	40	52
Very few of their patients	19	8
None of their patients	3	6
	100% (n = 301)	100% (n = 98)

[a]This question was asked only of those who reported having heard of manipulative treatment.

40% to 52% of all responses. And *very few,* presumably less than 32%, declined from 19% to 8%.

Seventh, as shown in Tab. 12.10, a positive evaluation of manipulative treatment correlated at .34 (on a scale from 0 to 1) with credibility assigned to D.O.s in 1981–1982. However, this correlation declined by 1991 to a low of .16 that could have differed from zero by chance 12 times in 100. Furthermore, analyses not shown here reveal that in 1981–1982, public evaluation of OMT and D.O. credibility correlated positively only among those who felt D.O.s manipulated some, very few, or no patients. Apparently even in the early 1980s, then, people endorsed OMT primarily when they felt it was used sparingly and with a narrow range of ailments (Culbertson & Stempel, 1985).

Eighth, Tab. 12.11 presents results from a question asking our 1991 lay people how important manipulative treatment and four other concepts were for American health care as a whole. Only 27% rated OMT very important, whereas the other four notions (wellness, treatment of the whole person, cost reduction, and caring physicians) fell in the range of 80% to 90%. Interestingly, when we asked a similar question of D.O.s in 1981, 61% rated manipulation as very important.

Ninth, also looking at Tab. 12.11, only 36% saw manipulation as closely linked to osteopathic medicine in 1991.

Tenth, Tab. 12.12 shows that the importance of OMT, the closeness of its linkage to osteopathy, and a third variable (linkage × importance) all failed to correlate with D.O. credibility as viewed by our 1991 lay respondents.

In sum, D.O.s and educators see manipulative treatment as important, albeit for treating a narrow range of ailments and not as a real hallmark of the profession. However, many feel OMT often does not get the emphasis it deserves in residency and clinical training or in overall medical practice. In the public eye, OMT is seen as a plus but as a slightly less salient part of osteopathy in 1991 than 9 years earlier.

We now turn to a seventh and final core concept of osteopathic medicine.

TABLE 12.10
Product Moment Correlations Between Osteopathic Credibility and Three Beliefs About
Osteopathy

Belief	1981-1982	1991
Perceived similarity between M.D.s and D.O.s[a]	.42 ($p = .001$, $n = 248$)	.36 ($p = .001$, $n = 204$)
Rated quality of osteopathic hospitals in Ohio[b]	.44 ($p = .001$, $n = 190$)	.35 ($p = .001$, $n = 110$)
Evaluation of manipulative treatment[c]	.34 ($p = .001$, $n = 114$)	.16 ($p = .12$, $n = 99$)

[a]Response options were *very similar, fairly similar, not very similar,* and *not similar at all.*
[b]Response options were *excellent, good, fair,* and *poor.*
[c]Response options were *good, neither good nor bad,* and *bad.*

TABLE 12.11
Importance Attached to Five Concepts and Perceived Closeness of Linkage to
Osteopathic Medicine[a]

	Perceived Importance in American Health Care				
	Manipulative Treatment	Wellness	Treatment of Whole Person	Lowering Costs	Caring Physicians
Very important	27%	82%	82%	89%	88%
Fairly important	58%	17%	17%	9%	11%
Not important at all	15%	1%	1%	2%	1%
	100%, (n = 314)	100%, (n = 376)	100%, (n = 375)	100%, (n = 375)	100%, (n = 376)

	Perceived Closeness of Linkage to Osteopathic Medicine Today				
Very close	36%	41%	45%	15%	39%
Fairly close	55%	52%	47%	49%	49%
Not close at all	9%	7%	8%	36%	11%
	100%, (n = 229)	100%, (n = 249)	100%, (n = 251)	100%, (n = 187)	99%, (n = 220)

[a]All data reported are from the 1991 general-population survey. These questions were not asked in 1981-1982.

The Human Body's Amazing Ability to Heal Itself

This notion was central to the thinking of Dr. Andrew Taylor Still, a Missouri physician and Civil War surgeon on the Union side who founded osteopathy in the 19th century.[1]

Still was highly critical of the crude treatment approaches of his day—things like having leeches suck one's blood to lower a fever. He observed that patients often got better no matter what physicians or the patients themselves did. He even hypothesized that the body contained its own chemical warehouse to aid it in fighting disease. Partly because of this insight, he is now regarded as something of a prophet, as modern research reveals many mechanisms in the body for self-healing.

Within osteopathy, the concept of self-healing has broadened over the years. For

---

[1]A man of strong passions, Still (1897) was both an outspoken abolitionist ("No man can have delegated to him by statute a just right to any man's liberty, either on account of race or color.") (p. 65) and a strong supporter of women's rights (. . . "[I]f man is the head of the family, his claim to superiority must be in the strength of his muscles, not his brain.") (p. 156). His American School of Osteopathy at one time prior to his death in 1917 had about 50% female students, a much higher percentage than any other coed medical school at that time (Denbow, 1978).

TABLE 12.12
Product Moment Correlations Between D. O. Credibility and Linkage as Well as Importance
Ratings for Five Medical Concepts

Medical Concept	Linkage or Importance Variable		
	Linkage to Osteopathy	Importance in Health Care	Linkage X Importance
Manipulative treatment	.01 *(nsd)*	.12 *(nsd)*	.07 *(nsd)*
Wellness	.20 (*p* = .005)	.04 *(nsd)*	.17 (*p* = .02)
Treatment of whole person	.25 (*p* = .001)	.14 (*p* = .03)	.29 (*p* = .001)
Cost reduction	-.01 *(nsd)*	.20 *(nsd)*	.01 *(nsd)*
Caring physicians	.23 (*p* = .002)	.01 *(nsd)*	.23 (*p* = .003)

All data are from the 1991 general-population survey. Correlations are based on subsamples ranging from 143 to 234 respondents.

its first few decades, the profession focused heavily on getting joints into alignment through manipulation so healing could occur naturally. Now self-healing is also thought to be enhanced by many other treatment and wellness procedures such as those discussed earlier.

In our 1991 study, one educator suggested the profession should do more to tell the public about the central role of self-healing in osteopathy. However, another worried that the area is very complex. Addressing the general public about it could create confusion, he said. Also, heavy emphasis on self-healing might lead some people to doubt the need for even important physician interventions!

An irony is apparent in the history of this concept. Although many credit Still with calling attention to the body's self-healing capacity and being far ahead of his time in hypothesizing about the immune system, M.D.s control most research facilities in the United States. Thus, as immunology grew and matured as a medical specialty, D.O.s found themselves largely on the outside looking in. As a result, many M.D.s would surely claim today that self-healing is standard stuff for them and not peculiar to osteopathy.

However, thinking about the body's self-healing capacity has undergirded the other concepts discussed previously in several ways.

First, wellness is important because it contributes to self-healing and illness prevention. As noted earlier, wellness requires that the physician play an adviser or counselor role. This, in turn, places special emphasis on a close, caring relationship between doctor and patient.

Second, the notion of self-healing suggests a somewhat humble role for physicians. They do not intervene and bring about a cure by themselves. Rather they seek to remove barriers to the body's own self-healing processes as provided by nature.

As D.O.s see it, the development of sophisticated technology and treatment has subtly led some physicians to lose this humility. Transplants and antibiotics seem to accomplish wonders. Although many or most M.D.s surely avoid such arrogance, citizens in a technological society such as the United States may accept it all too readily. As noted earlier, 42% of all 1991 respondents agreed that "Modern medicine can cure almost any ailment."

Such conceit about the role of medicine can lead both patient and doctor to see the latter as an all-knowing guru and not as a partner working with the patient. As noted earlier, this can hamper doctor–patient relations.

Third, self-healing requires integrated effort involving the entire body, mind, and soul. And, as noted earlier, most lay respondents bought the basic notion that doctors must treat and deal with the whole person.

Fourth, prevention of illness usually costs less than treatment of it once it arrives. Thus emphasis on self-healing relates closely to the public's number one health-care concern: cutting costs.

This concludes the discussion of seven key concepts in osteopathy. We now show how these concepts are linked to three issues facing the field. These are the role of osteopathic hospitals, cost containment, and the distinctive identity of the osteopathic health care school.

SOME KEY ISSUES FACING OSTEOPATHY

Beliefs warrant special attention if they meet two conditions. First, holding of them correlates positively with credibility assigned to D.O.s. (Such a correlation suggests gests it's possible that people view the belief object as good for osteopathic practice.) Second, physicians and the lay public hold differing views with respect to them.

In 1982, three beliefs met these two conditions. These were perceived similarity between M.D.s and D.O.s, evaluation of osteopathic hospitals, and evaluation of osteopathic manipulative treatment.

The discussion already shows that the linkage between OMT and D.O. credibility declined substantially by 1991. The absence of data about D.O. beliefs at that time makes it impossible to assess differences between physicians and lay persons then. However, the correlations between M.D.–D.O. similarity and hospital evaluation on the one hand and D.O. credibility on the other remained positive and significant in 1991 (see Tab. 12–10). Also, educators continued to see these matters as important for the field. Thus, we discuss them in some detail along with the central issue of cost.

Osteopathy—Its Distinctive Identity

Throughout its life, osteopathic medicine has been threatened from one side by allopathic medicine and from another by chiropractic, a school of health care that like osteopathy, deals with the musculoskeletal system. We now deal in turn with each of these.

Allopathic Medicine. In 1981–1982, we asked D.O.s whether they would like to emphasize similarities with M.D.s more than differences, differences more than similarities, or both about equally in addressing the general public.

About one fourth gave the *equal* response—perhaps the most appropriate in light of osteopathy's claim that it offers most of what allopathic medicine provides and more. However, other physicians voted for emphasizing differences rather than similarities by about a $2\frac{1}{2}$–1 margin (Culbertson & Stempel, 1982, p. 33).

That was not surprising in light of the history of osteopathy. It had come into being more than 100 years earlier as a rebel offshoot of allopathic medicine. D.O.s were rebels who challenged, among other things, the use of the unscientific drugs of that era. As often happens with rebels, the founders and their followers were ostracized. The American Medical Association that had at first labeled them as *quacks* and *cultists* eventually settled on another strategy: "If you can't beat'm, let'm join you."

Such an attempt to swallow up the smaller rival branch of medicine occurred in the early 1960s in California, where the local AMA affiliate, the California Medical Association (CMA), needed 3,000 more members to become the largest delegation at the AMA national convention. It was a complex issue, but in brief, here's what happened:

A bill to enact a new osteopathic-practice law was placed on the statewide ballot. During the campaign for its passage, D.O.s were threatened with the loss of all hospital privileges. Under this pressure, most of the state's D.O.s paid $65 to become M.D.s with newly awarded "degrees" from the state's former osteopathic college that had just been converted to an M.D. school. As a result of these defections, the CMA blanketed the state with a media blitz for a few weeks prior to the election with news that all parties, except for a handful of dissident D.O.s, totally agreed with the merger.

In this almost circus-like atmosphere, the referendum not surprisingly passed. The new law's effect, simply and devastatingly, was to deny new D.O.s the opportunity to take licensure examinations in California[2]. The profession seemed to be doomed to a Shaker-like extinction (Denbow, 1977). Furthermore, the D.O.s who had become M.D.s were viewed as second-class citizens within the allopathic community, particularly when they sought to practice in other states.

The California amalgamation, however, was not the wave of the future as it first appeared to be. Some felt the profession might die. Instead, it emerged stronger, both in that state and nationally, than it was before the merger (Berlfein, 1989). But to this day, many D.O.s look upon the idea of merger with horror, fearing the distinctive aspects of their school would more or less disappear within the huge, powerful AMA.

This concern has increased in some quarters recently as growing numbers of

---

[2]The 1962 Osteopathic Licensure Act was overturned in 1974 by the California Supreme Court on the grounds that it denied "equal protection of the law to graduates of osteopathic colleges."

osteopathic students have completed residencies in allopathic institutions. That trend developed for at least two reasons. First, the number of D.O. graduates grew to the point where there were not enough osteopathic residencies for all. At the same time, the number of allopathic graduates was going down. Second, osteopathic hospitals have declined in numbers.

Osteopathic educators differed in 1991 as to how many D.O.s are likely to desert their school of medicine, psychologically or in professional affiliation, after completing allopathic residencies. Most agreed that some such desertion has already occurred.

However, one respondent offered the following rebuttal to the doom sayers:

Those who run . . . internships within osteopathy say, "Our students are running off and deserting us. How can we punish them?" They should say, "Look at the diversity and strengths which these people (D.O.s with allopathic residencies) bring to our profession." D.O.s with such a background still have the unique things which osteopathic training has provided.

This debate is fueled by the previously-noted concern that D.O.s protect their identity by emphasizing differences between themselves and their allopathic sisters and brothers.

However, as shown in Tab. 12.10, the general public in the state studied appears to have a different view. The more similar people believe M.D.s and D.O.s are, the more credibility they assign to osteopathy. (The correlation between similarity and credibility ratings was .36 in 1991, down slightly from .42 9 years earlier, but still substantial.)

Taken as a whole, our data suggest that people see the dominant allopathic school as the standard in American health care, the primary creator of modern technology. Further, they feel it's important that physicians who treat them have some knowledge of the entire body. (After all, a back pain sometimes reflects an ailment in one's kidney or elsewhere.) And, unlike with D.O.s, who have sometimes been associated with the musculoskeletal system, M.D.s, as a whole, presumably have never been linked in people's thinking with particular treatments or ailments.

Tab. 12.13 suggests that most lay respondents perceive America's two schools of medicine as quite similar. Overall, 81% chose the *very similar* or *fairly similar* response in 1982, compared with 79% in 1991. However, these data also give some hope for advocates of osteopathic distinctiveness. Only 27% chose *very similar* in 1981–1982, and this figure declined to 17% by 1991. Obviously, then, at least three fourths of all respondents did see differences worth noting.

Table 12.14 indicates that competition with M.D.s in the court of public opinion need not work to osteopathy's disadvantage as some within the profession fear. In each survey, we asked about agreement or disagreement with the statement that "Osteopathic physicians are at least as well qualified, on the whole, as medical doctors (M.D.s)." In 1981–1982, 78% of all respondents agreed with this state-

TABLE 12.13
Percentage of Respondents Perceiving Various Levels of Similarity Between Osteopathy and
Both Allopathy and Chiropractic

Allopathy

How similar of different, on the whole, would you say D. O. s and M. D. s are in the practice of
medicine?

	1981-1982	1991
Very similar	27 ⎰ 81%	17 ⎰ 79%
Fairly similar	54 ⎰	62 ⎰
Not very similar	15	14
Not similar at all	3	7
	99% (*n* = 312)	100% (*n* = 276)

Chiropractic

On the whole, how similar would you say chiropractors and doctors of osteopathy are in the
practice of medicine?

Very similar	10 ⎰ 46%	9 ⎰ 47%
Fairly similar	36 ⎰	38 ⎰
Not very similar	35	33
Not similar at all	19	20
	100% (*n* = 286)	100% (*n* = 278)

TABLE 12.14
Percentage of Respondents Agreeing and Disagreeing With Statements About D. O. Credibility
as Seen by Respondent and as Attributed to Public

Respondent

Osteopathic physicians are at least as well qualified and trained, on the whole, as medical doctors
(M.D.s).

	1981-1982	1991
Agree strongly	42 ⎰ 78%	31 ⎰ 76%
Agree somewhat	36 ⎰	45 ⎰
Disagree somewhat	4	16
Disagree strongly	19	8
	101% (*n* = 296)	100% (*n* = 245)

Attributed to Public on the Whole

Overall, the osteopathic profession has a good image with the general public.[a]

Agree strongly		18 ⎰ 66%
Agree somewhat		48 ⎰
Disagree somewhat		27
Disagree strongly		7
		100% (*n* = 260)

[a]This question was asked only in the 1991 general-population survey.

ment, 42% strongly. In 1991, comparable figures were 76% agreement and 31% strong agreement. (It's important to note that 40% gave no response in 1982, compared with 50% in 1991. This doubtlessly reflects the most fundamental public relations problem of osteopathy—lack of awareness.)

In the same table, 66% agreed (18% strongly) with the statement that "Overall, the osteopathic profession has a good image with the general public." These results address the respondent's assessment of osteopathy's reputation among people as a whole, not simply in her or his own mind.

Taken as a whole, our data suggest that cooperation between M.D.s and D.O.s is increasing and will continue to do so. One educator put the matter succinctly in 1991:

> I think the entire profession is going through a major change. Most of our graduates now work in hospitals with both M.D.s and D.O.s on their staffs. Some osteopathic hospitals have earned dual accreditation. I see this as our future. We are not going to build any more osteopathic hospitals. Thus we are going to have a growing need for combined-staff operations.

At the same time, however, D.O.s appear to have strong pride in their profession and to work hard toward a separate identity.

Said one professor, "I argue that, if there were no significant differences in training or practice—if we were Fords and allopaths were Chevys—having two separate schools would still be healthy. Some competition and expression of differing viewpoints, providing a real choice, is needed."

Chiropractic.   Chiropractors are restricted by law to treatment of the bones, joints, and muscles. They rely largely on manipulation.

Interestingly, osteopathic educators with whom we talked said they knew little about chiropractic approaches. Most did not have firm opinions as to whether differences between osteopathic and chiropractic manipulation, on the whole, were profound or fairly minor.

Such separation between the two schools undoubtedly reflects, in part, the fact that D.O.s appear to have said little—critical or otherwise—about chiropractic practice. After all, if they discuss the rival school, D.O.s call attention to it.

Tab. 12.13 shows that only 46% of lay respondents in 1981–1982 and 47% in 1991 saw osteopathy and chiropractic as very or fairly similar. What's more, only 10% in 1982 and 9% in 1991 chose the *very similar* response.

Nonetheless, as shown in Tab. 12.8, people tended to associate manipulation with chiropractic more often in 1991 than 9 years earlier. This is consistent with the suggestion by one D.O. that chiropractors have marketed their services very effectively.

Educators reported some very tentative interaction between D.O.s and chiropractors ("Doctors of Stark County," 1987). Space precludes discussion of that here. It may be healthy, but problems could arise if competition becomes more intense.

We now turn to a second issue facing the field: the plight of hospitals.

Osteopathic Hospitals—A Dying Breed?

Many physicians say that hospitals play an important role in building awareness of and respect for osteopathy. A hospital serves as a training center for physicians and other professionals. It showcases the D.O.s practice of total health care as opposed to simply treatment of backaches and sore joints, etc. It provides modern health care when one is truly ill and most need it. And it can symbolize service at a time when may associate health care with large fees (Culbertson & Stempel, 1983a).

Tab. 12.10 shows a substantial positive correlation (.44 in 1981, .35 in 1991) between evaluation of osteopathic hospitals and osteopathic credibility. However, our data suggest a certain "softness" in the public relations posture of osteopathic hospitals. Specifically:

Tab. 12.15 indicates that two thirds of our 1981–1982 D.O. respondents rated osteopathic hospitals in their state as *excellent*. But they correctly believed that the most common response by residents of their state was *good*. This held with general-population data in both 1981–1982 and 1991.

Data (Culbertson & Stempel, 1985) not reported here suggest that the correlation between evaluation of osteopathic hospitals and D.O. credibility hinged on people's assessment of the hospital itself and not on awareness of osteopathic concepts that might have been learned there. Hospital public relations people told us their bosses tend to hide their osteopathic identities and not use their institutions very actively in telling the overall osteopathic story.

TABLE 12.15
Ratings that D.O.s Who Have Worked in Osteopathic Hospitals This ˙ ´ear Gave to Such Hospitals Compared With Assumed and Actual Ratings by General-Population Respondents in 1981-1982 and 1991

	Ratings by D.O.s for Osteopathic Hospitals That They Know of (1981-1982)	Ratings that D.O.s Feel People in Their Areas Would Give (1981-1982)	Ratings by General Population (1981-1982)	Ratings by General Population (1991)
Excellent	67	36	28	23
Good	28	51	48	53
Fair	3	10	20	16
Poor	2	3	4	8
	100% (n = 192)	100% (n = 189)	100% (n = 250)	100% (n = 133)

Why the hiding? There appear to be two basic reasons. First, some administrators fear (with little justification, based on our data) that the osteopathic label is a stigma and might hurt their reputations. Second, as noted earlier, most hospitals, osteopathic or otherwise, have at least some allopathic specialists on their staffs. Because the AMA had once defined D.O.s as quacks, these M.D. staff members might take a dim view of giving the institutions' osteopathic aspect a high profile. Political opposition within the hospitals could result (Culbertson & Stempel, 1983a).

Such factors aside, osteopathic as well as allopathic hospitals have had tough sledding in recent years. According to *D.O. Magazine,* the osteopathic profession lost 13% of its hospitals between 1982 and 1988 ("Closed," 1988). A 1988 article estimated that 700 of the nation's 5,700 (12%) hospitals would close by about 1995 (Sprovieri, 1988).

Some hospitals are surviving by merging with others and/or by providing specialized services that meet a particular need (Sprovieri, 1988). Unfortunately, osteopathic hospitals tend to be vulnerable, partly because they exist largely in small towns. A given institution can survive in a large metropolitan center by specializing in, say, heart or cancer problems. But a small town and surrounding rural area often lack a critical mass of nearby patients who could support such a unit.

One medical educator reflected the thinking of all we interviewed in saying, "I am worried about osteopathic hospitals. They are a gathering point for the osteopathic community. And without that, it will be hard to maintain that community."

We now turn to a very important problem: health care costs.

Health-Care Costs—Scary Business

In 1982, we asked lay people what they saw as the most important problem facing health care today. About 57% mentioned things connected with health-care costs, beating the second most oft-mentioned problem, an alleged shortage of health-care personnel, by more than 10-1. Nine years later, 55% mentioned costs by name whereas another 23% zeroed in on health care availability, surely tied closely to one's ability to pay.

Clearly the cost of catastrophic health care scares people greatly. Most people have had at least one relative with cancer or some other dread disease. Thus, one has learned first hand how quickly one might go broke if it weren't for health insurance. No doubt largely because of this, costs are at the top of the public's health-care agenda even though according to our 1981 content analysis, newspapers then gave rather modest attention to related issues (Culbertson & Stempel, 1983b).

Of course, the reasons for skyrocketing costs are numerous and complex. Technology and sophisticated techniques cost money. Malpractice suits have become common in our litigious society, forcing physicians to buy expensive malpractice insurance and order unnecessary testing largely so they might look good in court.

Furthermore, as noted in chapter 4, many people buy the cultural belief that costs don't matter because someone else will pay. Others accept a second cultural belief that technology and science can achieve most anything. This attitude has proven costly.

Health-maintenance organizations (HMOs) grew rapidly in the early 1980s, offering incentives to cut costs. Basically, an HMO provides a kind of insurance. The patient pays it a certain fee each year, and the HMO finds physicians and other professionals who provide care as needed. With certain exceptions, patients pay the same amount whether they require a lot of care or none at all. Thus, the HMO and physician shoulder some of the risk.

According to one estimate, HMOs served about 13% of all Americans by the mid- to late 1980s (Wogensen, 1990). The comparable figure for our 1991 sample was 15% (60 of 390).

However, many have gone belly up, basically because they couldn't cut expenses enough to compete successfully with traditional insurers while still covering their own operating costs (Wogensen, 1990).

Insurance companies have also set up rules and procedures designed to cut costs by shortening hospital stays. Educators saw this as a good thing in many cases. One commented that hospitals are for acute care, and it hardly makes sense to spend $400 a day for a place in which to lie down and eat!

However, such rules have disadvantages. Resulting bureaucratization hurts doctor–patient relations as discussed earlier. Also, patients occasionally have relapses after going home too early.

In our 1991 survey, 54% of all respondents reported that they, or at least one member of their immediate families, had been hospital inpatients during the past 3 years. Of these people, 41% felt rules pertaining to health insurance had a big impact on the length of hospital stays. Nineteen percent reported a small impact, whereas 39% saw no impact at all.

In total, 36% of the *big-impact* people felt they or their relatives had gone home too early, whereas 4% said they had stayed too long. Overall, then, about 15% (36% of 41%) of all respondents who had inpatient experience within their families felt insurance rules had shortened hospital stays too much. This is a small but significant minority.

Turning to health insurance as a whole, 86% of our respondents reported having it. And 80% of these people said their employers paid, at least in part, for their insurance.

Thirty-nine percent of the insured said they were very satisfied with their insurance, whereas 51% said *fairly satisfied* and only 10% *not satisfied at all*. Furthermore, 43% of the employer-paid insurees, but only 23% of the self-paid, described themselves as very satisfied.

Insured respondents were asked about their biggest single complaint regarding health insurance. In all, 23% had to do with the amount paid by the insurance company, 24% with loopholes (failure to cover dental, eye, and other problems).

About one fourth of the employer-insured respondents complained about the amount that their employers paid toward premiums.

In sum, people see a need for insurance but gripe about it a great deal. Educators told us emphatically, however, that insurance really doesn't cut or contain costs (though conceivably it could be designed to do so by encouraging wellness and preventive measures). Rather, it insures that "someone else will pay for them"—a somewhat dangerous mind set that often leads to extravagance.

It was suggested earlier that all seven basic concepts of osteopathy contribute to cost containment. OMT, immunization, wellness, diagnosis with attention the musculoskeletal system, and good doctor–patient relations cost the patient (and the doctor or insurer, for that matter) very little. Furthermore, whole-person treatment takes time and patience, not expensive equipment or expertise. Primary care physicians supposedly act as allies for their patients in containing costs as well as in other areas.

Unfortunately, most people do not appear to associate osteopathy with cost containment. Tab. 12.11 shows that in 1991, only 15% of all respondents linked osteopathy very closely to cost reduction, whereas 36% saw no linkage at all. Also, fully 89% rated cost factors as very important. Yet neither importance nor linkage ratings correlated with perceived D.O. credibility or image (see Tab. 12.12).

It appears, then, that osteopathy could gain appreciation in the years to come by emphasizing the economic values of its major tenets. How this can be done is not clear, but we now offer some suggestions in the concluding section of this chapter.

IMPLICATIONS

We now discuss several action plans relating to six general points flowing from our research. As with other chapters, the reader should draw on our results in discussing each action plan before looking at the rationales that we provide.

Point 1—D.O.s are their own best public relations people and adult educators. Doctor–patient contact, one-on-one and in small groups, appears to be the most effective means of telling the osteopathic story and teaching basic notions of good health care. The state and national osteopathic associations, hospitals, and colleges of osteopathic medicine should make a concerted effort to help physicians play these roles.

Our data suggest that, by and large, people see their own physicians as caring people. Also, most survey respondents gave their doctors high marks for taking the time to answer questions and explain diagnoses as well as treatments.

In both 1981–1982 and 1991, people who had family physicians seemed more happy about the "human side" of care they were getting than did people who relied on alternatives such as clinics. In 1991, we had too few respondents with D.O.s as family doctors (just 19) to permit meaningful comparison of M.D.s with D.O.s in this area. However, in 1981–1982, D.O. patients seemed slightly happier than M.D. patients about the overall care that they had received.

Physicians' dedication to serving patients as total humans surely helps explain these results. However, situational theory, discussed in chapter 4, gives added support to the idea that patients are especially open to new health-care information and ideas just before, during, and just after visits to their doctors. The theory predicts active information seeking given at least three conditions, all of which seem apt to hold when doctor and patient talk:

High problem recognition. Patients usually feel they have health-related problems and uncertainty about how to solve them or they'd not see their physicians in the first place. (Of course, regular examinations may not stem from a perceived ailment. But they do reflect a need to answer questions about one's overall condition in maintaining wellness.)

High involvement. Basically, this entails seeing a link between what one is doing at a given time and one's self. Surely a person's body lies at the core of herself or himself. Obviously, then, when one explores and seeks help with the well-being and treatment of one's own body, one normally feels highly involved. At such times, health care is very personal. It is not simply an abstract problem for society or humanity as a whole.

Low constraint recognition. No doubt many people see their physicians partly because they feel constrained; they cannot figure out how to solve or avoid health problems. However, the physician's job is to help them find a way. **And in playing the counselor or teacher role, a physician can help make the patient feel like a partner in this process.** Such a feeling, in turn, helps patients feel they **can** make a difference by learning and using health care information.

This line of reasoning suggests at least three broad courses of action.

Action 1—Strengthen training of physicians in patient and public relations, broadly defined. Continuing education in this area for practicing physicians is especially important.

Reasoning. Many physicians and educators told us that such training is often thin; it's crowded out of many medical curricula by the vast and growing amount of technical information that a physician must master. However, the college of osteopathic medicine at the researchers' university offered a required course focusing on doctor–patient relations. In this course, a psychologist, as co-instructor, helped physicians learn, partly through role playing, how to approach one's patient as a partner in health care.

As noted earlier, treatment of a range of problems from addiction to dying requires special emphasis on doctor–patient relations. Courses that deal with these matters need to present units on doctor–patient relations. In particular, we were told, many older physicians need to update themselves on recent developments in diagnosis and treatment of alcohol and drug abuse. That includes interpersonal aspects of the treatment process.

Workshops at medical conferences, continuing-education videos, and other channels are relevant here.

Action 2—Make videos and the VCR's needed to play them along with readable brochures presenting the osteopathic story available in clinics, doctors' waiting rooms, hospital lobbies, and other locations where patients and other involved persons may have the time and inclination to consume them.

Reasoning.   Patients and others close to them are likely to encounter these materials at a time when, according to situation-belief theory, they are inclined and able to read and listen actively.

Action 3—Encourage physicians to discuss patient communication thoroughly with nurses, medical therapists, and others who have frequent contact with patients.

Reasoning.   In hospital and clinical settings, physicians find only limited time to spend with their patients. During hospital rounds, a doctor often checks patients' charts, observes them briefly, makes a few (hopefully cheery) comments, and leaves. On the other hand, nurses take vital signs frequently, give shots and pills, and in hospitals, are available 24 hours a day so the patient may contact them by flicking a switch or pushing a button.

Nonphysicians are normally precluded from saying much about diagnoses, symptoms, and treatments. This is understandable; they might well mislead if they depart very far from the physician's "script."

However, we found hints that some physicians take a somewhat condescending attitude toward practitioners in other health-care professions. It is reasonable to suggest that teamwork among professionals as well as between doctor and patient helps patient relations. This is especially likely where, because of personnel shortages, physicians must rely heavily on so-called para-professionals.

These and other steps strengthen the all-important **social contacts** between doctor and patient. However, one obvious point is important. *All the training in the world will not aid doctor–patient relations very much unless the physician is a caring person at heart, unselfish and dedicated to serving humanity.* Our data suggest that by and large, D.O.s (as well as M.D.s) qualify here.

However, one osteopathic educator worried in 1991 that D.O.s are beginning to lose that minority feeling that had long made them try harder, as the rental car company Avis claims to do in dealing with customers. The educator stressed that physicians must be chosen and trained with this in mind.

Point 2—Most Americans hold certain cultural beliefs that work against their being effective health-care consumers. Such beliefs tend to be difficult to change, as they are imparted during socialization and receive considerable

social support. However, although D.O.s may seldom bring about such changes on a large scale, they and their organizations can question the applicability of these beliefs to health care.

One such belief holds that **technology and science can solve all of our problems.** Ellul (1965, pp. 90–105) among others, saw this as a deep-seated part of individualistic "mass" societies such as America. And, as noted earlier, 42% of our 1991 general-population respondents agreed that "modern medicine can cure most anything."

Educators often told us this belief creates unrealistic expectations. These, in turn, make people especially apt to bring expensive lawsuits. They also encourage health-care professionals to use sophisticated equipment and treatments where these things may not be needed or effective. They may suggest little need for patients to play an active, responsible role in wellness and prevention. (If medicine can cure an ailment quickly and easily, why bother to prevent it?) Such concerns suggest a type of action.

Action 4—Develop and market media features on and give physicians ammunition for discussion with patients about the long slow, discouraging process of preventing and/or curing AIDS, cancer, polio (in years gone by), and other health-care problems.

Reasoning.   Because those with such ailments suffer a great deal, features about these people have dramatic appeal. Communication theory (Galtung & Ruge, 1973) along with our own content analysis of newspapers (Culbertson & Stempel, 1983b) suggest the media are willing to run such stories.

Unfortunately, in our 1981 interviews with D.O.s, few reported taking the initiative in going to the media with story ideas. However, those who did so generally assessed resulting press coverage quite favorably (Culbertson & Stempel, 1982). These findings point up the need for training of physicians and other health care professionals in public relations as urged under Action 2 previously. The opportunity is there, but D.O.s and their organizations must be proactive to seize it.

Situational theory suggests that the mass media tend not to reach people in settings that favor re-thinking the validity or implications of basic beliefs. That's because media consumers tend to read, view, and listen casually. They seldom experience high problem recognition or involvement at the time. However, the theory also suggests they will attend to and remember messages whose dramatic appeal captures their attention. People may apply such information later when personal involvement leads them to recall and consider it.

Action 5—Media releases, training material for physicians, brochures and videos for patients, and other messages on care of elderly and the "right to die" issue should emphasize the limited success that health-care professionals have had in affecting the aging process.

Reasoning.   Modern medicine has lengthened lives. But is this always a blessing? Several educators said no. Lots of elderly people are bedridden invalids who lose their memories and can scarcely function mentally. Many suffer a great deal from bodily pain and from boredom that seems inevitable when they spend years staring at walls in front of their beds.

These matters can be discussed in the context of real human dignity and suffering. They deserve a full airing as physicians counsel with patients about living wills and death, as urged earlier, *before these people become ill and lose their ability to think clearly.* Also, because of their dramatic appeal, such matters can be presented so as to attract media coverage. *Furthermore, the issue can be linked to the overall question of modern medicine's limited capacity to cure all ailments or dictate the long-term course of human life.*

The belief that medical science is all knowing and all powerful is likely to undergird a second widely held belief that **doctors are superior to patients and dictate their treatment rather than working it out with them as partners.** Earlier, we noted that this view often detracts from doctor–patient relations. Here we suggest a series of related actions.

Action 6—Media releases, training material for physicians, brochures and videos for patients, and other messages showing doctor and patient working together to deal with health problems.

Reasoning.   Such messages might show doctors counseling AIDS victims and their families, working with local community leaders in the ghetto to improve people's social and physical and environments, etc. Because of dramatic appeal, this kind of material should interest even those who, at the time of message consumption, do not feel highly involved.

The belief that doctor is superior to patient goes along with another oft-noted idea that **the doctor, and not the patient, is basically responsible for the patient's health.** Counteracting this belief, especially important in wellness medicine, suggests another set of actions (Katz, 1984).

Action 7—Media releases, training material for physicians, brochures and videos for patients, and other messages should stress the importance of wellness and the need for patients to adjust their own lifestyles and behavior patterns to achieve it.

Reasoning.   Once again, we have a facet of health care that lends itself well to human-interest treatment by communicators, though perhaps it involves less gripping drama than is found with diseases and suffering of the type discussed earlier.

Physicians can play the noble role of teacher fully and obviously in the area of wellness. No doubt some doctors do not have personalities or goals that prepare them to succeed here. Urologists, radiologists, and other technical specialists may not need to play a teaching role, it is argued. However, educators and trainers need to emphasize the overall importance of this area.

Emphasis on patient responsibility is linked to another cultural belief that several educators saw as a problem. This is the idea that **we are all entitled to the very best health care and to have someone else pay for it.**

The implications of such entitlement beliefs in various aspects of American life were noted in chapter 4. Applied here, these implications suggest another set of actions.

Action 8—Media releases, training material for physicians, brochures and videos for patients, and other messages emphasizing patient responsibility, as noted in action 7, should consider the extent to which that responsibility entails providing dollars. Further, it is important to note that payment must come from somewhere. So where?

Reasoning.   Many argue persuasively that people in the United States **are** entitled to comprehensive health care, even if the government must provide it free, from cradle to grave. If the nation can afford to fly to the moon and to bomb Baghdad into submission, it ought to be able to insure first-rate health care for all as other less wealthy countries do.

Of course, this is an emotionally loaded topic. Physicians undoubtedly differ greatly on it in line with their diverse ethical and political views. However, in years gone by, the American Medical Association has used the phrase *socialized medicine* in an extensive and largely successful campaign to fight government-controlled-and-sponsored health care. Thus, it's apparent that professionals **can** take a stand on financing and institutional control of health-related service with considerable impact.

In interviewing educators, we asked if the American Osteopathic Association had taken a proactive stance on this matter. The response was generally negative. Perhaps this is defensible. However, in their role as educators, D.O.s need to go beyond slogans and help their patients look carefully at the question of just where the nation can find dollars to pay for the very best health care. That is obvious because many physicians were not comfortable with the idea that only the rich have the right to live.

We now look at cost more specifically from the standpoint of osteopathic medicine.

Point 3—When viewed closely, many elements of osteopathic philosophy can contribute to cost reduction and containment. There is need for a strong effort to link osteopathy to cost in people's minds.

Earlier we noted that the seven proposed elements of osteopathic philosophy contribute, in varying degrees, to economy. Furthermore, in both 1982 and 1991, most survey respondents saw cost as the most pressing problem in America. **Yet very few perceived a close link between cost containment and osteopathic medicine.**

Establishing such a link will not be easy. But we propose two general courses of action.

Action 9—Devise estimates, however rough, of costs, benefits, and savings connected with wellness, manipulation, immunization, and other health-care approaches linked closely to osteopathy.

Reasoning.   Journalists write and most people think in rather concrete dollars-and-cents terms. Thus, press coverage will be enhanced along with popular learning if D.O.s attach dollar values to specific aspects of their practice.

To be sure, this is not easy. It's hard to attach a dollar value to an illness when one prevents it or to feeling well partly because of wellness behavior. Our interviews and reading revealed only minimal progress and relatively little effort in this area. Apparently that stems in part from the fact that D.O.s do not do much research of any kind.

Two sociologists, Altheide and Johnson (1980) pointed up the need for varied service providers to express in concrete terms what they accomplish. Also, our chapter 6, in defining the economic context, discussed the need for assigning dollar values when making decisions about alternative needs and expenditures.

A good deal of research has gone into developing indices of success or failure for welfare departments, evangelical churches, tourism agencies, and other service units. Perhaps osteopathic physicians need to direct more attention to developing such indices, called **bureaucratic propaganda** by Altheide and Johnson (1980).

To be sure, these indices are often open to question. They are used in self-serving ways by the sponsoring agencies. Their surface-level sophistication often masks many highly subjective decisions that went into their creation and validation.

Nonetheless, Altheide and Johnson (1980) argued that bureaucratic propaganda is needed for many professions and groups to survive in today's world. Almost all organizations and individuals need resources to operate and must argue persuasively that the resource providers or stake holders get something in return.

Perhaps the profession could start by estimating lost work days and costs associated with them that certain health care practices help avoid.

Surely osteopathic associations and colleges can validate research on indices of achievement partly by checking to be sure that they pass muster with M.D.s and other interested groups, thereby protecting credibility. Also, researchers can stress the imprecision of and assumptions underlying their assessments.

Dollar values, of course, have limited appeal to the public and little clear meaning in a world where the media talk glibly about billion-dollar bombers and trillion-dollar debts. Thus, another type of action is needed.

Action 10—Develop analyses, perhaps looking in-depth at a broad range of specific cases so as to clarify human implications and decision-making dynamics, of ways in which primary-care medicine saves money. Such analyses can attempt to assess how much money is saved, in what way, and what steps are taken to avoid a resultant decline in health-care quality.

Reasoning.   Three points underlie this suggestion.

First, it's widely assumed that general practitioners charge less than specialists sometimes for the same service. If this can be documented, it points up the economies of osteopathic medicine given that school's heavy emphasis on primary care.

Second, educators told us that the good primary care physician serves as patients' allies, helping them make good use of an increasingly complex, bureaucratic health care system. Do general practitioners carry out their ally role with an eye to saving money? If so, how? And what savings result? If answers can be provided here, they should encourage people to link osteopathy with cost containment. If the referral process, in fact, fails to consider cost factors, educators and physicians should take a hard look at it.

Third, educators told us that cost-saving devices such as health-maintenance organizations and rules to shorten hospital stays generally work well. However, cutting corners does lead occasionally to inadequate testing, health-care delays, limited treatment, relapses, etc. Our general-population data suggest this happens often enough to create some controversy and public displeasure. The health-care professions need to explain candidly the frequency and severity of such problems along with how to solve them.

It is important to present related information in a personalized way, stressing suffering, relief, and expenses in terms that most people can understand. Hence the need for case study material as spelled out in action 10.

Point 4—A substantial number of people believe that osteopathic physicians deal primarily with ailments of the bones, joints, and muscles, Thus, it seems important to emphasize that D.O.s practice total health care.

Our 1981–1982 general-population data show that almost 40% of all respondents greatly overestimated the number of patients whom D.O.s manipulate. This problem appears to have abated somewhat by 1991. However, the total-care message deserves continuing emphasis.

Action 11—Media and other messages aimed at the general public need to portray D.O.s doing surgery, delivering babies, reading X-rays, and doing diverse things other than manipulating.

Reasoning.   One educator told us in 1991 that as a surgeon, he felt osteopathy had somewhat oversold its commitment to primary care. This occurred to him early in his career when some patients could scarcely believe that D.O.s perform surgery!

After our 1981–1982 survey, the osteopathic association of the state that we studied sponsored a pilot study to test this strategy. For several weeks, television spots in two medium-sized cities portrayed D.O.s giving varied treatments as noted previously. Survey data collected before and after the media campaign reveal increased awareness of osteopathy and a growing perception that D.O.s use all treatment modes well.

Of course, the demonstrated effect was short term and doubtlessly would dissipate in the absence of ongoing public relations and educational effort. Also, buying TV time is expensive, though producing and sending public service announcements and video news releases may not be. Our next point focuses on one other oft-ignored, inexpensive type of effort that might help sustain such views.

Point 5—D.O.s can best view the social and physical environments of their patients—matters relevant to treating the whole person—if they become familiar with and active in the communities where they practice.

This point is fairly obvious. At least two osteopathic educators told us that physicians need to develop closer relationships with and learn more about their patients by getting to know them socially outside the office. Unfortunately, our research did not investigate how many physicians did this or how they did it. But the need seems real, suggesting the following set of actions.

Action 12—Encourage D.O.s to become active in their communities. They may do so by serving as athletic trainers, addressing classes in school, speaking to civic groups, establishing physical fitness programs, and in many other ways.

Reasoning.   Coorientation theory, discussed in chapter 4, points up the need to do this. A physician can truly **understand** a patient only by observing what problems that person faces and how she or he deals with them day in and day out.

Many patients lack the opportunity or ability to explain these things while sitting in a doctor's office. Educators told us that such understanding is especially important in dealing with substance abuse, AIDS, the right to die, and other highly personal matters where (a) the social and physical contexts become very important and often create stress and (b) patients tend to withdraw and do not communicate fully unless physicians show tremendous skill and persistence. Perhaps a reputation as a caring human—not just a physician—helps here.

Going beyond health care per se, varied professionals have come to realize that community service boosts their public relations. As noted in chapter 6, exchange theory suggest that people tend to help you where you have helped them. Because savvy executives don't know when they may need favors, many take part in community affairs partly to make deposits in their favor banks. Perhaps more D.O.s could take this to heart.

Hospitals also can play a part in community service. As noted earlier, these institutions have come on hard times. However, educators and D.O.s, as well as lay citizens, look to them as symbols of the total health-care system. This brings us to a final point.

Point 6—Osteopathic hospitals can give high priority to telling the osteopathic story. Unfortunately, many appear to have largely avoided such activity while more or less hiding their osteopathic identities.

As noted earlier, osteopathic hospitals tended to avoid emphasizing their osteopathic aspects because: (a) M.D.s who work there might object and (b) administrators sometimes fear that osteopathy carries a stigma.

However, our research suggests that in general, people who are aware of osteopathy and its key concepts accept them. **Thus osteopathy should be an asset, not a liability, in the public eye.** This suggests a final set of actions.

Action 13—Osteopathic hospitals should develop and use open houses, displays, talk-show appearances, medical columns in local papers, brochures placed in lobbies, and many other channels to explain the seven key concepts of osteopathy, their importance, their advantages (as well as disadvantages), and how they interrelate.

Reasoning. People who visit hospitals tend to be highly **involved** with health-care problems. They or their loved ones often feel a need for help in solving **problems.** Thus, situational-belief theory suggests they should be open to and motivated to process health-care information and arguments. (Of course, some who go into hospitals are very ill or have anxiety that makes it hard for them to concentrate! But many do not have these burdens.)

One further point deserves emphasis here. A hospital can strive to tell the osteopathic story without actually placing the word osteopathic in its name. For the most part, M.D.s now ascribe at least some validity to most though not all osteopathic ideas and practices. Thus, political barriers resulting from the need to work with allopaths should be surmountable (Culbertson & Stempel, 1983a).

A final argument concludes this chapter. Professional communicators and citizens both tend to view entertainment and news as two distinct aspects of mass-media content. However, some scholars such as Mendelsohn (1973) and Singhal and Rogers (1989) demonstrated that entertainment programming can deliver serious educational messages. For example, soap operas have informed people about welfare programs and how to access them. Also, a televised driver's test made many people aware that they lacked knowledge about rules of the highway (Mendelsohn, 1973).

Obviously hospitals and doctors play a prominent role in the plots of soap operas and dramatic shows on television. However, such programs seldom emphasize health-care tips or information. One notable exception was "Marcus Welby, M.D.," a popular prime time show of many years ago. The American Osteopathic Association and other groups might explore this area more fully, perhaps even helping to develop a program called "M. T. Hollister, D.O."

REFERENCES

Altheide, D. L., & Johnson, J. M. (1980). *Bureaucratic propaganda.* Boston: Allyn & Bacon.

Belkin, L. (1990, February 19). Many doctors see themselves drowning in sea of paperwork. *New York Times,* pp. A1, A13.

Black, R. B. (1988, August). Presidential address: Be active in your profession, don't teach apathy. *Buckeye Osteopathic Physician,* pp. 23–25.

Bronstein, D. (1987, October). Treating AIDS patients: Physicians, too, have a choice. *Osteopathic Medical News,* p. 3.

Broom, G. M., & Dozier, D. M. (1990). *Using research in public relations.* Englewood Cliffs, NJ: Prentice-Hall.

Carlat, D. (1989, July–August). A rural awakening. *The New Physicians,* pp. 11–12.

Closed: Hospitals in Transition. (1988, March). *The D.O.,* p. 116.

Culbertson, H. M., & Stempel, G. H. III. (1982). *A study of the public relations posture of osteopathic medicine in Ohio.* Columbus: The Ohio Osteopathic Association.

Culbertson, H. M., & Stempel, G. H. III. (1983a, September). Stress the "osteopathic" in osteopathic hospitals. *Osteopathic Hospitals,* pp. 8–11.

Culbertson, H. M., & Stempel, G. H. III. (1983b, October). A study of medical coverage in eleven Ohio metropolitan newspapers. *Buckeye Osteopathic Physician,* pp. 4–11.

Culbertson, H. M., & Stempel, G. H. III. (1985). Linking beliefs and public relations effects. *Public Relations Research and Education, 2,* 23–35.

Denbow, C. J. (1977, May). Osteopathy: Packing more professional punch. *Medical Dimensions,* pp. 19–22, 24.

Denbow, C. J. (1978, July). The female physician. *Kirksville Magazine,* pp. 2–6.

Denbow, C. J. (1991, June 22). *1991 OU-COM alumni survey.* Unpublished report presented to officers, Ohio University College of Osteopathic Medicine Society of Alumni and Friends, Toledo, OH.

Denbow, C. J., & Feeck, R. (1988, January). The many meanings of "holistic medicine." *Journal of the American Osteopathic Association, 88,* pp. 15, 18.

Doctors of Stark County start pilot program with chiropractors. (1987, May). *Buckeye Osteopathic Physician,* p. 20.

Ellul, J. (1965). *Propaganda: The formation of men's attitudes.* New York: Vintage.

Fitzgerald, M. (1989, February). Addictionology academy offers a helping hand to private practitioners. *The D.O.,* pp. 117–119.

Gabe, C. (1987, December 6). The AIDS doctor. *Cleveland Plain Dealer Magazine,* p. 12.

Galtung, J., & Ruge, M. (1973). Structure and selecting the news. In S. Cohen & J. Young (Eds.), *The manufacture of news* (pp. 62–72). Beverly Hills, CA: Sage.

Gevitz, N. (1982). *The D.O.'s: Osteopathic medicine in America.* Baltimore: The Johns Hopkins University Press.

Grunig, J. E., & Hunt, T. (1984). *Managing public relations.* New York: Holt, Rinehart & Winston.

Katz, J. (1984). *The silent world of doctor and patient.* New York: The Free Press.

Mendelsohn, H. (1973). Some reasons why information programs can succeed. *Public Opinion Quarterly, 37,* 50–61.

Singhal, A., & Rogers, E. M. (1989). *India's information revolution.* Newbury Park, CA: Sage.

Sprovieri, J. (1988, March). Hospitals challenge tougher economic climate. *The D.O.,* pp. 118–120.

Still, A. T. (1897). *Autobiography of A. T. Still.* Kirksville, MO: Journal Publishing.

Wogensen, E. O. (1990, April). The HMO squeeze. *The New Physician,* pp. 12–17.

IV CONCLUSION

13 SPE-Context Theory in Action: An Overview

This volume provides practice in using 17 sets of theoretical concepts (6 sets each focusing on the political and economic contexts, and 5 on the social context, as shown in Tab. 13.1). Obviously, such use requires an understanding of concept meanings. This concluding chapter seeks to clarify meanings of the 17 perspectives. In doing this, we summarize interpretations and implications discussed in the three theoretical and six case-study chapters.

This chapter examines themes. It does not review all implications discussed earlier, but it does provide practice in concept use. This practice, in turn, should help the practitioner or student apply such notions as problem recognition, institutional leadership, externalities, and internalization quite easily and naturally. Practice makes perfect in using any tool—be it a hammer, a saw, or a theory.

One caveat. In this chapter, we do not give a coherent picture of the public relations postures of the six case-study clients reported on earlier. We hope chapters 7–12 do a reasonable job of this. Our purpose here is to focus on the **meaning and use of concepts,** taken one at a time, with some attention to their many interconnections. Only after the reader has studied chapters 1–12 will chapter 13 make much sense.

As noted earlier, particularly at the end of chapter 4, the theories overlap in meaning and interconnect in various ways. We now discuss some of these relationships.

SOME LINKS AMONG THEORIES

First, the economist's notion of opportunity costs and benefits can be viewed as an application of frame-of-reference or adaptation-level theory that falls under the social context.

TABLE 13.1
Sets of Concepts Used to Study Social, Political, and Economic Contexts

Social Context	Political Context	Economic Context
Cultural and subcultural beliefs	Group maintenance and task achievement	Competition
Situational beliefs	Institutional leaders, effectors, and activists	Exchange
Frame of reference	Politicians and technocrats	Value, marginal utility, and marginal returns
Quality and number of social contacts	Internalization, compliance, and identification	Opportunity costs and benefits
Coorientation processes	Central and peripheral information processing	Demand elasticity
	Relative power and coalition formation	Externalities

When considering opportunity costs, one first defines several alternative decisions or courses of action. She or he then assesses each option by comparing its actual or probable costs and benefits with those of all other options. The latter serve as adaptation levels or standards of comparison.

One point deserves emphasis here. Particularly in the service sector, it's often difficult to assign a cost or benefit value to a given option. As Sherif and Sherif (1956, pp. 40–66) noted, *perceptual anchors* that are vaguely defined or held with low certainty and conviction often get little use. Thus, a frequent goal of public relations—noted quite often in this volume—is to help people clarify the value of alternatives.

Second, involvement has roughly the same meaning and plays roughly the same role in the Grunigs' situational-belief theory (presented under the social context) and the elaboration likelihood model of Petty and Cacioppo (1986) (discussed as part of the political context because it focuses on persuasion). In each case, a highly involving situation is linked closely to a person's self.

However, key dependent variables differ somewhat in the two theories. Situational-belief theory predicts when one will be an active information seeker and processor or a passive consumer (Grunig, 1976, 1983). The elaboration likelihood model also deals with this question, but it goes on to investigate which elements a message consumer attends to. Specifically, this theory postulates that high-involved or central interpreters examine message content carefully and assess it on its own merits. Low-involved or peripheral folks, on the other hand, focus heavily on a message's source and on the setting in which they receive or consume the message. (For example, a person sometimes discounts even very credible speakers if their known vested interests suggest they have an ax to grind.)

Third, the notions of marginal value and returns in economics call attention forcibly to the importance of beliefs about situations, just as does situational-belief theory. A hamburger has very little value in a situation where the prospective eater has already downed 5–6 burgers. And so on.

Fourth, within the social context, cultural and subcultural beliefs frequently steer, stimulate, and constrain the consumption and interpretation of information. Thus such beliefs act as schemata. However, the two perspectives are not synonymous. Cultural and subcultural beliefs are quite stable, partly because they are products of prolonged socialization. On the other hand, schemata often are fleeting. They may be held only by one or a few individuals, whereas cultural and subcultural beliefs are shared by many and defined as "standard" within society as a whole or a substantial subgroup.

Fifth, cultural and subcultural beliefs often serve as anchors for personal values. Within the political context, Kelman (1961) said the influence strategy called *internalization* occurs when one links a behavior or belief to such values. Furthermore, Kelman regarded internalized behavior as stable (because it does not hinge on surveillance by others, as with compliance, or on one's self-defining relationship to role models, as with identification). He implied internalized behavior is authentic in that it relates closely to oneself. All of which points up the need to study cultural and subcultural beliefs when analyzing public relations strategies.

Sixth, power, a key element in the political context, is generally viewed within the context of competition, a central construct in economics. However, the political and social versions of competition often differ. As defined by economists, competition tends to be of the win–lose variety. That is, victory by one competitor makes victory by others less likely. However, within management (Argyris, 1974, pp. 1–33) and group-dynamics (Cartwright & Zander, 1960) theories, coalition formation focuses on win–win competition. Here individuals and groups strive to outdo each other as to salary and title, etc., while recognizing that in a collective endeavor, success by one participant contributes to success by all others. No chain is stronger than its weakest link.

One must appreciate such relationships to grasp fully the individual theories. No doubt many other such links exist, but we cannot identify them fully here. We now turn to some applications and interpretations of specific SPE concepts.

SOCIAL CONTEXT

Cultural and Subcultural Beliefs

As noted earlier, these beliefs are shared by all or substantial segments of a society or a subgroup that tends to socialize its members. Such beliefs are quite stable. They tend to fit together, forming what some call a *world view*. They frequently serve as schemata, influencing how people seek, process, and interpret information.

Many subcultural and cultural beliefs show up in the case studies reported. Taken as a whole, our data support at least four general conclusions.

First, the belief that government employees have a special obligation to serve citizens is widespread in the United States. It undergirds at least two public relations problems reported earlier.

Chapter 11 notes that a municipal worker sometimes gets into a public relations bind because of rules that preclude taking time to help cut down tree limbs on citizens' own property, unclog drains, etc. Such rules certainly may enhance apparent employee efficiency and task achievement. However, taxpayers find this hard to swallow in light of the public service norm.

Also, chapter 7 argues that because of this norm, police often get onto thin public relations ice when they impound cars until all fines are paid, refuse to unlock car doors, and rigorously enforce parking regulations. Such steps focus attention on citizen payment to the government and away from government service to citizens.

Second, some cultural and subcultural beliefs probably lead people to be passive and uninvolved when their involvement would be to everyone's advantage.

For example, Americans tend to have more or less blind faith in technology. Promotion of medical technology implies that health care people can cure almost any ailment. Thus, some folks see no compelling need to take personal responsibility for shaping their own lifestyles as required in wellness and preventive medicine.

In much the same vein, chapter 7 notes that many TV shows, movies, and novels portray law enforcement people as courageous, all knowing, and almost always successful. Although flattering to cops, such a view may contribute to citizen apathy about crime prevention. As a result, Neighborhood Watch, senior citizen volunteer, and other programs have enjoyed only limited success.

Third, cultural and subcultural beliefs quite often detract from the quality of interaction among citizens and between them and service-oriented professionals.

Chapter 12 reports that the attribution of very high status to physicians—learned by many Americans at an early age, and doubtlessly enhanced by health care promotion—can detract from doctor–patient relations. Patients all too often fail to question what doctors say as required in a responsible partnership. Also, doctors sometimes give unrealistically hopeful diagnoses and assessments partly to reduce patient anxiety. Such manipulative, if well-intentioned, tactics as telling white lies might be less common were it not for society's attributing semidivine power to doctors—power that some physicians are willing to assume. Unfortunately, even well-intentioned falsehoods may eventually reduce trust.

Also, chapter 10 notes that Blacks' belief in the centrality of their own racial pride and heritage has sometimes set the stage for them to distance themselves from the subcultures of Whites and other racial-ethnic groups. Such distancing detracts from understanding of non-Blacks. Unfortunately, Blacks in the United States must succeed or fail within an SPE context dominated largely by Whites.

Fourth and last, people within different occupational subcultures sometimes have dissimilar beliefs and world views. That, in turn, makes it difficult for these groups to work together effectively and harmoniously.

Chapter 7 shows this with special cogency. Police are taught to emphasize rules and their enforcement along with punishment of wrongdoers. On the other hand, social workers stress the need to support people and rehabilitate those who err. Rules of the social welfare system are often viewed by its case workers as barriers to progress, not virtues. These and other differences make it hard for the two groups to agree on diagnoses and work together.

However, police usually are the only government employees on duty 24 hours a day. When they encounter a wrongdoer, they must often define that person very quickly as a mental case or a crook. Unless they see the former interpretation as viable, they may never call the case to the attention of mental health personnel. Thus, their decision, although perhaps not completely irrevocable, can greatly affect eventual treatment and care.

In the corporate realm, chapter 9 indicates that open communication and involvement among all personnel—from motel-franchise managers to custodians—enhances organizational commitment. This, in turn, leads people to tolerate and better understand each other's differing beliefs so as to enhance breadth of perspective and creativity.

Situational Beliefs

The studies reported here reveal at least three recurrent themes relating to situational-belief variables.

First, perceived barriers to understanding and use of information often inhibit active information seeking. In such cases, it is important to help people remove constraints and/or recognize they aren't as formidable as they appear to be.

For example, many poor people feel unable to afford health care. Thus constrained, they often don't seek information that might help them obtain needed care at low cost or practice economical preventive medicine. Of course, illiteracy and the technical nature of many health care related messages act as further constraints.

On the positive side, the educational aspect of wellness emphasizes that people can improve their health through exercise, sensible diet, and other low-cost, easy-to-understand steps. Our data suggest that, by and large, people often learn about and practice wellness.

In the study of livestock magazines, farmers, especially younger ones, often report a need for how-to or mobilizing information. In part, certainly, such information may help them feel they can control their farms and their fates. Such a feeling, in turn, may contribute to the active information-seeking of livestock association members.

Also, Chapter 11 reports frustration among municipal employees who feel they have little impact on budgeting within city government as a whole or within their departments. We recommend strong steps to permit such impact and the open communication that it requires early in the budgeting process.

Further, in the very poor area served by Chief Glotz's police department, impounding of autos until their owners' fines levied by the city are paid could be quite devastating. Owners might have a very hard time earning the money needed to pay the fines! Given such barriers, many people probably would not attend very actively to messages about departmental policy. (Why bother? Ordinary citizens apparently have little impact, anyhow.)

Second, when addressing low-involved publics, one has two basic choices. Frame messages with large headlines, novel or bizarre words, colors, etc., so they catch the eye or ear of even low-involved audience members. Or seek to get audience members to link each message to themselves so they feel more involved with it.

Our data suggest that many young Blacks do not link Black studies programs to their own problems and aspirations. Consequently, they feel apathetic about such programs. In a similar vein, people tend to read or view media content about health care in a relaxed, escapist, low-involving way. Thus, in reaching Blacks as well as people with health care concerns via the media, programmers must (a) package programs in an appealing, conspicuous way, and (b) spell out sought-after conclusions and actions specifically and concretely so the casual reader or viewer will grasp them.

Third, one can safely give considerable detail and expect active, critical information processing when addressing audiences who have high problem recognition, high involvement, and low constraint recognition.

Patients waiting in doctors' offices tend to meet these conditions. Folks usually go to such offices, because they have health problems that they can't solve but believe their physician can. The problems clearly relate to themselves, suggesting high involvement. Likewise, in the police study, retirees, women, members of a Boy Scout Explorer post, and other groups are apt to score well on situational variables. The livestock magazine data suggest high reader involvement, as magazines provide information relating to people's livelihood. Active information seeking is apt to prevail within all these groups and settings.

Frame of Reference

As described in chapter 4, this notion focuses on two related concepts. A schema is a belief that helps determine how one seeks, processes, recalls, and interprets information. An adaptation level is a standard of comparison used to characterize something, on a continuum from low to high, with regard to some variable.

Our research uncovered three types of need or challenge relating to frame of reference.

First, we found at least four instances of felt needs by clients to change schemata (often a difficult task if they are widely used and held with intense commitment) or show that they do not apply in a given area as people assume.

Three examples showed up in the osteopathic-medicine research. To begin, primary care physicians are described as very important partly because specialists focus on one organ, organ system, or type of ailment. For example, a heart specialist is conditioned by training and basic beliefs (i.e., schemata) to look very hard at the role of the heart when diagnosing a wide variety of ailments. Primary care doctors, on the other hand, are taught to look at the whole person without placing undue emphasis on any one part of the body. In our research, members of a general-population sample endorsed the whole-person approach with enough unanimity to suggest that its endorsement acts as a schema for many.

Another example dealt with AIDS. People are conditioned to believe common-sense sanitary precautions can virtually eliminate the risk of catching AIDS. This schema, in turn, suggests that physicians, too, can safely treat AIDS patients. However, surgeons sometimes cut themselves during an operation, making it difficult, at best, to prevent the exchange of bodily fluids.

In a third and final medical instance, most Americans have great faith in technology and science to solve problems. This culturally based schema has at least two unfortunate consequences. First, people sometimes feel they need not take responsibility for their own health care, because if something goes wrong, doctors can easily fix it. Second, blind faith in doctors' ability to fix things sometimes leads to unrealistic expectations. When they aren't met, these expectations can create disillusionment and despair.

In a different realm, law-enforcement studies show a gradual swing away from the schema that police can and must assume sole responsibility for crime prevention. Rejection of this belief has been buttressed by the contention that societal forces such as poverty and divorce—beyond cops' control—contribute to crime. One result of such perceptions is the rather rapid growth of community efforts such as Neighborhood Watch groups.

Second, the studies reveal several instances in which practitioners need to discern and perhaps change adaptation levels.

In chapter 7, Police Chief Glotz dealt with zero-based budgeting. Essentially this means he had to justify every penny spent by discerning what the world might be like with that expenditure as compared with no expenditure at all. This stands in marked contrast to traditional budgeting in which managers view last year's budget as the standard and more or less assume it will remain constant unless conditions dictate a change.

Also in the law-enforcement study, respondents guessed that on the average, Glotz's town needs about 13 patrol persons on duty at any one time. Because the actual number of people on duty is just 4, the number 13 serves as a useful adaptation level for Glotz to discuss. He could use it to show his department's efficiency or to argue for additional funding.

The municipal employee study also reveals two important adaptation levels probably held by many citizens. First, the private sector has become more and more service oriented, generally (though not always) providing better and better service over time. It's only natural that people compare government services with those offered by, say, hotels and appliance dealers. Thus, government must keep pace to retain public approval and support. Second, people generally expect friends and neighbors to be considerate and serve them well. Such expectations are used to assess performance day in and day out. These assessments are especially salient in a small town, partly because many municipal employees' customers are their friends and neighbors.

Third, sometimes a public relations client needs to start from scratch in establishing expectations (i.e., adaptation levels) within key publics. At the time of our study, the Center for Afro-American Studies at Midwestern University faced such a problem. Like many other ethnic-studies institutes, it was born around 1970 largely to placate militant campus protesters. Partly because of a lack of university-level commitment and partly because of the haste with which such institutes came on line, no clear goals or objectives were established for steering and assessing programs. As a result, many Black and other ethnic-studies programs still flounder in near-aimlessness, with few standards of comparison useful in assessing them.

Quality and Number of Social Contacts

Many scholars have argued that fruitful human relationships generally require accurate two-way communication, with respectful listening, openness by both source and receiver to a wide variety of ideas, and a measure of spontaneity. Our research focuses on three related principles in this area.

First, space and time constraints often limit fruitful social contact and must somehow be surmounted. For example, the good physician takes time to listen respectfully, explain and answer questions fully, and show genuine concern. Such relations with patients have long been a hallmark of osteopathic medicine. Thus, as shown in chapter 12, D. O.–patient communication appears to enhance acceptance and understanding of basic osteopathic concepts. However, hospital settings provide few relaxed opportunities for such educational interaction. Our data suggest that people learn few basic medical concepts while in the hospital.

In fact, in hospitals, doctors talk with their customers only about once each day while on rounds. In contrast, nurses, therapists, and other health care personnel converse with patients quite often and are on call 24 hours a day. This points up the importance of human-relations training for many kinds of hospital workers.

Turning to law enforcement, cops typically walked beats and got to know people very well in years gone by. However, largely to enhance efficiency, walking beats has almost given way to riding in patrol cars. Unfortunately, it's pretty tough to ask how people are feeling or to help an old lady across the street while riding in a car! Various techniques have been instituted to re-establish the personal touch in police work, but most of these have limitations.

In a related vein, however, the municipal-employee study reveals no correlation between the amount of time spent talking with people and employee assessment of the utility and completeness of those contacts. Perhaps additional human-relations training for workers is part of the answer. In any case, it's obvious that quantity of contact does not insure quality.

Second, high-quality contact is most likely to occur in supportive, nonthreatening environments. In some service professions, special effort is needed to provide such surroundings.

When police ride in patrol cars, for example, they often wind up talking with citizens primarily where some misdeed has been alleged or where fear of crime is high. In such situations, many view the police as the source of the problem or a very inadequate solution to it. In light of all this, police now spend many working hours serving and educating people in "friendly" settings far removed from traditional law enforcement.

Municipal employees also lead stressful lives, partly because they must deal with many complaints. As noted earlier, a worker often doesn't know the needed answer or where to find it. Chapter 11 emphasizes the need to train city workers in this area and to provide user-friendly clues for both citizens and employees as to what the answers are and how to find them easily and quickly. Such clues may remove stress and anxiety where employee and citizen interact.

Third, the quality of social contacts often suffers because one or more interactants have stereotypic beliefs about and prejudices toward others.

Partly for such reasons, Black students on a White-dominated college campus sometimes interact primarily with other Blacks. Such segregation, in turn, often leads to incomplete, inaccurate understanding of and perhaps contempt for the broader culture within which contemporary Americans must function. Certainly Blacks need social support and a sense of their own heritage. In meeting these needs, Black studies programs carry out an important function. However, isolation from the broad culture is sometimes encouraged and is counter productive.

Stereotypic beliefs also hamper police public relations. In fact, many police come from families with relatively low socioeconomic status. However, cops frequently arrest citizens of low status, often leading such people to regard them as oppressors and representatives of the hated establishment rather than as allies and helpers. Such perceptions are hardly conducive to mutual understanding, respect, and cooperation.

Fourth, members and workers are sometimes too few in number to tell an organization's story effectively to broad general publics. This fact largely explains why the major public relations problem of osteopathic medicine is lack of awareness. Most people strongly approve of osteopathy's seven basic concepts described in chapter 12 when these notions are explained to them. However, M. D.s outnumber D. O.s in the United States by about 20–1. As a result, few citizens, on the whole, have intimate contact with D. O.s that might inform them about notions such as manipulative treatment and that might link osteopathic philosophy in people's minds to solving the all-important problem of health care costs.

As osteopathy has grown, this problem has declined somewhat. Certainly we found greater understanding of the field in 1991 than 10 years earlier. Also, in the municipal-employee study, workshops focused in part on the need to "multiply the city's voices" by training and encouraging more and more workers to explain why the city did what it did.

Coorientation Processes

As noted just previously, the quality of social contact plays a key role in establishing mutual understanding among organization members and stakeholders and of them by key publics. Also, we emphasize that client understanding of publics is every bit as important as the converse.

First, we uncovered several instances in which mutual understanding, and demonstration of it, is important politically for a client. In our 1981 health care study, for example, physicians perceived correctly that the population as a whole respected osteopathic hospitals but did not give them the "excellent" ratings that the physicians felt they deserved. We presented these data to osteopathic leaders to suggest that an educational program about hospitals would have support within the osteopathic community itself.

In the municipal-employee study, mutual understanding also proved important. It was argued that citizens respect city government as a rule enforcer and service provider only if they truly understand the reasons for rules and for service limitations from the perspective of the government and its leaders. A city worker can hardly serve citizens well unless she or he respects them.

In the Motel Inn study, chapter 9 shows that positive relationships enhance two-way communication and considerate behavior toward others. Without these elements, business people often react at an emotional level rather than logically examining factors that frame a situation. Corporate-level executives, franchise owners, and employees all have different perspectives on how to run a motel. Unless each group understands where the others are coming from, misunderstanding, lack of respect, and political infighting seem inevitable.

Second, high-quality social contact, as defined in the preceding section, contributes to accurate perception of one person or group by another. For instance, osteopathic educators often told us that too few physicians become involved in civic and community activities such as training athletic teams. Such effort enhances knowledge of patients' social environments. That knowledge, in turn, plays a key role in caring for the poor, AIDS victims, addicts, and others who need special attention.

In a related area, chapter 10 notes a lack of needed outreach to White, Hispanic, Asian, and other students by the Center for Afro-American Studies at Midwestern University. Such interaction is crucial if Blacks are to understand and adjust to the fast-changing larger society in which they live and work.

This concludes our discussion of the social context. We now move to the political realm.

POLITICAL CONTEXT

In discussing each of the first three concepts under this heading, we focus on the need for balance and quality regarding two or three types of leadership activity. In each case, it is crucial to avoid emphasizing one type of leadership at the expense of others.

Group Maintenance and Task Achievement

As explained in chapter 5, group leaders have two broad concerns. They must get certain tasks accomplished, and they generally must maintain conscientious, cooperative effort, avoiding jealousy and misunderstandings that might detract from that effort. It is crucial to lead well in both of these areas. Sometimes, operation in one realm makes it hard to achieve success in the other.

For example, the physician who seeks to help a patient overcome an addiction must view the two of them as partners in a group process. At times, however, a doctor feels compelled to use rather strong words so the patient will see the need to take responsibility for his or her own actions. Social support is important. However, in the final analysis, the alcoholic or other addict must keep his or her own life from going down the tubes. Physicians often feel they can achieve this only by "talking turkey."

Unfortunately, such confrontation sometimes leads to alienation. The doctor who loses contact with a patient during such a moment of truth may have no more chances to help that person in the future. Consequently, a physician must often make a difficult decision on when to become confrontational. If the decision is to go ahead, she or he may try to reduce stress and resentment with tact, promises of future support, etc.

In police work, administrators find it necessary to carry out a group-maintenance function—gaining community support—along with their primary task of controlling and preventing crime. Citizens and those who train law-enforcement officers have been slow to recognize the importance of such activity.

In the livestock magazine study, many editors felt they could enhance cohesion and support among association members—a group-maintenance function—by covering all sides of industry-related controversies. However, some leaders worry that presentation of diverse views in association magazines might suggest a lack of unanimity among members. Also, legislators sometimes do not take an organization seriously if they perceive only limited member support for stands espoused in lobbying. As a result, a free-wheeling publication may make it hard for government-relations people to complete their task of promoting or arguing against certain laws.

In the municipal government study, the Division of Public Safety received many complaints about missing street signs. As rules dictated, such complaints initially were passed on to the Division of Public Works that had responsibility for maintaining signs. However, the latter division did not do its job promptly. At this point, the Division of Public Works faced a dilemma. It could complete an important task quickly and effectively by putting up the signs itself. Unfortunately, such a step would involve "going over the heads and behind the backs" of Public Safety, perhaps causing morale and other group-maintenance problems within that division!

At Motel Inn, room occupancy is the chief goal. Sales representatives invoke a host of marketing techniques to achieve the task—a "full house." However, customer complaints arise and business declines if front-desk managers, clerks, and housekeepers fail to remember that customers are humans and, as the saying goes, are "always right." All too often, motel managers issue mandates on cleaning and sanitation but ignore the basic fact that all motel employees are "people persons" to a degree. All are members of a team and must work together to satisfy and attract customers.

Finally, at Midwestern University's Center for Afro-American Studies, students tend to turn inward and interact only infrequently with non-Blacks. This serves the group-maintenance purpose of maintaining a sense of cohesion and mutual support among Black-student members, possibly enhancing their support for the Center. However, such cohesion comes at the expense of progress on the important task of enhancing understanding of diverse racial and ethnic groups.

One final point deserves mention here. One can often tell from such indexes as sales, election results, and reduction of complaints received whether a given task is being achieved. In contrast, group maintenance involves many intangibles that are hard to gauge until a major crisis erupts. This argument leads to our recommendation, in chapter 11, that municipal governments set up early-warning systems to detect morale-related problems.

Institutional Leaders, Effectors, and Activists

Recall that institutional leaders motivate people because of their prestige and pave the way in accomplishing tasks because of their foresight and vision. Effectors, on the other hand, give orders, make assignments, arrange people and events so as to encourage high-quality communication, and generally take responsibility for figuring out how to complete tasks. Finally, activists lead by example, inspiring others with dedicated effort and telling in a convincing way the rationale for what's being done.

Several problems uncovered in our research reflect a lack of emphasis on and quality within one or two of these leadership categories.

First, we focus on institutional leadership. In the police study, a previous chief's rather bizarre behavior and other factors had damaged the reputation of Glotz's department. However, Glotz himself had obtained grants and provided long-term planning so as to enhance credibility with the mayor and other stakeholders. Such vision and prestige are primary concerns at the institutional level. By the time we did our study, Glotz's department seemed to score well in this area.

Second, effector leadership in group maintenance is lacking in one aspect of osteopathic education and training. Young D. O.s receive fine classroom training on manipulative treatment. They know how to carry out the tasks involved. However, trainers and supervisors in clinical and internship settings do little manipulating and say little to enhance student enthusiasm for this important treatment mode.

The livestock magazine study reveals a serious challenge for effectors in organizing tasks. New printing technology has largely eliminated full-time proofreaders, adding quality control to already heavy editorial workloads. Furthermore, computers make it possible for one person to lay out, as well as write, edit, and proofread, a story almost in the same operation. On the surface, these innovations are likely to enhance efficiency greatly. Unfortunately, they also increase the varieties of skills needed among and pressures upon harried, mortal journalists!

In the municipal-government study, it is noted that services have become more and more complex in recent decades. Consequently, effectors must take steps to insure that the right information gets into the right hands at the right time. Such "flow" is essential for city workers to carry out the task of serving people. It also has group-maintenance implications, as persons faced with complaints that they cannot effectively help solve are bound to become discouraged.

Chapter 9 also indicates that, in motel management, effectors must communicate well about clear goals and specific tasks that they take the lead in defining. Understanding of both short-term and long-term objectives helps employees realize they depend on each other—within and among departments and divisions—in providing a comfortable motel environment.

Third, Chief Glotz's primary leadership problem resides in the activist realm. Too few volunteers were available to meet personnel needs within the police department studied. Thus, we urged that Glotz focus on setting up an Explorer Scout Post, recruiting more retired volunteers (whom our data show to be willing, strong police-department fans), etc.

We conclude this section by noting that the Center for Afro-American Affairs at Midwestern University is deficient at all levels of leadership. The university has not provided the kind of commitment needed for the Center to do long-term planning and gain a reputation for a clear mission: both keys to institutional leadership. Administration within the Center has failed to spell out inspiring, helpful goals or means of achieving them: both concerns of the effector. Lack of faculty plus declining enrollment has signalled a lack of enthused, able activists (as defined by group-dynamics theory, though not necessarily as that term is used in the study of social movements!).

Politicians and Technocrats

To a large extent, politicians focus on group-maintenance concerns, whereas technocrats are task oriented. Recall that according to Bower (1983), politicians tend to be people-oriented generalists with diffuse, vaguely defined goals. Technocrats, on the other hand, specialize in tasks at hand, focus heavily on important parts of their organizations, and operate with narrow, precisely defined objectives.

As with other concepts tied to the political context, these call for a balancing and intermeshing of different types of leadership. In our research, one or both types of leadership, as defined within this framework, sometimes need bolstering.

First, in at least three cases, added emphasis on technocratic leadership was called for.

In the medical study, general practitioners and other primary care physicians—the hallmarks of osteopathy—qualify largely as politicians. They look after the whole person, emphasize patient acceptance (they had to as minority D. O. practitioners or risk losing their practices), and coordinate diverse specialties and professions so as to best serve each patient. In these respects, such doctors operate largely in the politician mode.

However, one educator noted that D. O.s do work as specialists, a fact sometimes forgotten in light of the public relations emphasis placed on primary care. This individual, a surgeon, reported that some of his early patients simply couldn't believe a D. O. was qualified to wield a scalpel!

Also, in the municipal-employee project, some officials with broad-ranging "politician" responsibilities (assistant mayors, public-service deputies, etc.) have job descriptions that require considerable technical training in public relations. In fact, the workshops reported in chapter 11 sought to meet just this need.

In the motel business, franchise general managers typically spend a great deal of time playing the political role of ambassador to customers and various groups in the community. However, managers need many technical and conceptual skills to maintain their units' viability. Honing of such skills is especially important for them and the firm, because the role of franchise general manager is often viewed as a training ground for franchise owners and corporate executives.

Finally, early leaders in Black Studies at Midwestern University performed as politicians with considerable zeal and initial success. These people linked their program to national and international movements and slogans such as Black Power, so as to gain impressive, if somewhat short lived, university support. However, the emerging Institute lacked hard-headed, competent technocratic leadership needed to define and implement goals.

Second, at least two case studies here pinpointed defects in and lack of needed emphasis on political leadership. In the police study, Chief Glotz and his subordinates have ironed out technical factors needed for cooperation with law-enforcement units in neighboring towns. Also, they have built a strong case on technical grounds for such cooperation. However, considerable work is still needed to achieve political support within those towns. The hilljack mentality there seemingly works against enthusiastic cooperation with outsiders.

In a related vein, one osteopathic educator railed against what he called "politicians" with great influence in his profession. According to this professor, narrow-minded politicians were seeking to discourage young D. O.s from taking allopathic internships. In his view, such exclusivity is a luxury that D. O.s could ill afford because financial and other forces lead irrevocably toward increased cooperation with M. D.s.

Third, the livestock magazine study reveals one classic confrontation between technocratic and political perspectives. Young readers express great need for service articles helpful in managing their farms. Such readers were quite numerous and undoubtedly have rather intense needs of the type described. Technocratically oriented editors now seek out audience segments that combine numbers with need intensity. However, although older farmers tend to score low in these realms, they have political clout because of their long service to and high-ranking positions within the sponsoring breed associations.

We now turn to a psychologically oriented theory relevant to political persuasion.

Internalization, Compliance, and Identification

To review quickly, Kelman (1961) defined three modes of influence in changing people's behavior. Internalization occurs when one is persuaded that a behavior pattern is consistent with values that she or he holds dear. With identification, the target person behaves in a certain way because of a self-defining relationship to a role model. Compliance hinges upon surveillance by people who may reward the sought-after behavior or punish the would-be behaver for its absence.

In general, most public relations practitioners surely wish to persuade by internalization. Influence wielded in this way often leads to consistent behavior, because it does not hinge on surveillance by would-be enforcers or the salience of a particular role model. Such surveillance and salience often develop only fleetingly and somewhat unpredictably. Furthermore, consistent behavior is essential for loyalty to a brand, organization, individual, or project. Inevitably, clients seek loyal support. Finally, active, responsible, creative behavior is most likely where it stems from authentic self-expression (i.e., linkage to ones personal values) rather than from obedient compliance or imitative identification.

Unfortunately, internalization often requires long-term education rather than short-term persuasion. Thus, it may not always be feasible. One may not be able to internalize the need to run from a burning theater and still have time to get out alive! Nonetheless, some of the most interesting challenges and problems faced by our clients require internalization.

As shown in chapter 9, Motel Inn owners and employees regard themselves as pioneers, constantly forging new ground. They perceive their brand name as the industry standard; an idea they feel has been confirmed during two decades of media attention. The firm's advertising campaign, "Stay with someone you know," expresses a philosophy that personnel at all levels must internalize and believe in deeply if the firm is to remain pre-eminent. Franchise relations efforts enhance such internalization.

In the osteopathic study, educators said repeatedly that doctor and patient must act as partners. As was noted earlier, patients often view their physicians as all-knowing figures whose proclamations should be accepted unquestioningly as in identification. On the other hand, patient understanding of basic health care concepts opens the door to internalization and a more fruitful relationship.

In much the same way, law enforcement based on surveillance and threats is impossible where police are badly outnumbered. Furthermore, such enforcement is unpalatable in a democratic society. Indeed, Americans tend to equate it with totalitarianism. The alternative is to educate about basic values and to improve socialization by working closely with schools, churches, families, and other institutions. As chapter 7 emphasizes, such education is a primary focus of modern, progressive police work.

In the livestock-magazine research, editors and association leaders sometimes emphasize human-interest content dealing with the rural way of life. Admittedly, this has entailed some counter-productive appeals to nostalgia. However, such content might also help young farmers internalize agrarian values as a foundation for staying in business despite hard times.

Chapter 11 emphasizes the importance of helping municipal employees develop basic values—often described in the private sector as corporate culture—that serve as linking pins for internalized productive-service beliefs. Presumably the worker who really believes that the customer is (almost, anyway) always right and that an organization must stick to its basic tasks has solid values. Job-related training may then consist largely of showing links between these values and specific activities or programs.

Finally, the Black-studies case serves as a classic demonstration that compliance, achieved under threat of rioting and burning, does not bring the deep, long-term commitment needed to establish a thriving academic program. Faced with rather hair-brained ideas about hiring and organizing, administrators at Midwestern University apparently complied, partly because they believed the early 1970s radicalism would soon pass. Then they could back away from their hasty commitments to the new academic unit on their campus.

We now turn to another psychological formulation, the Elaboration Likelihood Model of Petty and Cacioppo (1986), that distinguishes between central and peripheral information processing modes.

Central and Peripheral Information Processing

Central processing occurs where people are highly involved, that is, where they see a close relationship between themselves and the message topic. Here one processes a message carefully before assessing its validity and importance largely on the basis of content. In contrast, peripheral processing operates with low involvement. In this case, assessment of the source and of the context in which it is given plays a major role in interpretation.

The preceding section notes that internalization is generally viewed as the preferred influence mode within Kelman's model. Furthermore, when people internalize, they link behavior to salient personal values. Presumably such linkages are expressed in message content rather than through relating to source or context. It follows that in many cases, central processing and the involvement presumed to trigger it are highly desirable within public relations. As noted at the beginning of this chapter, central processing is most likely where values on the Grunigs' situational variables are favorable, where involvement and problem recognition are high and constraints appear to be surmountable.

In light of this, practitioners can often take advantage of publics' high involvement. Where involvement is low, they must choose between two courses. First, they may be able to increase involvement by showing that a client or program relates more closely to people's values than had previously been realized. Second, they can live with low involvement by designing and delivering messages so as to maximize attention-getting power.

First, livestock farmers and municipal employees are quite highly involved when consuming work-related messages. That's because both groups see their work as problematic and complex as well as involving. Chapters 8 and 11 indicate that, by and large, these two groups process work-related information actively. Both are willing to digest even complex information—provided they can understand it—and look carefully at its implications for them.

Second, in two cases, our research gives reason for optimism about the possibility of increasing audience involvement. First, in the police study, women and retired folks indicated strong support for local law enforcement. The local police department could harness that support by making it clear just how people can enhance community safety. Second, our 1991 osteopathic study suggests that citizens are more receptive than some physicians assumed to regimens of diet and exercise linked to feeling well.

Third and last, TV consumers, in particular, tend to view in a relaxed, escapist mode. Thus, presumably they rarely engage in central processing. It follows that the practitioner using TV must package messages in attractive, novel ways that grab people's attention. Information gained in this fashion is seldom processed actively right away. However, social-learning theorists suggest that at some later point, involvement may increase. Then one can retrieve information from memory and process it more actively.

We now turn to a sociological concept central to understanding political contexts.

Relative Power and Coalition Formation

A person with power has the ability to change or influence the behavior of others. Varied researchers noted that people often find it hard to work together in a creative, flexible way when some have far more power than others. Power discrepancies can inhibit communication. Also, they can hamper group maintenance and morale where they lead to excessive demands on the powerless.

Unfortunately, public relations can seldom alter power relationships very much. However, practitioners sometimes can empower the powerless by pointing up avenues for coalition formation.

First, we review four instances in which, according to our research, power discrepancies appeared to inhibit open, free, active communication.

To begin, M. D.s hold great power over D. O.s, largely as a result of superior numbers. Osteopathic officials fear being swallowed up by the huge American Medical Association. Some observers believe that anxiety led D. O.s to close the door prematurely on needed collaboration with their allopathic brothers and sisters.

In a closely related area, osteopathic hospitals enjoy positive reputations as hospitals. However, they seldom promote their osteopathic philosophy and identity. Public relations practitioners say this lack of activity stems in part from fear that osteopathic promotion might alienate M. D.s on whom their hospitals depend. We argue and several practitioners agree that such fears are largely unfounded. Hospital administrators could promote important elements of osteopathic philosophy vigorously without proposing many arguments with which large numbers of M. D.s might disagree strongly.

According to the literature, most law-enforcement institutions place low priority on police–community relations. As a result, PCR administrators often have little clout within their overall departments and are ineffective. A common result is press-agent hype rather than genuine two-way communication useful in planning programs. Here, as in health care, informed observers now see a great need for public relations training within crowded curricula to enhance management understanding of and respect for the field.

Finally, the evidence suggests—albeit somewhat inconclusively—that female journalists operate at a disadvantage while interviewing male news sources with high power and status. Our data indicate this might be a problem on livestock magazines.

Informing news sources about the increasing role of women in specialized journalism might help overcome such stereotypes. Also, it is important to train both male and female journalists in coping with evasive news sources. At present, formal classroom instruction in this area is quite limited. Perhaps more workshops such as the ones reported in chapter 8 are needed.

Second, morale problems arise where people with little power face demands that they see as excessive and unfair. Our studies uncover at least three instances of this problem.

Two of these examples arose in the livestock magazine study. First, some younger farmers apparently feel compelled to support their breed associations even though association magazines provided little service content that they need. Being young and lacking political clout, these farmers can do little to make their wishes count. Second, as with many other occupations, women often do at least as much work and do it at least as well as their male counterparts, but for lower pay.

A third and rather blatant example occurred at two levels within the Black community at Midwestern University. First, Black students feel isolated and resentful in a small town where they can not even find a barber willing and able to cut Afro-Americans' hair. Second, Black-studies professors face heavy demands partly because they are young, untenured, and few in number. They are expected to publish books and articles just as their White brothers and sisters are in other departments. Yet they also shoulder heavy advising, counseling, and other extracurricular loads for two reasons. Black students often need lots of advice because of severe adjustment problems on a White-dominated campus. In addition to meeting student needs and serving as important role models, Black faculty members generally feel obliged to take part in civil-rights related activity.

Third, coalition formation sometimes empowers the powerless to a degree. Our studies reveal two relevant cases. One appeared to be a blown opportunity, but modest progress was reported in the other instance.

On the down side, the Center for Afro-American Studies at Midwestern University has made little effort toward cooperation with the university's relatively new and quite successful women's studies program. Both programs are interdisciplinary. Each seeks to enhance understanding of and pride in a neglected heritage. Furthermore, a substantial group, Black women, live within the constituencies of both programs.

In a more positive vein, Chief Glotz reported some progress in working with school, welfare, and women's groups on projects designed to enhance community safety and quality of life.

Relative power often becomes an issue when people operate in a win–lose mode. That is, the powerless tend to resent a high-status contemporary who uses power to hurt them. However, coalition formation is usually successful only when the groups involved have a shared interest so one's success makes the other's success more, not less, likely. This leads into a brief look at the concept of competition as we begin the economic-context section.

ECONOMIC CONTEXT

Competition

Economists tend to assume that competition is in the win–lose mode. However, group dynamicists such as Cartwright and Zander (1960, pp. 414–448), and management theorists such as Argyris (1974, pp. 1–33) emphasized that it need not be cut-throat. For example, teammates in sports often try to outdo each other in terms of salary, title, batting average, or prestige. In that sense, they compete. But, as any fan knows, shortstops and second basemen must work together in completing double plays. Success by one contributes to rather than detracts from possible success by the other.

Public relations practitioners must often talk with key publics about competition in two ways to avoid destructive conflict. First they must show where people have shared needs and goals, justifying coalitions. Second, they must try to insure that people have complete information and understand it fully when making competitive choices.

Our research reveals several instances where various groups—cops and citizens,

M. D.s and D. O.s, Black and women-studies faculty, city Departments of Public Safety and Public Works, and other groups—could profit from working together. Shared goals deserve emphasis in communicating with such groups. Also, it's important to identify and explain needs for cooperation based on the fact that one group has resources that others do not.

Of particular importance here are professional and trade associations such as the American Medical Association, the American Osteopathic Association, and livestock breed organizations. For example, different types of physicians and farmers compete for customers. Unfortunately, in the heat of competition, people often lose sight of shared goals that they can achieve only by cooperating. Indeed, trade-and professional-association public relations has become a growth field in recent decades, partly because at last competitors have seen fit to collaborate in government relations and other areas.

The police study reveals one instance in which natives and university students in a small university town developed some hostility toward each other because intense win–lose competition seemed likely. This occurred partly because growth of the university and drives to encourage student voting suddenly made students a potential force in local politics. This alarmed natives, partly because it violated the notion of fair exchange, the next concept to be discussed.

Exchange

Thibaut and Kelly (1961), among others, noted that human relationships hinge on an underlying notion of fair exchange. This involves two premises. First, people are entitled to a reasonable return—however they may define it—on any money, effort, or other resources that they invest in any activity or relationship. Second, no one person should gain exorbitant profits at the expense of another.

Our research uncovered several instances in which exchange relationships are problematic, sometimes in ways not usually seen as economic. For example:

1. Health care professionals reportedly resent laws currently before American legislatures that would force them to get tested for the AIDS virus and reveal the results to patients. Many professionals undoubtedly agree that such testing is reasonable. However, some call for a two-way street. To be sure, the Hippocratic Oath and related documents dictate that physicians minister to all who need health care. However, the doctor with knowledge that a patient has tested HIV positive can take special precautions to avoid dangerous exchange of blood and other bodily fluids. How unfair, some say, that the physician is not entitled to know a patient's HIV status when, in fact, most health care workers who contract AIDS do so from patients! The reverse surely is not true.

2. Cultural beliefs that one is automatically entitled to social-welfare benefits obscure the fact that when health care is provided, someone must pay for it. Several

physicians pointed to this fact as a contributor to extravagant treatment. That, in turn, helps create skyrocketing health care costs.

3. In the community of our police study, as just noted, many townspeople fear student power at the polls, partly because students pay little in property or income taxes within the small town where they study. Thus, students might enact laws creating public services beneficial to them but for which they would provide little help in paying. This seemingly unfair exchange apparently contributes somewhat to hostility between students and townspeople. Such hostility can spell trouble for police. (Fortunately, perhaps, most students remained apathetic about local politics. Even those who voted seldom did so in blocs so as to overwhelm long-time citizens.)

4. In the livestock magazine analysis, female staffers feel they often fail to get equal pay for equal work when compared with their male counterparts. Unfortunately, quite a few males do not share and seem unaware of this female assessment.

5. In the Black-studies case, Midwestern University administrators allocated substantial funds for the new academic unit. However, they apparently felt the threat of a campus takeover by militants would soon go away. Then, from an exchange perspective, they'd have little to lose by cutting resources to the Black-studies unit.

6. In the municipal-employee study, careful prioritizing of programs is urged, in particular, for one basic reason. In tight economic times, which seemed to be coming when the research was done, citizens are especially apt to expect a fair return on their tax payments—or in colloquial terms, lots of bang for their bucks.

7. Motel Inn franchise owners' effort and skill constitute the life blood of the chain. In return, corporate headquarters provides a script for marketing. Many owners, as second-generation franchisees, have enjoyed a long, profitable relationship with headquarters. Considerable franchise autonomy has contributed greatly to the success of that relationship. However, problems sometimes arise where, partly because of this autonomy, a franchisee or a corporate executive loses sight of the other's role and importance. In such cases, lethargy may set in among individual motel units. Owners may fail to recognize that they have a communication problem with both employees and customers.

The notion of a fair return involves assessment of the **value** of a service, activity, or product. Value and related concepts comprise our next focus of attention.

Value, Marginal Utility, and Marginal Returns

The value that one assigns to a product or service depends in part on the intensity of needs that the item is presumed to help meet. Also, value depends on how much of that item a person already has. As noted in chapter 6, the price one has to pay hinges in part on what it costs to provide the item earned or purchased and on the plentifulness or scarcity of that item.

Diminishing marginal utility refers to the notion that as plentifulness of something increases, the value of additional units declines. For instance, a hungry person may be willing to give her or his left arm for one egg roll but much less for a 15th or 20th.

Turning to the producer's bookkeeping, the first unit of input provided for an undertaking (for example, the first thousand dollars spent on equipment for a farm) yields high returns. However, assuming all other inputs (land, labor, and management or entrepreneurship) are held constant, the 10th or 100th thousand dollars invested yields a relatively low return. This notion is called *diminishing marginal returns*.

Obviously, public relations people must often seek to clarify values of products and services. Our cases illustrate at least four major points about this area.

First, it's often difficult to evaluate services. How much is it worth to feel good? To have fun? To enjoy companionship? To receive social support? To have peace of mind provided by health insurance? To live? As suggested by the old adage that one can't put a price on life, few people can answer such questions clearly.

In some cases, practitioners and their clients can define at least reasonable minimal values. For example, chapter 12 suggests that D. O.s collect approximate data on the illness rates of people who practice wellness and on those who don't. Such information might provide some basis for guesstimating the number of missed work days each year that wellness helps avoid. And it's fairly easy to assign dollar values to work days.

To be sure, such interpretations are seldom beyond question. They do not do justice to "feeling good," an intangible result of wellness. Nonetheless, Altheide and Johnson (1980) argued that such attempts at assigning value to services are necessary if organizations are to gain support needed for survival.

Second, customers and constituents expect that an organization will give top priority to providing services that they view as most important. For example, there's considerable evidence that people view crime control and prevention as the most important functions of police. Chapter 7 suggests that Chief Glotz may encounter resentment if he focuses on ceremonial and educational activities without first doing a good job of catching crooks and preventing crime.

Third, diminishing marginal utility must often be understood as a basis for publics' priorities. For instance, older livestock farmers downgrade the importance of how-to or service information, helpful in farm management, within their breed-association magazines. Why this negative assessment? Apparently such established, experienced farmers have other sources of service information that are more complete and trustworthy. Thus, these people look to their magazines for other kinds of content.

Fourth, clients must be sure that, in fact, they are providing a service valued by relevant publics. Where value is not offered, no amount of public relations can "make a silk purse out of a sow's ear." For example, chapter 10 argues that

Midwestern University's Center for Afro-American Studies simply does not provide service of great value to actual or prospective students. The curriculum includes little job-related training. The Center's extracurricular component largely fails to enhance intercultural contacts and understanding as needed for survival in the modern world. Small wonder, then, that the number of new majors at the Center declined to zero and one in 2 recent years!

Discussions of value relate closely to two other economic concepts: opportunity costs and benefits and demand elasticity. We now look at each of these notions in turn.

Opportunity Costs and Benefits

As noted earlier, these concepts really represent an extension and application of the psychological notion of standard of comparison or adaptation level discussed under the social context. When deciding what to buy, use, or produce, one looks at all available options and selects the one with the most favorable profit (i.e., benefits vs. costs). In essence, this involves using all other options as standards of comparison when evaluating any given alternative.

Clearly public relations practitioners must often help publics and clients evaluate opportunity costs and benefits realistically. Our cases give many examples of such assessment. For example:

1. Some poor people do not seek medical help, because they need their few precious dollars for food and other necessities. Consequently, these folks choose illness and additional suffering rather than to go to a clinic. Although somewhat reasonable in the short term, such decisions have disastrous long-term consequences that the poor do not understand. If it's not treated, today's minor illness may become major in a few months or years. At that point, someone must pay a huge bill!

2. Wellness and preventive medicine, as well as osteopathic manipulative treatment, cost relatively little and entail few side-effects when compared with drugs and surgery.

3. In law enforcement, it costs less in suffering as well as dollars to prevent crime than to incarcerate criminals. Also, Chief Glotz's police department might point out to key stakeholders that in one typical recent year, it recovered stolen poverty valued at about 80% of the department's operating budget. Thus, if the department were crippled or eliminated, some $112,000 per year would not be returned to its owners.

4. In operating livestock magazines, new printing technology is not an alternative to hiring skilled editorial personnel. Desk-top publishing may cut some costs. But one cannot simply hand over pictures and stories to a computer and expect a high-quality magazine to appear magically!

Demand Elasticity

When demand is inelastic, people buy roughly the same amount of an item when prices are very low as when they are high. For example, the senior author regards much food as bland and distasteful unless it includes some salt. Thus, he would be inclined to buy this product even if the price went sky high. At the other extreme, however, he does not enjoy eating huge amounts of salt. Hence, he would not increase his salt purchases greatly even if that condiment were free.

Elasticity offers another way of looking at value. The concept relates closely to loyalty, a very important goal in public relations and advertising. Loyalty to a candidate implies willingness to support that person consistently through thick and thin. Loyalty to a brand involves buying it even when the mix of alternative brands changes. And so on.

Demand elasticity seldom came in for explicit discussion in our case studies. However, three related points did come to the fore.

First, elasticity hinges in part on opportunity costs. Clients must assess such factors accurately, and publics must also understand them. For example, beef-cattle farmers face marketing problems, partly because chicken is promoted as an alternative to beef. Recent concerns about animal rights as well as the healthfulness of red meat have raised the opportunity costs, as viewed by consumers, of buying beef.

Second, sometimes the pain of doing without something is so great that it becomes unthinkable. Then people refuse to consider it, even when it becomes a reality. For example, we take it for granted in the United States that all people are entitled to life and to top-quality health care. Yet citizens and government officials have only begun to talk about the life-and-death ramifications of skyrocketing costs. As noted in chapter 12, only the rich can sometimes afford life-saving treatment. At an abstract level, Americans abhor this. Yet they seem unwilling to pay the high price needed in practice to guarantee an equal chance at life for everyone. In short, demand for life-saving care is not perfectly inelastic!

Third, where people need a product desperately (i.e., they are willing to pay a very high price for it, as with highly inelastic demand), opportunities for exploitation and windfall profits exist. For example, petroleum companies have been accused of capitalizing on the fact that American lifestyles depend heavily on cars and petroleum. Thus, people apparently do not purchase much less gasoline than normal even when prices skyrocket. In such cases, responsible practitioners must insist on clarification of available options. Also, they may encourage clients to charge less today, as winning today's price battle may contribute to loss of tomorrow's war for governmental support and prestige.

We now turn to a final concept useful in defining the economic context.

Externalities

Externalities are benefits and costs that are not intended and usually are not taken into account as people consider opportunity costs and benefits when making decisions. Certainly stakeholders often ignore externalities, partly because they are hard to assess. However, public relations clients can often enhance their support and improve their socially responsible performance by considering externalities carefully.

In ethics externalities are especially important, because they often apply to the community or society as a whole and not simply to the client or narrowly defined publics. Culbertson (1973) and Kruckeberg and Starck (1988), among others, argued that ethics requires a concern for benefiting and serving society as a whole.

All of the cases analyzed here reveal important externalities. Following are some examples.

1. Preventive medicine helps people avoid contagious illness. When person A remains well, he or she is unlikely to spread that disease to others. This holds even though person A seldom considers the impact on associates when deciding to exercise faithfully, eat and drink responsibly, etc.

2. In law enforcement, community Neighborhood Watch programs are usually created to prevent crime. However the community effort involved often helps people develop camaraderie and a sense of social support. That, in turn, enhances quality of life within the community.

3. Success in farming helps farmers lead fruitful lives. In addition, it supports many stores and industries that sell to and buy from farmers. Drive through any town where an industry has died, and you find many empty, ghost-like buildings that once housed stores and businesses.

4. In municipal government, each service meets a specific need by providing clean water, disposing of garbage, etc. However, taken as a whole, such services give citizens a sense that they live in a thriving, caring community. This, in turn, contributes to that nebulous thing called *quality of life*. Unfortunately, officials sometimes do not consider such matters fully when preparing and justifying budgets.

5. The Black Separatist philosophy underlying Midwestern University's Center for Afro-American Studies emphasizes primarily service to Black militants. However, as noted in chapter 10, many Black students do not have militant political or social views. The Center's basic approach excludes them. Also, it provides students with few skills that help the larger minority population throughout the land. Such factors were negative externalities.

6. Motel Inn sponsors events that benefit their communities and enhance regional esprit de corps. Often, as a result of this process, general managers become community leaders, patrons of the arts, and supporters of various sports and civic activities. As a result, community groups become stronger. Also, such events showcase area businesses in ways helpful to them and to the community as a whole.

This concludes the discussion of specific concepts and perspectives related to the SPE context.

CONCLUSION

Here we make four points.

First, this volume offers practice in using and finding applications for a wide variety of social science theories. We hope our readers find it natural and fairly easy to find adaptation levels, externalities, cases of high problem recognition, instances of politician and technocrat performance, etc., as they serve and study their own public relations clients. Such a knack is far more important than specific conclusions drawn from our research. (Indeed, conclusions soon get outdated in the modern world!)

Second, as noted in chapter 1, we chose and used theories as we went along. In an initial paper (Culbertson & Jeffers, 1992), we focused on seven basic concepts. An additional year of reflection increased this to nine (Culbertson & Jeffers, 1991). And, when we sat down to write this book in earnest during 1991, we found it necessary to discuss all 17 perspectives covered in this chapter.

As a result of this process, our presentation may seem a bit disorganized. Certainly we could have covered all angles more thoroughly had we developed the full theoretical scheme prior to doing our research. However, Kaplan (1964, pp. 1–11) and others noted that intellectual inquiry is seldom neat and tidy. We hope to keep building a framework for the SPE context. We earnestly solicit others' comments and help in doing so.

Third, we believe our approach to studying clients' social, political, and economic contexts contributes to implementation of the two-way symmetric model of public relations proposed by Grunig and Hunt (1984, chapter 2). This model serves as a useful ideal for practitioners. However, only with contextual study can practitioners and their clients interpret what they hear as they listen respectfully to publics.

Fourth, our discussion of the political context focuses on how people persuade and exercise power as everyday use of the term political implies. In coming to grips with this, we focus heavily on fairly micro analysis of power and persuasion. We certainly do not do justice to macro concerns of overall systemic power and interdependency that bulk large in political science. Although they are important, such macro issues are central in only a fairly narrow range of public relations analyses.

REFERENCES

Altheide, D. L., & Johnson, J. M. (1980). *Bureaucratic propaganda*. Boston: Allyn & Bacon.

Argyris C. (1974). *Behind the front page*. San Francisco: Jossey-Bass.

Bower, J. L. (1983). *The two faces of management*. New York: Mentor.

Cartwright, D., & Zander, A. (1960). *Group dynamics: Research and theory*. New York: Harper & Row.

Culbertson, H. M. (1973). Public relations ethics: A new look. *Public Relations Quarterly, 17*, 15–17, 23–25.

Culbertson, H. M., & Jeffers, D. W. (1991). The social, political and economic contexts: Keys to front-end research. *Public Relations Quarterly, 36*, 43–48.

Culbertson, H. M., & Jeffers, D. W. (1992). The social, political and economic contexts of public relations: Keys in educating the true public relations professional. *Public Relations Review, 18*, 53–65.

Grunig, J. E. (1976). Organizations and public relations: Testing a communication theory. *Journalism Monographs, 46.*

Grunig, J. E. (1983). Communication behaviors and attitudes of environmental publics: Two studies. *Journalism Monographs, 81.*

Grunig J. E., & Hunt, T. (1984). *Managing public relations.* New York: Holt, Rinehart & Winston.

Kaplan, A. (1964). *The conduct of inquiry: Methodology for behavioral science.* San Francisco: Chandler.

Kelman, H. C. (1961). Processes of opinion change. *Public Opinion Quarterly, 25,* 57–78.

Kruckeberg, D., & Starck, D. (1988). *Public relations and community: A reconstructed theory.* New York: Praeger.

Petty, R. E., & Cacioppo, J. T. (1986). *Communication and persuasion: Central and peripheral routes to attitude change.* New York: Springer-Verlag.

Sherif, M., & Sherif, C. W. (1956). *An outline of social psychology.* New York: Harper.

Thibaut, J., & Kelly, H. (1961). *The social psychology of groups.* New York: Wiley.

Author Index

Subject Index

Q